1978

GROWING UP:

A Study of Children

A Study of

GROWING UP:

Children

Janice T. Gibson
University of Pittsburgh

**ADDISON-WESLEY
PUBLISHING COMPANY**

Reading, Massachusetts
Menlo Park, California
London
Amsterdam
Don Mills, Ontario
Sydney

Cover and text illustrations by Stephen Alexander.

ISBN 0-201-02914-6
ABCDEFGHIJ-HA-7987

To our continuing family:
our parents, our children, and someday,
their children

Preface

Growing Up is a study of children, a subject that should be important business to people concerned that our society be one of happy, healthy, socially alert youngsters and adults. *Growing Up* describes physical and functional characteristics of children as they increase in age, and explores the complex interrelationships that exist among these characteristics. It examines, in effect, the steps through which children advance as they grow and interact with the world around them. *Growing Up* also is a study of biological and social forces that impinge on developing children. Many of these make newspaper headlines as new evidence is found concerning the effects of malnutrition, drugs, changing parental roles, and family relationships. Advances in medical and biological research also, in many cases, affect development; these too are the subject of this text.

   Growing Up deals with two different issues as they relate to child behavior. First, it focuses on the major determinants of child behavior, factors whose effects often remain constant in relationship to the growing child. Second, it deals with how children change with age in the ways they learn to adjust to their environments. The arrangement of the text into parts and chapters reflects both of these issues. Early portions of the text deal with determinants of behavior, such as maturation, learning, and heredity. Theories that seek to explain how each of these variables affects behavior common to all children as well as individual differences between children are discussed. Many of the theories presented have recently been the subject of major controversy among psychologists, educators, biologists, and lay people. New research involving such questions as how to make use of new genetic information pose increasingly important and complex problems for society.

Since the most noticeable overt characteristics of the period we call "childhood" are associated with aging, much of the text has been arranged in chronological fashion, from the prenatal period to adolescence. Within parts devoted to each successive age period, individual chapters focus on the interests and concerns of children, parents, and caretakers at that age level. For example, Part 2, "The Prenatal and Infancy Periods," deals with effects of the uterine environment and the birth process on later development, as well as with a variety of topics related to care of the infant and the development of behavior. The possible adverse consequences of malnutrition even before conception are discussed here, as are the effects on later learning of drugs during childbirth and cognitive stimulation during infancy.

Since early childhood involves developing the first truly socialized behavior, language, and the beginnings of more complex problem solving, chapters in Part 3 of the text deal directly with these topics. Of particular concern are the effects of rapidly changing child-rearing methods in our society on socialization.

Middle childhood, the subject of Part 4, involves schooling, and with these years increased concern on the part of children, parents, and teachers for personal-social behavior, school learning, and achievement. Although sex-typing has always played a major role in shaping child behavior and is discussed throughout the book, at this point it assumes major importance. In recent years, also, with the advent of new educational policies such as mainstreaming, increased emphasis has been placed on the needs of special children in regular classrooms. The study of individual differences and methods for providing the most advantageous learning environments for all children are discussed in detail.

The end of childhood—adolescence—is an age often thought to bring particular problems and psychological changes. The adolescent in our society must deal with a newly developing identity, self-actualization, and greater responsibility for making moral and vocational decisions important to his or her life. The abilities of adolescents to achieve their goals during this period depend in great part on their experiences during childhood. Adolescence can be understood as the end of childhood. If the biological and social forces discussed earlier have interacted satisfactorily during the individual's childhood, adolescence is the beginning of adulthood and maturity.

How should *Growing Up* be used? Psychologists have shown that each individual learner can be described in terms of one most effective learning style. Because of different past experiences, no two people are likely to approach the problem of learning about children in exactly the same fashion. For those who wish to consider child behavior in terms of the aging process first and therefore want to study the interests and concerns of children in chronological order, the process is a simple one. Part 1 deals with determinants of child behavior that should be understood in relation to each chronological period. Parts 2 through 5 follow, dealing with each age level of childhood in turn. Part 2 begins not simply with conception as the beginning of childhood, but, interestingly, with issues that affect development even before conception has occurred. Part 5 concludes the text with a discussion of adolescence, the end of childhood.

Some readers may wish to consider child behavior in a manner other than chronological. These readers may find it more effective to study specific topics related to child behavior separately. For these readers, a "Topical Outline" follows this preface. The "Topical Outline" also appears on the text's front and rear endpapers. Each major topic relating to learning, development, and individual differences between children is listed together with the chapter or chapters where that topic is discussed. Students and instructors desiring a topical approach to the study of children should find the guide useful.

In addition to the topical outline, learning aides are provided throughout the text and also are available in supplementary learning materials. Because child behavior so often is the subject of news reports and articles appearing in the mass media, sections of the text are boxed off to highlight certain items of current social interest. Each issue discussed is related to the theoretical concerns of child psychologists. Case histories throughout the text provide additional, personal examples of topics discussed. A supplementary text, *Growing Up: Readings on the Study of Children*, edited by J. Gibson and P. Blumberg, offers timely and socially provocative research articles keyed to each chapter of the text. In both *Growing Up: A Study of Children* and *Growing Up: Readings on the Study of Children*, study questions accompany each chapter to stimulate thought about important issues. In addition, learning objectives precede each chapter and an annotated bibliography follows each chapter of the main text. For students who want help in preparing for examinations, a *Student Study Guide* reviews key concepts and provides self-administered quizzes and answers. An instructor's manual suggests varieties of class exercises that can be used effectively with both large and small classes.

ACKNOWLEDGMENTS

Children constitute exciting subjects for research, whether they are in classrooms, psychological laboratories, or sitting opposite you at your own dinner table. To prepare the material used in *Growing Up*, I have made use of children, both in the United States and abroad. To all of them, including my own children, I owe thanks for help in providing insights described in this book. The extensive research, in addition, of my many colleagues cited in this text posed a formidable challenge; to detail all of their most important new findings required considerable effort.

Certain of my colleagues have provided particular assistance, which should be mentioned here. Particularly, I should like to thank Charles A. Austad, Bemidji State University; B. Bethine Bigej, Montana State

University; Ann M. Bingham-Newman, California State University–Los Angeles; Meryl E. Englander, Indiana University; Jean D. Harlan, Ohio University; Sharon L. Hiett, Florida Technological University; Janet D. Kelley, Rio Hondo Junior College; Carole Rothberg, Western Illinois University; Nancy J. Spencer, Virginia Commonwealth University; and Kathleen M. White, Boston University, who read through and offered valuable commentary on the text as it was being prepared. Jane Simkin provided valuable assistance in helping me interpret the many effects of nutrition on development and simply keep up with the state of the field. Phyllis Blumberg provided aid in her role as research assistant and enabled me to complete my work speedily. Richard Atkins prepared the glossary. Finally, Elsie Squitieri typed the manuscript, flawlessly as usual, and, as usual, with time pressures.

Pittsburgh, Pennsylvania   JTG
November 1977

A Topical Outline

Growing Up is a psychological study of children from before conception to adolescence. The book's approach is chronological: each chapter deals consecutively with the interests and concerns of children, parents, and caretakers at each age level. Many topics, of course, appear repeatedly. It is important to note, however, that although interests and concerns may be similar in many respects across age levels, different variables affect the child at each age level. Some readers may wish to trace a particular topic through the life of a child without first inspecting other variables. For these readers, the major topics discussed are listed here with the chapters where they are examined.

Learning

Principles of learning: 3, 6, 10, 12

Effects of child-rearing methods: 3, 7, 8, 9
child abuse: 8
disciplinary techniques: 8, 11
divorce: 7, 8

Effects of stimulation and stimulus deprivation: 6, 7, 13

Sex differences, sex roles, and sex-typed behavior: 7, 8, 9, 11, 12, 14

Socialization: 8, 9, 11
effects of television: 9
peer influences: 8, 9, 11
play and creativity: 1, 7, 9, 10, 11, 12

Development

Principles of development: 2
Development of:
attitudes and values: 11, 13, 15
cognition: 2, 6, 7, 9, 10, 11, 12
identity and self-actualization: 3, 7, 14
language: 2, 3, 6, 9, 10, 13
moral reasoning: 2, 9, 10, 11, 14
perceptual and sensorimotor functioning: 3, 6, 7, 11, 12, 13
personality: 2, 7, 11, 14
physical functioning: 2, 5, 6, 11, 13, 14
social-emotional functioning: 6, 7, 8, 9, 10, 13, 14

Individual Differences

Individual differences (general): 6, 13

Cross-cultural studies: 1, 6, 7, 8, 9, 14

Effects of heredity; genetics: 2, 4

Effects of nutrition: 5, 6

Effects of the prenatal environment: 5

Learning disabilities: 13

Problem behavior: 3, 9, 13, 14

Tests used to measure individual differences between children: 6, 9, 10, 12, 13

Educational Programs: 2, 6, 9, 10, 11, 12, 13, 14   **Research Methods Used with Children:** 1

Contents

PART 1
Determinants of Child Behavior

PART 5
The End of Childhood

Childhood and Child Psychology

Learning objectives

After completing this chapter, you should be able to:

1

describe some of the characteristics of the period of childhood in terms of their importance to the developing person;

2

identify the major societal factors that affect child development and are of concern to psychologists;

3

select methods of research best suited for answering different types of questions related to the ways children grow and develop;

4

differentiate between research methods considered ethical and unethical by psychologists for study of children.

The study of children should be important business to all Americans. If we are to be a nation of happy, healthy youngsters and adults, it is essential that we seek insight into the factors that contribute to sound development. As children grow, they present us—as adults, parents, and teachers—with unique opportunities to respond to them in ways that can either deter or facilitate healthy growth. By discovering how we can help children learn to use their bodies, to think and to problem solve, to develop healthy attitudes and productive interests, and to interact successfully with others, we take an important first step toward ensuring that they will become useful, happy adult-citizens of tomorrow.

Urie Bronfenbrenner stressed the importance of studying children when he asked the question," How can we judge the worth of a society? On what basis can we predict how well a nation will prosper?" Bronfenbrenner's own answer was: "the concern of one generation for the next" (Bronfenbrenner, 1970, p. 3).

What *is* our concern for the next generation? Unfortunately, many studies of the ways we raise our children in America have produced distressing results. We now know that damage can result from ignoring children as they grow up. By not providing sufficient things for babies to

THE IMPORTANCE OF STUDYING CHILDREN: AN INTRODUCTION

Psychologists today are more aware than ever of the importance of early development to later life experiences.

see and touch and taste when they are very young, it is possible to impair later mental ability. By socially rejecting children or by depriving them of parental attention, it is possible to destroy otherwise healthy personalities. By providing less-than-adequate educational procedures and facilities, it is possible to decrease a child's intellectual potential. We know all this, but often choose not to act on our knowledge. American psychologists and educators have expressed deep concern about this apparent apathy. Their views were summed up in a Report to the President in 1971. Authors of the report noted their fear of "a national neglect of children" (*Report to the President: White House Conference on Children*, 1971, p. 252). Psychologists, educators, and parents are just now beginning to understand what this neglect means and are seeking ways to do something about it.

Psychologists today are more aware than ever of the importance of early development to adult life experience. In this book, we examine the development and behavior of children through adolescence. A large portion of Chapter 4, "Heredity," is devoted to behavioral genetics, the study of the effects of genetic variables on development. In this chapter, we look at factors that affect the developmental process even before conception takes place. Other chapters discuss the effects of different child-rearing methods, different educational procedures, and the spiraling effects of social change. The study of children has many implications for a theory of human behavior. At a time in history when we are reminded daily of the potential and immediate threats of environmental pollution, overpopulation, and war, a thorough understanding of human behavior may well be critical to survival of the human race.

A HISTORICAL LOOK AT CHILDHOOD

Margaret Mead once said that "our descendants will regard as one of the great accomplishments of our age the discovery of the nature of childhood and the attempt to put this new knowledge to work in the upbringing of our children" (Mead, 1972, p. 49). Interestingly, this concern for children as a separate and important part of society is a comparatively new phenomenon. Until very recently, children were not even considered legally to be persons. They had no legal rights and were usually considered property of their parents until they were grown. Children of the ancient Spartans were considered property not of their parents, but of the Commonwealth. Infanticide of children considered defective was practiced in Sparta as well as in many other societies (Gordon, 1973, p. 16).

Infant death was so common just a few hundred years ago as to be expected among all levels of society throughout the world. In Europe, in the mid-eighteenth century, one in every four newborn infants did not

Young children, until recently, were dressed as small replicas of adults. (Courtesy Museum of Fine Arts, Boston)

survive. Less than half the children born were expected to reach adulthood. Children who did survive infancy had little to look forward to. There were no special nurseries, no playgrounds for children, certainly no special children's toys. Things we now consider part and parcel of every child's growing up—like fairy tales and nursery rhymes—were unknown 400 years ago. Books for children in language they could understand and about things of special interest to them did not even begin to appear until the nineteenth century. Indeed, our ancestors of just 100 years ago would have been aghast at Dr. Seuss!

Until recently, very few adults seemed to pay much attention to children—until these children grew sufficiently to become productive members of society. Growing up was, at best, a haphazard experience. The ancient Spartans, as many ancient peoples, practiced infanticide whenever it was useful for the adult members of that society. Their fellows, the ancient Athenians, left much of their culture for the modern world to marvel at, but left nothing that reflects any particular concern for their children, either in their writings or their many statues. In medieval European society, writings at least acknowledge the existence of children, but not as unique human beings. Rather, children of medieval times were thought of as small replicas of the adults they would become. Their clothing, their recreation, and the behavior expected of them reflect the notion that they were but small and inadequate grown people.

Young children, instead of learning to play games, learned the vocations of their parents. For the relatively few members of the wealthy, leisured classes of each society, this might have involved such activities as dancing, singing, or watching "farces" with the adults (Aries, 1962, pp. 70–97). For most children in the world, however, it involved heavy manual labor. The extreme briefness of childhood is confirmed by literary descriptions of how children spent their time. Many took over adult responsibilities at early ages, replacing the labor of their parents (whose life spans were shorter than those of today). Accordingly, it's not difficult to picture such youth taking part in all adult affairs, including marrying and bearing children while still practically children themselves. In Shakespeare's *Romeo and Juliet*, Romeo was not yet sixteen years old, Juliet not fourteen. This young age for an adult love relationship was quite understandable to theatergoers of the time.

Western society seems to have watched the trampling of childhood with indifference. Historical descriptions depict children engaging in various types of physically destructive labor. In England, children of both sexes worked in coal mines and in factories alongside adult workers Even today, in some Western countries, children of very young ages legally work at full-time jobs. (As late as 1973, in Greece, I saw eight-, nine-, and ten-year-old boys of poverty backgrounds working late at

As recently as this century, children were employed in textile mills, coal mines, and factories. This photograph of a young girl at her spinning machine was taken around 1909. (Courtesy of The Bettmann Archive)

Childhood in America 200 years ago began at home rather than in the hospital. Infants usually were delivered in a special room in the house, known as "the borning room." Historians estimate that about a third of the babies born during that era died in infancy—of diseases for which there were then no cures (*Time*, December 1975). For children lucky enough to survive, life was harder than it is for today's children in America. Many of the stern, Puritanical parents were suspicious of play and games—indeed, they were suspicious of anything that prompted laughter and enjoyment. Children were permitted, however, to engage in sports for their health. They had some toys: dolls for girls, marbles for boys. As in other societies, children used their time to copy adult activities. Boys learned to fish and hunt. Girls played house and learned to cook. Children of slaves learned to wait on their masters and mistresses. Rich children learned the avocations of the leisure class—they were given dancing and riding lessons, were taught proper manners, and learned how to give orders to underlings. One educational diversion for children of all classes was the watching of public executions of criminals, considered a vital part of their moral education.

night in tavernas to serve food to the adults of the community. These same young boys attended required school classes during the day.)

In colonial America also, children labored in mills, mines, and factories. It was not until the mid-nineteenth century that children in the United States were given special legal protection through child labor laws and other social reforms. And not until 1959 were the rights of children of the world unanimously proclaimed by the UN General Assembly (Declaration of the Rights of Children, *United Nations Yearbook*, 1959).

In America, as elsewhere, acknowledgment of children's special needs and recognition of childhood as a special and separate part of development came very gradually. Important changes, such as separate play and learning experiences, gradual exclusion of children from work as well as other adult activities, and, finally, governmental regulation of labor and education, are relatively recent.

In the eighteenth and early nineteenth centuries, western educators, such as Pestalozzi, first began to suggest major changes in the child-training methods of that time. Pestalozzi and Rousseau, the philosopher whose works so greatly influenced him, proposed that training ought to follow the "inherent nature of children's minds" (DeGuimps, 1906).

Early study of children centered about the developmental process itself —attempting to describe what it was that made children special. In 1891, G. Stanley Hall published a landmark study devoted to children's thinking. The material for Hall's manuscript, *The Content of Children's*

The Beginnings of Scientific Study of Children

Minds, was derived from interviews with children first entering school (Hall, 1883, in Dennis, 1949).

In 1891, Hall founded the *Pedagogical Seminary,* the first journal devoted to child studies. A second major milestone in the history of child study came in 1905 when Alfred Binet published the Binet Scale of Intelligence. Binet's work clarified for the first time the relation of chronological age to the thought processes.

Binet's techniques quickly spread to the United States. His early scale was revised for use in this country in 1937 and now is known as the Stanford-Binet Scale of Intelligence (Terman and Merrill, 1937). The Stanford-Binet and other scales devoted to measurement of intelligence will be discussed later in this book.

From the turn of the century through 1930 in the United States, many major research programs, devoted primarily to the study of long-term physical and mental growth of children, were undertaken. Institutes and research stations were opened to conduct "growth studies" at such places as the University of Iowa, Harvard, Yale, the University of Chicago, the Fels Institute, and others.

Interest in childhood was not confined to universities. Governmental interest was shown in a series of White House Conferences on Children, the first convened in 1909. One of the major outcomes of that first White House conference was the U.S. Children's Bureau, officially established on April 9, 1912. The stated purpose of the Children's Bureau was to focus on "the continuing process of growth and development, biologic and behavioral, from conception and prenatal development through infancy and childhood and on into maturation and aging" (*U.S. Government Manual,* 1975, p. 238). In 1920, continuing governmental and academic interest led the Committee on Child Development of the National Academy of Sciences to form a special Society for Research in Child Development.

Somewhere between 1935 and 1945, new interest in the effects of experience on development, spurred on by increased interest in Freudian studies, produced research on the effects of child experience on personality formation. Studies of different methods of child rearing—weaning, toilet training, parental rejection—began to appear. With them came greater concern for child welfare.

CONTEMPORARY STUDY OF CHILDREN

S tudies of children carried out today reflect concern for development and for the effects of different types of experience on child behavior. Included in the study of child psychology are studies of physical development; language development; the development of cognition (the abilities to think and understand); the development of moral reasoning; and the

Contemporary studies of children focus most frequently on problems of interest to society.

development of attitudes, interests, and personality characteristics. Both educators and psychologists have begun to devote considerable attention to the possibilities of changing the course of development by more thoroughly understanding and affective the mechanisms that direct it (Eysenck et al., 1972).

The impetus for current research comes from a variety of sources, including academic concern for the nature of children and pragmatic concern for the welfare of children. Academic concern has been expressed in basic laboratory studies of child and adolescent behavior. Theoretical models of behavior have been developed to allow psychologists to predict behavior on the basis of chronological age, as well as on the basis of environmental factors. Several such models—for example, those of Piaget, Erikson, and Kohlberg—will be discussed later in this book. Some researchers are concerned most specifically with the effects of experience on behavior. Some of these researchers conduct their studies in laboratory settings; others study children in real-life settings. Some researchers are primarily concerned with treatment of problem behavior. These child psychologists often work with families, in schools, directly in the community, and in guidance clinics.

Contemporary child psychology centers most frequently on problems of interest to society. With increasing evidence of the great importance of prenatal and early infancy environment, attention is being given to such questions as: How do we provide the best prenatal environment possible for the developing infant? What specific effects do early child care and infant learning have on later development? How do child-rearing patterns affect personality development? The special problems of child development characteristic of low-income groups also have been of deep concern, particularly in the past few years. Applied research in this area includes studies of growing up in an urban ghetto environment and in rural poverty. Other studies include the effects of poor nutrition and of deprivation of early stimulation and learning in infancy and early childhood.

Current Governmental Interest in Childhood

The concern of the federal government for childhood and for the "psychology of poverty" as it relates to children has been expressed in a number of ways. The Office of Economic Opportunity (OEO) was established within the Executive Office of the President by the Economic Opportunity Act of 1964. The purpose of OEO was to open to everyone the "opportunity for education and training, the opportunity to work, and the opportunity to live in dignity." The Head Start Program, sponsored by OEO, was begun in the summer of 1964 at 13,400 educational centers. 560,000 preschool-age children were enrolled in the first year. Head Start initially was designed to orient preschool children of economically poor backgrounds to school situations similar to those they would encounter when they entered public school (Gibson, 1972, p. 207).

The Office of Child Development (OCD) was opened in 1969 as part of the Federal Department of Health, Education, and Welfare. OCD assumed the duties originally assigned to the Bureau of Children. Population research, aging, mental retardation, and sudden infant death are among the Office's areas of special concern (*U.S. Government Manual*, 1975, p. 238). The National Institute of Education (NIE) opened its doors later in 1972 as part of the Educational Ammendments of that year. NIE was created to provide "leadership in the conduct and support of scientific inquiry into the educational process, to provide more dependable knowledge about educational quality, and to improve education."

METHODS OF STUDYING CHILDREN

The first "studies" of children involved observations followed by philosophical writings. Educators observed children and then suggested ways to improve their educations. Rousseau's famous treatise on education, *Emile, or Concerning Education* (1762) is an example of this

Descriptive researchers observe the behavior of children in natural settings.

approach. In *Emile,* Rousseau began with the philosophical conviction that man is born good. He maintained that the major concern of education ought to be to preserve and develop these original "good instincts." This could be accomplished, Rousseau suggested, through guidance away from the "nefarious influence" of society, until the young adult was strong enough morally to act according to his conscience.

Descriptive child research involves the study of children in natural settings, without experimental manipulations of outside conditions. Descriptive research describes what takes place; the researcher makes no attempt to alter conditions so as to study their effects on behavior.

Descriptive Child Research

Prenatal research Descriptive research in child behavior begins before birth with study of the individual still in utero—that is, still in the mother's womb. Study of the developing individual from conception to birth has been done in a number of different ways. Physical and behavioral studies of prenatal development have been made possible when, in certain emergency situations, fetuses have had to be surgically removed while still alive for the protection of the mother. In some situations in which fetus, amnion, and placenta were removed by Caesarian section and the fetus was kept alive for some time in solution at normal blood temperature, the fetus was studied for the duration of its life (Thompson, 1962, p. 61).

Infants born prematurely also have been a source of study for developmental researchers. The pronouncement of Crump et al. (1958) that premature infants have been born with callouses on their thumbs from sucking in utero came from just such a study.

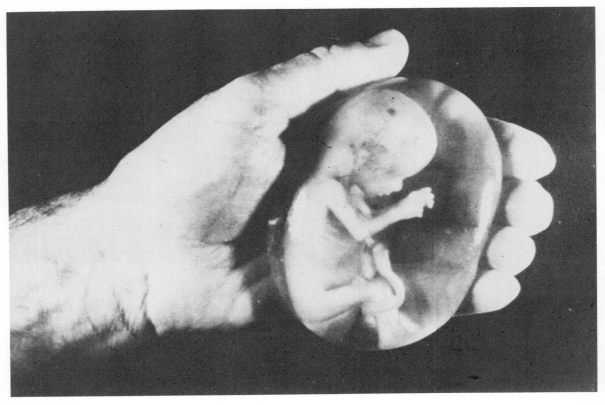

Physical and behavioral studies of development begin as
early as the prenatal stage. This human embryo is twelve
weeks of age.

Observation of fetal activity also has been made possible through use
of special equipment attached to the mother's abdomen. Using this procedure to measure amount of fetal movement, Richards and Newberry
(1938) of the Gesell Institute reported a strong relationship between
amount of prenatal movement and activity after birth. Schmeidler (1941),
measuring fetal movement during the course of pregnancy, reported
that the number and intensity of fetal movements clearly increase as the
fetus gets older.

On July 12, 1974, the National Research Act (Public Law 93-348) was
passed. This law prohibited United States government-sponsored research on a living human fetus, except for the specific purpose of ensuring the fetus's survival. Even though the moratorium on research was
lifted a year later, its impact on all fetal research, as well as on studies
of premature infants and newborns, continued to be felt. Later in the
chapter, we will discuss this issue in more depth.

Studies of children after birth Of course, most descriptive studies of child behavior deal with children after they are born. As of 1960, a full 94 percent of these studies dealt with children of preschool age (Wright, 1960, p. 75). Some of the methods of study used by researchers are described below.

Biographical methods. Over the years, description of early child behavior has taken many forms. One method used in Rousseau's time and, indeed, until recently, is the *baby biography.* Pestalozzi published in 1774 a diary describing the behavior of his son during the first forty-two months of life (DeGuimps, 1906). Pestalozzi used the diary as the basis for his description of child development. Later, the diary was used as a rationale for procedures used in his famous experimental schools.

Another famous baby biography published a century later was that of Charles Darwin (1887). Darwin used his descriptive diary to produce evidence for his theory of evolution. Darwin's baby biography is of particular interest to psychologists because of the impressiveness of detail, as well as the many hypotheses it contains regarding the nature of development. However, both Pestalozzi's and Darwin's biographies, as those of other writers of that time, were limited in the same respects. The philosophical biases, the selective perceptions of the viewers, and the fact that each biography studied one case only, made it impossible to generalize from these studies to studies of other children.

The biographical method still appears today in various forms. One variation is the *anecdotal record* kept by many public-school systems to describe incidental observations of student behaviors. Teachers prepare these records by describing on a day-to-day basis behaviors they consider sufficiently important to be remembered and passed on to future teachers.

Since students' files follow them from school to school, it is possible for anecdotal records to follow as well. Anecdotal records are viewed today with some alarm, both by educators and by parents. Critics point out that many teachers are unable to describe objectively what they see in the classroom, or to put down in the record *all* factors critical to the observed behaviors. In some cases, anecdotal records are extremely selective and serve only to prejudice the next teacher who comes in contact with them. The following excerpt was taken from the anecdotal record of an eighth-grade boy in a large Eastern public elementary school. This excerpt is typical and illustrates why many educators and parents view the anecdotal record with concern.

Friday, November 5
Jimmy tends to be totally disinterested in his schoolwork. Nothing that I do to motivate him seems to work. He is rude and is noticeably bored with everything going on about him. As an example, he was late for school four days this week. Yesterday, when I gave him a note describing

his behavior to take to his mother for her signature, he returned the next day (late again!) without the note and maintained that he had lost it. He seems incapable of even trying to learn. I do not expect him to complete high school unless he changes his attitude.
Sarah Jones, eighth-grade teacher

Let's assume that the description of Jimmy's behavior in Miss Jones's class is factually correct. He is rude. He often is late. He returned to school without the note, and maintained that he had lost it. Do these behaviors justify Miss Jones's conclusion that Jimmy simply is bored and disinterested in school? Perhaps not. Perhaps Jimmy really is interested in learning, but has rather serious personal problems at home. Perhaps Jimmy's mother has a serious or terminal illness; Jimmy may often be late because of duties associated with her care. If these facts, unknown to Miss Jones, are the case, the information now in Jimmy's permanent anecdotal record conveys an erroneous and unfair picture of the problem. A ninth-grade teacher reading the report with no more information certainly might be prejudiced.

The possibilities for harm caused by factually incorrect or incomplete student records led directly to passage in 1974 of Public Law 93-380, an extension and amendment of the Elementary and Secondary Education Act of 1965. The Buckley amendment insured that federal funds would not be made available to any state or local educational agency that does not give students or their parents access to cumulative-record folders. Provision of opportunity to challenge content of school records was also made by the amendment.

Anecdotal records are sometimes referred to long after the fact. One interesting example of observers making use of anecdotal records many

An unplanned result of the Buckley amendment

The right of students and their parents to examine academic records, as granted by the 1974 Buckley amendment, may result in increasingly bland recommendations from high-school teachers and principles. According to a 1975 Nation's School Report, the new law has caused many educators to be very guarded in their comments about students, for fear of potential lawsuits. Interviews with high-school counselors and college admissions officers seem to confirm that, since the law took effect, fewer negative comments have appeared in letters of recommendation. The result, according to admissions officials, is that students are tending to look more and more alike. The only way, apparently, to tell them apart is on the basis of their grades, test scores, and class standing (*Pittsburgh Press*, 8 December 1975).

years after they were written involves the case of Lee Harvey Oswald, the accused assassin of President John F. Kennedy. After Oswald's arrest, statements made years before by Oswald's teachers and placed permanently in his records were made available to the public. At least one of Oswald's teachers had considered him seriously emotionally disturbed and had so reported in his record. In this case, no follow-up was apparent.

Case histories. Another descriptive tool used after the fact is the case history. The researcher using the case-history method describes, often many years later with the assistance of the subject, previous events that are thought to have contributed to the subject's current situation. The case-history method often is used by psychiatrists and clinical psychologists. It permits study over time of the behavior of just one individual.

Excerpt from "Protection of the Rights and Privacy of Parents and Students," Education Amendment Act of 1974

Sec. 438. (a) (1) No funds shall be made available under any applicable program to any State or local educational agency, any institution of higher education, any community college, any school, any agency offering a preschool program, or any other educational institution which has a policy of denying, or which effectively prevents, the parents of students attending any school of such agency, or attending school, or other educational institution, the right to inspect and review any and all *official records, files, and data directly related to their children,* including all material that is incorporated into each student's cumulative record folder, and *intended for school use or to be available to parties outside the school or school system,* and specifically including, but not necessarily limited to, identifying data, academic work completed, level of achievement (grades, standardized achievement test scores), attendance data, scores on standardized intelligence, aptitude, and psychological tests, interest inventory results, health data, family background information, teacher or counselor ratings and observations, and verified reports of serious or recurrent behavior patterns. Where such records or data include information on more than one student, the parents of any student shall be entitled to receive, or be informed of, that part of such record or data as pertains to their child. Each recipient shall establish appropriate procedures for the granting of a request by parents for access to their child's school records within a reasonable period of time, but in no case more than forty-five days after the request has been made.

(2) Parents shall have an opportunity for a hearing to challenge the content of their child's school record, to insure that the records are not inaccurate, misleading, or otherwise in violation of the privacy or other rights of students, and to provide an opportunity for the correction or deletion of any such inaccurate, misleading, or otherwise inappropriate data contained therein.

Like the anecdotal record, the case history is subject to bias—in this case, due to the selectivity of both the biographer's and the subject's memories as well as differences in their points of view. When interpreting information, the unskilled biographer may infer too much, oversimplify, or make generalizations or judgments on the basis of too little evidence (Ralston and Thomas, 1972).

As with other biographical methods that study one individual only, it is impossible to use the case-history method to make broad generalizations about the behavior of people. When used objectively by a trained observer, and with all sources of information specified, the case-history method still can be an extremely useful tool in understanding the roots of problem behavior. Focusing attention on and attempting to understand the behavior of a single person can be a challenging task. The author of a case study must take special care not to be influenced by his or her own biases, and must not permit his or her own past experiences to color presentation of the material.

Opposite is a case study of a second-grade child, together with recommmendations for teachers and parents. The study was completed by a graduate student in clinical psychology, using a procedure and format developed and tested extensively by two educational psychologists (Ralston and Thomas, 1972).

Consider how much more useful this case history is in interpreting Alice-Lu's behavior than a brief anecdotal record describing only the difficulties Alice has had in class—such as the anecdotal record of Jimmy that we read earlier. The reader of Alice-Lu's case study does not have to agree with the study recommendation in order to find the report useful. On the basis of the systematic, detailed information provided, he or she is free and able to draw a number of conclusions.

Questionnaires, interviews, and other observational tools. So far, we have discussed descriptive methods used to study one person at a time. Descriptive measuring instruments are used also to study many people at the same time, to describe how groups of people tend to behave. One such instrument is the *questionnaire*, first developed by G. Stanley Hall and his students to explore "the content of the mind" (Hall, 1891). The questionnaire method utilizes series of questions that can be administered to large groups of people. Persons being studied may be asked to write down their answers or, in some cases, to respond orally. As with the other methods we described, the questionnaire is useful only when it is complete and objective. Persons writing questionnaires must prepare each question with extreme care to make certain the wording does not bias the person answering.

When administered orally, a questionnaire is called an *interview*. Interviews can provide useful information, particularly when the inter-

A case study of Alice-Lu Parker

I. *Identification and sources of information*
Name: Alice-Lu Parker, 67 Selbourne St.,
Pittsburgh, Pa.
Sources of Information:
1. Personal observation
2. Interview with student
3. Interview with child's mother
4. Interview with teacher
Race: Black
Sex: Female
Age: 7 years, 3 months
School: Colbrook Elementary, grade 2

II. *Family history*
Youngest of three children, all students at
Colbrook. Two male siblings, in grades 4 and 5.
All children in good health and doing well
academically. None with grade lower than B.
Alice-Lu is physically attractive. Reads well
above grade level, seems to enjoy her work.
However, this year for the first time, seems to be
having some trouble getting along with class-
mates, and sometimes gets into fights in class.

Mother is young, very serious-appearing
woman. Quite agreeable at coming in to be interviewed, although somewhat concerned that
Alice-Lu wasn't getting along in class. Reported
no problems at home. Completed two years of
college, majoring in philosophy, before leaving
school to marry. Reported that she was sorry
that she had dropped out, and that she hopes
one day to complete college. Adamant that her
children be educated. Husband completed three
years of college. After marriage, began to work
full time. Continued in night school. B.A. in
accounting. Now works for local firm. Has second night job to supplement the family income.
Rarely at home. Unavailable for interview. Economic status of the family moderate, although
more "well-to-do" than most in neighborhood.
Mother expresses desire to help. She has served
as room mother for class. Last year was vice-
president of the PTA.

III. *Case history*
Child born in County Hospital. Normal delivery.
No complications. Began to walk at eleven
months. Talked in sentences at three and one-
half years. Eats well. No major illnesses. Appears happy in her interactions with her family.
Many friends in the neighborhood. Only recently began "fighting with some of the kids in
the class." Isn't sure why this is happening.
Thinks possibly it's due to fact that teachers
know her older brothers. No one else in the class
has older siblings. Says she is not "the teacher's
pet." Reports that one of the children in the class
had said she was.

Child learned to read in kindergarten with
mother's help. Chosen as a peer teacher in the
first grade. Reports she likes school. Favored
play activities include riding her bicycle with
friends in the neighborhood, and reading books
about travel and adventure.

IV. *Present status; diagnosis and prognosis;
recommendations*
For the present, no substantial difficulty seems
noticeable in child's life, other than concern reported by both the child and her teacher in relation to not getting along with others. She is
bright for her age and a good student, and has,
perhaps, been emphasizing this aspect of her
schooling to the detriment of social activities.
She has good rapport with adults. In the future,
it is hoped that she will talk more with them
about insecurities. Mother is advised to provide
help, through encouraging child to bring her
classmates home to play.

viewer is skilled. The open-ended interview technique, for example, allows the interviewer to continue on in discussion of a particular question when the results seem meaningful to the study. Of course, the interviewer, as the developer of a questionnaire, must be objective in questioning and careful in selecting subjects to study.

It is extremely important that the sample subjects selected are representative of the larger population being studied. For example, if we wish to determine the attitudes of American children toward their fathers, it is important that we question all sorts of American children—from different racial backgrounds, different areas of the country, different socioeconomic backgrounds, and so on. We cannot study children from our own community only in order to describe the views of all American children. This is true regardless of the evaluation tool used, whether it is a questionnaire, interview, rating scale, or other measuring instrument.

Cross-sectional and longitudinal studies. There are several ways that child psychologists can gather information about changes that take place in development, no matter what measuring instrument they decide to use. One way to study developmental change is to study the same person or persons over time, and then to observe and measure systematically changes in behavior. This type of study is called a *longitudinal study.* One very famous longitudinal study of the behavior of gifted children observed the behavior of the same individuals over a thirty-five-year period (Terman, 1925–1959). Another famous study of individuals raised in stimulating and nonstimulating environments during early childhood followed the behavior of these people over thirty years, as they married and began adult professional lives (Skeels, 1966).

Longitudinal studies clearly pose one major problem to developmental researchers interested in human beings. It takes a very long time, as long as a human lifetime, to describe life-span development. In addition, the high mobility rate of Americans today makes it extremely difficult to keep close track of one individual's activities over an extended period of time.

The *cross-sectional method* of research is designed to help solve these problems. When large numbers of children of different ages are studied all at the same time, so that behavior at these different ages can be compared, the method is called cross-sectional. Piaget used the cross-sectional method to observe the behavior of children while they solved problems requiring the ability to think and to understand. Piaget systematically observed and described both verbal and nonverbal behavior in his studies. He attributed differences found to differences in age. Although Piaget often referred to the method he used as "clinical," interpreters of Piaget have termed it "anecdotal" (Flavell, 1963, p. 30).

Comparative research. Comparative researchers—those who study child development in different cultures—often employ cross-sectional methods of research. Such researchers sometimes have taken extreme positions in assuming that culture is clearly the all-important factor in the development of personality. The statement that "cultures transcend the minds and bodies of individuals living within them" (Hsu, 1972, p. 3) is an example of such a position. However, because of the obvious impossibility of effectively manipulating cultures so as to determine whether or not they actually affect personality, comparative researchers must be cautious in interpreting their data. Methods used in comparative research usually are descriptive: many cultures are studied; behavior of children at different ages within each of the different cultures is compared. Comparative study of child development is just now beginning to afford American psychologists new glimpses into our own cultural contributions to child rearing. We are beginning to ask questions such as: How does the behavior of children raised from infancy in preschools, such as those in the Soviet Union and on kibbutzim in Israel, compare to that of American children raised by their mothers in their own homes?

During six visits to the USSR to study Soviet children in preschool programs, I consistently observed them to be happy, healthy youngsters. If the Soviet babies I visited had problems, these problems did not relate to health or to apparent enjoyment of life. Perhaps there is much we can learn from Soviet methods of infant care. In Chapter 7, we examine child rearing in a number of other societies, and discuss the behavior of children at various ages as part of our study of American methods of child rearing.

Comparative studies of child development afford psychologists new insights into child-rearing techniques. These Soviet infants are being cared for in a state-operated boarding school.

Experimental Study of Children

Descriptive studies are used to investigate how children behave in natural, real-life situations. Some researchers study child behavior in carefully controlled situations. Such researchers—called experimental researchers—not only describe *what* children do, but also use their research to explain *why* they do it. Experimental researchers manipulate and control features of the environment important to behavior, then measure the consequent behavior.

To explain the experimental method, let's use one famous experimental study as an example. Hilgard (1933) devised this study to answer the question of whether development of certain basic skills is due to training or to normal maturing processes. Hilgard's subjects were sets of young identical twins. He assumed, because they were identical twins, that their heredity component was identical. Any differences in behavior had to be due to learning rather than to normal maturing processes controlled by heredity. The basic procedure used with each set of identical twins was as follows. First, one young twin was given training at some skill, while the other was not. Sometime later, the skill was measured in both twins. If Hilgard found that training one child increased that child's skill competence above that of the other, he concluded that the skill was developed through training. If both twins performed equally well, even though only one was given special training, then Hilgard concluded that the increase in skill was due to identical maturation processes. Hilgard's experiments involved a variety of relatively simple motor skills, such as tossing a ring over a peg and walking along a narrow board.

Since most sets of twins performed equally well at the skills when they were measured, Hilgard concluded that ability in these skills increases normally with age and cannot be enhanced through early training. Hilgard's findings were used much later by advocates of readiness theories, as we will discuss in Chapter 2.

Independent and dependent variables In Hilgard's study, as in all experimental studies, one feature of the environment was manipulated by the researcher. This manipulated feature is known as the independent variable. In the case of Hilgard's co-twin control study, the feature manipulated—i.e., the independent variable—was the training experience. The variable that might be affected by this independent variable is known as the dependent variable. In Hilgard's study, the dependent variable measured was skill at performing the required tasks.

Experimental and control subjects Two types of subjects, experimental and control, are used in an experimental study. The experimenter must ensure that they are as alike as possible in all respects but one: the experimental subject has access to the independent variable; the control subject does not. In the Hilgard study, the twins receiving training were experimental subjects. The twins receiving no training were control subjects. Identical twins, of course, are perfect control subjects, for they are as identical as any two human beings possibly can be, both in terms of genetic makeup and also in terms of most other family experiences.

Using animals for experimental study Human beings are very complicated creatures. In experimental research with humans, it is impossible for the experimenter always to control all outside conditions affecting behavior. Invariably, some variables that might possibly affect the behavior of the subjects cannot be controlled by the experimenter. In studying child behavior, the experimenter often is limited in ability to evaluate accurately the child's present environment, the child's history of interaction with his or her past environment, and, in most children, exact genetic endowment. In the case of Hilgard's co-twin study, Hilgard could tell that, because the subjects were identical twins, they were identical in genetic characteristics. However, he could not control all of the personal experiences that each of the twins might have had during the courses of their lives outside the experimental situation. And, even if it were theoretically possible to control all of these outside experiences, Hilgard would have been prohibited from doing so by ethical considerations.

For these reasons, many researchers concerned with questions related to the nature of development have relied on subhuman subjects for their experimental data. Initially, it may seem meaningless to study the effects of changing environments on the development of chimpanzees or puppy dogs or rats if one is interested in child development. On the other hand, particularly when researchers are interested in studying the effects of independent variables that might produce long-term harmful effects on the subjects being studied, as, for example, sensory deprivation, it is advantageous to study lower species first.

Many experimental studies conducted with lower animals have major relevance to human child psychology. One famous example is a classic series of studies done by Harlow with baby monkeys (Harlow, 1958). In one of these studies, Harlow used an experimental group of baby monkeys reared in cages alone. Instead of their live mothers, each monkey was given two substitute mothers, one made of hard wire and one made of soft terrycloth. A control group of monkeys was raised in cages together with their own natural mothers. These monkeys spent a large proportion of their days clinging to their mothers, both during feeding and at other times as well. In the experimental group, the wire mother was the sole source of food. Nursing bottles were built into the center of the wire mothers' chests with the nipples protruding. To nurse, the baby monkeys had to climb onto the fronts of the wire mothers and hang on with all four limbs. When not eating, they spent much of their time clinging with all four legs to the comfortable, soft-padded mother substitute. Other than when nursing, not much time was spent in close contact with the wire mother.

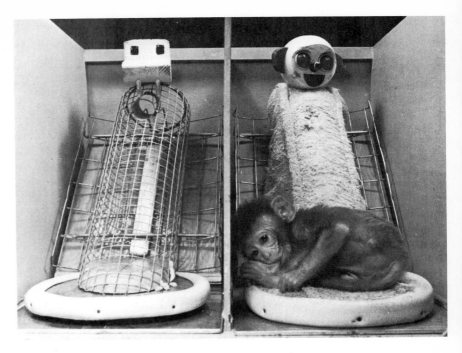

Harlow's baby monkeys spent much time clinging to their soft, padded mother substitutes. (From H. Harlow, The nature of love, *American Psychologist* 13, 1958: 675. Copyright © 1958 by the American Psychological Association. Reprinted by permission.)

Harlow's study made clear that his independent variable, type of mother or mother substitute, strongly affected the baby monkey behavior. It showed something else as well. In the experimental group of monkeys, even when food did not come from the soft cloth mother, the latter provided an apparently necessary contact and was uniformly preferred by her "monkey children." Harlow showed that when baby monkeys are offered both hard and soft substitute mothers, even though the hard mother "feeds" the baby, the baby still prefers contact with the soft, padded "mama." Harlow's study thus demonstrated that contact comfort is more important to the development of a strong affectional response in baby monkeys than is satisfaction of the hunger drive.

The results of Harlow's study are important. Equally important are the dangers implicit in such a study had human babies been used for research. In a later report, Harlow noted that all baby monkeys who were raised with live monkey mothers eventually developed normal adult heterosexual responses (Harlow, 1962). However, none of the babies raised with wire or cloth-mother surrogates developed either normal adult heterosexual behavior, or, in females, maternal responses toward their young—results Harlow had not predicted initially. Imagine the possible sad outcomes for humans had they been experimental subjects in Harlow's experimental design.

It is generally agreed that research involving children is good for society as a whole, and that many important gains for humanity have come from such research. Yet, together with increased understanding of the benefits of research has come the additional responsibility of providing moral and legal protection for subjects.

Out of the famous Nuremberg trials of Nazi War criminals came descriptions of cruel experimentation performed on concentration-camp victims. Many of us have read reports of research on the effects of various aversive drugs on prisoners, studies of the length of time prisoners could remain alive immersed in cold water, and worse. To ensure that such atrocities could never again be permitted under the guise of scientific research, the Nuremberg Code was formulated (Reynolds, 1972). The Nuremberg Code established the right of any human subject participating in clinical research to give or withhold what was termed "informed consent." Informed consent, according to the Code, means that the subject clearly and fully understands what the research entails for him or her before agreeing to participate.

Ethical Problems in Studying Children

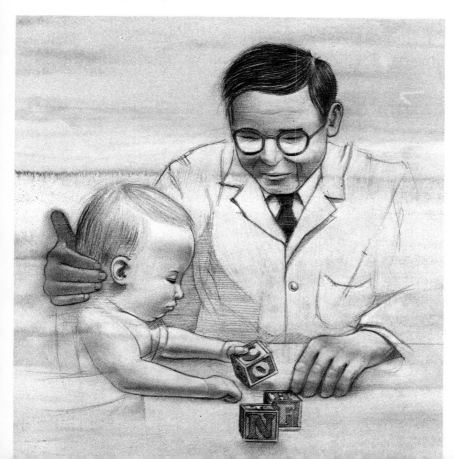

Child research poses a number of ethical and legal questions for psychologists.

The question of informed consent is a complicated one. When researchers are studying the behavior of individuals with restricted ability to understand what the research is all about, as in the case of small children, the mentally incompetent, or even simply uneducated adults, or when they are studying the behavior of individuals who do not have the freedom to give or withhold consent, as in the case of prisoners, this question becomes difficult, indeed. When does volunteering for an experiment change from a free decision to coercion? When the researcher is a teacher "requesting" students in the class to volunteer for a study in learning, how many students feel they "must" volunteer? If an experimenter is paying poverty subjects to volunteer for a study and the subjects are clearly in need of money, is this really freedom of consent or is it coercion? And if a researcher requires consent of parents to study the behavior of small children, how much information about the study must be given these parents before the requirements of informed consent are met? Should parents be given the responsibility for making decisions regarding the welfare of their children without understanding each and every implication of these decisions? We mentioned earlier in this chapter that studies of fetal development have been performed. Fetal research presents another major problem in ethics. How we can ever possibly guarantee the rights of consent of a fetus?

Children's rights groups stop Harvard research project

Observational studies of children, as well as experimental studies, can cause ethical crises. According to an article in the *New York Times* (20 June 1975), a study by a Harvard University psychiatrist screening newborn children for the presence of extra chromosomes was halted. A Boston group called Science for the People together with the Children's Defense Fund in Washington and a number of Massachusetts advocacy groups had charged that the study stigmatized the children and did them more harm than good. They further charged that the research findings could yield very little information useful either to the children or their parents.

The study had used a longitudinal approach.

Children who were identified as having the extra chromosome were studied over time to determine what adverse effects might have been associated with the aberration. In order to do this, parents had to be informed of the extra chromosome and the possibility that it might be related to behavioral aberrations. Some psychologists suggested that the study might provide a self-fulfilling prophecy. The chief investigator of the study reported in an interview that he had halted the research because of harassment, unrelenting controversy, and the threat of further opposition to his work by groups supporting children's rights.

Ethics codes established by psychologists for research with children All of these extremely complicated questions led the United States government in the 1960s to enact the first federal law and agency regulation on medical experimentation of humans (Durran, Smhyg, and Beecher, 1969, p. 77). The American Psychological Association, after considerable debate on the advantages and disadvantages of controlling human behavioral research, developed a code of ethical standards for research with human subjects. Because of the special implications of conducting behavioral research with children, the Division on Developmental Psychology of the American Psychological Association established its own statement of ethical standards, a portion of which appears on pages 26–27.

Much, of course, has happened since the late 1960s relating to the use of human subjects in research. Federal guidelines governing the use of children in research were still being established in 1976 when this text was being prepared. In addition, many universities have developed their own explicit procedures for conducting research with children. Basically, however, all of these ethical codes make the same several requirements: that parents be notified, given all details and facets of the proposed research important to the child, and be told the use to which the information obtained from the child will be used. Despite these requirements, however, in the case of psychological research with uneducated populations in our country, major ethical problems still remain for researchers to resolve.

Psychologists today agree that research with human beings should not involve invasion of privacy. It would be considered an invasion of privacy, for example, for a researcher to ask a child questions concerning the sex life of his or her parents, or their personal attitudes toward one another, without parental permission. Human psychological research must maintain respect for the individual.

Psychologists agree also that research involving children should involve procedures guaranteed safe for the subjects being studied. Studies involving the effects of frustration on children, for example, have been criticized by many authorities, because of the possibilities of the child subjects suffering long-term detrimental effects. The APA Code states that researchers must avoid at all costs the possibility of exploiting subjects in the name of science.

The problem of safety, however, is a complicated one. In some cases, psychological research may be made unsafe simply because of inexperienced or naive researchers. An example of just such a research project was observed by the author. It was conducted in a university laboratory under controlled, and apparently safe, conditions. However, because of a lack of appropriate screening devices for subjects, an obvious danger was present. The children used as subjects in the study were asked to observe a series of words focused on a movie screen by a tachistocope, a device that presents images for extremely short periods of time. The screen on which tachistoscopically presented images appear alternately brightens (when the image is on) and darkens (when it is off)—the effect is similar to a flashing light. One of the subjects in the study was a ten-year-old girl, who, unknown to the researcher, was an epileptic. Both the child and her parents had been told the nature of the study. However, the researcher had neglected to inform them that the tachistocope causes light flashes dangerous to epileptics. The child spent fifteen minutes in the room with the other children in the study, then fell to the floor in an epileptic seizure. Luckily for this subject, the seizure was a short one and was not followed by additional reactions. However, the incident clearly could have been avoided by more careful screening of subjects and by providing more information to the parents. Without presenting information regarding the potential dangers of the equipment involved, the researcher, in this case inadvertently, violated the rights of consent of this subject, and, in addition, threatened her safety.

APA Division of Developmental Psychology excerpt on ethics

Children as research subjects present problems for the investigator different from those [posed by] adult subjects. Our culture is marked by a tenderness of concern for the young. The young are viewed as more vulnerable to distress (even though evidence may suggest that they are actually more resilent in recovery from stress). Because the young have less knowledge and less experience, they also may be less able to evaluate what participation in research means. And, consent of the parent for the study of his child is the prerequisite to obtaining consent from the child. These characteristics outline the major differences between research with children and research with adults.

1 No matter how young the subject, he has rights that supersede the rights of the investigator of his behavior. In the conduct of his research the investigator measures each operation he proposes against this principle and is prepared to justify his decision.

2 The investigator uses no research operation that may harm the child either physically or psychologically. Psychological harm, to be sure, is difficult to define nevertheless, its definition remains a responsibility of the investigator.

3 The informed consent of parents or of those legally designated to act in loco parentis is obtained, preferably in writing. Informed consent requires that the parent be given accurate information on the profession and institutional affiliation of the investigator, and on the research, albeit in layman's terms. The consent of parents is not solicited by any claims of benefit to the child. Not only is the right of parents to refuse consent respected, but parents must be given the opportunity to refuse.

4 The investigator does not coerce a child into participating in a study. The child has the right to refuse and he, too, should be given the opportunity to refuse.

5 When the investigator is in doubt about possible harmful effects of his efforts or when he decides that the nature of his research re-

Clearly it is unethical for a researcher to conduct an experiment that has the potential of causing a ten-year-old child to have an epileptic seizure. But other studies, possibly of great importance to psychologists and educators, pose problems that are not so clear-cut. For example, take a child-development researcher who wishes to establish an early-intervention program to teach disadvantaged children skills necessary for later success in public school. Is this researcher conducting humanitarian research? Or is he instead exploiting these children by imposing his own goals and values on them, perhaps even destroying their cultural heritage?

The problems psychologists have encountered in applying and interpreting ethical codes have generated considerable debate. Some psychologists have been deeply concerned that restrictions imposed on researchers at best take a considerable amount of work and planning to implement. Further, there is the danger that research important to humanity may be stopped because of misinterpretation of the code. Indeed, there is evi-

quires deception, he submits his plan to an ad hoc group of his colleagues for review. It is the group's responsibility to suggest other feasible means of obtaining the information. Every psychologist has a responsibility to maintain not only his own ethical standards but also those of his colleagues.

6 The child's identity is concealed in written and verbal reports of the results, as well as in informal discussions with students and colleagues.

7 The investigator does not assume the role of diagnostician or counselor in reporting his observations to parents or those in loco parentis. He does not report test scores or information given by a child in confidence, although he recognizes a duty to report general findings to parents and others.

8 The investigator respects the ethical standards of those who act in loco parentis (e.g., teachers, superintendents of institutions).

9 The same ethical standards apply to children who are control subjects, and to their parents, as to those who are experiment subjects. When the experimental treatment is believed to benefit the child, the investigator considers an alternative treatment for the control group instead of no treatment.

10 Payment in money, gifts, or services for the child's participation does not annul any of the above principles.

11 Teachers of developmental psychology present the ethical standards of conducting research on human beings to both their undergraduate and graduate students. Like the university committees on the use of human subjects, professors share responsibility for the study of children on their campuses.

12 Editors of psychological journals reporting investigations of children have certain responsibilities to the authors of studies they review: they povide space for the investigator to justify his procedures where necessary and to report the precautions he has taken. When the procedures seem questionable, editors ask for such information.

13 The Division and its members have a continuing responsibility to question, amend, and revise the standards.

From *Newsletter*, American Psychological Association, Division on Developmental Psychology, 1968, pp. 1–3. Reprinted by permission.

dence that this may have occurred in some situations. For example, in 1974, the National Research Act (PL 93–348) was passed, prohibiting research on living human fetuses. Even though the ban, mentioned earlier in this chapter, was intended only to protect living fetuses before or after induced abortion, it was interpreted by researchers so broadly that most fetal research in the United States ended (Hart 1975, p. 72). In 1975, a legislatively created panel reported to the Secretary of Health, Education and Welfare that "ethically acceptable research that might yield important biomedical information has been halted," and, for this reason, "it is considered in the public interest that the moratorium be lifted." The panel urged further that HEW "take special care . . . that the commission's concerns for the protection of the fetus as a research subject are met, and that the fetus be treated with the respect due to dying subjects" (*Report of the National Commission for the Protection of Human Subjects of Biomedical and Behavioral Research*, 1975). The views of the panel led the Department of Health, Education and Welfare in August, 1975 to lift the moratorium. The new ruling stated that a woman "need not be presumed to lack interest in her fetus even when she has decided to terminate her pregnancy; thus, she may validly be asked for consent for research involving the fetus." The rules ban experiments that "of themselves would terminate the heartbeat or respiration of a fetus," or that would artificially maintain the vital functions of a nonviable fetus, except to develop "new methods for enabling fetuses to survive to the point of viability" (Department of Health, Education and Welfare, 1975).

Obviously, questions that psychologists have concerning the ethics of research will never be answered by any code of ethics alone. Judgments often must be subjective. For this reason, many universities and governmental research agencies today require that any proposal involving human subjects be reviewed by an ethics advisory committee made up of research colleagues, in order to ensure that highest ethical standards are used, that the integrity of all subjects is preserved, and that helpless subjects, such as children, are protected.

SUMMARY

History shows that interest in childhood as a separate and important part of the individual's life span is a relatively new phenomenon. Only very recently have psychologists, educators, and parents focused attention on this period. Factors affecting children as they grow are now recognized as essential to the development of happy, healthy, sane adults.

In the past, research methods used to study children have included descriptions of what children do. Biographical methods, case histories, questionnaires, and interviews have been made more useful to researchers in recent years through the development of systematic and objective

procedures. Studies of children may be conducted longitudinally, in which the same children are studied over time, or by cross-sectional methods, in which children of different ages are studied at the same time and then compared. Comparative researchers study children of different backgrounds and cultures.

Experimental child study is a most recent development in the study of children. Experimental researchers manipulate variables within a controlled environment in order to observe the effects on the behaviors being studied. Experimental child psychology answers the question of why children behave as they do. At the same time, it poses provocative ethical questions for the researcher and the scientific community.

QUESTIONS FOR THOUGHT AND REVIEW	

QUESTIONS FOR THOUGHT AND REVIEW

1 Compare and contrast the societal role of children in earlier times with the position of children today. What advantages do American children enjoy now that were not available to their ancestors? Conversely, were there advantages in the past that children no longer have? (For review, see pages 4–7.)

2 What are the major issues of concern to child researchers today? Why are these issues important? (For review, see pages 8–10.)

3 Assume you are a child psychologist interested in answering the question: What effects does consistent picking up of a young baby and holding the baby upright have on later motor development? What research method would you use to answer this question? Describe how you would conduct the study. (For review, see pages 10–22.)

4 What limits do you think should be placed on researchers studying the behavior of school-age children? Why? (For review, see pages 23–28.)

FOR FURTHER READING

Anderson, J. The methods of child psychology. In C. Murchison, *Handbook of Child Psychology*. New York: Russell & Russell, 1967, pp. 3–30. Anderson provides in this relatively short reading an excellent overview of techniques used in studying children. He describes a series of evaluative instruments in some detail. The article is useful reading for students planning to design their own research projects.

Ethical aspects of experimentation with human subjects. *Daedalus* 98 (1968): 211–598. This special issue of *Daedalus* is concerned entirely with the problems of ethics in conducting human research. Medical research, as well as research in the social sciences, is discussed. Many points of view are considered, including legal aspects of the problem.

Readers who are provoked by discussion in this chapter of ethical issues may well find some of their questions answered here.

Mussen, P. *Handbook of Research Methods in Child Development*. New York: Wiley, 1960. This handbook provides a major reference source for research methodologies. Sections related to methods of research in biological, cognitive, personality, and social development are included.

Reese, H., and L. Lipsitt. *Experimental Child Psychology*. New York: Academic Press, 1970. Reese and Lipsitt are concerned in this text primarily with experimental methods of research. The review of child research literature includes studies of sensory and learning processes, language learning, emotional and perceptual learning, intelligence, and socialization.

REFERENCES

American Psychological Association, Committee on Ethical Standards in Psychological Research. Ethical standards for research with human subjects. *APA Monitor*, May 1972, pp. i–xix.

American Psychological Association Division on Developmental Psychology. Statement on ethical standards. *Newsletter*, 1968, pp. 1–3.

Aries, P. *Centuries of Childhood*. New York: Knopf, 1962.

Brody, J. Screening for extra chromosomes ends in Boston. *New York Times*, 20 June 1975.

Bronfenbrenner, U. *Two Worlds of Childhood*. New York: Russell Sage Foundation, 1970.

Coles, R. Growing up in America then and now. *Time*, 29 December 1975, pp. 27–29.

Crump, E., P. Gore, and C. Horton. The sucking behavior in premature infants. *Human Biology*, 30 (1958): 128–141.

Darwin, C. A biographical sketch of an infant. *Mind* 2 (1887): 285–294.

Declaration of the rights of the child. Proclamation by the UN General Assembly, November 20, 1959. *United Nations Yearbook*. New York: Columbia University Press, 1960.

DeGuimps, R. *Pestalozzi, His Life and Work*. New York: Appleton-Century-Crofts, 1906.

Dennis, W. Historical beginnings of child psychology. *Psychological Bulletin*, 46 (1949): 224–235.

Department of Health, Education, and Welfare, Office of the Secretary. Protection of human subjects: fetuses, pregnant women, and in vitro fertilization. *Federal Register* 40 (8 August 1975): 33525.

Durran, W., J. Smhyg, and H. Beecher. Experimentation in children: a reexamination of legal ethical principles. *Journal of the American Medical Association* 10, no. 1 (1969): 77–83.

Eysenck, H., W. Arnold, and R. Meili, eds. *Encyclopedia of Psychology*. London: Search Press, 1972.

Flavell, J. *The Developmental Psychology of Jean Piaget.* New York: Van Nostrand & Reinhold, 1963.

Gibson, J. *Educational Psychology: A Programmed Text.* New York: Appleton-Century-Crofts, 1968.

Gibson, J. *Educational Psychology.* 2d ed. New York: Appleton-Century-Crofts, 1972.

Gordon, H. Genetics and civilization in historical perspective. In H. Porter and R. Skaldo, eds., *Heredity and Society.* New York: Academic Press, 1973.

Gray, S. Ethical issues in research in early childhood intervention. *Children,* 18 (1971): 83–89.

Hall, G. The contents of children's minds on entering school. *Pedagogical Seminary,* 1 (1891): 139–173.

Harlow, H. The nature of love. *American Psychologist,* 13 (1958): 673–685.

Harlow, H. The heterosexual affectional system in monkeys. *American Psychologist* 17 (1962): 1–9.

Hart, D. Fetal research and antiabortion politics: holding science hostage. *Family Planning Perspectives* 7 (1975): 72–82.

Hilgard, J. The effect of early and delayed practice on memory and motor performances studied by the method of co-twin control. *Journal of Genetic Psychological Monographs* 4 (1933): 493–497.

Hsu, F. *Psychological Anthropology.* Cambridge, Mass.: Shenkman Co., 1972.

Mead, M. A new understanding of childhood. *Redbook Magazine,* January 1972, pp. 49–50.

Mussen, P. *Handbook of Research Methods in Child Development.* New York: Wiley, 1960.

Ralston, N., and G. Thomas. *The Child Case Studies for Analysis.* Scranton, Pa.: Intext Educational Publishers, 1972.

Report of the National Commission for the Protection of Human Subjects of Biomedical and Behavioral Research. Conference held at Bethesda, Md., March 14–15, 1975.

Report to the President: White House Conference on Children. Washington, D.C.: U.S. Government Printing Office, 1971.

Reynolds, F. On the protection of human subjects and social science. *International Social Science Journal* 24 (1972): 693–719.

Richards, T., and H. Newberry. Studies in fetal behavior: III. Can performance on test items at six months postnatally be predicted on the basis of fetal activity? *Child Development* 9 (1938): 79–86.

Rousseau, J. *Emile, or Concerning Education, Book 2.* (First published 1762) New York: Dutton, 1938.

Schmeidler, G. The relation of fetal activity to activity of the mother. *Child Development* 12 (1941): 63–68.

Skeels, H. Adult status of children with contrasting early life experiences. *Monographs Research in Child Development,* October 1966.

Terman, L., and M. Merrill. *Measuring intelligence.* Boston: Houghton Mifflin, 1937.

Terman, L. *Genetic Studies of Genius.* Vols. 1–4. Stanford: Stanford University Press, 1925–1959.

Thompson, G. *Child Psychology* 2d ed. Boston: Houghton Mifflin, 1962.

United States Government Manual 1974–1975. Washington, D.C.: Office of the Federal Register, National Archives and Records Service, General Service Administration, U.S. Government Printing Office, 1975.

Wright, H. Observational child study. In P. H. Mussen, *Handbook of Research Methods in Child Development.* New York: Wiley, 1960, pp. 71–139.

PART 1

Determinants of Child Behavior

Development

Learning objectives

After completing this chapter, you should be able to:

1
explain the relationship between maturation and learning and outline the so-called critical period in the life of the child in terms of this relationship;

2
describe some of the developmental tasks expected of children in our society and relate each to the development of "readiness";

3
describe the major developmental stages through which children go and explain the major principles governing this development;

4
consider the stage-dependent explanation of development; compare and contrast some of the major developmental theories in light of their utility to parents and/or educators.

As people get older, both their bodies and their behaviors change. They grow physically larger; their body proportions change; they gradually become stronger; and they become more and more capable of making intricate responses and solving more and more complex problems. They develop different interests, attitudes, and abilities.

Many child psychologists are concerned with describing and explaining these and all the other changes that take place as people age. They view changes in growth and development as a series of progressively more complex stages. The causes of these changes are physiological and environmental, or both. In this chapter, we examine the principles that govern growth and development in children and consider several theories that attempt to explain why these changes take place.

MATURATION

Some changes that take place with age are due simply to our biological inheritance and to the fact that we are human beings. It is these changes that make us different from all other living creatures. Whatever the environment, a puppy will grow to be a dog and a baby will become an adult human being. Some development is controlled by the genetic materials contained in each of the cells of our bodies. This development takes place independent of interaction with the environment—that is, regardless of outside influences—and is termed *maturation*. In Chapter 4, we discuss the specific mechanisms through which heredity controls development. We also examine how defects in the genetic material caused by such factors as viruses, X-rays, and chemicals can drastically alter the course of development. Some authors have stressed the fact that maturation sets limits on development (Hurlock, 1972). However, for most of us, maturational limits are never met. We never reach our true potentials.

Maturation affects all types of development, behavioral as well as physical. Child psychologists have shown that many human behaviors develop through maturation. The ability to walk, for example, is affected only minimally by learning experience. Evidence for this was reported in studies of Hopi Indian babies. Hopi mothers used to bind their babies to cradle boards that they would carry on their backs. Babies remained attached to these boards most of the time during the first three months of their lives, and for part of each day after that. Because they were unable to move their legs while attached to the boards, they had almost no experience using the muscles required for walking. Yet, when removed from the cradle boards, they walked at approximately the same age as other children. Apparently, lack of opportunity to practice moving their arms and legs did not hamper development of walking (Mussen, 1973).

Hopi Indian babies carried on cradle boards for the first
three months of life had no difficulty learning to walk.

**The Relationship
between Maturation
and Learning**

From the instant of conception, the developing individual is interacting
in certain ways with the environment. When interaction between the
child and the outside world leads to changes in behavior, we say that
learning has taken place. Humans are capable of very simple forms of
learning even before birth (Spelt, 1948). It is extremely difficult, therefore, for psychologists to determine which behaviors are due to maturation and which to learning. Clearly, maturation and learning are closely
interrelated in their effects on human development. Maturation explains
the many similarities between human beings; the interrelationship between maturation and learning explains the individuality of human behavior.

One method child researchers have used to distinguish the effects of
learning and maturation on development is the identical-twin study
(Gesell and Thompson, 1929; Strayer, 1930; Hilgard, 1933; and others).
Fraternal twins are the result of simultaneous fertilization of two different

egg cells or ova by two sperm. As we shall discuss in Chapter 4, persons with genetically different characteristics are created when this happens. Identical twins, on the other hand, are the result of the splitting of one fertilized ovum. Two genetically identical individuals are thereby created. Since identical twins have exactly the same genetic inheritance, differences noted in their behavior can be attributed to different life experiences. Investigators have found many behavioral differences in identical twins. They have also found many similarities, even when individual learning experiences related to these behaviors have been quite different (Gesell, 1954). To complicate this issue, identical twins spend more time together, are more likely to be placed in the same classrooms, have more similar health records and reputations, and, in general, share a more common physical and social environment than that experienced ordinarily even by fraternal twins. In short, it seems that environmental influences are more similar, at least in some ways, for identical twins than for fraternal twins. Thus, we cannot always be sure that similarities in behavior of identical twins are due to heredity alone. However, we do know that differences must be due to environment and not heredity.

As described in Chapter 1, Hilgard (1933) used identical twins to study specific effects of maturation on memory and motor performance. The basic procedure used in this and other identical-twin studies is the co-twin procedure. (For a review of this procedure, see p. 20.)

Hilgard studied one pair of identical twins from the age of fifty-four months to sixty-six months, focusing on a series of specific skills that involved both memory and motor responses. Specific tasks included memorizing lists of objects and digits, tossing a ring over a peg, and walking the length of a narrow board. At the beginning of the study, neither twin demonstrated ability in any of these skills. Later, twin T was given specific training. Twin C was given no training. Three months later, both twins were tested. Hilgard found that the twin without early practice quickly caught up with the other; almost nothing had been gained from the early practice. Hilgard assumed that the skills studied had developed through maturation alone. He further assumed that practice did not aid in their development.

One chief effect of maturation on the developing child is to make new kinds of behavior possible. Some new behaviors, such as those studied by Gesell, appear to be self-generated. We call these *autogenous* behaviors. Autogenous behaviors seem to appear spontaneously, without preparation or practice. Walking is a good example. It is possible to delay by artificial methods the age at which a young child begins to walk—for example, by not providing proper nourishment, so that the baby's legs do not grow strong enough to carry his weight. However, without deprivation of this sort, we can expect all babies to walk at roughly the same stage of development, regardless of whether we provide any sort of special learning experience.

Evidence gathered so far by child psychologists indicates that autogenous behaviors that mature without any necessary training or practice are limited to very simple skills. As the complexity of a skill increases, so does the relative influence of learning. More complex behaviors may require a certain degree of maturation, but do not appear at all without the addition of special learning experiences. Speech is an example of such a behavior. According to many authors, learning rather than maturation is the major determinant in the development of highly complex classroom skills, such as reading and writing.

Readiness

Maturation and learning have been described by one author as being "in a circular relationship, each feeding into the other" (Stone and Church, 1973, p. 162). Another way of saying the same thing is that maturation brings with it *readiness* for the appearance of new and more complex behaviors. In some cases, readiness refers to behaviors of which the developing child is capable, on condition that certain kinds of learning experiences are provided. We call this readiness to learn. According to many child psychologists, children cannot learn until they are ready to do so. The effectiveness of teaching, according to this approach, depends on proper timing of experiences. It also depends on a thorough knowledge of the developmental stage of the child.

Critical Periods of Development

Maturation leads to readiness for new behaviors. Developmental psychologists theorize that there are *critical* or *sensitive periods* in children's development during which learning new behaviors first becomes possible. They further theorize that certain interactions with the environment are required during this period in order for development to proceed normally. The crucial factor here is timing. If appropriate interaction does not take place during this critical period, development may be slowed or stopped. In other words, there are more favorable and less favorable periods in development for learning different skills. Children who receive attention and praise for early verbal attempts will be likely to speak more fluently and at an earlier age than children who do not receive verbal stimulation when ready to learn. A young child deprived of opportunity to learn can be expected to have difficulty later in developing other learned responses helpful to school learning.

Learning deprivation occurs when caretakers do not provide a child with suitable attention. Children from every socioeconomic, religious, ethnic, and racial background in this country have been subject to such deprivation. Certain other types of deprivation during critical periods of development can actually cause permanent damage. Such is the case with severe protein malnutrition at early ages, which can lead to irreversible retardation (Coles et al., 1967).

Much developmental research has been devoted to specifying exact time periods when stimulation will be most useful (Lavatelli and Sten-

Konrad Lorenz, the "imprinted mother" to these goslings, leads his charges on a morning stroll.

Imprinting: maturation or learning?

A research topic of major interest to psychologists concerned with the relationship between maturation and learning is *imprinting*. Dr. Konrad Lorenz, the pioneer researcher in the area of imprinting, noted that some animals are born with a tendency to accept a certain range of "mother figures." Once a mother figure has been accepted by the young animal, it will follow that mother figure everywhere. Imprinting is the term used to refer to the bond that apparently develops between the young animal and the mother figure it adopts. Lorenz's most famous research involved geese (Lorenz, 1952). He discovered that, shortly after hatching, young goslings will follow the first moving object that comes into their field of view. They thereafter "imprint" that object. Of course, normally, the first moving object present is the mother goose. Lorenz, however, was able to produce artificial situations in which the first moving object the baby goslings saw was Lorenz himself. Imagine this great ethologist waddling across a field, waving his arms, followed by his troupe of imprinted goslings!

Lorenz and colleagues found that many animals, including geese, chickens, goats, and sheep, exhibit this imprinting response. They discovered a number of interesting phenomena related to this event. Apparently, there is a critical period in the life of the young animal for imprinting. In geese, approximately three days after hatching, imprinting no longer takes place. However, the critical period seems to be extended considerably if the animal is kept in an almost structureless environment after hatching (Moltz and Stettner, 1961).

The relationship between imprinting in lower animals and the development of attachment in humans is being considered by many psychologists. They are intrigued by the relationship between a response that clearly matures with age and important environmental effects on that response.

Many advocates of the critical-period argument favor infancy intervention programs.

dler, 1972). Many psychologists argue that the preschool years are particularly important for intellectual development. These same psychologists advocate systematic early intervention programs to help children who have received little cognitive stimulation in infancy (Glaser and Resnick, 1972). However, many advocates of the critical-period argument have pointed out that even the preschool years may be too late. These psychologists favor infancy intervention programs for babies disadvantaged from lack of stimulation. They suggest that education should begin "in the cradle" (McGraw, 1970).

· Many early intervention programs have been designed to help make up for a lack of early stimulation. Another reason given for early childhood education is to accelerate the critical-period schedule and decrease the age at which new behaviors ordinarily appear. Some psychologists and educators, however, question the advantage of this type of acceleration. They suggest that accelerating one pattern of development might disrupt another. Some answers to the question of the specific effects of acceleration, as well as the significance of early childhood programs in the United States, will be discussed at length in Chapter 10.

The concepts of readiness and critical periods have been used widely by psychologists concerned with social and emotional development, as well as with cognitive development. Psychoanalytic theory suggests, for example, that delaying formation of close attachments much past the age of six months may impair the baby's later ability to form close personal attachments to other people. Many psychiatrists are greatly concerned with effects of social and maternal deprivation, particularly in the first year of life. Some problem behaviors that appear in later life have been attributed to this type of deprivation. The case history of Albert B., a six-year-old boy, is similar in many respects to many histories reported by Bowlby and others (see p. 46).

Bowlby lists what he calls typical characteristics of the deprived child (Bowlby, 1965, p. 55):

superficial relationships;
no capacity to care for people;
inaccessibility;
no emotional response to situations where it is normal;
deceit and evasion, often pointless;
stealing;
lack of concentration at school.

According to Bowlby, changing behavior related to these characteristics is extremely difficult. However, the earlier that deprivation is removed, the greater the possibility for correcting at least some of the damage.

Children are, of course, remarkably flexible. With the exception of really extreme cases, no one argues that withholding training until a critical period has passed necessarily will cause irreversible damage. We

Delaying formation of close maternal attachment may impair a baby's later ability to form close personal relationships.

The case of Albert B.

Albert B. was six years old and in the first grade when his teacher called in his parents because of her concern about Albert's behavior in school.

Albert was the youngest of three children in the Brown family, all adopted. Both Beth, age ten, and Philip, age eleven, had been adopted at three months of age. Neither child exhibited any behavior problems and both were doing well in school. Albert was adopted when he was three years old.

According to information given the Brown family by the adoption agency, Albert, an unwanted child, had been shunted from family member to family member, none of whom had been interested in keeping him, until the authorities took him. His natural mother was unmarried and left the city shortly after his birth. Her whereabouts were not known. Albert's maternal grandmother took him home from the hospital. After six months, however, she decided that taking care of her daughter's baby was simply "too much work for someone her age." Albert was then sent to the home of his grandmother's sister, where he remained another few months.

At this time, pleading illness, his great-aunt requested that the authorities take him. Albert was made a ward of the state and placed in a foundling home. At one year of age, Albert moved to a foster home, the first of several. In the last home he stayed, his foster parents requested that he be returned to the foundling home because of what they called his "antisocial behavior."

The Browns took Albert from the foundling home when he was three years old. Both Mr. and Mrs. Brown were warned that he exhibited a number of antisocial behaviors, such as stealing and destroying property. The Browns felt, however, that this behavior would "go away" when Albert became accustomed to being a permanent family member, and when he learned that he was wanted and loved. Mrs. Brown was not employed outside the home and said she was prepared to "work full time at making Albert know that he was loved."

In talking over Albert's classroom behavior with his teacher, both Mr. and Mrs. Brown remembered many examples of behaviors that concerned them, also. For example, when Albert

do not know at this point just what brings a critical period to an end, or what exactly are the consequences to each child of delaying learning beyond the end of a critical period. Earlier, we described the failure of many intervention programs for young children. Similar failure of later compensatory programs suggests the great difficulties in teaching skills after these optimal learning periods have passed.

Developmental Tasks

So far we have been discussing development in terms of the capability of a child to perform new behaviors. Another way to examine the development of children is in terms of their abilities to perform "the developmental tasks of life." At each period of their lives, people are confronted with certain and different tasks they are expected by society to achieve. Havighurst (1952) divided the life span into six basic periods. He then described the "developmental tasks" expected of people in our arrived the first day in his new home, he was introduced to the family and to Brownie, a large Irish setter. He was shown his new room, the first room that he had ever had all to himself. Albert was well behaved that evening, but appeared almost disinterested. He told his new family that he was happy to be there; he petted Brownie; he dutifully kissed his new parents goodnight. Mrs. Brown later remembered reporting to her husband, however, that "something was wrong." She said that Albert appeared too casual, almost as if he "didn't care about anything." Mr. and Mrs. Brown hoped then that attention would solve the problem.

Another instance, occurring the same year, involved a stack of empty chewing gum wrappers Mr. Brown noticed lying on the floor in the back of Albert's closet. He asked Albert why he had left them there, and suggested that Albert put them in the wastebasket. According to Mr. Brown, Albert looked up blandly and said, "But I never put them there—it must have been Beth or Philip." When Albert was five years old, the boy next door accused him of stealing his new ball. Albert denied taking it, although later that day Mrs. Brown found the ball in Albert's waste-basket. She returned it to the neighbors with apologies. She was sure that there had been some mistake, because Albert had a brand new ball of his own. There seemed no reason that he might steal another ball. Albert said he didn't know how the ball had gotten into his wastebasket and suggested that his friend must have put it there.

In the first grade, Albert's teacher reported to his parents, Albert was doing less than satisfactory work even though, according to his score on an IQ test, he was brighter than average. He seemed to get along with the other children and caused no serious problem in the classroom. He didn't seem to make friends easily, however, and, unless prodded, spent his playtime by himself. What bothered his teacher was his seeming lack of interest in everything that went on around him. She felt that if it continued, he might well have to repeat the first grade. She was worried about Albert, she said, because she didn't ever really know "what he was thinking about or what he was feeling." He just "didn't seem to care."

society. According to Havighurst, developmental tasks must be mastered at the proper and accepted developmental stage if the individual is to develop normally. Tasks vary from society to society; what is acceptable in one society may not be acceptable in another. Children successful at accomplishing each task prescribed by their own societies at the appropriate age are rewarded. Failure at any developmenal tasks is punished and is likely to hamper development in succeeding stages.

The accompanying chart describes each of the major periods established by Havighurst. Included are some of the important physical, cognitive, social, and emotional tasks considered by different psychologists to be required by our society. All periods described by Havighurst are listed, from infancy to aging, in order to show the tasks in proper relationship to the life cycle. Looking at the list of tasks, we can see that early mastery of tasks is the result of accelerated maturation. Energy

Developmental tasks of infancy include learning to walk and
exploring the environment.

Developmental tasks of life

Birth to six years (infancy and early childhood)
Learning to take solid foods
Learning to walk, talk, and control elimination of wastes
Developing trust in one's self and others
Exploring the environment
Learning to identify with one's own sex
Learning to relate socially and emotionally to others
Learning to distinguish right from wrong

Six to twelve years (middle childhood)
Expanding knowledge of the physical and social world
Learning appropriate sex role
Developing confidence and self-esteem
Acquiring academic skills, reasoning, and judgment
Learning physical and social skills

Twelve to eighteen years (adolescence)
Developing self-assurance and a sense of identity
Adjusting to bodily changes
Acquiring sexual interests and more mature relationships with peers
Achieving emotional independence from parents
Exploring interests and abilities; selecting an occupation

Eighteen to thirty-five years (early adulthood)
Completing formal education and beginning profession
Finding and learning to live with a mate
Developing responsibility to care for family needs
Developing basic philosophy of life

Thirty-five to sixty years (middle age)
Accepting greater social responsibility
Establishing a pattern and standard of living
Helping one's children become effective adults
Adjusting to one's aging parents
Accepting the physiological changes of middle age

Later life (aging)
Adjusting to increased physical limitations
Adjusting to reduced income
Affiliating with one's own age group
Accepting retirement

This list of tasks is compiled from data described by Havighurst in *Developmental Tasks and Education* (New York: Longman-Green, 1952).

plays an important role in the mastery of developmental tasks, particularly at earlier stages of development. Children whose environments offer the opportunity to learn, as well as reward for learning, tend to accomplish developmental tasks more rapidly than children who have not had this opportunity. Children who receive guidance from family and teachers are likely to learn more rapidly than children who must rely on trial and error or imitate childish models (Hurlock, 1972).

Some developmental psychologists study children for the purpose of describing and explaining the principles by which they develop. The purpose of this research is not only to help explain the behavior of any individual at a particular age, but also to help make predictions

PRINCIPLES GOVERNING CHILD DEVELOPMENT

about how groups of people will behave at any given stage in their development. The principles listed below govern all aspects of development, whether we are talking about physical or behavioral development, or motor, cognitive, or social-emotional development.

1 *Development proceeds qualitatively, from simple to complex.* In order to explain this principle, it is first necessary to distinguish between what we have been calling "growth" and what we have been calling "development." All humans increase in size as they get older. At the same time, the number of different responses they are able to make increases as well. These are both examples of quantitative change—what we call growth. To give one example of growth, children increase the number of words they can produce and respond to, from an average of three words at one year of age to 2,562 words at six years (Smith, 1926).

At the same time, development proceeds qualitatively. That is, it progresses from simple to complex. Not only do humans grow larger, they change from single-celled organisms at conception to highly complex creatures of varied structure and function. The process by which this occurs is development. Similarly, while children increase the size of their vocabularies (quantitative growth), they are simultaneously developing the ability to use their words in more complicated ways and to give them more involved meanings (qualitative development).

2 *Development proceeds from the general to the specific.* Together with the change toward complexity comes an increase in specificity. In terms of physical development, as the cells of the body change in character, specific kinds of tissues with specific functions are developed —skin, bones, blood, etc. In an example of behavioral development, the baby makes general arm movements long before specific responses, such as reaching for objects. Similarly, as children increase the numbers of ways they use words, at the same time they develop very specific uses for certain words. For the baby, "Mama" refers to anyone who helps take care of him or her. For the older child, however, "Mama" means a single, very specific individual.

3 *Development proceeds directionally.* The *cephalo-caudal principle* refers to the fact that development (as well as growth) always proceeds directionally from head to foot. We can see this principle demonstrated in physical growth simply by comparing the changes that take place in the comparative sizes of different parts of the body. At birth, babies' heads are large in comparison to the rest of their bodies. As children grow older, the rate of growth increases in the lower extremities of the body. As this occurs, the head gradually begins to look smaller in relation to the rest of the body (see Fig. 2.1).

Some approximate comparisons between newborn and adult bodies are: Infant's head is one-half the length of adult head. Infant's trunk is one-third the length of adult trunk. Infant's legs are one-fifth the length of adult legs.

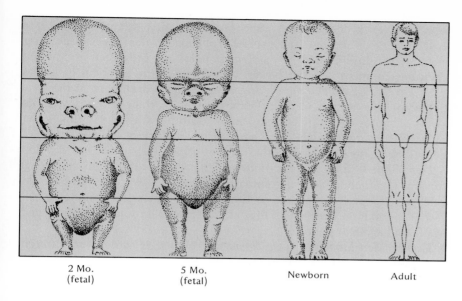

Fig. 2.1 Changes in body form and proportion.

2 Mo.
(fetal)

5 Mo.
(fetal)

Newborn

Adult

In terms of the timing of qualitative development, the first part of the body to develop in complex fashion is the brain. As noted above, behavioral development proceeds directionally from head to foot. Babies are able to use their hands in complex fashion, as, for example, in holding a rattle and bringing it to their mouths, long before they are able to use their legs and feet to stand and walk.

Development also proceeds in a *proximo-distal* fashion—that is, it proceeds from areas closest to the central nervous system outward to the extremities of the body. For this reason, arm muscles develop before finger muscles; babies learn to control arm movements long before they can manipulate their fingers at will. In fact, they will not develop control of their fingertips sufficiently to make the very fine movements required in writing until somewhere near the age of six years.

4 *Development continues throughout life.* Changes that are controlled by the developmental process are orderly and tend to occur in an unvarying sequence. This means that a person's body and behaviors continue to change in predictable ways as long as the person lives. Every baby can be expected to sit before standing, to stand before walking. All aging persons can be expected gradually to lose the abilities they once had. It is this fact that led Havighurst and other psychologists to outline the developmental tasks expected for all of the life span. It has led one researcher to describe death as "the last stage of development" (Kubler-Ross, 1975).

Since development is continuous, what happens at one stage influences all ensuing stages. People change as a result of a combination of maturation and experience. Psychoanalytic theorists point out that the child who receives little maternal affection in the first year of life can be expected to exhibit predictable social problems in later stages of development. Accordingly, many psychologists today are interested in studying child development in order better to understand the behavior of adults.

5 *The rate of development varies.* Any two children born at the same time can be expected to differ somewhat as to their heights, weights, levels of motor development, and so on. Another way to say this is that each child is unique; children tend to be distinctive in both their inherited characteristics and in the rates at which they grow and develop.

Development also is discontinuous. That is, it varies from age to age for any given child; it is not smooth and gradual. Sudden spurts in development appear from time to time. This is particularly noticeable at certain periods in everyone's life, as, for example, during the first year of life and again at puberty.

Finally, *developmental rate is asynchronous;* it varies for different aspects of development. For example, the development of speech patterns in a very young child tends to slow down at the same time that motor development seems to be speeding up. (This often happens at the same time that a baby takes a few hard falls in learning to walk. For this reason, many inexperienced mothers become frightened by this speech delay, fearing that a head injury may be the cause.)

Relationships exist between different aspects of development. For example, there is a marked correlation between the rates of physical and mental development. This is exemplified in the relationship between sexual maturation and patterns of interest and behavior. Certainly we see all sorts of new patterns of behavior developing in the sexually maturing adolescent. It is important for teachers and parents to be aware of the different levels of development of children of this age, in order to help predict what will be interesting and exciting for them.

THE STUDY OF DEVELOPMENTAL STAGES

Johnny, age four, is playing in the yard with his younger sister, Susie. All of a sudden, she picks up Johnny's favorite teddy bear and throws it in a mud puddle. Johnny raises his arm as if to hit Susie, then looks back at the house where his mother is looking out of the window. He wants either to hit his sister or, at least, throw one of her toys in the mud puddle. But he has been told by his mother that he will get a spanking if he hurts his sister. Johnny picks his teddy bear up out of the mud puddle and begins to wipe it off. He is obedient not because he doesn't want to hurt Susie, but because he wants to avoid a spanking.

Lawrence Kohlberg, an investigator interested in the development of moral judgment, would describe Johnny's behavior as characteristic of a "premoral stage of development, Stage 1," which he calls "punishment and obedience orientation" (Kohlberg, 1963).

The concept of developmental stages grows logically from the principles of development outlined in the previous section. According to these principles, the child develops in a systematic and orderly fashion. Although development is continuous throughout life, it is not perfectly correlated with age. Researchers have been able nevertheless to specify fairly distinctive stages characterized by special behaviors.

Exploration of broad aspects of behavior have led psychologists to make generalizations about the sorts of behavior we can expect of children at various ages. Some researchers point out that the concept of the developmental stage becomes most useful when it is used to describe not just one behavior, but rather an interrelated or unifying set of behaviors associated with a given age level (Wohlwill, 1973). Inhelder (1953) calls this set of behaviors "a structured whole as opposed to any isolated pieces of behavior." An example of such a set of behaviors is that associated with infancy or adolescence.

Developmental stages are used to provide descriptions of the sequences of changes expected as children get older. The term "adolescence," for example, brings to mind a particular sequence of behaviors. Adolescence means to most of us behaviors associated with developing sexuality, with achieving greater independence from home and parents, with increased time spent away from home with peers, and so forth. Descriptions of developmental stages are based on the "average" person's behavior—that is, behavior expected of most people at any given age. They serve as a kind of concise summation of what is happening to individuals at that point in their development. Such a description is important to both parents and teachers in understanding an individual and in planning suitable learning experiences.

Keniston (1970) described what he considered a developmental stage between adolescence and adulthood. He called it the "stage of youth." Youth, he said, is characterized by behavior associated with tensions between self and society, pervasive ambivalence, alternating estrangement and omnipotentiality. The term "youth," as defined by Keniston, describes so many people in our society today—many of whom are no longer very young in years.

Developmental stages are more than simply descriptions of age-related behavior. Piaget (1956, 1960) argued that developmental stages, by definition, describe certain sequences of behavior. That is, they describe behaviors that gradually and predictably change in some specific order. Inhelder (1953) reported that in passing from "inferior" to "superior" stages, the inferior becomes part of the superior. She assumed that earlier stages are not forgotten; the skills learned within each stage are used later on.

Developmental stages thus describe behaviors that are related one to another in different ways. In order to describe a developmental stage, researchers must do more than describe behaviors common to a general age level. They must also be able to describe and explain the "interpatterning among the changes of responses" (Wohlwill, 1973, p. 219).

Gesell and others pointed out that the stages of development are affected by what they called *reciprocal interweaving*, that is, repeated alternation of opposing or contradictory forces (Gesell et al., 1974). According to Gesell, this interweaving creates a shuttlelike pattern of movement, as though the child takes two steps forward to gain new experience, and then one step back while he or she consolidates goals. Some stages affected by this interweaving may be characterized by what Gesell and others have called *equilibrium*. Others are characterized by *disequilibrium*. The majority of children in equilibrium stages show signs of good social adjustment. They easily adapt to people and to environmental demands; they tend to be happier and more relaxed than during other developmental stages. The majority of children in stages characterized by disequilibrium tend to be more tense, indecisive, and

Children in equilibrium stages tend to be happier and more relaxed than children in disequilibrium stages.

insecure. They may exhibit many problem behaviors that do not occur during other stages of their development. They have difficulties in adapting to people and to life in general. Hurlock points out that many parents associate these changes in behavioral patterns with environmental changes. Worse yet, they associate them often with just plain "brattiness." But behavioral difficulties, she states, may not be individual aberrations at all, but rather predictable behaviors characteristic of the developmental stage through which the child is passing (Hurlock, 1972, pp. 40–41). Ames (1972) put it another way: "At certain stages, all children tend to be out of balance, if not out of bounds. It's just a normal part of growing up." The fortunate parent who understands this is the one who learns to take it in stride.

There has been much controversy among psychologists over the roles of heredity, maturation, and learning experience in development. (We will discuss this controversy at length in Chapter 4.) Psychologists agree, however, that developmental stages, as we have been describing them here, are the result of a combination of maturation and learning. Characterization of stage is rarely, if ever, free of the environment in which the child acts. For this reason, many developmental stages cannot clearly be separated from one another. Transitions from one stage to the next are gradual and occur at slightly different times for children with different learning experiences. Psychoanalytic researchers are particularly concerned with experiences children have at particular periods of their lives. Timing is critical. A child deprived of maternal affection during infancy is expected to be affected quite differently than a child deprived of maternal affection in middle childhood. In this way, the developmental stage is used to explain individual differences in behavior as well as to explain average behavior.

Research conducted at major developmental institutes—for example, the Gesell Institute at Yale—has yielded information concerning motor, cognitive, and personality development. At this point, we will examine very briefly just a few of the findings and theorists in each area. Later chapters discuss each approach in greater detail.

All the theories discussed here assume that development proceeds in specified stages. Although these stages may vary sometimes as to timing and may even overlap, the same stages occur in a fixed, sequential order that does not vary. They change systematically in complexity and specificity with age. We call this approach to development the *stage-dependent* approach. Many developmental researchers—Gesell, Ilg, and Ames to name a few—have been concerned with the many different types of development and the complex interrelationships that exist among them.

SOME STAGE-DEPENDENT APPROACHES TO DEVELOPMENT

The Development of Motor Behavior

Contributions of Gesell, Ilg, Ames, and their colleagues Arnold Gesell, founder of the Institute of Child Development at Yale University, proposed that development occurs in an unvarying sequence. In describing how posture, postural sets, prehension, and locomotion develop in humans, Gesell and his co-workers at the Gesell Institute were particularly concerned with the first five years of life. Researchers in this area point out that the first five years comprise changes that are "so swift and variegated that they cannot be taken in at a single glance" (Gesell, Ilg, Ames, and Rodell, 1974, p. 19). Indeed, in motor behavior alone, the changes from birth to five years are so dramatic that it is difficult to believe we are dealing with only one kind of creature. From their observations of children, Gesell and his colleagues described the changes they saw as follows: In the first fifteen weeks, control is developed by the infant primarily in visual-motor areas. Specifically, the twelve oculomotor muscles develop. From sixteen to eighteen weeks of age, the infant gradually gains control of the muscles that support the head and allow arm movement. By eighteen weeks, the baby reaches out for objects in the environment. Development at this age, as always, proceeds in cephalo-caudal and proximo-distal directions. From twenty-eight to forty weeks, the infant gradually gains command of trunk and hands; sitting and grasping objects now occurs. It is not until the end of the first year, from forty to fifty weeks, that development of ability extends to legs and feet, and to forefingers and thumbs. It is at this age that the infant "points and plucks" (Gesell et al., 1974, p. 20).

Infants sixteen to eighteen weeks of age gradually gain control of the muscles used to support the head.

Gesell and his colleagues were interested in the development of motor behavior, language, what they called "adaptive" behavior (learning to use present and past experience to adapt to the environment), and personal-social relationships. To continue their description of observed changes, by the end of the second year, the child can be expected to walk and to run, to speak in words, to be toilet trained, and to gain the beginnings of personality identity.

Gesell and his colleagues suggested many interrelationships between different aspects of development. For example, degree of motor development affects ability to learn the developmental tasks of a particular age. By three years, the child is expected to speak in sentences, to think with words, and to show greater propensity for coping with the environment. The four-year-old's behavior adds questioning as part of the process of learning to develop analogies, to conceptualize, and to generalize. This is the age during which the mother frequently is used as a sounding board for examining the world. "Why does it get dark out at night? Why is the sky blue? Why doesn't it snow in the summer? Why? Why? Why?" The questions gradually stop with the fifth year. Time now is spent developing finer motor control, learning to do things like hopping and skipping, socializing, and learning to conform to a socialized world. The influence of previous stages on this year of development is important. Without having developed all of the preceding behaviors, it would have been impossible for the child to reach this stage. Similarly, the influence of this stage on all later stages of development is enormous.

Arnold Gesell was especially interested in studying the rapid changes that take place during the first five years of life.

Piaget's theory of cognitive development Jean Piaget, a Swiss researcher, spent the bulk of his long career observing the ways that children of different ages think and solve problems. Piaget watched infants and children react to problem situations of many kinds. He was interested not in whether they solved these problems correctly, but in the *reasons* they responded as they did. From his painstaking, detailed observations, Piaget derived a theory to explain the development of the thinking processes. According to Piaget's theory, the thinking processes change in many different ways with age. He proposed a progression of different cognitive stages, each stage permitting children to solve problems using qualitatively different processes.

Piaget did not picture the stages as entirely discrete and nonoverlapping. Nor did he specify exact ages at which they occurred. Instead, he described a series of stages that varied somewhat in their timing. They sometimes overlapped one another slightly, depending on the type of problem solving studied. But they always occurred in the same fixed order, more complex or higher stages always following less complex ones.

Piaget did not explain stages strictly in terms of either maturation or learning, but rather as a mixture of the two. His detailed descriptions, as well as his theoretical writings, make clear his belief that interaction with the environment is necessary for cognitive change to occur. Piagetian theory would predict that children reared in isolation from outside stimulation would have significantly slowed rates of cognitive development.

Following is a brief overview of Piaget's description of the major cognitive stages. Each will be discussed in greater detail in Chapters 6, 9, 10, and 12.

A child's first two years are devoted to the development of sensorimotor skills. Piaget called this the *sensorimotor period* of development. Throughout this period, infants learn to make use of the sensations coming to them from the outside world and to manipulate and control the muscles of their body. Young infants use responses that do not require use of symbols or language.

Like Gesell, Piaget saw many major and predictable changes taking place during the sensorimotor period. He described them in terms of a number of smaller substages. These include an early *reflexive stage* in which innate responses become efficient. *Circular-reaction stages* follow, in which babies willfully repeat acts over and over again, first for their own sakes, later to watch the results, and finally to obtain particular goals. At this stage, babies will throw toys out of their cribs repeatedly, to the consternation of their caretakers. Not until children reach about eighteen months do they learn to think about the effects of responses before they make them—a relief to those caring for them. This is the final stage of sensorimotor functioning: the *stage of mental combinations*.

Children, according to Piaget, enter the *stage of preoperational thought* at the end of the second year. During the early part of this stage, they develop the use of language. At the same time, they develop ability to use signs and symbols. Language opens many new doors: children begin to be able to solve many more complex problems, sometimes without the need for the subject of their conversation to be present.

At Piaget's *intuitive stage*, children are able to solve a variety of complex problems that involve what Piaget called image-based thinking. Children of four, unlike children of two, can play with baby dolls and use them to represent live babies. After age four, they continue to add information and to use symbols.

Children at four can solve problems, but still have a great deal of difficulty solving them logically. According to Piaget, during the intuitive period, children's problem solutions are likely to be based on one stimulus dimension only. That is, only one aspect of the problem is used to help find the solution. For example, a four-year-old might decide that the taller of two containers always contains "more" liquid, even though the shorter container is wider and holds a greater volume. Piaget would say, in this case, that the only stimulus dimension the child is considering is height. (This example reminds me of an experiment I tried out on my own three-year-old daughter when I was a graduate student studying Piagetian theory. Robin was sitting at the kitchen table eating an oatmeal cookie and began complaining that she wanted "two cookies." Remembering Piaget's notion that three-year-olds base problem solving on one stimulus dimension only, I broke the cookie and presented her with two halves. It worked! Robin based her happy conclusion on the fact that there were, indeed, "two cookies" in front of her and not that the actual amount of cookie had not changed.)

According to Piaget, each successive cognitive stage permits a child to solve problems using qualitatively different processes.

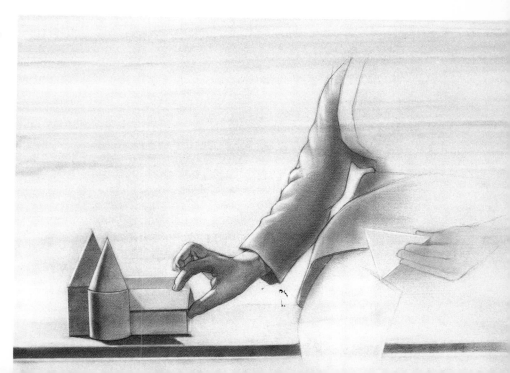

The intuitive stage ends with what Piaget called the *operational stage* of development, at about seven years of age. This is the beginning of the development of true reasoning, first with reasoning requiring concrete examples and, later, with reasoning using abstract or formal operations. Now children can think about and solve problems of many varied and complex types.

How do all the changes that Piaget describes take place? According to Piaget, cognitive development is, in many respects, comparable to organic development. That is, it consists essentially of activity directed toward *equilibrium* (Piaget, 1967). Equilibrium, in the sense that Gesell used the term, means "well-balanced adjustment." Equilibrium, in the sense that Piaget used the term, means a well-balanced set of ideas, organized into a coherent mental system that can be used to solve new problems. Piaget called this system a *cognitive structure*.

According to Piaget, children go from one cognitive stage to the next in each type of problem solving. At the same time, they go from periods of disequilibrium, in which the environment is not matched by their capabilities to use it, to periods of equilibrium, in which they are maximally capable of using the environment and prepare to learn more. For example, six-month-old children sitting in playpens have available to them the means of pulling themselves up to standing positions. However, at six months, they are not yet ready to make use of this aspect of the environment. Later, when they have developed better use of their arms and legs, they will use the playpen bars to pull themselves up. From here, their opportunities to learn and to problem solve are widely extended.

The process by which increases in ability to respond takes place was called by Piaget *equilibration*. Equilibration assumes the interplay of two separate processes, each following the other. These are called *assimilation* and *accommodation*. Assimilation occurs when children use new stimuli in their environments to perform activities they already know how to do. An example of assimilation in the sensorimotor period would be reaching out of the playpen and finding an orange, then using the orange to perform a series of acts that have already been done with other round objects—rolling it across the playpen floor, for example.

Accommodation occurs when children add new activities to their repertoires or modify old behavior. A child may stay in a playpen for a long period of time before suddenly realizing that he or she might use the bars of the playpen to perform a new activity. The first pulling to a standing position by the child in the playpen is a good example of accommodation.

Assimilation and accommodation follow one another, the first increasing the number of stimuli to which responses are made, the second increasing the number of responses made to the already assimilated stimuli. In other words, as children assimilate, they increase ability to accommodate. It follows logically that without suitable stimulus input from the environment, both processes necessarily would stop. Suitable stimulus input, according to Piaget, consists of stimuli *matched* in complexity to the child's cognitive structure. Piaget was skeptical of attempts to teach children advanced and complex concepts at early cognitive stages. He felt that such attempts too often do not provide stimuli properly matched to the cognitive structures of the children and thus are not likely to succeed. According to Piaget, with suitable stimulus input, assimilation and accommodation follow each other in increasing complexity. More and more complex cognitive structures are thus formed.

Kohlberg's theory of the development of moral reasoning Piaget, because of his interest in explaining the development of cognition, was interested also in the development of moral reasoning. He hypothesized that mature moral reasoning, like other forms of cognition, occurs in stages. A refined extension of Piaget's concepts was proposed by Lawrence Kohlberg, who also hypothesized stages that form an invariant and universal sequence. Kohlberg gathered his information in the following fashion. He interviewed boys aged ten to sixteen and asked them to respond to problems containing hypothetical moral dilemmas involving conflicts. The problems posed were complex; there were no "correct" answers. In each problem, the boys could give answers based on anything ranging from conformity to societal expectations or adherence to law to certain higher considerations—for example, the welfare and rights of others.

Kohlberg described stages ranging from what he considered the lowest stage of moral development, obedience and punishment orientation, to a sixth and highest level involving conscience or principle orientation (Kohlberg, 1969, p. 376). Like Piaget, he found a positive relationship between age and stage. He also noted that moral stages, like cognitive stages, seem to be the product of an individual's interaction with the environment. Kohlberg stressed that increases in the development of moral reasoning do not occur through direct teaching—that is, they cannot be taught through traditional school-type lessons. Rather, they develop through complex processes involving, among other factors, interaction with others. Kohlberg notes that most people in our society do not reach the highest stage, that of morality based on universal ethical principles. He suggests that perhaps only 5 to 6 percent of us reach this highest level (Sanborn, 1971). We will discuss some of the reasons for this and the implications of Kohlberg's research later in Chapters 9, 11, and 14.

Many theorists have described the development of personality. Earlier, in our description of reciprocal interweaving, we discussed Gesell's explanation of regularized changes in children's "relationships to others and to their environment" (Gesell et al., 1974). Two other developmental theorists also deserve consideration at this time.

The Development
of Personality

Kohlberg's stages of moral judgment

Kohlberg believes that individuals acquire and refine the sense of justice through a sequence of invariant developmental stages. In 1957, while working on his dissertation at the University of Chicago, Kohlberg began testing the moral judgment of a group of seventy-two boys, aged ten through sixteen, by asking them questions involving moral dilemmas. A typical question raises the issue of stealing a drug to save a dying woman. The inventor of the drug is selling it for ten times what it costs him to make. The woman's husband cannot raise the money, and the seller refuses to lower the price or wait for payment. What should the husband do? From the answers given by the group, Kohlberg distinguished six basic types of moral judgment, which he found corresponded to developmental stages. Subsequent retesting of the group at three-year intervals has shown growth proceeding through the same stages in the same order.

The stages are:

1 Orientation to punishment and reward, and to physical and material power.
2 Hedonistic orientation with an instrumental view of human relations. Beginning notions of reciprocity, but with emphasis on exchange of favors—"You scratch my back and I'll scratch yours."
3 "Good boy" orientation; seeking to maintain expectations and win approval of one's imme-

diate group. Morality defined by individual ties of relationship.
4 Orientation to authority, law, and duty, to maintaining a fixed order, whether social or religious, which is assumed as a primary value.
5 Social-contract orientation, with emphasis on equality and mutual obligation within a democratically established order—e.g., the morality of the United States Constitution.
6 Morality of individual principles of conscience which have logical comprehensiveness and universality. Highest value placed on human life, equality, and dignity.

The stages are not defined by particular opinions or judgments, but by ways of thinking about moral matters and bases for choice. Stages 1 and 2, which are typical of young children and delinquents, Kohlberg describes as "premoral," since decisions are made largely on the basis of self-interest and material considerations. The group-oriented Stages 3 and 4 are the "conventional" ones at which most of the adult population operates. The final "principled" stages are characteristic of 20 to 25 percent of the adult population, with perhaps 5 to 10 percent arriving at Stage 6.

From S. Sanborn, "Means and ends: moral development and moral education," *Harvard Graduate School of Education Association Bulletin*, Fall 1971.

Freud's psychoanalytic theory Another major developmental theorist was Sigmund Freud, an Austrian psychiatrist whose major works were written during the early part of this century. Freud's observations and the theories developed from them have been described by his followers as "more differentiated and specific" than any other work (Baldwin, 1967, p. 349). Freud's classic work, *Three Essays on the Theory of Sexuality* (1905), was based on only a few observations. But the characteristics he observed were confirmed by him later in thousands of additional obser-

During Freud's oral stage, the organized source of gratification is sucking.

vations that allowed him to amend, refine, and clarify his concepts. Freudian theory, also called psychoanalytic theory, assumes a stage-dependent approach. In addition, it stresses the vital role of experience. Psychoanalytic theory maintains that unless basic needs for food, love, warmth, and security are met at early stages in life, development of personality will be arrested. Freud called this *fixation*. He felt that fixation at early stages—caused by frustration of basic needs—affects personality at all later stages. In this sense, each stage constitutes a critical period in the life of the child. Without fixation, Freud thought that children would pass through the stages of development in specific sequential order. With fixation, however, the basic personality structure of the child would be flawed in whatever area the deprivation occurred.

Freud hypothesized five basic stages of development, each stage characterized by a new socialization problem confronting the individual. The first stage, occurring during infancy, is characterized by passive and dependent behavior on the part of the child. The organized source of gratification at this age is sucking. The child's life centers about the mother, the nipple, and the thumb. Freud called this the *oral stage*. We described earlier, in discussing the work of Bowlby, another psychoanalytic theorist, some characteristics of children fixated at the oral stage through inadequate maternal attention. The case of Albert B. (see p. 46) also exemplifies the effects of deprivation during the oral stage.

The next period of development, according to Freud, is associated with concerns for control of bladder and bowels. Freud called this the *anal stage*. Children at this stage are learning to exercise power over their environments. They are able to give or not give feces. They are acquiring language and communication skills. Fixation at this stage of development causes different characteristics than oral fixation. According to psychoanalytic theory, the child may become overly controlled, orderly, and rigid. Or, he or she may do the reverse and become extremely messy, disorderly, and irresponsible.

The *phallic stage* occurs when the child becomes aware of genital differences and the pleasures associated with them. Freud thought that this occurred in early childhood. At this time, the child develops increased affection for the parent of the opposite sex. Personality, according to Freud, now begins to take shape. The child begins to explore the world and to internalize a value system.

The phallic stage is followed by what Freud termed the *latency stage* of middle childhood. The child now begins to divert primary love attentions to those outside of the home. Interest in peers increases. Some authors have referred to this stage as the "calm before the storm of puberty" (Westlake, 1973). Freud's fifth stage, the *genital stage*, is that storm. With adolescence, he said, comes an upsurge of instinctual sexual drives, a need to dissolve parental attachments, and a set of conflicts only too well known in our society.

Erikson's psychosocial theory Erik Erikson, another psychoanalyst representative of neo-Freudian views, has expanded and elaborated on Freud's theories. Erikson, one of the first child analysts in the Boston area, outlined *psychosocial* stages of development to parallel Freud's stages. Erikson said these stages describe the child's orientation to self and to his or her social world. Erikson, unlike Freud, felt that personality is not defined in early childhood, but continues to develop throughout life. In this sense, many feel that Erikson has rectified Freud's "one-sided emphasis on childhood" as the beginning and end of personality development (Elkind, 1970).

Erikson, as Freud, believed in critical periods of development. These periods, he felt, are characterized by crises or potential turning points. They are due to radical changes taking place in the perspectives of the child. If a problem is not resolved, it will appear again and again at each successive stage. However, unlike Freud, Erikson was optimistic in his belief that failures at one stage can be corrected by successes at later stages. Further, he felt that resolution of problems at one stage does not necessarily require resolution of other past problems.

Erikson described eight stages of psychosocial development, each increasing in complexity and developing directly from the preceding stage. The first stage is characterized by children's learning to *trust or mistrust*

According to Erikson, if children's needs are met by warm, loving mothers during the first two years of life, they will learn to trust.

the environment. During the first two years of life, according to Erikson, if children's needs are satisfied by warm, loving mothers, they will learn to trust; cold, unsupporting mothers or mother surrogates will create mistrusting personalities in their children.

The second stage of childhood, from age two to age three, is characterized by the learning of either *autonomy or doubt*, as children emerge from total dependence on a mother or other caretaker. The child may learn to control the environment successfully during this period if adequate support is given by parents or caretakers. An overprotected child may learn to fear the environment. Too little protection and resulting unpleasant experiences may produce similar fear.

Initiative or guilt is developed in the fourth and fifth years, depending on the responses of individuals around the child to his or her continued experimentation with the environment. This stage of development corresponds to Freud's genital stage.

The early school years, ages six to eleven, are the years in which the child develops *industry or inferiority* feelings. It is in these years that the child learns to relate with peers, to play by the rules, to perform academic tasks. Reward for learning and assistance in learning leads to industry. Inability to deal with this environment leads to feelings of inferiority.

Erikson probably is known best for descriptions of adolescent development. According to Erikson, adolescence, the period from twelve to eighteen years, is used by teenagers to learn who they are. They may learn either *identity or role confusion* at this time, depending on what happens in their interactions with the world. (We will discuss the many problems of adolescence in Part 6 of the text.)

Erikson's sixth, seventh, and eighth stages of development, describing the concerns of adults, deal first with developing either *intimacy or isolation* during young adulthood, *generativity or self absorption* during middle age, and, finally, *integrity or despair* in old age.

SUMMARY

Human beings develop gradually during their lifetimes in systematic and orderly fashion from tiny and helpless infants to full-sized, mature adults. Although the process of development is continuous, it is not perfectly correlated with age. Development is affected not only by a maturation process internal to the organism, but also by interaction between the organism and the environment.

Psychologists who study the developmental process and describe it in terms of a series of stages through which individuals pass as they increase in age are called stage-dependent theorists. These psychologists characterize each stage in terms of generalizations about the sorts of behaviors that can be expected, as well as the underlying principles that govern behavior. Stage-dependent psychologists have studied many different aspects of development, including psychomotor development, cognitive development, and the development of personality, interests, and attitudes.

QUESTIONS FOR THOUGHT AND REVIEW

1 What do you think constitutes the critical periods in the life of the developing child? What evidence do you have that these periods are really critical? (For review, see pages 42–46.)

2 Does readiness mature, is it learned, or does it appear because of a combination of learning and maturation? How does readiness relate to what we call "developmental tasks?" Give evidence for your answers. (For review, see pages 42 and 46–49.)

3 List the main principles governing growth and development of the child. Go out and observe some children ranging in age from three to six

years. Write down descriptions of behaviors they exhibit which illustrate these principles. (For review, see pages 49–52.)

4 Select one of the following theorists and review his approach: Erikson, Freud, Gesell, Kohlberg, Piaget. What does this approach contribute toward the understanding of development? What roles do maturation and learning play in development, according to this theorist? (For review, see pages 52–66.)

FOR FURTHER READING

Erikson, E. Identity and the life cycle. *Monographs of Psychological Issues* 1 (1959). This article is an excellent primary source for readers interested in Erikson's theory of development. It deals with the issue of identity, not only in adolescence, but throughout the life span of the individual.

Gesell, A., F. Ilg, L. Ames, and J. Rodell. *Infant and Child in the Culture of Today.* Rev. ed. New York: Harper & Row, 1974. All students interested in developmental theory should take the opportunity to read a firsthand account of the research of these famous psychologists. The description of child development afforded by Gesell and his colleagues is extremely thorough; their attention to detail is unparalleled.

Itard, J. *The Wild Boy of Aveyron.* New York: Century, 1932. Itard's book is a detailed account of a now-famous boy who, as a child, was reared with animals and not with people. Itard's study brings to life the maturation-learning controversy in developmental psychology, and asks questions that psychologists cannot afford not to answer. (For those excited by the book, the story has been made into a film by Truffaut entitled *The Wild Child.* The movie, in French with English subtitles, was produced by United Artists in 1970. It is 85 minutes long, in black and white.)

Rohrer, W., P. Ammon, and P. Cramer. *Understanding Intellectual Development.* Hinsdale, Ill.: The Dryden Press, 1974. Cognitive as well as psychoanalytic theories are discussed in this volume. Emphasis is on the growth of intellect.

Wohlwill, J. The study of developmental stages. In J. Wohlwill, *The Study of Behavioral Development.* New York: Academic Press, 1973, Chap. 9. This chapter in Wohlwill's text on developmental psychology presents arguments for and against stage-dependent approaches to child development. Wohlwill first advances an argument for what should be included in a developmental stage, then examines the research of famous theorists in light of this argument. The book offers challenging reading for interested students.

REFERENCES

Ames, L. Is your child a brat or is he just going through a stage? *Family Circle*, May 1972.

Baldwin, A. *Theories of Child Development*. New York: Wiley, 1967.

Bowlby, J. *Child Care and the Growth of Love*. Harmondsworth, Middlesex, England: Penguin Books, 1965.

Coles, R. et al. Hearings before the U.S. Senate Subcommittee, July 1967. In *Hunger and Malnutrition in America*. Washington, D.C.: U.S. Printing Office, 1967.

Elkind, D. Erik Erikson's eight stages of man. *New York Times Magazine*, 5 April 1970.

Erikson, E. *Childhood and Society*. 2d ed. New York: Norton, 1963.

Freud, S. Three essays on the theory of sexuality. In *The Complete Psychological Works of Sigmund Freud*. Standard Edition. Vol. 5. 1905. Reprint. London: Hogarth Press, 1953.

Gesell, A., and H. Thompson. Learning and growth in identical twins: an experimental study by the method of co-twin control. *Journal of Genetic Psychological Monographs* 6 (1929): 1–124.

Gesell, A. The ontogenesis of infant behavior. In L. Carmichael, ed., *Manual of Child Psychology*. New York: Wiley, 1954, pp. 335–373.

Gesell, A., F. Ilg, L. Ames, and J. Rodell. *Infant and Child in the Culture of Today*. Rev. ed. New York: Harper & Row, 1974.

Glaser, R., and L. Resnick. Instructional psychology. In P. Mussen and M. Rosenzweig, eds., *Annual Review of Psychology* 23 (1972): 207–276.

Havighurst, P. *Developmental Tasks and Education*. 2d ed. New York: Longman-Green, 1952.

Hilgard, J. The effect of early and delayed practice on memory and motor performances studied by the method of co-twin control. *Journal of Genetic Psychological Monographs* 4 (1933): 493–567.

Hurlock, E. *Child Development*. New York: McGraw-Hill, 1972.

Inhelder, B. Criteria of the stages of mental development. In J. Tanner and B. Inhelder, eds., *Discussions on Child Development: A Consideration of the Biological, Psychological, and Cultural Approaches to the Understanding of Human Development and Behavior. Vol. I of the Proceedings of the First Meeting of the World Health Organization Study Group on the Psychological Development of the Child*. Geneva, Switzerland: International Universities Press, 1953, pp. 75–96.

Keniston, K. Youth: A "New" stage of life. *The American Scholar*, Autumn, 1970.

Kohlberg, L. Stage and sequence: the cognitive-developmental approach to socialization. In D. Goslin, ed., *Handbook of Socialization Theory and Research*. Chicago: Rand McNally, 1969, p. 376.

Kohlberg, L. The development of children's orientation toward a moral order: sequence in the development of moral thought. *Vita Humana* 6 (1963): 11–33, 82, 83.

Kohlberg, L. The development of moral character and moral ideology. In M. Hoffman and L. Hoffman, eds., *Review of Child Development Research*. Vol. I. Hartford, Conn.: Russell Sage Foundation, 1964.

Kubler-Ross, E. *Death: The Final Stage of Growth*. Englewood Cliffs, N.J.: Prentice-Hall, 1975.

Lavatelli, C., and F. Stendler. *Readings in Child Behavior and Development*. New York: Harcourt Brace Jovanovich, 1972.

Lorenz, K. *King Solomon's Ring*. London: Methuen, 1952.

McGraw, M. Major challenges for students of infancy and early childhood. *American Psychologist* 25 (August 1970): 754–756.

Moltz, H., and L. Stettner. The influence of the patterned-light deprivation on the critical period of imprinting. *Journal of Comparative and Physiological Psychology* 54 (1961): 279–283.

Mussen, P. *The Psychological Development of the Child*. Englewood Cliffs, N.J.: Prentice-Hall, 1973.

Piaget, J. Les stades du developpement intellectual de l'enfant et de l'adolescent. In P. Osterrieth, ed., *Le Probleme des Stades en Psychologie de l'Enfant*. Paris, France: Presses Universitie de France, 1956, pp. 33–42.

Piaget, J. *Psychology of Intelligence*. Patterson, N.J.: Littlefield and Adams, 1960.

Piaget, J. *Six Psychological Studies*. New York: Random House, 1967, pp. 100–115.

Sanborn, S. Means and ends: moral development and moral education. Cambridge, Mass.: *Harvard Graduate School of Education Bulletin*, Fall 1971.

Smith, M. An investigation of the development of the sentence and the extent of vocabulary in young children. *University of Iowa Studies on Child Welfare*, No. 5 (1926).

Spelt, D. The conditioning of the human fetus in utero. *Journal of Experimental Psychology* 38 (1948), 338–346.

Stone, L., and J. Church. *Childhood and Adolescence*. New York: Random House, 1973.

Strayer, L. Language and growth: the relative efficacy of early deferred vocabulary training studied by the method of co-twin control. *Journal of Genetic Psychological Monographs* 8 (1930): 209–219.

Westlake, H. *Children: A Study in Individual Behavior*. Lexington, Mass.: Ginn and Co., 1973.

Wohlwill, J. *The Study of Behavioral Development*. New York: Academic Press, 1973.

Learning

3

Learning objectives

After completing this chapter, you should be able to:

1
describe similarities and differences between stage-dependent and learning-environmental theorists;

2
describe how children learn using the concepts of behavioral psychology; explain how different types and schedules of reinforcement can be used to increase learning;

3
describe in motivational terms how child behavior develops; explain how motives develop and how they can be used to help children learn;

4
differentiate among the separate domains or types of learning and describe the environmental factors that contribute to each learning type.

C hapter 2 described the changes that take place in children as they get older. It also discussed theories relating these changes to aging. We call this approach to development the stage-dependent approach, because it describes behavior change as a series of stages increasing in complexity with age.

In this chapter, we consider another explanation of behavior change: the *learning-environmental* approach to development. Learning is a relatively permanent behavior change resulting from the child's interactions with the environment. Psychologists, no matter what theory they use to explain behavior, agree on one thing: children need to interact continually with their environments in order to develop normally. For example, babies do not develop the ability to hold a nursing bottle by themselves during feeding solely because of the maturing of motor ability. If we watch carefully, we will see that babies learn this skill gradually through series of interactions with their mothers and the bottles. Learning begins with a feeding in which the mother holds tightly to the bottle and tilts it properly, so that the baby will receive milk. This behavior is followed with a series of intermediate steps in which she gradually relinquishes hold as the baby's grip becomes stronger and more sure. Finally, she lets go altogether; the baby has *learned* to hold the bottle without help. By gradually helping her baby to hold the bottle properly and gradually removing that help as the baby's responses become more appropriate, she has helped behavior change (learning) to take place.

Children need to interact continually with their environments in order to develop normally.

Learning-environmentalists agree with stage-dependent theorists that behavior changes relate in some ways to chronological age. However, they disagree as to the cause of that relationship, as well as to the emphasis placed on it.

One learning environmentalist, Robert Gagne, suggested that Piaget's stages of cognitive development depend on two factors: (1) what the child already knows, and (2) how much still has to be learned in order to reach the goal. According to Gagne, "the child progresses from one point to the next in his development . . . because he learns an ordered set of capabilities which build on each other in progressive fashion . . ." (Gagne, 1968, p. 181). Every higher level of learning requires previous lower-level learning. As children get older, they are more likely to have completed more lower-level earning. Thus, the older the children, the more often they will be able successfully to solve problems requiring these lower levels of learning. Piaget's cognitive structures, according to this view, are not evidence of qualitative differences, but rather combined capabilities acquired through experience with the environment. In this sense, stages of cognitive development are not related so much to age as to the fact that *learning takes time.*

Learning and Readiness

Developmental readiness is described by learning-environmental theorists in similar fashion. According to the learning-environmentalist, readiness is the accumulation of previously learned skills. At young ages, children may not be able to perform given tasks. This is not because they are not maturationally ready, but because they have not yet acquired the necessary prerequisite skills. If we properly sequence the learning of these prerequisite skills, we can provide learning programs in which children become capable of highly complex tasks at younger ages. According to this view, development is "behavior change which requires programming." Programming, of course, takes time, but "not enough of it to call age" (Baer, 1970).

Many learning-environmentalists have proposed that it is possible to teach young learners to solve abstract problems, as long as the necessary skills are taught beforehand. One psychologist, Jerome Bruner, proposed that children never should wait in order to learn. He stated that "any subject can be taught effectively in some intellectually honest way to any child at any stage of development" (Bruner, 1960, p. 26). Bruner does not expect this learning with any kind of curriculum; he attaches great importance to both the design and structure of curriculum materials, as well as to the method of teaching used. Curricular materials, according to Bruner, should contain problems that progress logically from simple to complex. Early learning should require simple levels of understanding and serve as preparation for later learning. Teachers should provide children continually with problems one step ahead of their present learning. Bruner suggests that teachers using this method can help children to solve complex problems more rapidly than we ordinarily think them capable of doing. He believes that his method, which he calls "the spiral curriculum," can increase considerably the rate of intellectual development.

We have known for a long time that children can learn highly complex tasks at earlier ages than generally expected. Maria Montessori reported as long ago as the turn of the century that she could teach extremely young children to solve highly complex problems (Montessori, 1914). Montessori was able to teach Italian children as young as four years to read and write in about a month and a half of "definite preparations" (Fisher, 1965, p. 87). (We will discuss what this "definite preparation" entailed in Chapter 10.)

The Montessori method is unusual in its effectiveness. However, many countries other than the United States have also developed educational programs in which children learn extremely complex tasks at early ages. Children reared in preschools in the Soviet Union are taught to perform many cognitive tasks at much younger ages than their American counterparts (Bronfenbrenner, 1970). (We will examine these Soviet preschool programs in detail in Chapter 7.) But it is not only highly organized and costly child-rearing programs such as those of the Soviet Union that effectively teach concepts to very young children. Unusually effective methods can be found in smaller and less wealthy countries as well. Indeed, in a trip made in 1971 to Cyprus, I was amazed to visit a class of Turkish-Cypriot preschool-aged children in Nicosia who were learning and solving advanced abstract alegbra problems.

Researchers have found that children also can learn motor tasks at earlier ages than normally expected in the United States. Researchers at the Institute for Research in Early Child Education at Moscow have indicated that motor development can be speeded through exercising and massaging of infants' muscles. Evidence was given some time ago, for example, of infants learning to turn themselves over "four months ahead of schedule" with this technique (CBS News Presents the 21st Century). In visits to the Soviet Union, I examined preschool centers where children as young as three months of age are enrolled. Frequently, I have been awed by the rapid motor development of these children. The photograph below shows a nine-month-old baby in Alma Ata, USSR, shown off by a proud caretaker as she walks.

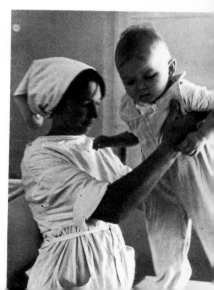

Nine-month-old baby and caretaker in Alma Ata, USSR.

Much American research has centered on the effects of learning experience on child behaviors usually anticipated as part and parcel of normal development. Brackbill (1958), for example, studied the effect of operant conditioning on the smiling response. Rheingold, Gewirtz, and Ross (1959) conducted similar studies of speech development. The ability to socialize and interact with others has also been carefully examined by learning theorists.

Many learning-environmentalists, such as Gagne and Bruner, believe that age makes a difference in how people learn. They believe that adults do not learn in the same way as children, because of the differences in experience at the two age levels. Not all learning-environmentalists hold this view, however. B. F. Skinner, as many other psychologists, agrees that some behaviors are typical for members of a given age group. However, Skinner feels that many principles of learning are universal and apply equally well to persons of all ages. These different approaches to learning are examined in the following section.

TWO LEARNING-ENVIRONMENTAL EXPLANATIONS OF CHILD BEHAVIOR

Many learning-environmentalists are interested in identifying principles common to learning in all people. In this section, we examine two different explanations of how children learn. The first explanation, that favored by behaviorists, restricts the study of children to that which can be *observed*: child behavior itself. The second, motivation theory, explains behavior by describing what goes on *inside* the child: his or her needs, drives, and motives.

Behaviorism

J. B. Watson, often called the father of behavioral psychology, wanted the study of psychology to become indisputably scientific and objective. To be objective, Watson said, psychologists should study only what they can observe (Watson, 1930). Behavioral psychologists today agree with Watson that human behavior is real and objective; they study only observable and measurable behavior.

Classical conditioning Watson showed in laboratory experiments that learning occurs when objects in the environment are associated one with another. In a now-famous study, Watson and Raynor (1920) demonstrated that an eleven-month-old baby could be taught to exhibit fear responses to a white rat. To accomplish this, they first showed that their subject, Baby Albert, responded without fear (smiling and cooing) when a white rat was presented to him. At the same time, he exhibited fearful responses (crying) when subjected to a loud noise. After Watson and Raynor presented the rat many times together with the loud noise, Baby Albert began to show fear when the rat was presented alone. Later, Watson and Raynor noted that Baby Albert generalized this fear to all white furry animals.

Baby Albert's learning is called *classical conditioning;* we say that he was classically conditioned to fear rats and other small furry animals. (Many people know of classical conditioning as *respondent conditioning.* It is called respondent conditioning because, in this type of learning, responses are elicited by certain stimuli in the environment.) Classical conditioning occurs when an initially neutral or *conditioned stimulus* (in this case, the white rat) is associated with an *unconditioned stimulus* (the loud noise). Albert's learned fear response to the conditioned stimulus is called a *conditioned response.* His initial, unlearned fear response to the unconditioned stimulus is called an *unconditioned response.* In Watson and Raynor's study, Albert's conditioned fear response *generalized* to other stimuli similar to the conditioned stimulus. He thus became fearful of all white furry animals.

Classical conditioning occurs frequently in the everyday lives of children. For example, the sound of a school bell usually will not evoke any particular response in the very young child who has not yet been to school. In most classrooms, however, this initially neutral stimulus comes to be associated with the beginning of the school day and students respond to it by taking their seats and paying attention to the teacher. In some cases, classical conditioning does not produce such a socially desirable response. When teachers are frequently punitive, students often associate fear of punishment with being in the classroom. These children develop classically conditioned fear responses. Small children who have experienced pain and illness during a stay in the hospital often come to associate pain with doctors and nurses, the people who were present when they were hurting. These children may develop generalized fear responses associated simply with visiting a hospital—perhaps even visiting a doctor's office—a most unfortunate state of affairs for children with many years of medical visits still ahead of them.

Students respond to the sound of a school bell by taking their seats and paying attention to the teacher—an everyday example of classical conditioning.

Social approval from peers is a powerful reinforcer for adolescents and teenagers.

Operant conditioning   Classical conditioning is learning caused by stimuli that precede the learned response. In the case of Baby Albert, presentation of both the white rat and the loud noise preceded Albert's fear response. In another type of learning studied by behaviorists, the learned response is followed by certain kinds of stimuli. This second type of learning is called *operant conditioning*. Operant conditioning can take place at the same time as classical conditioning.

B. F. Skinner stressed the fact the behavior is affected by what follows it. He noted that behaviors followed by certain kinds of stimuli are more likely to occur again in the future (Skinner, 1953, 1968). For example, if you study this chapter carefully tonight, and receive an A on a quiz in class tomorrow, you will be more likely to use this same careful method of studying for future quizzes than if you had received a lower grade. Careful study behavior, in this example, is called an *operant response:* you are operating on your environment in order to produce what, for you, is a desired result. Operant conditioning sometimes is referred to as *instrumental* conditioning because the response made is instrumental in producing a given result.

A *reinforcement,* according to the operant theorist, is any stimulus that has the effect of increasing the immediately preceding response. Feedback on a test, if good news, is a reinforcement. The value of any particular stimulus as a reinforcer depends on the person being reinforced. To most college students who want to achieve in school, high grades serve as potent reinforcers. To a teenage gang leader, on the other hand, social approval from peers is likely to be a much more powerful reinforcer than any feedback a teacher is able to give. Among preschool children, peer approval, rather than teacher approval, has been found to be the more potent reinforcer (Clark, Viney, Waterhouse, and Lord, 1974). Sometimes, too, what we think is an unpleasant stimulus may prove to be a strong reinforcer.

Primary and secondary reinforcers. Some stimuli, called *primary reinforcers,* are necessary to physical survival. Examples of primary reinforcers are food for a hungry person or shelter for an individual lost in the wilderness. Other stimuli, such as grades and social approval, are unnecessary for physical survival, but still strongly affect behavior. These are called *secondary reinforcers.* A secondary reinforcer initially is not reinforcing, but comes to be so through repeated association with one that is. A newborn infant certainly will not change behavior because of a high grade. Nor are infants at very early ages affected by parental approval. It is only later, when approval has come to be associated with satisfaction of primary needs and grades have come to be associated with approval, that these become secondary reinforcers. Money is a powerful secondary reinforcer for many people in our society because it is closely associated with the primary reinforcers it can purchase.

Reinforcement may occur immediately after a response is made, or it may occur sometime later. Psychologists have discovered that the longer the delay of reinforcement, the less its effect on the response. Thus, your good grade in child psychology will have a stronger effect on your future study habits if your instructor grades your quiz immediately than if he or she waits two weeks to tell you how you did. The ability to learn with delayed reinforcement develops only gradually. Promises that studying will lead to great success in adult life will have very little effect on the behavior of a first grader. The same is true of promises of good health in later life as the child observes the doctor preparing to vaccinate him with that big, long needle! A much more effective reinforcer might be strong social approval exhibited openly by everyone—parents, doctor, and nurses—for receiving the shot without commotion.

Finding the reinforcer: using operant theory to get rid of unwanted behavior

Rodney was an extremely active ten-year-old in the fourth grade. Mrs. Murphy, his teacher, reported to the school psychologist that Rodney was a "behavior problem." He continually jumped out of his seat and disrupted the class. It had gotten to the point, she said, that she had to stop what she was doing every few minutes to ask Rodney to sit down. Mrs. Murphy had called in Rodney's mother, who agreed to punish Rodney for his misbehavior. Rodney's mother, however, was not able to provide the help Mrs. Murphy needed. She was recently divorced and looking desperately for a job. She was terribly preoccupied with her own serious problems and seemed to have very little interest in Rodney's classroom misbehavior. Mrs. Murphy reported to the school psychologist that she was at her "wit's end."

Dr. Huff stayed in Mrs. Murphy's classroom all that morning to observe. Later, the psychologist gave Mrs. Murphy a sheet of paper and asked her to write down the time whenever Rodney jumped out of his seat. She also told her to write down exactly what occurred immediately after this happened. When Dr. Huff and Mrs. Murphy sat down together a day later to look at the paper, Mrs. Murphy said, "Each time he jumped up, the same thing happened: I stopped, told him to sit down, and went back to my work."

The psychologist explained to Mrs. Murphy that any stimulus in the environment can be a reinforcer to some children. Often the only way we can find out what the reinforcer is is to find out what always follows the unwanted behavior. "In this case," Dr. Huff said, "probably the attention given to Rodney when he jumps up is the reinforcer. Let's test it by ignoring the jumping up response." Dr. Huff recommended that Mrs. Murphy continue recording the times that Rodney jumped up and showed her how to plot the responses on a graph.

A week later, Dr. Huff and Mrs. Murphy studied the graph Mrs. Murphy had drawn. It looked like this:

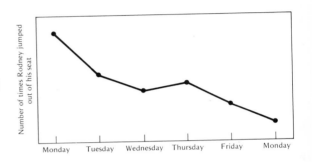

The first day, Rodney jumped out of his seat almost every two minutes. Mrs. Murphy had trouble simply counting Rodney's jumping responses, because they occurred so frequently. The second day, he jumped up half the number of times and spent most of the remaining time sulking. By the third day, Rodney began to spend his time looking at his schoolwork. It was clear by now that Mrs. Murphy's attention was the reinforcer. On the fourth day, Rodney first tried to get attention by raising his hand. He was greatly surprised and delighted when Mrs. Murphy smiled at him. It was a very pleasant and novel (for him) type of attention. By the time Dr. Huff came back to the class, Rodney was jumping up from his seat only a few times per day. The unwanted behavior was almost completely extinguished.

Teacher approval is a highly effective secondary reinforcer for some children.

Schedules of reinforcement and extinction. In any learning situation, reinforcements can be provided after each individual desired response is made. They also can be provided after every few desired responses occur. The pattern by which reinforcements are provided is called a *reinforcement schedule.* Researchers have conducted extensive study on the effects of different types of schedules on behavior. A continuous or 100-percent reinforcement schedule provides reinforcement after every single desired response is made. Researchers have found that continuous schedules of reinforcement lead most rapidly to regular patterns of responding. In early stages of learning, it is most useful to provide reinforcement each time the learner makes a desired response. This will produce a steady rate of responding. However, once reinforcement is stopped, a continuous schedule leads to most rapid *extinction* or disappearance of the response. If Alice is accustomed to receiving praise each time she makes her bed, and suddenly her mother stops praising her, Alice will quickly extinguish her bed-making response. It will not be long before she becomes sloppy again.

In most learning situations, other than ones in which there is a one-to-one learner-teacher ratio, it is impossible to follow every desired response with reinforcement. Once we withhold continuous reinforcement, rapid extinction will occur. Other schedules of reinforcement, therefore, are more suitable if we want permanent learning.

Interval schedules provide reinforcers only after specified intervals of time have passed. If a classroom teacher decided to give a quiz every Friday and provide feedback once a week, we would say that the students in that class were on a *fixed-interval* schedule of one week. Researchers have shown that fixed-interval schedules lead to increased responding at the end of each interval. We can predict that, in this class, students preparing for a quiz each Friday will tend to study heavily only on Thursday evenings.

Extinction of a fixed-interval schedule can be rapid, but not so rapid as with a continuous schedule. If the classroom teacher stops giving quizzes each Friday, it will not take the students long to learn to begin to use their Thursday evenings differently. Sometimes teachers give "pop" quizzes—they may give them every week on the average, but never notify the students in advance. This schedule is called a *variable-interval schedule*. Variable-interval and fixed-interval schedules using the same number of quizzes produce very different response rates: the student preparing for the pop quiz is likely to study before each class, while the student on a fixed schedule will study just before the exam. Extinction, occurring when the teacher stops giving quizzes, occurs more slowly on variable schedules than on fixed schedules. The student used to pop quizzes never knows when the next quiz might come; the student expecting quizzes each Friday learns very quickly when they have stopped.

Another type of schedule less frequently used in formal learning situations is the *ratio schedule,* in which reinforcement is contingent on a specified number of desired responses. If Alice's mother decides to reward her for keeping her bed made and her room neat for seven consecutive days, Alice has been placed on a ratio schedule. Like variable schedules, ratio schedules may be fixed or variable.

Shaping behavior. In the beginning, children often do not know how to make the response desired. For example, in teaching children to print their names, we first have to teach them how to hold their pencils. Then, we must teach them how to make the movements required for each letter. Finally, we teach how to print the letters in proper sequence. Reinforcement following each step of the way ensures that learning occurs. The process of reinforcing successive approximations to the final desired response is called *shaping.* Learning to make complex responses requires shaping of successive approximations to the final response.

Positive and negative reinforcers. All the reinforcements we have been talking about so far have led to increases in the immediately preceding responses. These reinforcements are pleasant; the learner wants them to occur. We call these *positive reinforcers.* Many stimuli in the environment affect learning in a very different way. *Negative reinforcers* are stimuli that the learner tries to stop. Such stimuli strengthen escape responses. That is, whatever the learner does to escape the negative reinforcer will be more likely to occur in the future (Hilgard and Bower, 1975). Researchers have shown that socially desirable escape responses *must* be available to the learner if negative reinforcement is to teach what we want (Holz, Azrin, and Ayllon, 1963; Solomon, 1964). Thus, we won't be teaching Tommy to come home for supper on time if the only thing we do is spank him after he comes home late. It would be far better to explain to Tommy before he goes off for the afternoon just what socially desirable behavior he can use to avoid the negative reinforcer.

What *does* happen when Tommy is spanked after coming home late for dinner? Most probably his mother spanks him because she assumes that spanking will decrease the probability of his coming in late. Behavioral researchers have shown, however, that punishment alone without any other learning never completely suppresses the unwanted behavior (Estes, 1944). Psychologists report that "a response cannot be eliminated from an organism's repertoire by the action of punishment alone" (Hilgard and Bower, 1975, pp. 135–136). When punishment is removed, the individual simply gradually returns to his or her prepunishment response rate. Without teaching Johnny a socially acceptable escape response, his mother can expect him frequently to come home late, no matter how many spankings she gives him.

Misunderstanding of how punishment works has encouraged some teachers to continue to demand corporal punishment as classroom behavior becomes more and more unmanageable. It probably has led mothers to say over and over again, "How many times am I going to have to spank you before you learn?" If all we do is spank and nothing else, according to the behaviorist, we may have to spank forever! But before we take this route, we should remember one other known effect of continued unpleasant stimuli in our environments: when our environment is associated with unpleasant stimuli, we develop associated fear responses. The generalized fear or anxiety caused by continued punishment or negative reinforcement often suppresses other undesirable responses. According to most behaviorists, even though negative reinforcement may effectively produce learning in some controlled situations, Tommy's mother would benefit by trying methods other than spanking alone to teach Tommy to come home on time.

Behavior management. When we intentionally reinforce desired behavior and ignore or punish undesirable behavior, we are engaging in what is called *behavior management.* The process goes on daily in homes and in classrooms. Parents reinforce socially desirable behaviors usually with social approval and love. School teachers use praise and good grades to the same end.

In order to apply behavior-management principles in systematic fashion, it's necessary first to study carefully the child's repertoire of responses. Obviously, we cannot reinforce behavior that doesn't appear. When the desired response does not appear initially, we know that we will have to shape that response, slowly and carefully reinforcing successive approximations to the desired behavior until it finally appears. When the desired response appears only sporadically, we have to be extremely careful always to follow it with reinforcers to ensure that it is not extinguished.

Anyone using behavior-management techniques with children must exert extreme care in selecting reinforcers. No single stimulus will reinforce all children equally. Praise is a highly effective secondary reinforcer for some children; stars attached to foreheads or to behavior charts are extremely effective for others. For most adolescents, peer approval is the most potent reinforcer of all.

One method for selecting reinforcers in a learning situation is to allow children to do the selecting themselves. One procedure for doing this is called the Premack principle (Premack, 1959). Persons making use of the Premack principle first carefully observe child behavior during free play and note behaviors that occur most frequently. Later, during learning, they will use that same behavior for reinforcement; that is, they will allow the children to practice that behavior as a reinforcement. For example, children who have spent most of their free time reading comic books now will be allowed to read comic books as reinforcement for desired behavior; children who spent their free time playing games will be given access to the game table.

Some people have expressed concern over the ethics involved in behavior-management programs. They ask: Should anyone have the right to exert control over the behavior of others? These ethical concerns, just as those discussed in Chapter 1, merit serious consideration by researchers. Children's rights, as well as adults', must always be considered. Behavior managers stress the importance of planning programs to benefit learners, not teachers.

Motivation Theory

Many learning theorists feel that the behavioral approach does not offer a full explanation of what takes place when a child learns. Motivation theorists attempt to describe what goes on inside children in order to explain their actions. They feel that all behavior has meaning and purpose. Without describing that purpose, we leave out important aspects of learning.

Motivation theorists, of course, cannot observe and measure purpose directly. Instead, they infer its existence from knowledge of what they can observe. In order to explain this approach to child behavior, it is important to understand three concepts basic to the theory: needs, drives, and motives.

Using parents as treatment agents

One of the problems in dealing with juvenile delinquency and other unwanted behaviors among school-aged children is the shortage of skilled psychological practitioners. One solution for dealing with this shortage is to use parents as treatment agents. Psychologists for years have been giving American parents advice on how to raise their children and how to deal with problem behavior. Recently, two psychologists set out to determine whether teaching specific behavioral-management skills would help. Wiltz and Patterson (1974) used for their study parents of boys referred to a behavior clinic for help in dealing with antisocial aggressive behavior.

Wiltz and Patterson chose for their study parents who had demonstrated willingness and ability to collect objective information about the behavior of their children and report it to a therapist daily by telephone. Parents demonstrating their desire to help their children in this way were divided into two groups. One group of parents, the experimental group, was given training in specifics of behavior management. This included the concepts, language, and data collection skills necessary to carry out behavior-management programs. A randomly selected second group, the control group, was not given special training. This group was, instead, placed on a waiting list for help.

The target behaviors selected for study included such unwanted responses as teasing, yelling, general noncompliance with authority, and general negative behaviors. Three goals were selected by the therapist for the experimental group: (1) to reduce unwanted target behaviors of the children to 30 percent of their original baseline occurrence; (2) to select other unwanted behaviors and similarly reduce their occurrence; and (3) later, to teach these same behavior-management techniques to new sets of parents.

Outcome of the program was measured by trained observers who studied all of the families in their homes in order to determine whether or not the boys reduced their undesirable behavior. Undesirable behavior of boys in the experimental group was significantly reduced. Boys whose parents remained on the clinic's waiting list continued, during observations, to exhibit the same antisocial behavior. The trained parents successfully met behavioral goals that parents, willing to help but placed on waiting lists, could not meet.

An explanation of needs, drives, and motives A *need* is a condition within the individual that must be reduced for satisfactory adjustment to the environment. Some examples are the needs for food and love. Needs necessary to physical survival are called *primary needs*. Food is a primary need; love is not. But for normal development, children must reduce more than primary needs alone. For example, the needs to be loved and, in our society, to achieve are both important. These are called *secondary needs*. They are not necessary for physical survival, but come, through learning, to be important to optimal adjustment.

According to motivation theory, a child's need gives rise to a *drive*, an internal state compelling the child to activity. When babies have

When babies have a primary need for food, they cry. Motivation theorists call this evidence of a hunger drive.

primary needs for food, they become active, squirm about, and cry. Motivation theorists call this evidence of "hunger drive." When students have secondary needs to achieve, they become activated in a different way: they study. It is important to note that the direction taken by drive activity initially (before learning) is indiscriminate. That is, although there may be high activity level, the individual at the outset has no particular goal in mind. A good example is the newborn baby (Gibson, 1972, pp. 276–78). A few hours after birth, newborn babies have a strong need for food. At this age, we certainly cannot assume that babies *know* their mothers' breasts reduce this need; they haven't yet had the opportunity to receive food through their mouths. The hunger drives, however, compels them to general activity; they squirm and cry. As a need increases, according to motivation theory, so does the resultant drive. The longer babies go unfed, the more we can expect them to cry. Only after they are fed and their needs for food are reduced can we expect their activity to cease. Of course, as babies get older, they will experience drive reduction through the mother's breasts many times. Later, when they cry, it will be for the purpose of obtaining those breasts. We call this now-directed behavior *motivation*. Motivation occurs only when the baby learns through pairing of a goal object with drive reduction to direct activities in such a way as to obtain a particular goal.

Maslow's hierarchy of needs

One original attempt to deal with the complexity of need systems is found in the work of Maslow (1943, 1954). According to Maslow, needs can be described most clearly in terms of hierarchy arranged from simple to complex, so that each need becomes dominant only when needs lower on the hierarchy are gratified.

According to Maslow, physiological needs, the foundation of motivation theory, are dominant unless they are satisfied. Children who are hungry will not be concerned, for example, with meeting needs for social approval. The usual social reinforcers will have little effect on their behavior. Safety needs—the needs for a safe, stable environment—follow. These needs dominate the existence of some unfortunate children whose lives are in turmoil because of broken households or parental separation. Love and belonging needs come next. Youngsters who feel unwanted, who feel no rapport with peers in school, often become major behavior problems. Esteem needs are met through achievement; teachers and parents can help by rewarding success and by providing opportunities for success. However, even if these needs are satisfied, according to Maslow, the child will feel "discontented and restless" unless he does "what he wishes and what he is capable of doing"—what Maslow calls self-actualization needs. It is only then that children can begin to satisfy the needs to know and to understand.

Maslow's hierarchy makes a great deal of sense when we attempt to explain why many peoples in underdeveloped countries have accepted American financial aid, only to then back nondemocratic governments. Until hunger drive is reduced, we cannot expect people to consider needs for self-actualization, according to Maslow.

Intrinsic and extrinsic motivation Psychologists have differentiated between what they call extrinsic motivation and intrinsic motivation. *Extrinsic motivation* occurs when activities are directed toward goal objects external to the learning experience, as, for example, money rewards given for good behavior. *Intrinsic motivation* refers to motivation for which the experience itself serves as the goal. Children may be intrinsically motivated to learn to read because reading is fun. Intrinsic motivation in this sense refers to what behaviorists call "self-reinforcing activities."

Harlow et al. (1950) proposed that humans often are motivated by curiosity and need for stimulation. This suggests that the novelty of a learning experience by itself can serve as a goal. Children seem to enjoy exploring without requiring any noticeable extrinsic reward. This fact supports the notion that intrinsic motivation can be a major source of learning.

Many new teaching methods make use of intrinsic motivation. For example, the famous and successful Suzuki method of teaching children as young as two-and-one-half years to play the violin relies heavily on making violin playing rewarding rather than on providing external rewards (Pronko, 1969). Many innovative curricula, such as the responsive environment developed by O. K. Moore (1968), also make use of intrinsic motivation. In the responsive environment, motivation comes through the children's knowledge that they are learning. The open-education approach, in which children help structure their own curricula, also relies almost exclusively on intrinsic motivation (Central Advisory Council for Education, 1967; Kohl, 1969).

The explanations given thus far of needs, drives, and motives help to clarify why many children today seem unmotivated to learn. Motivation of students to achieve develops in much the same way as motivation of babies to obtain their mothers' breasts. That is, it develops only when a child has learned to direct activity toward a particular goal. Whether this goal is extrinsic (as a good grade) or intrinsic (as fun in solving a new problem), motivation can occur only after drive reduction has taken place. Children who, in the past, have failed at everything they've attempted never have had an opportunity to experience drive reduction in

Children may be intrinsically motivated to learn to read because they find reading fun.

learning situations. Such children can be expected never to achieve until major changes have been made in the learning situation. Instead of saying, "Johnny isn't learning because he isn't motivated," the teacher much more accurately should say, "Johnny isn't motivated because he isn't learning."

We often assume that children will be motivated by a desire to avoid failure or punishment. This approach can be successful occasionally with children who already have learned how to avoid failure. But for the child who always has failed, motivation theorists, like learning theorists, would predict continued lack of motivation.

Gagne (1970, pp. 284–289) suggests more positive ways by which children might be motivated to learn—for example, motivating through the desire to gain social approval of peers, to establish positions of social esteem, to master skills, to develop the abilities to function independently, and to achieve. Another suggestion given by many psychologists is to make learning meaningful. Meaningfulness has been shown to be extremely important to learning (Underwood, 1964a, 1964b). When children understand the uses to which their efforts can be put, motivation is increased. When they are able to describe and reach their goals, motivation is increased. Arranging learning in small steps, so that the next step can easily be understood and reached by the child, is a far more effective teaching method than using aversive stimuli.

Motives and developmental change Developmental psychologists tell us that different types of motives predominate at different ages. According to Kagan (1971, p. 64), "the motives that are preoccupying are usually those linked to goals that one is uncertain of attaining. These foci of doubt change as the child matures." Kagan suggests that, in the beginning months of life, the infant is not guided by ideas of any goals, with the exception of those associated with satisfaction of physiological needs. By the end of the first year, however, as long as these needs are met, motives associated with nonphysiological goals begin to appear. Nine-month-old babies who express surprise and upset when a toy is hidden from view are showing us that they want that toy. Similarly, eighteen-month-olds who cry when their mothers leave the room are showing need for maternal presence. They are motivated to seek their mothers' return. When children reach three, they begin to seek not just the presence of their mothers, but maternal approval as well. Three-year-olds want to be hugged. Later, at four, they will not so much want to be hugged as to make their mothers hug them. At four, children are motivated primarily to control rapidly expanding and potentially more threatening environments.

The early school years are characterized by growing needs for competency, according to Kagan. During this period, desire both for com-

First graders have a growing need to feel competent in school.

petence and for acceptance from peers is strong. First graders have great needs for evidence that they are valued. Praise is as effective as a hug; they often will work hard at school tasks just to receive praise from the teacher. First graders who have difficulty learning to read not only feel unworthy because of lack of achievement, they also are keenly aware that peers can see their failures.

Adolescence brings strong sexual motives to the forefront. In our society, sexual attractiveness is extremely important. The adolescent, growing awkward and gangly at this period, needs evidence of sexual attractiveness in order to feel desirable. The adolescent who feels insecure in matters related to sexuality has a great deal of difficulty adjusting to peers and to the school environment. Sex-typed behavior, learned gradually through childhood, now becomes extremely important. Behaviors unacceptable to peers are disapproved of. The high school girl who seeks strongly to gain her father's or boyfriend's praise at this age may do so in a variety of ways, including spending hours combing her hair and experimenting with makeup. An adolescent boy who thinks that his father will be proud of him for his athletic ability may work out long hours in the gym. Of course, changes in cultural stereotypes affects sex-typed behaviors. But the need for acceptance exists, no matter what behavior is chosen as culturally correct. The following statement made by a fifteen-year-old girl to her high school counselor illustrates this need for acceptance, as well as the adolescent's extreme fear that acceptance will not be forthcoming:

> No matter what I try to do, I never seem to be able to be what every-one wants. My father wants me to get good grades and go to college. What's he going to say when he finds out that I got all C's on my re-port card? And Johnny wants me to stay out at an all-night party next week! Fat chance I'll be allowed. Then all the kids will know I'm a real jerk. I can't seem to do anything right!

Modeling and motivation Beginning at early ages, children are motivated by the need to obtain their mothers' presence. Later, as they get older, children seek not only their mothers' presence, but their approval and acceptance as well. It is not surprising, therefore, that psychologists have shown that children can be taught new behaviors simply through imitating their mothers or caretakers (Bandura, 1969). Children learn first to listen and then to imitate the sounds of their parents' or care-takers' voices. Imitation, when reinforced by approval, leads to language (Hursh and Sherman, 1973). Children select models who are similar to them in some way. According to Kagan (1971), the greater the number of similar features, the firmer is the belief of the child that the model is similar. For this reason, children tend to imitate the behavior of the same-sexed similar-appearing parent. The three-year-old boy who imitates his father's behavior by using the sponge to wash the family car, just as he has seen his father do it, is exhibiting sex-typed behavior. The little girl who imitates her novelist mother's behavior by sitting down at the table and trying to write a story is exhibiting a modern form of sex-typed behavior.

Children tend to imitate the behaviors they see exhibited by the same-sexed parent.

Many personality patterns are acquired through children's imitation of parental activities. Often parents are not even aware of the behaviors that are being imitated. Sometimes they are not behaviors desired by the parent at all. A classic case is that of the most punitive mother on the block who severely punishes her child for aggressive behavior. As a result, of course, she has the most aggressive child on the block.

Imitation involves copying the act, not the person. Imitation of the same-sexed parent is just a first step in the learning process. As children get older, imitation is followed by what psychoanalytic theorists call *identification*. Identification is a process in which children adopt for themselves not just the behavior, but the standards of the model by which to judge their own behavior. By the time that children begin this process, they are capable of seeking symbolic goals. One symbolic goal achieved through identification is vicarious pleasure. Children who identify with a model believe that some of the characteristics of the model belong to them; they exhibit vicarious involvement with the model (Kagan and Phillips, 1964). The three-year-old imitates his father by copying his car-washing movements. The six-year-old may try to wash the family car by himself when he hears that his grandmother is coming to visit. He does so because he believes that his father would want the car clean on such an occasion. In the event that his father takes the car to the carwash for a professional cleaning, the six-year-old child still will be pleased to hear his grandmother give praise for the clean car. By the same token, the little girl whose mother is a novelist will be excited and proud when the story about her mother's best-selling novel appears in the newspaper. The adolescent boy who now tries to please his dad through working out in the gym recalls earlier feelings about his father:

> When I was in the first grade, I thought I had the strongest dad in the whole world. When his bowling team won the trophy, and his picture was in the paper as top scorer for the team, I was the proudest kid in the class. I used to love to go bowling with my dad. He always used to beat the men he played with.

Children identify not only with models who are similar to them, but with models who provide love and attention. Studies have shown that children pay attention more to warm, loving models than they do to models who do not provide warmth (Yussen and Levy, 1975). Thus, children are more likely to imitate warm, happy mothers and ignore cold, unresponsive ones.

Children also identify with models who are powerful. This is called identification with the aggressor. Not only do parents usually serve as sources of reinforcement for young children, they also serve as sources of punishment and control. All the "don'ts" of our society are taught through what has been called *prohibition learning*. Prohibition learning is the term given to learning the "don'ts" in our society. "Don'ts" are often taught through identification with a powerful model who says "don't!" Johnny says to his best friend Bill, after the teacher has announced that Bill will have to be kept after school, "It's your own fault. You should have done your homework. The teacher said so!" Johnny receives vicarious pleasure by identifying with a powerful, punitive teacher. By identifying with the teacher instead of with Bill, he receives vicarious feelings of strength. Resistance to temptation and self-instruction to obey are taught by the same means. Thus, the small child who is tempted to take a candy when his mother isn't looking, reaches into the bowl, says "No! No!" and withdraws his hand.

DIFFERENT TYPES OF LEARNING

In discussing different theories of learning, we have not distinguished among the many types of learning possible. Gagne (1972) differentiated among five separate domains or types of learning—perceptual-motor learning, verbal information, intellectual skills, cognitive strategies, and attitudes—each characterized by a different successful instructional method. We examine each domain in the sections that follow, and will refer to them many times in later chapters as we describe child behavior.

Perceptual-Motor Learning

Perception involves making meaning out of the stimuli in the environment. Motor learning involves using the body in such ways as to make best use of what is perceived. Increasing both perceptual and motor skills is important for children. This is true in both the early years, when basic skills such as crawling and walking are learned, and also later during the

Learning to ride a scooter involves a series of perceptual-motor tasks.

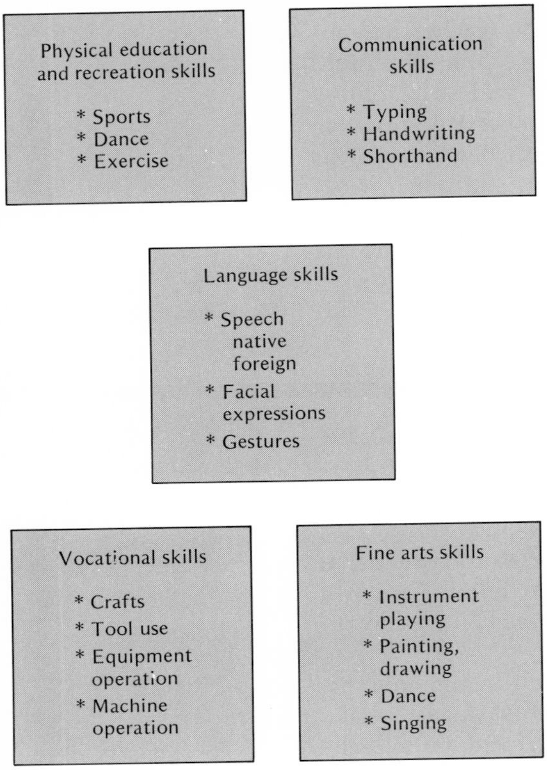

Physical education and recreation skills	Communication skills
* Sports * Dance * Exercise	* Typing * Handwriting * Shorthand

Language skills

* Speech
  native
  foreign
* Facial
  expressions
* Gestures

Vocational skills	Fine arts skills
* Crafts * Tool use * Equipment operation * Machine operation	* Instrument playing * Painting, drawing * Dance * Singing

Fig. 3.1 Representative psychomotor behaviors classified by traditional subject-matter categories. (Reprinted by permission from M. Merrill, Psychomotor taxonomies, classifications, and instructional theory. In R.N. Singer, ed. *The Psychomotor Domain: Movement Behaviors.* Philadelphia: Lea & Febiger, 1972.)

school years. During middle childhood, many fine skills are developed, such as those required in reading and writing. Perceptual-motor activities enter into all spheres of life. For adults, as well as children, highly developed skills are necessary for socially acceptable performance. The abilities to throw a baseball and to drive a car are just two examples.

Merrill (1972) differentiated among five basic areas of motor-skill learning. These, together with the uses to which they ordinarily are put, are shown in Fig. 3.1.

A motor skill is a smoothly integrated series of movements undertaken for a specific purpose. Psychologists have shown that motor learning, like other types of learning, is strongly affected by reinforcement. Knowledge of results is known to be a strong reinforcer to a child who wants to develop motor ability (Merrill, 1971). Clarification of end goals —that is, knowing just what the perfected skill should look like—also improves performance. The difficulty of goals also is an important variable in learning motor skills. A goal that is too easy to reach will produce boredom. A goal that is so difficult as to be almost impossible to achieve will produce only frustration (Locke and Bryan, 1966).

Perception involves extracting meaning from the world around us. So many stimuli are present in the child's world that, to be able to get meaningful information from what is there, the child first must learn to select and discriminate. Perceptual learning is important in many types of tasks ranging from simple sensory discrimination to complex acts with many component parts, such as reading. According to Eleanor Gibson (1965, 1968), learning to discriminate among and identify distinctive features of each of the letters of the alphabet is the first step in learning to read. Gibson taught four-year-old children to "read" a chart showing the distinctive features of each letter of the alphabet. Incorrect answers were given to letters containing larger numbers of features shared with other letters much more often than were letters less similar to the rest of the alphabet. Gibson concluded that errors resulted from perceptual confusion.

Meaning is also critical to learning to read. Studies of the perceptual processes involved in learning to convert letters to sounds have shown

Movement theory: a model to describe learning

Educators recently have developed a new model to interpret the learning process. Movement theory describes the movements through which a child must go in order to make a learned response. All learning, according to this approach, requires movement, from very young children's early reaching-out and touching behaviors to see how the world differs from themselves, to much more complex responding, such as verbal communication.

Movement theory is based on the distinctive characteristics of motor learning and on the premise that readiness does not develop by itself. Readiness, according to movement theory, results from early learning of specific prerequisite motor skills.

According to movement theory, children need instruction in the motor skills prerequisite to learning. This goes for all types of learning, not just those associated with physical education. We call this developing readiness. For example,

in learning to print, children must first learn to make their arms go where they want them to. Then they must learn to control their wrists. Finally, they must learn to control the muscles of their fingers, so as to hold the pencil properly. Then, and only then, are they ready to learn to print. Once readiness has been learned, each of the little components required in the complex skill of printing can be taught (Gentile, 1972; Hunter, 1972).

Preschool children in the Soviet Union are taught to draw and to print using essentially this same principle. They are taught at extremely young ages to use the muscles of their fingers to hold very fine hairline brushes and pens. According to their teachers, this is "to learn to make very small movement with very small hands." American children, conversely, usually are given extra-large crayons to use, because they have not yet developed the readiness to make such fine movements.

that pronounceable words are perceived correctly more often than unpronounceable and meaningless groups of letters (Gibson, Pick, Osser, and Hammond, 1962).

Learning Verbal Information

By verbal information, Gagne means learning the facts, principles, and generalizations contained in what we call "bodies of knowledge." Psychologists have shown that making verbal material meaningful makes it easier to learn. Thus, if a child today is asked to learn a passage from Chaucer written in Old English, he or she will have much more difficulty than if asked to learn the same passage written in modern English. (Many adult Americans still remember the pain in high school of having to memorize long passages written in unfamiliar Chaucerian language, only to receive low grades because of missing punctuation.) One psychologist has suggested that the reason that meaningful material is more easily learned than nonmeaningful may simply be that the meaningful material already is partly learned (Travers, 1967). Thus, to some extent, the child is relearning the modern English passage rather than learning it for the first time.

Spacing and timing learning sessions in which verbal information is taught also is important. Apparently, mental fatigue builds up in massed learning more quickly than it does when learning is spaced systematically (Gibson, 1968). No wonder that cramming for exams rarely produces the desired result!

Learning Intellectual Skills

A concept is a class of stimuli with common attributes—that is, distinctive features that vary from one concept to the next. Concept learning requires the ability to classify stimuli according to these common attributes. Discrimination learning, conversely, requires the ability to distinguish between stimuli on the basis of their differences. Intellectual skills, as defined by Gagne, include both concept and discrimination learning. The learning of intellectual skills is a continual process. Each child, because of a unique past history of experiences, classifies those experiences in a unique way. Thus, Mary's concept of "policeman" might include the attributes warmth, protection, and assistance, while Sylvia's concept of "policeman" might include hurt, arrest, and danger.

Ability to use language is important to development of intellectual skills. According to stage-dependent theories, conceptual thinking increases in complexity with chronological age. According to learning-environmental theories, it develops through a lifetime of meaningful experiences, in which the concept is described in many different forms (Gagne, 1965 and 1970). Practice by itself or without meaning does not improve intellectual skills. Concept learning is increased by teaching applications to new situations rather than by repetitive practice (Gagne, 1965, Markle and Tiemann, 1970).

One way school children may learn the concept of "freedom" in social studies class is first by considering political, personal, and social freedom as it exists in our society. Then, to thoroughly understand the concept, children should practice what they have learned in new situations—for example, by establishing a student-controlled government that allows them to test these various individual freedoms.

According to Gagne, cognitive strategies include internally organized skills that govern the child's behavior in learning, remembering, and thinking. Some psychologists call these learning styles (Gibson, 1976) or cognitive styles. Cognitive strategies are evidenced by individual differences in the ways problems are solved. In addition, some investigators feel that they are related to personality and motivation differences.

Learning Cognitive Strategies

Nations (1967) suggested that cognitive strategies are affected by three components: sensory orientation, response mode, and thinking patterns. Sensory orientation refers to the sensory mode used most easily in learning. Children differ in their visual, auditory, and tactile experience and tend to use that mode most familiar to them. The response mode refers to that type of response used most easily. Response mode, according to Nations, is measured by children's abilities to work most effectively in groups or independently. Thinking pattern refers to the manner in which children tend to learn: by getting many details together and organizing them into a pattern or, conversely, by making major intuitive leaps.

Riessman (1966) emphasized the importance of cognitive strategies or learning styles in planning educational experiences. He pointed out that some children clearly learn more easily through reading, others through

The child who works best alone should be encouraged in this independence.

listening, still others through doing things physically. Riessman and others (discussed in Chapter 12) noted that, once developed, these learning styles are extremely difficult to change. Riessman suggested therefore that, rather than trying to change the child to fit the learning system, a more practical procedure is to change the learning system to fit the child. The child who solves problems most effectively by discussing them in a small group together with other students should be kept in such a group as much as possible. Similarly, the child who works best alone with a piece of paper and a pencil should be encouraged in this independence. The message here, clearly, is that the most effective teacher is the flexible teacher.

Attitude Learning

Attitude learning constitutes Gagne's fifth domain. Although attitudes are learned, they do not seem to be affected strongly either by practice or by meaning. They are strongly affected by strong model figures from whom children receive what Bandura has called "vicarious reinforcement" (Bandura, 1967). Thus, children who see their strong and powerful father denouncing the black janitor in the apartment building are likely to develop similar attitudes toward black janitors and, unfortunately, perhaps toward all black people. Social reinforcers such as smiles, parental approval, praise, and encouragement all serve as reinforcers for attitude learning. Thus, children who are encouraged by their parents for positive attitudes toward school are likely to enjoy school much more than children whose parents feel that education is a waste of time. Acquisition of parental values occurs most fully in an atmosphere of love. Children who grow up in warm, loving homes are most likely to adopt their parents' values.

Attitude development, of course, is affected by many other variables. The age, race, and sex of a child clearly are related in many ways to attitude formation.

SUMMARY

The learning-environmental approach to development explains the behavior of children in terms of their interactions with their environments. Learning-environmentalists may be classified as behavior or motivational theorists. Behavioral psychologists restrict their study to that which can be observed: the responses of the child to stimuli in the environment. Two basic types of learning have been identified through behavioral studies. These include classical conditioning, in which learning is caused by stimuli that precede the learned response, and operant conditioning, in which the learned response is affected by stimuli that follow it. Operant conditioning can occur at the same time as classical conditioning. Motivation theorists differ from behaviorists in their attempts to explain learning by describing what goes on inside the child. Motivation theorists

Acquisition of parental values occurs most fully in an atmosphere of love.

feel that all behavior has meaning and purpose. From their observations of children, they infer their needs, drives, and motives.

Both behaviorists and motivation theorists study many domains of learning, including perceptual motor learning, verbal learning, the development of intellectual skills, the learning of cognitive strategies and attitude learning.

QUESTIONS FOR THOUGHT AND REVIEW

1 Both stage-dependent and learning-environmental theorists use the term readiness to explain why some children are able to learn new tasks while other children do not seem to be able to do so, no matter how much help they receive. How do each of these two theoretical approaches explain readiness? What are the main similarities and differences between these explanations? (For review, see pages 73–76.)

2 Explain how positive and negative reinforcers affect child behavior in different ways. Make use of operant theory to describe in detail a method that would be successful in teaching a six-year-old to add and subtract. (For review, see pages 78–84.)

3 The following statement was made earlier in this chapter: Instead of saying, "Johnny isn't learning because he isn't motivated," the teacher much more accurately should say, "Johnny isn't motivated because he isn't learning." Explain this statement using motivation theory. (For review, see pages 84–89.)

4 Kenneth Clark once reported, "It seems apparent that individual students respond to different approaches, methods, and materials, and also that individual teachers teach effectively with different approaches, methods, and materials" (Clark, 1970, p. 41). What evidence do psychologists have to support this statement? (For review, see pages 97–98.)

FOR FURTHER READING

Bandura, A. *Social Learning Theory*. New York: General Learning Press, 1971. In this text, Bandura summarizes the research and theory relating imitation learning, identification, and modeling. He discusses how social and personal competencies relate to real-life social situations. Principles of behavior management are described in some detail.

Gelfand, D., ed. *Social Learning in Childhood*. Monterey, Cal.: Brooks/ Cole, 1975. Gelfand has collected in this volume a large number of theoretical and research studies dealing with social learning, imitation, and identification in children. The text provides an excellent survey of the literature in the field.

Kagan, J. *Understanding Children's Behavior, Motives, and Thought.*
New York: Harcourt Brace Jovanovich, 1971. This practical book contains essays emphasizing the roles of behavior, motives, and thought in child development. The text provides an easy-to-read description of motivation theory.

Skinner, B. F. *Beyond Freedom and Dignity.* New York: Knopf, 1971.
This relatively short work is an excellent and extremely controversial discussion of Skinner's notions of the implications for mankind of a behavioral approach toward the solving of societal problems. A major asset of the book is that Skinner prepared it for lay readers and kept psychological jargon to a minimum.

REFERENCES

Baer, D. An age-irrelevant concept of development. *Merrill-Palmer Quarterly* 16 (1970): 238–245.

Bandura, A. The role of modeling processes in personality development. In W. Hartrup and N. Mothergill, eds., *The Young Child: Reviews of Research.* Washington, D.C.: National Association for the Education of Young Children, 1967, pp. 42–58.

Bandura, A. *Principles of Behavior Modification.* Montreal: Holt, Rinehart and Winston, 1969.

Brackbill, Y. Extinction of the smiling response in infants as a function of reinforcement schedule. *Child Development* 29 (1958): 115–124.

Bronfenbrenner, U. *Two Worlds of Childhood.* New York: Russell Sage Foundation, 1970.

Bruner, J. *The Process of Education.* New York: Vintage, 1960.

CBS News Presents the 21st Century. *From Cradle to Classroom, Part I.* New York: McGraw-Hill Films.

Central Advisory Council for Education. *Children and Their Primary Schools.* Vols. I and II. London: HMSO, 1967.

Clark, A., L. Viney, I. Waterhouse, and J. Lord. Instrumental learning in preschool children as a function of type of task, type of reward, and some organismic variables. *Journal of Experimental Child Psychology* 17 (1974): 1–17.

Clark, K. *Appendix to a Possible Reality.* New York: Metropolitan Applied Research Center, Inc., 1970.

DeCecco, J., and W. Crawford. *The Psychology of Learning and Instruction: Educational Psychology.* 2d ed. Englewood Cliffs, N.J.: Prentice-Hall, 1974.

Estes, W. An experimental study of punishment. *Psychological Monographs* 52, no. 263 (1944).

Fisher, D. *Montessori for Parents.* Cambridge, Mass.: Bentley, 1965.

Gagne, R. The learning of concepts. *School Review* 73 (1965): 187–196.

Gagne, R. Contributions of learning to human development. *Psychological Review* 75 (1968): 17–191.

Gagne, R. *The Conditions of Learning.* 2d ed. New York: Holt, Rinehart and Winston, 1970.

Gagne, R. Domains of learning. *Interchange.* Toronto: Ontario Institute for Studies in Education, Vol. 3, no. 1 (1972).

Gentile, A. A working model of skill acquisition with application to teaching. *Quest* 17 (1972): 1–23.

Gibson, E., A. Pick, H. Osser, and M. Hammond. The role of grapheme-phoneme correspondence in the perception of words. *American Journal of Psychology* 75 (1962): 554–570.

Gibson, E. Learning to read. *Science* 148 (1965): 1066–1072.

Gibson, E. Perceptual learning in educational situations. In R. Gagne and W. Gephart, eds., *Learning Research and School Subjects.* Itasca, Ill.: Peacock, 1968.

Gibson, J. *Educational Psychology.* New York: Appleton-Century-Crofts, 1968.

Gibson, J. *Psychology for the Classroom.* Englewood Cliffs, N.J.: Prentice-Hall, 1976.

Harlow, H., M. Harlow, and D. Meyer. Learning motivated by a manipulation drive. *Journal of Experimental Psychology* 40 (1950): 228–234.

Hilgard, E., and G. Bower. *Theories of Learning.* New York: McGraw-Hill, 1975.

Hill, W. *Learning: A Survey of Psychological Interpretations.* Scranton, Pa.: Chandler, 1971.

Holz, W., N. Azrin, and T. Ayllon. Elimination of behavior of mental patients by a response produced extinction. *Journal of Experimental Analysis of Behavior* 6 (1963): 407–412.

Hunt, J. McV. Experience and the development of motivation: Some reinterpretations. *Child Development* 31 (1960): 489–504.

Hunter, M. The role of physical education in child development and learning. In H. Behrens and J. Maynard, eds., *The Changing Child.* Glenview, Ill.: Scott, Foresman, 1972.

Hursh, D., and J. Sherman. The effects of parent-presented models and praise on the vocal behavior of their children. *Journal of Experimental Child Psychology* 15 (1973): 328–339.

Kagan, J. The concept of identification. *Psychological Review* 65 (1958): 296–305.

Kagan, J. Reflection-impulsivity; the generality and dynamics of conceptual tempo. *Journal of Abnormal Psychology* 70 (1966): 17–24.

Kagan, J. *Understanding Children: Behavior, Motives and Thought.* New York: Harcourt Brace Jovanovich, 1971.

Kagan, J., and W. Phillips. Measurement of identification. *Journal of Abnormal and Social Psychology* 69, no. 4 (1964): 442–444.

Kohl, H. *The Open Classroom: A Practical Guide to a New Way of Teaching.* New York: Random House, 1969.

Locke, E., and J. Bryan. Cognitive aspects of psychomotor performance: the effects of performance goals on level of performance. *Journal of Applied Psychology* 4 (1966): 286–291.

Markle, S., and P. Tiemann. Problems of conceptual learning. *British Journal of Educational Technology* 1 (1970): 52–62.

Maslow, A. A theory of human motivation. *Psychological Review* 50 (1943): 370–396.

Maslow, A. *Motivation and Personality.* New York: Harper & Row, 1954.

Merrill, M. Psychomotor and memorization behavior. In M. Merrill, ed., *Instructional Design.* Englewood Cliffs, N.J.: Prentice-Hall, 1971.

Merrill, M. Psychomotor taxonomies, classification and instructional theories. In R. Singer, ed., *The Psychomotor Domain.* Philadelphia: Lea and Febiger, 1972, pp. 385–414.

Montessori, M. *Dr. Montessori's Own Handbook.* New York: Schocken, 1914.

Moore, O., and A. Anderson. The responsive environments project. In R. Hess and R. Bear, eds., *Early Education.* Chicago: Aldine, 1968.

Morrison, B. The reactions of external and internal pupils to patterns of teacher behavior. *Dissertation Abstracts,* 1967, 27A, 2072A (University Microfilms No. 66-14,560).

Mowrer, O. *Learning Theory and Personality Dynamics.* New York: Ronald Press, 1950.

Nations, J. Caring for individual differences in reading through non-grading. Lecture at the Seattle Public Schools, May 3, 1967.

Premack, C. Toward empirical behavior laws: I. Positive reinforcement. *Psychological Review* 66 (1959): 219–233.

Pronko, N. On learning to play the violin at the age of four without tears. *Psychology Today,* May 1969, pp. 52–53.

Rheingold, H., J. Gewirtz, and H. Ross. Social conditioning of vocalizations in the infant. *Journal of Comparative and Physiological Psychology* 52 (1959): 68–73.

Riessman, F. Styles of learning. *National Education Association Journal* 55 (March 1966): 15–17.

Shumsky, A. *In Search of Teaching Style.* New York: Appleton-Century-Crofts, 1968.

Skinner, B. F. *Science and Human Behavior.* New York: Macmillan, 1943.

Skinner, B. F. *The Technology of Teaching.* New York: Appleton-Century-Crofts, 1968.

Skinner, B. F. *Beyond Freedom and Dignity.* New York: Knopf, 1971.

Solomon, R. Punishment. *American Psychologist* 19 (1964): 239–253.

Travers, R. M. W. *Essentials of Learning.* 2d ed. New York: Macmillan 1967.

Travers, J. *Learning: Analysis and Application.* 2d ed. New York: McKay, 1972.

Underwood, B. The representatives of rote verbal learning. In A. Melton, ed., *Categories of Human Learning.* New York: Academic Press, 1964a.

Underwood, B. Laboratory studies of verbal learning. In E. Hilgard, ed., *Theories of Learning and Instruction, Part I of the 63rd Yearbook of the National Society for the Study of Education.* Chicago: University of Chicago Press, 1964b.

Watson, J. *Behaviorism.* Rev. ed. New York: Norton, 1930.

Watson, J., and R. Raynor. Conditioned emotional reactions. *Journal of Experimental Psychology* 3 (1920): 1–4.

Wiltz, N., and G. Patterson. An evaluation of parent training procedures designed to alter inappropriate aggressive behavior of boys. *Behavior Therapy* 5 (1974): 215–221.

Yussen, S., and V. Levy. Effects of warm and neutral models on the attention of observational learners. *Journal of Experimental Child Psychology* 20 (1975): 66–72.

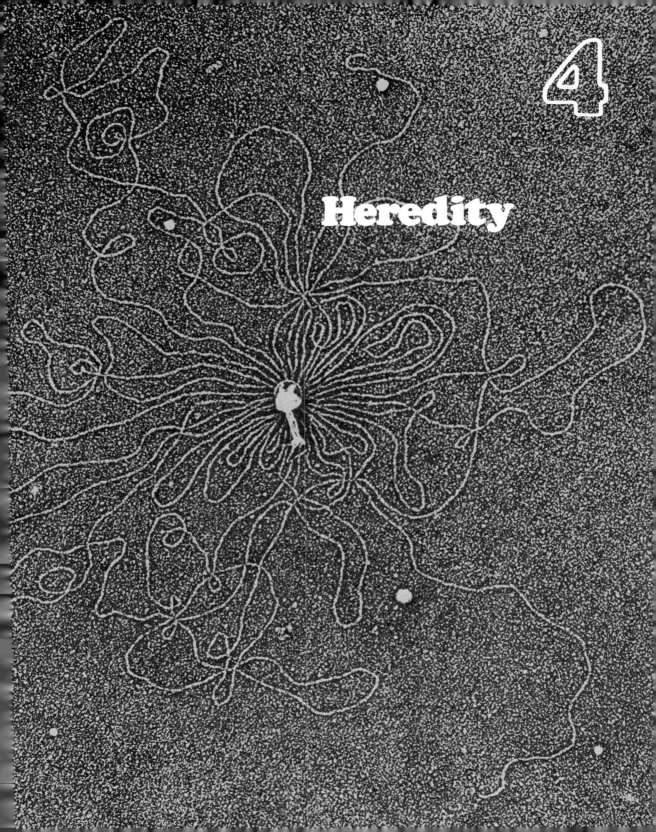

4

Heredity

Learning objectives

After completing this chapter, you should be able to:

1
identify some of the genetic factors that contribute to the development of the child;

2
explain how these factors interact with environmental factors to help shape individual courses of development;

3
discuss some of the ethical problems involved in genetic research;

4
describe some of the factors to consider in determining family size; use this information to help make personal decisions about your own family.

(G) eneticists have shown that heredity affects the developing child in a number of ways. The resemblance of children to their parents is taken for granted. We know that heredity controls the color of our eyes, hair, and skin. It obviously affects our adult heights. Many physical characteristics, both useful and harmful to the developing child, are passed from one generation to the next. This chapter focuses on the mechanisms of inheritance and their importance to society.

Children's abilities, like their physical characteristics, are affected by heredity. However, the link is not always quite so direct. Inherited abilities are influenced and shaped in various ways by the outside world. As a result, each child exhibits unique capabilities and behaviors. The mechanisms by which this takes place are not always clearly understood. In our society, unfortunately, this lack of understanding and information sometimes leads to confusion and fear. The example of Mary-Lou, described on the following page, is a case in point.

The so-called heredity-environment controversy has been an issue hotly debated by geneticists and social scientists. For some physical characteristics, such as hair and skin color, parent-child similarity is explained by very specific and well-understood genetic mechanisms. Inheritance of intellectual capability, personality, and susceptibility to disease are more complicated. Which is more important to Mary-Lou, the hereditary characteristics determined by parents she never knew or her present life with her adopted family? The question is a complex one and has been answered in different ways by different theorists.

The Heredity-Environment Controversy

Which is more important, heredity or environment? Just a few years ago, social scientists engaged in a debate of this question that mushroomed into public furor. Using mean differences in IQ scores between black and white populations in the United States as evidence, Arthur Jensen (1969, 1972) proposed that heredity far outweighs other factors in explaining differences in mental ability. Jensen, and later others, proposed further that differences in innate ability are the reason that compensatory education programs in this country often have failed to produce IQ or achievement gains.

Response to Jensen's position by learning-environmental theorists was swift. Their criticism was on several grounds. They charged that Jensen and others supporting him had failed to take into account environmental factors, such as educational differences known to affect IQ scores. They pointed out the cultural bias of the tests used. Learning-environmentalists as well as geneticists criticized also the statistical bases of Jensen's arguments. Public criticism charged that Jensen's position served to retard hard-won social improvements in our country rather than adding to our information base. Literature on the topic and public discussion in the mass media fueled the debate. (For a review of the controversy, see

The case of Mary-Lou, an adopted child

Mary-Lou is a first grader at Westfield Elementary School. Last year, Mary-Lou seemed in most ways to behave like the other children in kindergarten. This year, however, she has been "acting out" in class. Her reading and writing are poor. At the suggestion of her teacher and with the consent of her parents, the school psychologist has brought Mary-Lou in to be psychologically evaluated.

Later, meeting with Mary-Lou's parents, the psychologist, Dr. Huff, reports that tests show Mary-Lou to be operating socially and intellectually well below her age-mates. Dr. Huff asks about Mary-Lou and her behavior at home. Mr. and Mrs. L., both college graduates, tell Dr. Huff that Mary-Lou is an only child who was adopted when she was six weeks old. The family lives just outside of town where they run a small farm. Mr. L. also is employed part-time as an accountant. Because they live in the country, Mary-Lou has had little opportunity to play with other children.

Mr. and Mrs. L. believe that parents "should not interfere with what the teacher does at school." Therefore, they have not supervised Mary-Lou's reading and writing activities. They have taught their daughter many skills related to farm living, however. Mary-Lou is handy with a hammer and saw, and also is in charge of her own vegetable garden at home.

Both Mr. and Mrs. L. express extreme dismay at Dr. Huff's report. They both had been aware of what seemed to be slow school progress. But they had assumed that this would pass as Mary-Lou got older. Now they reveal deep, hitherto-unspoken fears that no matter what they do, her behavior will not change. Because she is adopted and they know so little about her natural parents, they are terribly afraid that the real cause of her slow learning is genetic. To them, genetic means unchangeable. Dr. Huff points out to Mr. and Mrs. L. that IQ scores and other test scores are not unchangeable measures of ability, but rather are estimates of what a child is capable of doing at the time the test is given. Psychologists do not know the exact extent to which heredity plays a role in developing intelligence. But they do know that the thinking processes can be helped considerably by environmental stimulation. Furthermore, there is a great deal of evidence to show that children's abilities are strongly affected by parental expectations. Dr. Huff calls this the "self-fulfilling prophecy."

Dr. Huff is extremely optimistic about Mary-Lou's future progress, but only if certain steps are taken. She reminds Mr. and Mrs. L. that Mary-Lou displayed exceptional skills on the farm when her parents helped her. She reports that with additional help in developing perceptual and social skills, Mary-Lou should gradually be able to pick up what she needs to do average or even above-average work. She suggests that right now Mary-Lou be placed in a special class for slow learners where she will be given extra individual attention. She also tells Mr. and Mrs. L. to devote regular playtime to games involving perceptual skills, and also to invite other children over to play.

The psychologist strongly cautions Mr. and Mrs. L. that their own fears concerning Mary-Lou's heredity could indeed become a self-fulfilling prophecy if they allow them to affect attitudes or behaviors toward their daughter. Unfortunately, however, Mr. and Mrs. L. remain terribly afraid that no matter what Dr. Huff says and no matter what they do, Mary-Lou will be a slow learner all her life. It has always been assumed in their own social circles that ability is totally inherited and it is hard for them now to think otherwise. Since they know nothing of Mary-Lou's heredity, their fears are strong—and so, unfortunately, is the danger of the self-fulfilling prophecy.

critics Bodmer and Cavalli-Sforza, 1970; Bronfenbrenner, 1970; Crow, 1969; Hebb, 1970; Hunt, 1969. See also Jensen advocates Eysenck, 1971; Herrnstein, 1971.)

In considering the controversy and its importance to society, it is important to note that, over two decades ago, social scientists had reviewed this same literature. They concluded then that the "nature-nurture" question simply is not answerable. It was decided that neither hereditarian nor environmental purists (those who accept either absolute hereditary or environmental choices) were providing a complete picture. In a classic article, psychologist Anne Anastasi pronounced that "the reacting organism is a product of its genes and its past environment, while the present environment provides the immediate stimulus for current behavior" (Anastasi, 1958, p. 197). Anastasi was concerned with the complexities of the interactions between heredity and environment. She stated that it is this interaction that is most important to the developing child.

Anastasi distinguished between hereditary influences that are directly responsible for specific traits and influences that are indirectly responsible. We have discussed already examples of direct hereditary influence. Eye color, for example, is due to the *genotype* or genetic makeup of the individual and is irreversible.

Indirect hereditary influences, like direct influences, are determined at conception. The direction that they take, however, is affected by environmental interaction. A *phenotypic* trait is the visible expression of the interaction between the genotype and the environment. Many visible characteristics of children are phenotypic. Phenotypic traits, such as artistic talent, social ability, and ability to perform on man-made tests of intelligence, are caused by the interaction of a large number of factors. Persons with inherited susceptibility to certain physical diseases must actually encounter the specific disease germs to be visibly affected. In other words, an individual with an inherited susceptibility (genotype) might become diseased (phenotype). Or, he might live out his life fortunate enough never to encounter the germ. In this case, the person's phenotype, the detectable expression of his inheritance, would not reflect his genotype. We probably would never discover his susceptibility. Some psychologists have suggested that schizophrenia may be a phenotypic trait. They suggest that susceptibility to this mental illness may be inherited, but that certain environmental conditions are necessary for the susceptibility to manifest itself (Eisenberg, 1968).

Many personality characteristics have been classified as controlled "in part" by heredity. One psychologist (Nash, 1970, p. 20) put it this way:

We can modify personality by environmental manipulation, and even by the individual effort previous generations called "will power," but we must do this within the constraints imposed by our evolution and present genetic endowment.

Musical ability is a phenotypic trait.

Environmental influences may be direct or indirect. An example of a direct environmental influence on the developing child is severe protein deficiency at certain stages of development, which is known to cause brain damage (Dobbing and Smart, 1974). An example of an indirect environmental influence on the developing child is infant hospitalization. Although the illness causing the hospitalization by itself may have no direct aftereffect, maternal absence associated with hospitalization might well permanently affect the developing personality.

Hereditary characteristics, as well as environment, clearly affect all of an infant's experiences with his or her world. What Jensen and his followers neglected to make clear is that it is impossible to separate out the two effects. Take, for example, a hereditarily defective infant born without eyes and ears. The life experiences of this child will differ so drastically from those of a more normal child that it *always* will be impossible to determine precisely which effects were caused by heredity and which by experience. Or, consider a more subtle (and common) example of a child born with skin color different from most other children where he or she lives. This child also will be affected by the environment in many subtle ways. The issue is complex and important. Neither heredity or environment alone govern the developing child, as the purists would have us believe. Rather, it is a complicated interaction between the two variables that is critical to development.

The heredity-environment controversy clearly shows that there is no consensus on the relative importance of heredity and environment to the developing child. All researchers agree, however, that heredity plays a major role. To understand the importance of heredity, it is necessary to understand just what happens at conception and how the genotypic pattern is determined at that instant.

The Hereditary Basis of Development: Conception

Biological inheritance of traits begins when two *gametes*, a male sperm and a female egg cell, unite to produce a fertilized egg or *zygote*. If we were to examine these gametes under a microscope, and the cells were stained with dye so as to make their separate parts visible, we would see twenty-three rod-shaped bodies in each. These are the *chromosomes*. Each chromosome is composed of thousands of smaller genetic units called *genes*. Genes carry the genetic information from parent to child.

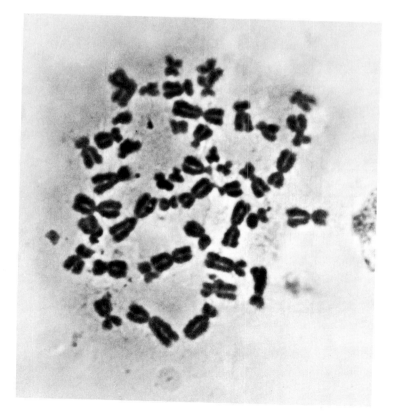

Human chromosomes.

Genes are made up of a complex chemical compound called *deoxyri bonucleic acid* or DNA, a compound composed of nitrogen bases. The way that these nitrogen bases are arranged within each gene provide the specific genetic information that results in what we have called the *genotypic pattern*. In some cases, the DNA within a single gene may determine one or even several inherited traits. Eye color is an example of a trait determined by just one gene. More often, however, a combination of genes, forming larger DNA chains, establish what are known as complex or *polygenic traits*. Skin color is a polygenic trait caused by a combination of many genes. A single gene may simultaneously affect a number of traits, leading to an amazing complex of interactions. In some cases, a gene derived from one parent may interact with one from the other to produce a trait that does not appear in either parent. It is therefore possible for children to bear little resemblance to either of their parents.

Earlier in this chapter, it was mentioned that some components of mental disorders and personality characteristics might be inherited. Can a gene pass on specific behavior? What actually intervenes between gene and behavior is not known. It has been hypothesized, however, that genes pass on certain patterns of constitutional organization related to body type, autonomic differences, certain types of endocrine balance and neural organization. Such hereditary characteristics by themselves do not necessarily lead to particular behaviors. Specific environmental stimulation is necessary for this to occur. Thus, as stated earlier, behavior can be indirectly affected by heredity.

To complicate this issue still further, there are two basically different types of genes: *dominant genes* and *recessive genes*. If a pair of dominant genes appear in the fertilized egg, the trait or traits determined by those genes will appear in the child. We know, for example, that the gene responsible for brown eye color is dominant; the gene responsible for blue eye color is recessive. A child who receives one brown eye-color gene and one blue eye-color gene will have brown eyes. This is true because brown eye color is dominant over blue. Only children who receive two genes responsible for blue eye color will have blue eyes. It is clear from this example that all brown-eyed children do not carry the same genetic pattern for eye color; some carry recessive blue-eyed genes. Two adults with brown eyes are able to produce a blue-eyed baby. It is not possible, however, for two blue-eyed parents to produce a brown-eyed child. The same rule applies to other traits controlled by dominant and recessive genes.

A defect in a single gene may interrupt normal development of both simple and polygenic traits. The gene that causes lack of iodine in the body essential to the development of thyroid hormones is an example of such a defective gene. This gene results in the genetic defect known as cretinism. Infantile amaurotic family idiocy results from a peculiar hereditary defect in the nerve cells of the brain and spinal cord. The disorder appears to be caused by the inheritance of specific recessive genes from both mother and father. Another type of hereditary defect occurs in abnormalities of chromosomal structure. An example of this is mongolism, a genetic defect caused by forty-seven rather than forty-six chromosomes. Mongoloid children are mentally retarded.

All of us carry some defective genes. Luckily, for most of us, these defective genes represent only a tiny proportion of our genes. Furthermore, most of these are recessive and therefore are less likely to affect our children. The average number of seriously defective recessive genes for each of us is thought to be between four and twelve. The existence of so many different defective genes together with continual mutations (changing of genes) causing possible additional genetic defects has been of great concern to geneticists, and will be discussed further in this chapter.

With the forming of the zygote, the genotypic pattern is set. Each of the forty-six chromosomes now duplicates itself in a process called *mitosis*. When the newly formed cell divides, each of the two new cells formed receives forty-six chromosomes matching the originals. Eventually, with repeated cell division, a totally new child develops, carrying in each body cell identical chromosomes, genes, and DNA.

No two children developing from different zygotes have exactly the same combination of chromosomes—or genes. With each chromosome containing approximately 20,000 genes, it is no wonder that each of us grows in unique ways. The only time that two children will be born with identical hereditary characteristics is when identical twins develop from the same zygote. Brothers and sisters, even fraternal twins developing at the same time in the same uterus from different eggs, have different heredities. They may have some genes in common, but they never are completely identical.

Each body cell has forty-six chromosomes. This is not true, however, of the reproductive cells or gametes. Sperm and egg cells are produced by

No two children developing from different zygotes have exactly the same combination of chromosomes.

a process called *gametogenesis*. During gametogenesis, a cell division called *meiosis* takes place, in which four cells rather than two are produced. Each of these four reproductive cells has twenty-three chromosomes. Sex of the developing individual is determined at conception by one special pair of these chromosomes. The female egg cell carries only what are known as X chromosomes; the sperm cell carries either X or Y chromosomes. If the zygote carries an XX combination, the resulting child will be a girl. If the sperm cell has contributed a Y chromosome, the developing child will be a boy. In one special sense, boys inherit more from their mothers than from their fathers. The Y chromosome coming from the father and responsible for producing males carries fewer germs than does its X counterpart. Thus, some of the X chromosome genes are unmatched by genes in the Y chromosome. Some sex-linked characteristics are passed on through the unmatched genes only through the mother. Two examples are hemophilia and color blindness, two sex-linked disorders inheritable only from mother to son.

MAKING USE OF GENETIC INFORMATION

How is information about heredity and conception used to affect development? One way that we have used what we know about genetics to change development is selective breeding. We all know that domestic animals are bred for different characteristics. Animal husbandmen long have used breeding procedures to produce "superanimals"—i.e., animals with characteristics humans find desirable. Examples would be cows that produce great amounts of milk or chickens with great amounts of breast meat.

Selective Breeding of Domestic Animals

Some of the problems encountered by animal husbandmen breeding "superanimals" should be apparent from our discussion of recessive genes. Breeding for desired phenotypic traits takes a great deal of time. In the process, recessive genes may cause many undesirable traits at the same time that they produce desirable ones. Most phenotypic traits occur because of the presence of combinations of genes interacting with one another. Breeding two animals with the desired phenotypic trait does not guarantee that the same desired array of genes will be present in the offspring. Recessive genes also may exist undetected for many generations, suddenly appearing without warning in a later generation. In addition, genetic mutations continue to occur in all living organisms. Statistically speaking, however, the probability of the appearance of the desired trait increases with each generation bred for that phenotype. In the case of undesirable traits filtering through in breeding domestic animals, it is a relatively simple matter for the animal husbandman; he or she rejects the carriers of physically undesirable traits from the breeding sample.

What about selective breeding of phenotypic behavioral traits? As pointed out earlier, psychologists can't determine exactly the specific roles of heredity and environment in determining behavior. The inter-relationship obviously is complex. Psychologists believe, however, that many behavior traits are affected indirectly by heredity. One example given earlier in this chapter was schizophrenia. Psychologists believe that schizophrenia may be a phenotypic trait that manifests itself only when certain types of environmental conditions are present. Another trait that interested psychologists long before Jensen conducted his research is intelligence.

Tryon (1940), almost forty years ago, purported to show that "bright" and "dull" strains of rats could be developed by successive selective breeding through many generations. Tryon measured differences in what he called brightness and dullness in maze-solving ability after selectively breeding eighteen generations of rats on the basis of their abilities to learn maze problems. Although Tryon referred to the differences he obtained between the two strains as brightness and dullness, other researchers noted that many other behavior differences also existed in the two eighteenth-generation strains. They pointed out that performance differences in the maze by the two groups could be accounted for in terms of motivational and emotional patterns (Searle, 1949; Thompson, 1953).

Interest in selective mating has not been restricted to domestic or lower animals. Selective mating has had a long and well-known presence in the history of humans as well. The prescribed marriages that took place in ancient times and that still occur in some societies today are an example. Prescribed marriages are formal mating procedures rooted in the belief that careful selection of partners will improve future generations. Prescribed marriages have not always been decided within the immediate families. Although the ancient Spartans did not understand thoroughly the mechanisms involved in hereditary control of phenotypic traits, they believed that traits are passed from parent to child. The governing body of the Spartans quite often arranged marriages of people in the common-wealth they considered "fit" to produce future citizens.

A method of selective mating similar in some ways to that of the Spartans was practiced by one community in the United States within the last century. The Oneida Community, an experiment in communal living, was founded in 1848 in Oneida, New York. In the Oneida Community, marriage and sexual relations were strictly regulated; the propagation of children was a matter of community control. Those selected to produce children were carefully mated with those supposedly carrying the most desirable characteristics. John Noyes, the leader of the group, referred to the selective marriage practice as "stirpiculture," a term meaning the "breeding of special stocks or races." The experiment was short-lived. Hostility to the marriage practices of the community grew rapidly in neighboring villages and finally forced Noyes in 1879 to advise the group to abandon the system.

Selective Mating of Humans

Although most societies do not practice so formal a selective mating procedure, informal selective mating occurs whenever a society prizes a visible human trait. Whenever this happens, males and females possessing the desired trait are at what is called a "statistical reproductive advantage." They are wanted by the opposite sex and chosen as mates statistically more often than are those without the desired characteristics.

Eugenics: Improvement of the Human Species through Controlled Genetics

Attempts to improve the human species through genetic control have occurred both formally and informally throughout history. The idea was given support in western society in the nineteenth century. Sir Francis Galton gave it the name *eugenics* and described it as follows:

> *We greatly want a brief word to express the science of improving stock, which is by no means confined to questions of judicious mating, but which, especially in the case of man, takes cognizance of all influences that tend, in however remote a degree, to give to the more suitable races or strains of blood a better chance of prevailing speedily over the less suitable than they otherwise would have had (Galton, n.d., p. 24).*

Galton, Director of the British Laboratory for National Genetics, was a proponent of positive eugenics, the increase of desirable characteristics in the human population through selection and breeding of desired traits. Galton was interested in more than this one form of eugenics, however. Another type of genetic control of interest to Galton was negative eugenics, the improvement of the human species through elimination of undesirable characteristics.

Negative eugenics is practiced to some extent in all societies today. For example, no contemporary society allows marriage between siblings or other close relatives. Incestuous inbreeding is considered a serious crime, for although inbreeding may increase desired traits, at the same time it greatly increases the probability of harmful recessive genes appearing. (Notably, in the few exceptions to the rule against incestuous mating—as, for example, in royal families—trends toward genetic defects exist. Hemophilia among royal families today is an example of such a defect. Among the ancient royal families of Egypt and Hawaii, in which incestuous mating commonly was practiced, infanticide to remove defective offspring was condoned. Only those babies carrying desired characteristics were allowed to survive.)

Galton's successor at the British National Laboratory, Karl Pearson, also was greatly interested in negative eugenics. Pearson felt that carriers of genetic defects had a moral responsibility to humanity to prevent the passing of these defects to the next generation. An American researcher, Charles Davenport, Director of the Station for Experimental Evolution and the Eugenics Record Office at Cold Spring Harbor, Long Island, New York, carried this interest in negative eugenics one step further. Davenport was concerned with the influx of immigrants to the

Sir Francis Galton was a proponent of positive eugenics, the selective breeding of desirable traits.

United States from southeastern Europe. He warned of the imminent danger of biological degeneration of the human race if human breeding were allowed to "proceed without control." (Davenport's ideas were reported as "quite fashionable" in the United States in the first several decades of this century. The station itself and the eugenics program was funded by the Carnegie Institute of Washington until 1940 [Gordon, 1973; Rosenberg, 1961].)

Eugenics and the Nazi programs While the theory of eugenics was preached at the Laboratory for National Genetics in Britain and the Station for Experimental Evolution in America, the law of eugenics was practiced by the Nazi government before and during the Second World War. The Nazi eugenics programs provide firsthand evidence of the horrors created by inappropriate use of genetic control.

The negative eugenics programs of the Nazis are now infamous. The Nazi party, when first gaining power, pronounced as unfit for procreation all individuals carrying "hereditary diseases." On January 1, 1934, legislation implementing both voluntary and compulsory sterilization of unfit persons was enacted. In the following years, large numbers of individuals were sterilized under this act's provisions. Later, the Nazi negative eugenics program was extended to include the total extermination of all people whose characteristics, according to Hitler, made them "unfit." Millions of so-called "racially impure" people were killed in labor and extermination camps.

The Nazis' positive eugenics programs matched in horror their negative programs. *Lebensborn* was a positive eugenics program begun in 1933 by the Nazi government. Lebensborn (meaning "life source") was designed as a major part of Hitler's larger program to produce a super-race. It began with careful selection of German women carrying what were considered "Aryan genetic characteristics" to bear children fathered by equally carefully selected SS men. At first, only German women who could prove their Aryan birth and the Aryan credentials of the father of their children were accepted to the program. Later, to increase the number of "pure-blooded" children more rapidly, the program accepted "Aryan-type" women from the occupied countries whose physical characteristics matched Hitler's requirements. The children born in these especially established homes were turned over to the Nazi government to be raised. Local authorities never were notified of the 50,000–100,000 births of what Hitler called "pure-blooded" Aryan children.

What genetic characteristics actually were bred by this program? In a Public Broadcasting Service documentary film, *In Pure Blood*, a nurse who worked in one Lebensborn home and remained there after the war stated for interviewers, "Superrace? Well, not really. . . . There were intelligent and ordinary children there. Also mentally defective children. But they were all withdrawn—typical institution children" (Henry and Hiller, 1975). Not surprising, when we consider the importance of environment relative to heredity.

In addition to the thousands of children born in Lebensborn homes during World War II, "Aryan-looking" children who passed so-called anthropological tests of hair and eye color, size of forehead, length of nose, and profile were taken from their families in occupied countries to be raised in German families as Germans. It was reported that 200,000 such children were kidnapped from Poland alone. Millions of children who did not meet these so-called genetic requirements were exterminated through negative eugenics programs (Henry and Hiller, 1975).

Genetic counseling today The Nazi atrocities produced evidence that eugenics can be used as a genocide weapon. Still, many theorists maintain, eugenics, if used for the right reasons and with adequate controls, may be of great benefit to mankind.

The past twenty years have brought major increases in scientific knowledge of genetics and biomedicine. Reliable screening of infants for genetic diseases has increased dramatically and treatment of genetic diseases has improved (Hsia, 1975). In addition, methods have been devel-

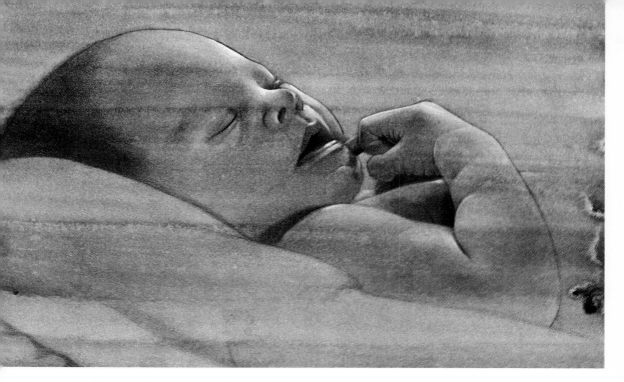

The recent development of amniocentesis has enabled doctors to gather certain genetic information before birth.

oped to help childless couples bear their own children. Most dramatic is the recent development of a procedure known as amniocentesis.

In 1955, researchers first reported the discovery of chromosomes of fetal cells in fluid surrounding the fetus in utero. Only eleven years later, a technique known as karotyping was developed which made it possible to study the number, form, and size of the chromosomes in these cells (McCormick, 1974). Amniocentesis is the procedure for removing fluid from pregnant women and studying the fetal cells.

Before amniocentesis, it was possible only to estimate the probability that defects would occur in children of known carriers and of individuals with higher probabilities of carrying defects than normal—as, for example, women over forty years old. The fact that recessive genes may be hidden made accurate prediction impossible. It is always possible also that new defects caused by new gene combinations or mutations can occur.

With amniocentesis, doctors are able for the first time to study individuals before birth for possible genetic defects. This procedure, together with the United States Supreme Court decision of January 22, 1973 to legalize abortion have made possible a reliable eugenics program in which infants can be selected for specific characteristics before birth. Each year, in the United States alone, there are more than 20,000 live births with recognizable chromosomal defects. The lifetime cost in dollars of just one seriously defective individual has been estimated at more than $250,000—an estimate that does not take into account the psychological and emotional costs also exacted (Milunsky and Atkins, 1975). Amniocentesis and abortion provide together one approach to solving the problems generated by the possibility of such births.

The controversy over the Supreme Court decision legalizing abortion is well known. At the same time, amniocentesis and other genetic and biomedical knowledge pose major social, legal, and ethical concerns for society. Concern of religious groups has been strong. To begin to appreciate the many types of problems that this new knowledge presents, it is helpful to consider the case of Mr. and Mrs. R., who had had one seriously defective child and wanted a second chance.

New genetic and biomedical information offered by amniocentesis presents prospective parents with new and difficult moral decisions. With knowledge that an unborn infant is defective, prospective parents now are faced with the decision of whether or not to allow the infant to be

The R. family: a case in genetic counseling

Mr. and Mrs. R. are parents of Donald, a mongoloid child with very low mental ability. Mrs. R. is Protestant; her husband is Roman Catholic. During the first three years of Donald's life, Mr. and Mrs. R. were able to raise him at home. However, the stress and strain of Donald's problems led to marital difficulties. Mrs. R. began to drink heavily; Mr. R. stayed away from home much of the time. When Donald was three years old, it became too difficult for Mr. and Mrs. R. to care for him at home and he was placed in an institution for the mentally retarded. After Donald's placement in the institution, Mr. and Mrs. R. began to resume their earlier happy relationship. Mrs. R. stopped drinking. Now, four years later, they both want another child, but are anxious about the possibility of its being mongoloid.

Before Mrs. R. becomes pregant, they make an appointment with her obstetrician. With the new process of amniocentesis, the obstetrician tells them, a second pregnancy can be monitored in utero. If the procedure shows that the fetus does not carry the additional chromosome associated with mongolism, Mr. and Mrs. R. can continue the pregnancy with no anxiety. But suppose amniocentesis shows that the fetus is defective? The physician points out that Mr. and Mrs. R. then will have the choice of aborting the fetus. In the interview, Mrs. R. announces that she does not want to go through with the pregnancy if the fetus is defective. She feels that the strain would destroy her and the family. Mr. R., because of his religious beliefs, is not sure what he would want to do. The obstetrician tells Mr. and Mrs. R. that they *must* decide together what they will do in either situation before making an appointment for the amniocentesis.

International concern for genetic disease

Doctors, social scientists, and religious leaders met in 1975 at the first International Conference on Tay-Sachs Disease to discuss medical, social, and religious implications of this genetic illness and to plan worldwide methods for eliminating the disease entirely.

Tay-Sachs Disease, passed from generation to generation in a very small percentage of Ashkenazic Jews, attacks children usually within the first few months of life, cripples, and usually causes death before age five. The disease generally causes severe degeneration of the brain within the first six months of life.

According to researchers, methods used to eliminate Tay-Sachs can be used also to elimi- nate other genetic diseases, as, for example, sickle cell anemia, which strikes mostly blacks. The criteria for removal of this genetic disease are: (1) it exists in a definite population; (2) blood tests can pinpoint carriers of the disease; and (3) the enzyme causing the disease can be detected in pregnancy, so that the fetus can be aborted if infected.

Worldwide screening programs and genetic counseling now are being used to combat Tay-Sachs. The 1975 conference reported on these screening efforts and also delved into the religious ethical implications of genetic counseling and abortion.

born. In the event that the parents disagree as to whether to continue the pregnancy, they must decide also who has the right to make the decision. Some people feel no one has the moral right to decide whether or not an unborn child should be permitted to live. Some feel that the decision should be made by the woman who carries the fetus; others feel it should be made jointly by the two parents who carry equal legal and financial responsibility. Still others have proposed that at least part of the decision should be made by the state, since it would carry the burden of the defective child, unless Mr. and Mrs. R. are extremely wealthy.

Deciding on how genetic counseling should be made available also presents problems. In the United States today, genetic counseling is done "on request." This means that if prospective parents come to a doctor to request such information, it is made available. Genetic-counseling programs run the gamut from private "passive counseling" programs in which this information is provided only when specifically requested to programs in which mass advertising is used. In most cases, it is agreed that counseling should be "nondirective"—that is, the counselor should give the prospective parents facts only and should never advise parents on what course of action they should take. Critics charge that even nondirective counseling of this sort can be considered psychological compulsion. Critics of free or low-cost advertised genetic screening programs point out that psychological compulsion exists whenever it is financially beneficial for prospective parents to make one decision rather than another.

Amniocentesis: a moral dilemma for geneticists

It now is possible for parents to select the sex of their child. But is it ethical? Geneticists report that when prenatal genetic diagnosis first was developed, they realized that eventually it would be used for sex selection. Some opposed it then and many still oppose it now.

Dr. Neil MacIntyre, Professor of Anatomy and Genetics at Case Western Reserve University, expressed his personal conviction that amniocentesis for the purpose of sex determination is morally wrong (Lazarevic, 1976). He believes that amniocentesis should be restricted to diagnosing disease and defects, such as hemophilia, muscular dystrophy, and mongolism, in the unborn.

While MacIntyre feels that physicians have the right to refuse to do what they feel is morally wrong, he believes geneticists are in a far different position. The geneticist ethically must provide information to the best of his or her ability. According to MacIntyre, by not providing a requested test, the geneticist actually is interjecting his or her own bias, and thereby is denying the right of informed free choice to the prospective parents.

Geneticists able to perform amniocentesis who refuse on moral grounds to perform the test for sex determination are trapped into choosing between what MacIntyre calls being "unethically moral" and being "ethically unmoral."

Certainly the specific information selected by a counselor to present to prospective parents will affect their decision making, no matter how objective the counselor tries to be. Some critics have stressed that it is important for the counselor to make clear the physical risk of amniocentesis as well as the advantages. In one study (Milunsky and Atkins, 1975), approximately 3.3 percent of women using amniocentesis were reported to have had major complications, such as spontaneous abortion or fetal death. Others point out that prospective parents should be made aware of the fact that, with today's knowledge, absolute diagnosis of fetal characteristics cannot be guaranteed (McCormick, 1974). Certainly the genetic counselor must be highly knowledgeable about every aspect of the procedure. The complex interaction of patient, family, and society; medical knowledge; and religious and moral issues must be considered.

What makes society consider a child defective? What are the criteria by which parents or a society have the right to consider a child "defective"? Some people say that no one has the right. Others respond in terms of the problems of living faced by that child and his or her family. Most of us are aware of the problems facing a very seriously mentally retarded or physically disabled child, but what if the retardation or disability is less? Amniocentesis can detect many characteristics of the unborn infant, including its sex. Today it is possible legally for parents to use amniocentesis to determine the sex of their unborn child and then to decide whether or not they will allow it to develop to a baby. Preselection of sex may be desirable for parents, but is it desirable for the child? If amniocentesis and genetic counseling come into common practice, where do we draw the line?

All these questions must be considered by specialists and lay people alike. Clearly, there are no easy answers. Such issues are only the first of the many major social and ethical questions that will undoubtedly arise as scientists continue to learn about genetics.

Researchers tell us to expect in our lifetimes the possibility of genetic surgery. Some biologists and physicians predict that, within five or ten years, advances in *euphenics,* the direct manipulation of genetic material (Stone and Church, 1973), may allow us to repair defective genes or to replace them with normal ones. Already human eggs have been collected, fertilized, and allowed to grow for a number of days outside the human body. One day soon, we face the possibility of embryos growing into babies in test-tube wombs. Biologists already have replaced the nucleus of a fertilized frog egg with the nucleus of a blood cell from another frog in a process called *cloning.* The cloned egg grew into cells genetically matching the frog from which the new cell came. Cloning in-

Euphenics: Changing Genetic Heritage through Manipulating Genetic Material

Genetic engineering: present danger and future potential

Research on DNA has been in limbo since 1974 when a handful of extremely well-known molecular biologists, in an unprecedented action, asked their peers to halt certain of their experiments until the risks could be fully assessed and guidelines established. The work these scientists were doing involved the transfer of genes from one organism to another. The fear was that laboratory strains of bacteria used in these studies might accidentally let loose on the world new virulent strains of bacteria resistant to antibiotics, or even cancer-producing genes.

If genetic engineering is potentially so dangerous, why do it at all? Scientists answer that genetic engineering might offer opportunity for therapy of genetic diseases. For instance, sickle-cell anemia results from a defect in the structure of hemoglobin, the blood component that carries oxygen. Research might develop means of supplying victims of this disease with equipment to produce normal hemoglobin. Dr. Robert Sinsheimer, Chairman of the California Institute of Technology's Division of Biology, reported to the *New York Times* that gene manipulation may allow the development of biomedical factories to produce complex substances of medical importance, such as insulin. Other scientists report that genetic engineering may lead to biologically produced antibiotics and antibodies to such illnesses as malaria and tuberculosis. Food production is also an area of potential research for genetic engineering. According to the *New York Times,* researchers are investigating ways to transplant cow genes into bacteria, a potentially inexpensive way of making cheese, a high protein food (Powledge, 1976).

troduces the possibility of recreating organisms genetically matching already existing organisms. Imagine the possibility of taking cells from a particular person, culturing them, and growing exact genetic replicas. No one yet knows if scientists ever will be able to clone a human being. Indeed, most consider it unlikely (Hsia, 1975; Ingle, 1973). But if cloning actually becomes possible, not only will we increase the possibilities of changing the human species, we will multiply our moral and social responsibilities as well.

CHOOSING WHETHER TO BE PARENTS

The early part of this chapter was devoted to people who wanted to be parents: Mr. and Mrs. L. adopted a little girl, Mary-Lou; Mr. and Mrs. R. wanted a second chance to have a baby after their first was born hopelessly defective. Apparently, very few Americans never want to become parents. One study (Pohlman, 1970) showed that more than 90 percent of American married women want children. Estimates of childlessness among married people in this country have varied from 6 to 15 percent (Kunz et al., 1973). There are people, however, who don't want to become parents. There are also others who, after having children, decide they don't want any more.

Changing lifestyles in the United States, coupled with increased public information about family planning, have given Americans greater control than ever before over the sizes of their families. Services provided in the last few years by family-planning agencies through the Population Growth Act of 1970 have made birth-control information readily available to the public. Decreases in the United States birthrate have followed. With more family-planning information available, the percentage of childless and one-child families in this country is expected to increase.

Family planning has not been restricted to the use of contraceptive devices, such as diaphragms, birth-control pills, IUDs, and condoms. In New York State, where the most liberal abortion laws became effective as early as July 1970, and particularly in New York City, where major hospitals first performed free abortion, a sharp drop appeared immediately in the birthrate. There also has been an increase in the United States in sterilization of both males and females. Between 1965 and 1970, the number of Americans requesting sterilization more than doubled (Osborne and Bajema, 1972). By 1970, more than one in six couples who had had their desired number of children already had been sterilized. Nearly 50 percent more indicated that they would seriously consider sterilization to prevent future unwanted pregnancies (Kohli and Sobrero, 1973). Today, for the first time in the United States, we appear to be stabilizing our population rate with our birthrate at replacement level or even below (Bajema, 1973; Osborne and Bajema, 1972).

With more family-planning information available, the number
of one-child and childless families in the United States is
expected to increase.

To understand the family that prefers to remain childless, or at least prefers to keep its size small, we must examine the costs of parenthood
today. In earlier generations, a family's wealth often was considered in
terms of the number of available hands to do the work. Whether this
wealth was measured in actual dollars or whether it, in fact, was only
psychological wealth has been discussed by historians (Vinogradoff,
1975). Interestingly, the popularly held stereotype that the poor tend to
have more children than do the rich has been found untrue. Kunz et al.
(1973) report that lower-income families tend to have fewer children
than do families with higher incomes. They report further that many low-
income families have no children at all. It is clear today that the nature of
our career expectations has made both the economic and the psychological cost of large families increase enormously.

The Costs of
Parenthood

Costs of parenthood from crib to campus

According to 1975 Bureau of Labor statistics, the cost at that time of raising the average baby to adulthood in the United States was $70,000.

In round figures, parents spent an average of $2,500 on recreation for each of their children, $4,000 for medical expenses, $6,500 for hous-ing, $7,000 for clothes, $13,000 for food, and $14,000 for miscellaneous expenses. The total cost of education for children through college in 1975 was $24,000. Today, all of these average figures are higher.

Changes in family economics are not the only changes that have oc-curred recently. Major changes in the status of women, lifestyles, and parental roles have taken place. Increasing numbers of women have entered the labor force. In 1970, a full 65.7 percent of married women were gainfully employed (Hedges, 1970). During the past eight years, an increasing number of mothers with young children began working. It is not unusual today for public-school teachers to ask mothers to help out with lunchroom or playground activity, only to find that virtually all of the mothers are occupied during lunchtime with professional activities.

Working mothers must make special provision for childcare, espe-cially when their children are small. Yet the number of day-care pro-grams providing adequate health and educational care, while sufficient in some countries, has not kept pace with need in the United States. A national survey by the U.S. Census Bureau reported in 1968 that nearly half the children of working mothers were cared for by fathers, older siblings, grandparents, or neighbors. Only 10 percent were provided health and educational care in daycare centers (Low and Spindler, 1968). In the 1970s, working women still complain about the shortage of ade-quate day-care facilities for their children.

With fewer adults at home to care for small children and few outside facilities to care for them, it is not surprising that child-rearing today often is described by mothers in terms of noise, mess, confusion, and confinement.

Women do not, of course, leave the home purely out of economic necessity. Many women today seek outside work for self-fulfillment, per-sonal satisfaction, and diversion. Because of the difficulty of providing adequately for their babies, it used to be the practice of many of these professional women to stop their careers during the early years of child rearing and reenter the professional world when their children were older. Many professional women today find this plan of action inade-quate or infeasible. Often, after a ten-year absence from the job, they find that their training is deficient or out-of-date; in some cases, they even may need to return to school if they hope to be successful professionally. The in-and-out career status, therefore, is often unacceptable to women with serious career interests (Gass, 1975).

Many women, attempting to combine home and professional careers, have developed what some researchers call "role overload" (Rapoport and Rapoport, 1969). They discover that they are taking on too many roles to perform them all satisfactorily. In families where both parents are employed, role overload can occur for both wife and husband. Role overload is a major factor leading to reported marital dissatisfaction (Giele, 1971). The following comment was made to a marriage counselor by a young woman who was studying full-time and pursuing a Ph.D. degree in English literature while simultaneously caring for two small children:

Sometimes I feel as if I am a workhorse instead of a human being. When I want to be reading Herman Hesse, I find myself washing diapers; when I think I need to spend a few hours extra time in preparing a term paper, one of the kids gets sick, and I spend the afternoon instead at the pediatrician's. Sometimes I feel as if I never should have gotten married or had children.

Working mothers must make special provision for child care.

Young women now postpone marriages longer than their mothers did. In 1960, only 28 percent of women ages 20–24 were unmarried. By 1974, this percentage had jumped to 40 percent (Glick, 1975). In 1971, more people under the age of 35 were single than at anytime since the turn of the century—an explanation in itself for decreased birthrate (U.S. Census Bureau, 1972).

The women's liberation movement has helped free childless couples from social stigma. Articles presenting their personal reasons for deciding not to have children appear often in the mass media today. "Child-free" is a term coined by the women's movement to negate the idea that "if one is without children, one is 'less'" (Peck and Senderowitz, 1974).

Today married families may select lifestyles in which children play no part, with less pressure from family and friends to "fulfill their parental duty." The statement of one young professional woman typical of this new lifestyle follows.

> *John and I decided before we were married that child rearing just wasn't our thing. I was interested in pursuing my own career which involves a lot of traveling. And John just wasn't interested in staying home and changing diapers while I was on the road. We haven't felt that we've missed much. Compared to our friends with children, we lead a much more exciting life—we take more vacations, travel, and socialize. Many of our friends admit that they are envious.*

Coupled with costs of parenthood to the family are the costs to society. Even with the decreased birthrate reported earlier, the present rate of increase in world population is unprecedented in history. If sustained, in less than 700 years, there would be one person for every square foot on the surface of the earth (Freedman and Berelson, 1974). Demographic data on population rise has led the zero-population-growth movement to campaign actively for smaller families. Coupled with concern for overpopulation is a pessimism related to political and ecological problems of today. The class speaker for the 1969 Mills College graduating class described this view in her statement, "Our days as a race on this planet are numbered. . . . I am terribly saddened by the fact that the most humane thing for me to do is to have no children at all" (Peck and Senderowitz, 1974).

The Rewards of Parenthood

The trend in the United States today is toward smaller and, in some instances, childless families. Still, in spite of the economic and psychological costs of parenthood, the percentage of couples who voluntarily elect not to have children remains small. Most married couples today still want to be parents. In one study of women who already had had two children each, 90 percent reported that they had wanted the second child (Pohlman, 1969).

Most adults in our society want children, regardless of the costs. Why? What are the rewards? Psychologists suggest that being a parent has

Many adults in our society want children, regardless of the costs.

many rewards. Psychoanalytic theory, for example, proposes that child bearing is proof of virility. Margaret Mead (1949) once suggested that women have an "innate need" to have children. Although role overload often is a problem in parenthood today, child rearing still provides what psychoanalytic theorists consider an important role need for many men and women in our society. According to psychoanalytic theory, motherhood still may be a major source of feminine identity. The woman who can fulfill both professional and maternal roles satisfactorily may well feel quite remarkable—perhaps even "superfeminine."

Social pressures to produce children have their origins in Judaeo-Christian tradition. Today, the popular media, while acknowledging women's rights and the population explosion, still depict the family as the ideal unit. Even though social stigma is decreasing, women deliberately deciding on childlessness frequently are viewed by society as being "self-involved and neurotic" (Rainwater, 1965).

Some writers point out that child rearing can decrease loneliness and alienation in dreary, nonrewarding lives. This is especially true in low-income families where parents are not able to find enjoyment in satisfying employment, education, or other alternative rewarding roles.

Marriage relationships also may influence desire for children. Adults may want children in order to have someone toward whom to express love and affection. In one study, wives separated from their husbands expressed a greater interest in having more children than did other wives (Pohlman, 1969).

Finally, for many, watching a child develop from an unseeing, helpless infant to a happy, healthy, responding youngster can be an exciting, rewarding experience in itself—worth all of the costs discussed earlier and more rewarding than all the alternative methods of self-fulfillment available in our society. When a representative sample of Americans was asked by a researcher, "What are some of the things that you feel happy about these days?" more responses were related to children than any other type of response (Gurin, Veroff, and Feld, 1960). As one married couple who decided to have children put it, "Mostly we wanted children because they are fun to watch and be with. And they give you an excuse occasionally to act like a child yourself. When there's a kid around, you can play with electric trains, and make funny noises at the dinner table" (McGrath and McGrath, 1975).

Psychoanalytic theorists suggest that motherhood still may be a major source of feminine identity.

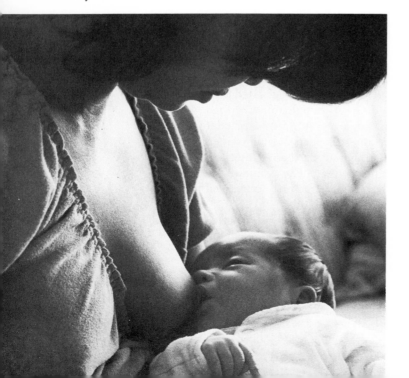

The behavior of the developing child cannot be understood completely without understanding the role of heredity and its effects on behavior. The heredity-environment controversy, involving the question of the relative importance of heredity and environment in determining capabilities and behaviors, is still an issue hotly debated by psychologists and geneticists. To understand the complexity of the issue with which the debaters are dealing, it is necessary first to realize that heredity and environment both directly and indirectly affect behavior and, in addition, that heredity and environmental influences interact with one another in highly complicated ways to critically influence development.

Biological inheritance begins at the instant of conception with the genes that carry genetic information from parents to child. Information about the mechanisms of inheritance has been used in a variety of ways to affect development. Selective mating long has been practiced by the human race. Eugenics, the attempt to improve the human species through controlled genetics, led to the atrocities of the Nazi World War II sterilization programs. On the other hand, it more recently has led to genetic counseling programs, which many people feel will be of great benefit to mankind.

The costs and rewards associated with the decision to become parents are affected by new possibilities introduced by genetic counseling, as well as by changing lifestyles, economics, and marriage relationships.

1 Describe the process by which each parent contributes to the development of the child. Use in your description the terms listed below. (For review, see pages 111–114.)

  Chromosomes
  DNA
  Dominant and recessive genes
  Gametes
  Genetic defect
  Heredity
  Polygenic traits
  Zygote

2 Explain why neither theorists proposing purist hereditary explanations nor theorists proposing purist environmental explanations give complete answers to the question of why we each develop as we do. (For review, see pages 107–110.)

3 Do the advantages of genetic research outweigh the potential dangers? What stance should society take in regard to such research? Why? (For review, see pages 118–124.)

4 List the most important reasons why birthrate in the United States has decreased in recent years. (For review, see pages 125–128.)

FOR FURTHER READING

Howe, L., ed. *The Future of the Family.* New York: Simon and Schuster, 1972. This excellent text reviews the current and future status of the family from the viewpoints of mother, father, children, and society. The short articles included in the book deal with alternatives to traditional family and child-rearing patterns.

Ingle, D. *Who Should Have Children?* Indianapolis: Bobbs-Merrill, 1973. This is an introduction to selective population control. Both genetic and environmental approaches are discussed as they relate to health, intelligence, education, crime, aggression, and social welfare.

Journal of Marriage and the Family. This journal is published quarterly by the Educational Office, University of Southern California, Los Angeles, California 90007. Articles focus on the changing patterns of families and population control and growth.

Milunsky, A., ed. *The Prevention of Genetic Disease and Mental Retardation.* Philadelphia: Saunders, 1975. Genetic components of disease and mental retardation are explained in this text. The book presents an unbiased view of the "hows" and "whys" of genetic counseling, together with discussion of the ethical issues society must consider.

REFERENCES

Anastasi, A. Heredity, environment, and the question, "how?" *Psychological Review* 65 (1958): 197–208.

Bajema, C. Some thoughts concerning the direction and intensity of natural selection with respect to human physical health and behavior patterns in industrial welfare state democracies. In I. Porter and R. Skalko, eds., *Heredity and Society.* New York: Academic Press, 1973.

Bettelheim, B. *Children of the Dream.* New York: Macmillan, 1969.

Biglass, E. Implications of the new reproductive technologies. *Social Biology* 19 (1972): 326–336.

Bodmer, W., and L. Cavalli-Sforza. Intelligence and race. *Scientific American* 223 (1970): 19–30.

Bronfenbrenner, U. *Two Worlds of Childhood.* New York: Russell Sage Foundation, 1970.

Bronfenbrenner, U. *Influences on Human Development*. Hinsdale, Ill.: Dryden Press, 1972.

Crow, J. Genetic theories and influences: comments on the value of diversity. *Harvard Educational Review* 39 (1969): 301–309.

Dobbing, J., and J. Smart. Vulnerability of the developing brain and behavior. *British Medical Bulletin* 30, no. 2 (May 1974): 164–168.

Eisenberg, L. The intervention of biological and experiential factors in schizophrenia. In D. Rosenthal and S. Kety, eds., *The Transmission of Schizophrenia*. London: Pergamon, 1968, pp. 403–412.

Eysenck, H. *The IQ Argument: Race, Intelligence and Education*. New York: Library Press, 1971.

Freedman, R., and B. Berelson. The human population. *Scientific American* 231, no. 3 (1974): 31–39.

Galton, F. *Inquiries into Human Faculty and its Development*. 2d ed. London: Dent, n.d., p. 24.

Gass, G. Equitable marriage. *The Family Coordinator* 23 (October 1974): 369–372.

Gibson, J. *Psychology for the Classroom*. New York: Prentice-Hall, 1976.

Giele, J. Changes in the modern family: their impact on sex role. *American Journal of Orthopsychiatry* 41 (1971): 757–765.

Glick, P. A demographer looks at American Families. *Journal of Marriage and the Family* 37 (1975): 15–26.

Gordon, H. Genetics and civilization in historical perspective. In I. Porter and R. Skalko, eds., *Heredity and Society*. New York: Academic Press, 1973.

Gurin, G., J. Veroff, and S. Feld. *Americans View Their Mental Health*. New York: Basic Books, 1960.

Hebb, D. A return to Jensen and his social science critics. *American Psychologist* 25 (1970): 568.

Hedges, J. Women at work. *Monthly Labor Review* 93 (1970): 19–29.

Henry, C., and M. Hiller. *Of Pure Blood*. A film documentary. Paris, France: Ageoce Franchaise d'Images. Presented on TV by Public Broadcasting Service, Washington, D.C., 1975.

Herrnstein, R. IQ. In *The Atlantic* 228, no. 3 (September 1971): 44–64.

Herrnstein, R. *In the Meritocracy*. Boston: Little, Brown, 1973.

Hsia, Y. Treatment in genetic diseases. In A. Milunsky, ed., *The Prevention of Genetic Disease and Mental Retardation*. Philadelphia: Saunders, 1975.

Hunt, J. McV. Black genes—white environment. *Transaction* 6 (June 1969).

Ingle, D. *Who Should Have Children?* Indianapolis: Bobbs-Merrill, 1973.

Jensen, A. On "Jensenism": A Reply to Critics. Address for the AERA Annual, Chicago, April 7, 1972.

Jensen, A. How much can we boost IQ and scholastic achievement? *Harvard Educational Review* 39 (1969): 1–123.

Kohli, K., and A. Sobrero. Vasectomy: a study of psychosexual and general reaction. *Social Biology* 20 (1973): 298–302.

Kunz, P., M. Brinkerhoff, and V. Hundley. Relationship of income and childlessness. *Social Biology* 20 (1973): 139–142.

Lazarevic, J. Ethics bug scientist in child sex choice. *Pittsburgh Press*, February 29, 1976, B-4.

Low, S., and P. Spindler. *Child Care Arrangements of Working Mothers in the United States*. Washington, D.C.: Children's Bureau Publication no. 161, 1968.

McCormick, T. Ethical issues in amniocentesis and abortion. *Texas Reports on Biology and Medicine* 32, no. 1 (Spring 1974): 299–309.

McGrath, N., and C. McGrath. Why have a baby? *New York Times Magazine*, May 25, 1975.

Mead, M. *Male and Female*. New York: Morrow, 1949.

Milunsky, A., and L. Atkins. Prenatal prevention of genetic disease and mental retardation. In A. Milunsky, ed., Philadelphia: Saunders, 1975.

Nash, J. *Developmental Psychology: A Psychological Approach*. Englewood Cliffs, N.J.: Prentice-Hall, 1970.

Osborne, F., and C. Bajema. The eugenic hypothesis. *Social Biology* 19 (1972): 337–345.

Peck, E., and J. Senderowitz. *Prenatalism: The Myth of Mom and Apple Pie*. New York: Crowell, 1974.

Plutarch, L. *In the Lives of the Noble Grecians and Romans*. Translated by J. Dryden. New York: Modern Libary, n.d., p. 61.

Pohlman, E. *Motivations in Wanting Conceptions in Psychology of Birth Planning*. Cambridge, Mass.: Schenkman, 1969.

Pohlman, E. Childlessness, intentional and unintentional. *Journal of Nervous and Mental Disease* 151 (1970): 2–12.

Pohlman, E. *The Psychology of Birth Planning*. Cambridge, Mass.: Shenkman, 1969.

Powledge, T. The genetic engineer still awaits guidelines. *New York Times*, February 15, 1976, E-8.

Rainwater, L. *Family Design: Marital Sexuality, Family Size, and Family Planning*. Chicago: Aldine, 1965.

Rapoport, R., and R. Rapoport. The dual career family: a variant family and social change. *Human Relations* 22 (1969): 3–30.

Rosenberg, C., and Charles Benedict Davenport. The beginning of human genetics. *Bulletin of the History of Medicine* 35 (1961): 266–276.

Searle, L. The organization of heredity maze-brightness and maze-dullness. *Genetic Psychological Monographs* 39 (1949): 279–325.

Stone, L., and J. Church. *Childhood and Adolescence*. 3d ed. New York: Random House, 1973.

Thompson, W. The inheritance and development of intelligence. In *Genetics and the Inheritance of Integrated Neurological and Psychiatric Patterns. Proceedings of the Association for Research of Nervous and Mental Diseases*. Vol. 33. Baltimore: Williams and Wilkins, 1953.

Tryon, R. Genetic differences in maze-learning ability in rats. *Yearbook, National Social Studies Education* 39 (1940): 11–119.

United States Dept. of Commerce, Bureau of the Census. *Series P-20,* September 1972, no. 239.

Vinogradoff, E. Personal communication.

Wattenberg, B. *The Real America.* New York: Harper & Row, 1974.

PART 2

The Prenatal and Infancy Periods

5

The Prenatal Period

Learning objectives

After completing this chapter, you should be able to:

1
describe the three stages of prenatal development in terms of structure and functioning ability;

2
explain some of the ways that the uterine environment affects the development of the fetus; describe the major changes that must take place in the mother in order for normal fetal development to take place;

3
list the variables that contribute most significantly to defects in the developing fetus and discuss some of the ways to reduce the possibility of these defects;

4
describe what should be expected to occur during the birth of an infant; discuss difficulties that might occur during the delivery process and advantages and disadvantages of alternative methods of childbirth designed to reduce these difficulties;

5
describe the procedures used to care for the infant immediately after birth and explain why these procedures are used.

I n Chapter 4, we discussed how male and female gametes—spermatozoon and ovum—together form the zygote (fertilized ovum). Conception occurs when a male sperm, injected during sexual union into the female vagina, moves through the fallopian tube and succeeds in piercing the wall of the egg or ovum.

The egg is a round cell large enough to be visible to the naked eye. We learned in Chapter 4 how, even though the egg is much larger in size than the sperm, both contribute almost equally to the inheritance of the developing offspring. We also learned how hereditary characteristics are carried through DNA in the genes of each chromosome. Immediately after conception, the nuclei of sperm and egg unite. The chromosomes of each gamete join to form twenty-three pairs of chromosomes, forty-six chromosomes in all. One chromosome in each pair comes from the mother, one from the father. Each chromosome contains approximately 20,000 genes, the basic units of hereditary transmission. Genes are, in turn, composed of deoxyribonucleic acid (DNA), which contains the genetic instructions that control body processes and form new tissues.

In this chapter, we watch the developing individual change from a one-celled zygote at conception to an indescribably complex human being with approximately 200 billion cells at birth. During the forty-week prenatal or intrauterine period in which this intricate process takes place, the organism lives in the protective and nourishing environment of the mother's uterus. In recent years, there has been growing realization that the period between conception and birth is a crucial one for the developing individual. If uterine conditions are favorable, the child is more likely to develop normally and to get a good start in life. If conditions are unfavorable, the child might be lastingly handicapped. We examine in this chapter both the stages through which the developing individual goes, and the extremely important effects on development of the uterine environment.

THE PRENATAL PERIOD

T he prenatal period can be divided into three basic periods or stages of development, each characterized by certain phenomena. What is called the *period of the ovum* begins with conception and lasts for two weeks until the developing cluster of cells attaches itself securely to the lining of the uterus. The *embryonic period* follows and continues for the next six weeks. During the embryonic period, essential body systems develop. The cluster of cells becomes recognizable as a partially functioning human being. During the *fetal period*, from eight weeks after conception until birth, the body organs, muscles, and nervous system mature, and the organism increases in size and takes on clearly human characteristics. We will examine each of these periods only briefly as preparation for studying the child after birth. Students are encouraged to study the articles and books listed in "For Further Reading" at the end of the chapter for more detailed descriptions of the prenatal period.

The Period of the Ovum

We learned in Chapter 4 that, within twenty-four hours after conception, the process of cell division called mitosis occurs; at twenty-four hours of age, the zygote already has doubled itself by forming two identical cells. During the two week period of the ovum, the zygote lives off its own yolk, dividing over and over again until it forms a cluster of cells the size of a pinhead. This cluster gradually moves down the fallopian tube. In the process, it forms a ball of cells in which a cavity, called a *blastocele*, appears. At this stage of development, the zygote is known as a *blastocyst*. The outer layer of cells of the blastocyst later will develop into nutritive and protective structures. An inner cell mass will develop into the embryo.

While the blastocyst is developing, the menstrual cycle thickens the uterine wall and increases its blood supply so as to prepare for reception of the new organism. (If the ovum had not been fertilized within the previous month, this supply of blood would have sloughed off, resulting in female menstrual flow.) On about the fourth day, the blastocyst reaches the uterus where it drifts about for several days. By the end of the week after conception, tendrils developed by the organism attach themselves to the uterine wall and finally penetrate the blood vessels within. From this instant, the developing organism is able to receive nourishment from the mother. The blastocyst is now ready to develop into an embryo.

The Embryonic Period

During the third week or early embryonic period, two cavities begin to develop in the inner mass of the cell cluster, now called the *trophoblast*. One cavity later will become the *amniotic sac*, filled with fluid. This will serve as a protective cushion, equalize pressure, and prevent adherence of the embryo to the wall of the uterus (Iorio, 1967). The other, the *yolk sac*, will feed the embryo until the umbilical cord is developed. Between these two cavities is the embryonic area from which the embryo now begins to develop.

Cells within the embryonic area gradually form three layers: *ectodem*, *mesoderm*, and *endoderm*. Later in development, the ectoderm will give rise to skin, certain mucous membranes, and the central nervous system. Blood, muscles, bones, and some internal organs will develop from the mesoderm. The endoderm will turn into lungs, bladder, alimentary mucosa, pancreas, and liver (Keay and Morgan, 1974).

The umbilical cord, formed by the sixth week of development, is designed to carry food from the mother's blood to the embryo and waste substances from the embryo to the mother. It passes both nutritive substances and waste through an area of the uterine wall called the *placenta*. As the circulatory system of the organism develops, blood is pumped by the fetal heart to the placenta. There the fetus exchanges carbon dioxide

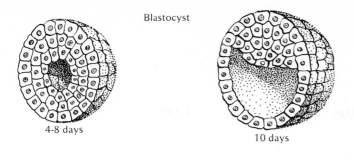

Blastocyst

4-8 days

10 days

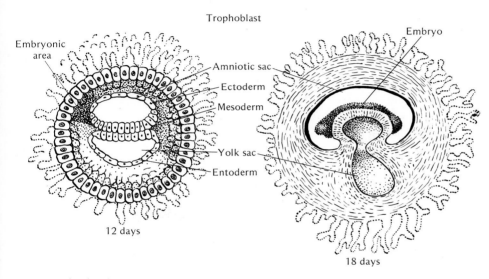

Trophoblast

Embryonic area

Amniotic sac

Ectoderm

Mesoderm

Yolk sac

Entoderm

12 days

Embryo

18 days

Fig. 5.1 The development of the fertilized ovum.

for oxygen, which is carried to the fetus by the mother's bloodstream.

It is very important to note that maternal blood and fetal blood never mix in the process of exchanging food and waste materials. Instead, the exchange occurs through the porous walls of closed blood vessels. The placenta, a semipermeable cellular membrane, serves as a protective barrier, selecting and absorbing those substances necessary for nourishment of the fetus and passing them to the fetus from the mother's blood. Similarly, the placenta passes waste materials from fetus to mother. The placenta will tend to reject many potentially dangerous substances in the mother's blood. However, some drugs and other potentially harmful substances sometimes are able to pass through the placenta to affect the developing organism. We will discuss the implications of this possibility later in the chapter.

Fig. 5.2 Actual size of fetus at approximately four weeks, eight weeks, and twelve weeks.

Growth and development during the embryonic period is rapid. By the end of the third week after conception, the organism is composed of a cluster of cells totaling only about one-quarter inch from head to the tip of what looks like a taillike protrusion on the embryo (see Fig. 5.2). Even at this stage, the organism is highly complex: a rudimentary heart is just beginning to pulsate; an embryonic brain with two lobes appears.

By the fourth week, the embryonic backbone is apparent. At this point, however, it is so bent that the head almost touches the "tail." The head, at this stage of development, is almost one-third the total length of the embryo. The cephalocaudal (head to tail) growth trend (discussed in Chapter 2) causes the head to develop in size and complexity long before other parts of the body. The nervous system already has developed extensively and cartilage and muscle development has begun. However, neuromotor activity (activation of muscles by nerve impulse) has not yet appeared. Rudiments of eyes, ears, and nose, as well as stubby arms and legs, are noticeable. Even the beginnings of respiratory organs, digestive tract, and stomach are apparent.

By the eighth week after conception, the embryo has a noticeably human appearance. It still is extremely tiny—small enough to fit in a walnut shell and about the same weight as a book of matches. It still is a long way from being able to live without an intimate lifeline to the mother. But it has a well-formed body with a very large head and unmistakably human face, arms, and legs. Fingers have developed on hands. The slower-growing legs have recognizable knees and ankles. The heart has been beating for several weeks, and a brain and nervous system sends out impulses. The reproductive system has begun to develop. The embryo at this age is growing at the rate of one millimeter per day. At eight weeks, it is approximately one inch in length from head to buttocks and weighs approximately one-thirtieth ounce.

During the fetal period, from eight weeks after conception to birth at forty weeks, the skeletal system becomes mature. Embryologists have chosen the appearance of bone cells as the criterion for defining the end of the embryonic period, because bone formation coincides with essential completion of the body. Perfection of function will follow perfection of structure.

The Fetal Period

Bodily systems mature during the fetal period. No brand-new features appear. Rather, growth and development progress in a steady and sequential pattern following the principles of development outlined in Chapter 2. We have already seen that development proceeds in a cephalocaudal direction. It proceeds also in proximodistal (from near to the central nervous system out to the body extremeties) and mass-to-specific directions. These principles of development are apparent not only by the size and complexity of the body components of the fetus, but also by its developing abilities to function.

By the end of twelve weeks in utero, the fetus has developed sexuality. A swelling appears that will eventually become a penis, if hormones are manufactured by a male testes, or a clitoris, if male hormones are not developed. Interestingly, the anatomy of the female reproductive system seems to be basic to human development: female sex organs will develop if either testes or ovaries are removed or do not function. Extremities of the body develop; fingers and toes are differentiated during this period. Fingernails and toenails now appear. The umbilical cord often has been found twisted around the fetus at this stage, evidence of the fetus's ability to move. The first movements detected by shock-recording devices placed on the mother's abdomen are generalized or mass movements, beginning with head movements.

The fetus develops gradually the capability of responding to touch. The exhibition of this capabiilty is shown by a gradual flexion movement of the head. The fetus also can move its thumb in opposition to fingers and is beginning to be able to make swallowing movements. Not until later will the fetus be able to make specific movements or move a particular limb in response to a touch.

It is interesting that the fetus already shows distinct individuality in behavior. This individuality is due, in part, to the fact that muscle structure varies from fetus to fetus. However, as we shall see, variations in the uterine environment also lead to differences in fetal behavior. The fetus is now approximately three inches long and weighs about three-quarters of an ounce.

By twenty weeks after conception, heart, stomach, and internal organs near to the nervous system have developed. Obstetricians report that, at this stage of development, they can feel the heartbeat of a fetus in the mother's womb using an ordinary stethoscope (Babson and Benson, 1971). If there are twins, the physician may be able to pick up the sounds of two different hearts at this stage. The lungs, although developing, are not yet sufficiently mature to allow the fetus to survive outside the protective environment of the uterus. At this stage, mothers first report that they feel movement in the womb. This feeling of movement, caused by arms and legs moving independently, is called the "quickening." Some mothers learn to recognize the different parts of the fetus's body and learn to distinguish head or buttocks from arms or legs. Some mothers report feeling "knocking" like a series of rhythmic jolts. This is due to hiccuping. The fetus may have hiccups that last as long as a half hour. Basic reflexes involving body extremities are now developed. By

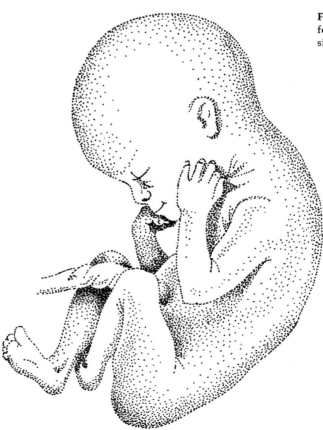

Fig. 5.3 Actual size of fetus at approximately sixteen weeks.

the end of twenty weeks, the fetus is approximately ten inches long and weighs about eight ounces.

By twenty-four weeks in utero, the fetus begins externally to look like a miniature baby. Eyes are completely formed and the fetus can open and close them. Hair has begun to grow on the head. Eyebrows and lashes now appear. Deposits of subcutaneous fat are beginning to give the fetus a babylike appearance. Quiet and active episodes are ex-

Fig. 5.4 Actual size of fetus at approximately twenty weeks.

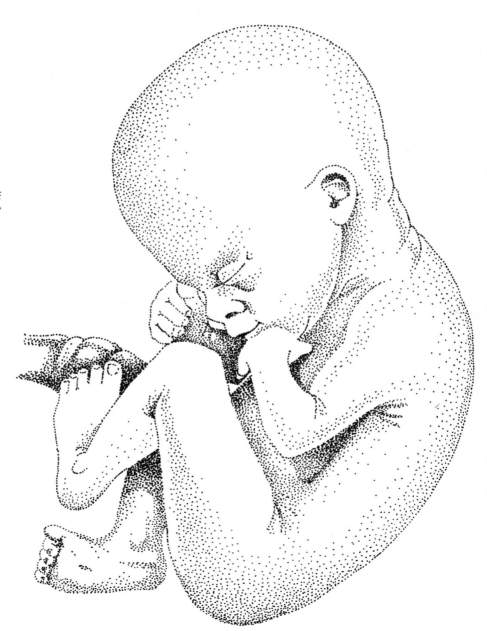

perienced by the mother as the fetus alternately sleeps and wakes. The fetus at this stage can be awakened from sleep by loud noises. He or she now is approximately twelve inches long and weighs about twenty-four ounces.

From the twenty-eighth to the fortieth week after conception, the fetus will mature in all respects, so that various body systems will be able to survive outside the protective environment of the uterus. By the twenty-eighth week, the nervous and circulatory systems and other organs are developed sufficiently that the fetus, if born prematurely, will have a chance to survive with special care.

In the last twelve weeks before birth, behavioral development proceeds at a rapid rate. Movements become active and sustained. In the ninth month, when the fetus moves, the contours of arms and legs make moving bulges on the mother's abdomen. A kick by the fetus at this age has been known almost to knock a book from the mother's lap (Flanagan, 1962). Hands develop the ability to grasp strongly. Finally, before birth, a strong sucking reflex develops. Size changes in these last weeks are dramatic. The fetus increases from an average length of twelve inches and weight of twenty-four ounces at twenty-eight weeks of age to an average length of twenty inches and weight of 7¼ pounds at birth. In the last month in utero, the fetus gains an average of one-half pound per week!

INFLUENCERS OF PRENATAL DEVELOPMENT

At one time, there was widespread belief that the unborn child could be affected by the mother's thoughts and experiences. One example of this belief is the idea that going to art museums or attending symphony concerts during pregnancy will help produce artistic or musically talented children. There is, of course, no evidence to support these old wives' tales. On the other hand, there is substantial evidence for a newer concept of prenatal influence on the unborn child: the child's health and development can be affected profoundly by uterine conditions, as well as by the state of health of the mother.

We learned earlier in this chapter that maternal and fetal blood do not mix. Instead, the placenta serves as a protective barrier, absorbing those substances from the mother's blood necessary for fetal nourishment and passing waste materials from fetus to mother. The placenta tends to reject potentially dangerous substances in the mother's blood. Inadequate placental absorption of necessary nutrients as well as absorption of abnormal dangerous elements clearly and adversely affect fetal development.

Nutrition

Let's begin by discussing cases in which necessary nutrients are not absorbed by the placenta. It once was believed that reserves accumulated in the mother's body would "spare" the fetus from possible nutritional

Very young mothers are sometimes not able to provide a prenatal environment adequate to nourish the developing fetus properly.

deficiencies, even if the mother didn't eat well during pregnancy. We know now that this is not the case. Good nutrition during pregnancy, as well as before pregnancy, actually can be a matter of life and death for the fetus. At the least, serious malnutrition of the mother affects the growth and health of her children (Shank, 1970). In periods of great famines, the babies that have been born were abnormally small in size. For example, babies born during the long and severe famine that occurred during the siege of Leningrad in World War II had birth weights 400–500 grams lower than normal. A less severe famine at the same time in Holland led to a reduction by 240 grams in average birth weights of Dutch children (Sterman, McGinty, and Adenolf, 1971). Vitamin deficiency in the diet of expectant mothers is known to produce rickets as well as general physical weakness and mental deficiency in newborn infants (Goldenson, 1970). Poor maternal diet during pregnancy is known to produce anemia, toxemia, miscarriages, prematurity, and still-births. The fragile infants of undernourished mothers are also more vulnerable to serious disease.

Perhaps most frightening is the recent finding that protein deficiency during the period of most rapid brain growth can damage irreparably the fetal brain. The cerebellums of individuals deprived of adequate amounts of protein during the fetal period actually have been found to weigh less and to have less than the normal complement of nerve cells (Altman, 1971; Stone, Smith, and Murphy, 1973).

Specific effects of a malnourished prenatal environment, as any aspect of that environment, is dependent on timing. At some stages of fetal development, gross changes in the environment may produce little or no effect on the fetus. In others, even minor alterations can produce severe complications. Adequate nourishment is most critical during periods of rapid growth. Any interruption of development during these periods may result in complete disruption of the organism. Since different bodily organs and parts develop at different rates, the effect of malnutrition at one period may be very different from that of another.

In the case of brain development, the brain grows most rapidly between twenty weeks after conception and two years after birth. During this period, called the critical period for brain development, inadequate nutrition inflicts the greatest damage. Damage to the cerebellum caused by malnutrition during its critical growth period has been used to explain clumsiness and greatly reduced motor ability (Cragg, 1974; Dobbing and Smart, 1974). Unfortunately, it's quite clear that in the United States, as elsewhere, people from low-income and low-education backgrounds, and with little ability to provide adequate diets, are most affected.

Because of the importance of maternal diet to the developing fetus, obstetricians recently have reversed earlier recommendations that pregnant women should gain as little weight as possible (Siegel and Morris, 1970). But it is not only the diet of the pregnant women that determines whether or not the fetus is nourished properly; the maternal metabolic system also has a major effect on the nourishment of the child. Metabolic

What is proper diet during pregnancy?

Proper diet during pregnancy is important to the well-being of both mother and child. A good diet that provides all the necessary nutrients is a deceptively simple thing. Lack of knowledge, poverty, mores, and motivation are a few of the reasons why many pregnant women do not receive well-balanced, high-protein, high-vitamin, and high-mineral diets. Excessive carbohydrates, especially sweets, should be limited.

Following are the daily basic food requirements in pregnancy and lactation frequently cited by researchers (Brewer, 1970; Simkin, 1976):

1 one quart of milk or more;
2 three or more servings of eggs, fish, liver, cheese, chicken, lean beef, lamb, or pork;
3 one or two servings of fresh, dark, green, leafy vegetables or deep yellow vegetables;
4 four or more servings of whole grain or enriched bread or cereal;
5 two servings of citrus fruit or fruit juice;
6 one pat of margarine, vitamin A enriched.

problems in the mother can result in a prenatal environment that is incapable of supplying everything the fetus needs. From the first hours of pregnancy, the maternal metabolic system begins a vast readjustment to provide nutrients to support fetal growth (Wishik and Lichtblau, 1974). Unhealthy or undernourished women with metabolic problems apparently are less able to produce prenatal environments for fetal growth.

Poverty, nutrition, and fetal and infant mortality Statistics relating fetal deaths to income level in the United States are quite clear. Thirty percent of pregnant mothers account for 67 percent of the serious pregnancy complications. This thirty percent of the population comes from lower socioeconomic groups and includes disadvantaged ethnic groups, low-education groups, undernourished or unhealthy mothers, and extreme ages (both very old and very young mothers) (Butler and Alberman, 1969; Novy, 1973). College-educated mothers have only one-third the chance of having undersized infants born to them as mothers with only grade-school education (Babson and Benson, 1971). These statistics relate directly or indirectly to nourishment and proper medical care.

Sadly, the United States, one of the most affluent countries in the world, has relatively higher rates of death and low birth weights among its children than many apparently less affluent countries. In the last decade, the United States ranked only thirteenth in the world in lowest infant mortality rate (U.S. Dept. of HEW, 1970). That is to say, twelve nations had lower mortality rates than the United States.

Maternal Age and Spacing of Births

No matter what the overall level of health care during pregnancy, risks for mother and child vary with maternal age. It has long been known that very young women and older women run a greater risk of having a defective child. The high incidence of mongolism in children of mothers over forty years of age was discussed in Chapter 4. Mongolism is due to chromosomal damage and apparently is unrelated to prenatal environment. However, the high risk rate of very young mothers (under sixteen years of age) apparently is much more directly related to the inability of the young mother to provide a prenatal environment to properly nourish her child. Young mothers, still growing themselves, have high nutritional requirements. It is difficult to meet the requirements of both a growing mother and a growing fetus (Siegel & Morris, 1970). Babies of young mothers are known to have lower birth weights and are more likely to be stillborn or to have birth defects than are babies of mothers in their twenties (Hulka and Schaaf, 1964; Nortman, 1974).

Timing of births also may affect fetal development. Close spacing of children (less than two-and-one-half years between births) has been related to decreased ability levels later in life. It is unclear, of course, whether such decreased levels are due to experiences after birth. However, some researchers have hypothesized that close spacing of children,

Are we damaging our children?

just as early age of mother, may result in an inadequate prenatal environment. In the case of spacing of children, it is hypothesized that the mother's body may have had insufficient time for a full "physiological readjustment" and "optimal readiness" for a new pregnancy (Holley, Rosenbaum, and Churchill, 1969). In the case of extremely young mothers, it is possible that their bodies have not yet matured sufficiently to provide adequate sustenance.

Disease

Maternal infection from bacteria, protozoa, and viruses also may have adverse effects on prenatal development by restricting nutrients to the fetus (Scrimshaw, Taylor, and Gordon, 1959). As in the case of malnutrition, timing is crucial. If the mother does not take in a sufficient amount of oxygen because of acute respiratory infection or chronic anemia during the first three months of pregnancy, the child could be born with a cleft palate or hair lip.

Diabetes, a metabolic disease in which glucose cannot be used as an energy source, always has caused high mortality rates in both mothers and children. Only in the past forty years have medical advances, including judicious use of insulin, made it possible for diabetic mothers to expect to bear live children. Even today, infants of diabetic mothers whose disease is not well controlled are more likely than other infants to have congenital abnormalities and are more subject to infant infections. Researchers hypothesize that these, as many other complications, are due to insufficient nutrients provided to the fetus. Diabetic mothers must metabolize fats and amino acids to meet their energy requirements, and thus might restrict the supply of amino acids to the fetus (Fletcher, 1975).

Maternal disease can affect the fetus in direct as well as indirect ways. For example, rubella (German measles) occurring in the mother during the first three months of pregnancy is known to invade placenta and fetus, infecting the fetus and causing defective or undersized infants. Fetal infection with gonorrhea or syphillis from an infected mother, unfortunately, is not at all uncommon today, and is increasing in frequency throughout the world. Fetal gonorrhea used to be the major cause of congenital blindness. The incidence has been greatly reduced through the use of silver-nitrate eyewash administered shortly after birth. Fetal syphillis can lead to abortion, fetal death, prematurity, and deformity. Since the fetus under eighteen weeks of age is not susceptible, treatment of the mother during early pregnancy could well save the life of the newborn child. Unfortunately, mothers, particularly young and uneducated mothers of poverty backgrounds, often do not avail themselves of necessary medical help.

The mother's state of health during pregnancy can profoundly affect fetal development.

Smoking	Recent research clearly relates maternal smoking after the fourth month of pregnancy to premature births, stillbirths, and decreased weight at birth (Babson and Benson, 1971; Ounsted, 1969). Researchers hypothesize that carbon monoxide replaces a great deal of oxygen in the mother's blood and hence in the placenta, thus affecting fetal growth adversely (Butler and Alberman, 1969).

Drug and Alcohol Use	Many commonly used and commercially available products now are known seriously to affect the fetus, both directly and indirectly. Directly, many products, by crossing the placenta, can affect the fetus in ways similar to those in which they affect the mother. Indirectly, such drugs alter the maternal physiology and thereby change the uterine environment. An example is the drug thalidomide, now known to affect fetal development and to produce severe abnormalities. Thalidomide was taken from the market only after a series of widely publicized tragedies, in which women who had taken the drug gave birth to severely deformed infants.

The U.S. Food and Drug Administration has been increasingly concerned that drugs commonly used in the United States have adverse effects on fetal development. In a recent study of pregnant women, 82 percent reported that they received prescribed medication. Almost as many took self-prescribed medication. The major drug categories used included iron, analgesics, vitamins, barbiturates, diuretics, antibiotics, cough medicines, antihistamines, and tranquilizers (Marx, 1973). Physicians now consider it possible that large doses of antihistamines, of some antiinfectant drugs, and even of vitamin D during pregnancy can produce serious defects in the baby. The use of some commonly used sedatives by pregnant women has been related to neonatal bleeding and to retardation in the infant (Babson and Benson, 1971; Vulliamy, 1972).

One of the most disturbing problems caused by the perplexing array of drugs taken by pregnant women is that damage can occur before mothers are even aware of being pregnant—that is, before they have missed their first menstrual periods. Most women whose babies were born with thalidomide-caused defects were taking the drug long before they knew they were pregnant (Bowes, 1970).

The use of illegal drugs also is an increasing problem to health experts. The use of hallucinogens such as LSD or mescalin has been associated with chromosomal damage capable of injuring the fetus even before conception (Dishotsky et al., 1971). Researchers have had some difficulty establishing the exact relationship between chromosomal defects and specific illegal drugs, however. One reason is that users of such drugs tend ordinarily to use more than one drug. In addition, the fact that these drugs are illegal usually makes it impossible to know the purity of the drug used. In the meantime, the number of defective children born to drug users increases.

The number of children affected by narcotics, such as heroin, cocaine, morphine, and alcohol also is increasing. Reports by the National Institute of Drug Abuse (1976) indicate that the 1960s epidemic did not abate in the 1970s. For several drugs, like cocaine, it is on the increase. Alcohol continues to be the national drug of choice. Drug or alcohol dependence occurs in 50 percent of infants born to dependent mothers. It has been estimated that the incidence of drug-dependent infants has increased in recent years from one out of two hundred deliveries to one out of fifty deliveries in large urban hospitals (Driscoll, 1973). Prenatal dependence can lead to prematurity, infant mortality, and withdrawal symptoms after birth. A now well-recognized syndrome frequently occurs in babies born to narcotic-dependent mothers. It is fundamentally a withdrawal syndrome, manifested by hyperirritability, trembling, shrill crying, rapid respiration, and vomiting. It can be fatal. In 1965, in New York City alone, 300 newborn infants were diagnosed as suffering from neonatal physical dependence on drugs or alcohol. Now, annually, the number expected is 400–500 babies (Kornetsky, 1970).

The infant still in utero can be affected in adverse ways by modern technology also. For example, radiation is known to be a hazard to the newborn. In the atomic explosions at Hiroshima and Nagasaki, women in the first twenty weeks of pregnancy who were within one-half mile of the center of the blasts and who later gave birth found their babies to be physical or mentally abnormal (Plummer, 1952). The number of defective babies born after the blasts was directly proportional to the distance of

Radiation

Is there a genetic component to alcoholism?

Reports by the National Institute of Drug Abuse (1976) show that alcoholism is increasing in the United States. Drug or alcohol dependence occurs in 50 percent of infants born to alcohol-dependent mothers. But neonatal alcohol dependence seems to be the least of the worries of these unfortunate children. Recent studies at the Washington University Addiction Research Center in St. Louis have shown that persons with one or more biological parents who were alcoholics are much more likely to become alcoholics themselves than are individuals who had nonalcoholic parents. This effect seems to occur even in individuals who were adopted as infants by nonalcoholic parents.

According to *Science Digest* (Alcohol inheritance, June 1975), data was gathered by Dr. Goodwin, Director of the Research Center, from thirty-year-old adopted adults who had been born to parents admitted to psychiatric hospitals for alcoholism. The study corroborated earlier findings by Goodwin that showed that American children of alcoholic natural fathers who did not live with these fathers still were six times as likely to become alcoholics as adopted or foster children brought up by alcoholics.

the mothers from the blast areas. In the United States, the Federal Radiation Council has estimated that 110 American children will show effects of nuclear fallout from experimental explosions in our atmosphere for the period 1950–1961 alone (Goldenson, 1970).

X-ray treatments, commonly used to treat a variety of illnesses in the United States, also can cause damage to unborn infants. It is well-known that X-ray treatment in the pelvic region—as, for example, in therapeutic treatments for tumors or cancer—is extremely dangerous. Fallout from X-ray treatment in other body areas also can be harmful. Pregnant women therefore are advised to avoid routine X rays during pregnancy. As a further precautionary measure, young women often are advised to avoid X rays during the latter half of their menstrual cycles, because of the possibility that they might be pregnant.

Rh Factor

Rh factor is the name given to genetically determined differences between blood types that make fetus and mother incompatible. Medical researchers have explained the difficulties to the fetus caused by the Rh factor as follows: the Rh positive fetus produces antigens which enter the mother's bloodstream through the placenta. The mother's blood in turn produces antibodies with the capability of destroying red blood cells. Miscarriages, stillbirths, defects, and early death all have been attributed to the Rh factor. In recent years, medical research has developed ways to deal with the problem. Afflicted infants now have a much greater possibility of living normal lives than did infants just a few years ago. Expert attention and parental education are, of course, required.

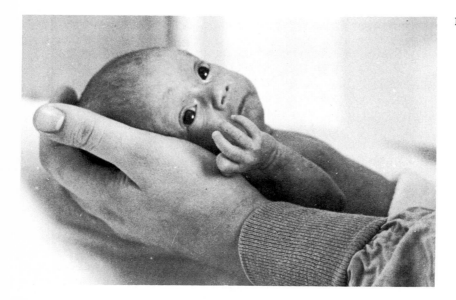

Newborn infant.

Can emotional stress of the mother affect fetal development? Researchers are not absolutely certain. Many believe, however, that "while there is no guarantee that a happy mother will have a happy and healthy child, it is quite possible that emotional disturbance will have a negative effect" (Goldenson, 1970, p. 1001).

It is known that fetuses move more actively within the uterus while the mother is in a state of stress than when she is calm and, further, that maternal stress is related to colic in the infant. Some researchers suggest that tension during pregnancy may alter hormonal balance and affect the delicate maternal-placental-fetal relationship. Tension also may affect the fetus by liberating chemicals in the bloodstream and modifying cell metabolism. Evidence for this possibility is provided by the fact that, while anxiety before pregnancy is unrelated to prenatal complications, anxiety during pregnancy has a clear relationship to later-found abnormalities (Gorsuch and Key, 1974).

Of course it is also possible that maternal tension affects fetal development in other more indirect ways. Tense mothers are more likely to smoke and to use tranquilizers, for example. And, as we have seen, both smoking and drug use are related to complications. Whether tension produces problems directly or indirectly, however, it appears that tense women are more likely to suffer complications in their pregnancies.

Stress, of course, cannot always be eliminated. Stress related to fears regarding pregnancy, however, can be reduced by good prenatal care and education. There is no substitute for a good physician-patient relationship that allows for adequate prenatal counseling. It was reported earlier that the 30 percent of pregnant women who account for 67 percent of complications during pregnancy come from low-socioeconomic and low-education backgrounds. Such women, unfortunately, are much less likely to obtain adequate medical attention or education regarding their pregnancies. One researcher has suggested that "the best prescription for reducing reproductive mortality and morbidity . . . is to improve living conditions and access to competent medical care" (Nortman, 1974).

THE BIRTH PROCESS

The end of prenatal development comes usually forty weeks after conception. The baby is squeezed out of the uterus and through the vagina by a series of uterine contractions known as labor. The birth sequence involves three stages. The first stage of labor dilates the cervix to permit passage of the baby's head through the vagina. The second stage allows the baby to pass through the vagina and enter the outside world. The final third stage, afterbirth, expels the placenta, remaining amnionic sac, and whatever is left of the cord. From the start of labor contractions to actual delivery of the newborn infant, the entire process takes about fifteen hours, on the average. Generally, first births take longer than later births.

Dangers during the Birth Process

Labor is a normal event in the life of mother and child. Nevertheless it may be a hazardous experience if both mother and child are not in good health or not given proper attention.

Anoxia Anoxia is inadequate oxygenation of the blood. All infants are subjected to varying degrees of oxygen deprivation during labor. In most births, this is tolerated without difficulty. In some situations, however, inadequate uterine environments pose additional risks, such that normal changes of labor are more than the infant can tolerate successfully. If supplies of oxygen to the nerve cells of the brain are reduced sufficiently, serious brain damage or death can result. Milder anoxia has proportional effects. Anoxia can produce irritable infants, muscular tension, rigidity, and motor defects (Graham et al., 1956; Lewis et al., 1967). Fetal and newborn anoxia are related to a variety of factors; we will discuss certain of these factors later in this section.

Hemorrhaging Another danger during the birth process comes from excessive pressure exerted on the fetal head during delivery. Excessive pressure can cause hemorrhaging (internal bleeding) and destroy brain cells. Some critics of traditional childbirth techniques in this country express concern that forceps, used unnecessarily, may in some cases be the cause of brain damage (Arms, 1975).

Prematurity A newborn infant is considered premature if it is born less than thirty-seven weeks after conception, or, more commonly, if its birth weight is less than five-and-one-half pounds. By this definition, 7.6 percent of hospital births in the United States are premature. Approximately twice as many American infants as Swedish fall into this category; twice as many of these are nonwhite as are white babies (Behrman, 1973).

Prematurity is predictive in many respects of later development. Although recent medical advances have greatly increased their chances, premature infants still have considerably less chance to survive than babies born at full term or at average birth weights. Today, prematurity accounts for one-third of the deaths in the first year. Mortality in the first two years for infants who survive to be discharged from the hospital is three times that of full-term infants.

In general, the lower the birth weight, the greater the likelihood of difficulties. Until very recently, extremely premature babies (born before thirty weeks after conception) almost always died. Those who survive frequently are neurologically or physiologically handicapped. There also

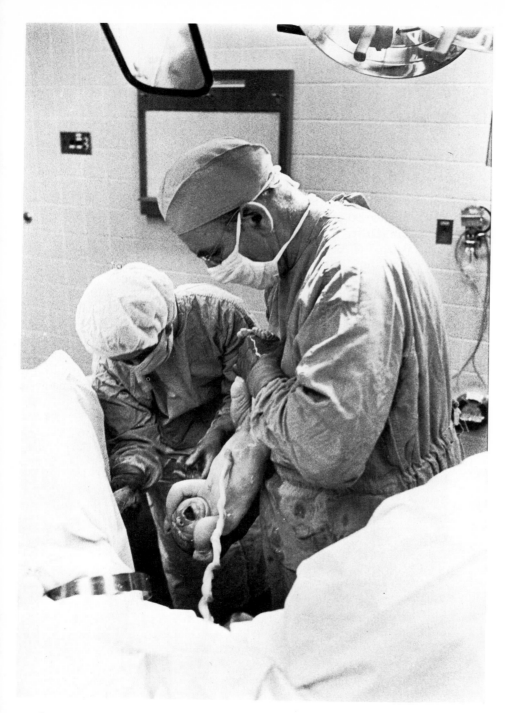

Newborn is still attached to mother by umbilical cord.

is an increased incidence of "sudden death syndrome" (crib deaths) among these infants. (Crib deaths are discussed in detail in Chapter 6). Today, moderately premature infants (born 31–36 weeks after conception) and borderline prematures (born 37–38 weeks after conception) frequently have serious respiratory difficulties. Danger of infection among these infants still is high (Usher, 1975). Children born prematurely tend later to score lower on tests of cognitive ability and gross motor development (Braine et al., 1966).

We discussed earlier the relationship between poor maternal diet and low birth weight. Illness and malnutrition, both associated with poverty, clearly are related to prematurity. Also related are excessive smoking and drinking (Goldenson, 1970). Drug abuse is related to prematurity; approximately 50 percent of infants born to drug-dependent mothers are premature (Driscoll, 1973).

Medication during labor and delivery Although a normal event, labor usually is associated with pain. Even the Bible (Genesis 3:16) records that, after eating the forbidden fruit, Eve was told, "I will greatly multiply your pain in childbearing; in pain you shall bring forth children. . . ." In more modern times, pain for the mother usually is reduced through medication in one form or another. Regional anesthesia has been used in obstetrics since the beginning of the twentieth century. Today, most infants born in private hospitals in the United States are delivered with the mother receiving some form of inhalation anesthesia or analgesia (Bowes, 1970).

Moments after birth.

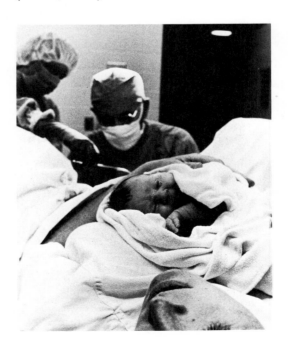

What effect does medication to relieve maternal pain have on the newborn infant? There is increasing information that medicated deliveries affect the uterine environment and the newborn infant. When a drug is given to the mother in labor, the extent of its effect on the baby depends on a number of factors. Let's begin with the mother's health. The blood level of the drug in the mother will remain high if her liver or renal functioning is impaired and, therefore, the drug will pass more readily to the fetus. Similarly, if maternal serum protein is low, any protein-bound drug will reach the fetus in greater quantity.

Effects on the infant also depend on choice of medication. All of the inhalation anesthetics commonly used today are known to cross the placenta easily and enter fetal circulation (Giacoia and Yaffee, 1975).

Helping parents of extremely premature infants

Until very recently, extremely premature infants (born before thirty weeks after conception) usually died. Today, with modern technology, more survive, but many still face severe problems. Being the parents of an extremely premature infant can be the most emotionally draining experience of a lifetime. First, the infant is taken away immediately after birth and placed in an incubator. The first meeting of parents and child is a frightening one: the infant, tiny and strangely colored, rests among a mass of tubes and wires. Parents immediately are faced with very realistic fears that the infant may not survive or that he or she may be abnormal. The physician can give no assurance. Parental feelings often include guilt as well as anxiety. They fear that somehow they are at fault. Often, for weeks after birth, sudden ups and downs in the infant's responding keep this fear strong.

What can be done to relieve parental anxiety and to help parents gain rapport with their newborn infant? Physicians suggest, first, that the baby should be shown to the parents immediately in the delivery room, even before being placed in the incubator. From then on, parents should be encouraged to visit the nursery often.

They should be counseled as to what modern medical care now can do. All good news should be reported immediately (Usher, 1975).

Parents also should be counseled as to what to expect of their infant when they are able to take the baby home. Many parental fears relate to the doctor's careful precautions in the hospital. Parents, already anxious, fear they might not be capable of caring for the infant properly away from the hospital. Many premature infants later become excessively timid children and exhibit behavior disorders related to overprotection—for example, nail biting, thumb sucking, and temper tantrums. When lasting effects of a psychological nature are found in "preemies," they are likely to be due to parental attitudes related to parental fear rather than to the prematurity itself. Physical development of the premature infant can be expected to be retarded in the first few months of life. Parents should be fully informed as to what to expect: extremely premature infants sit, stand, and walk considerably later than do full-term babies. Speech development is apt to be delayed, baby talk persists longer, and stuttering is more frequent than among full-term infants (Goldenson, 1970).

Barbituates, if short acting and given well before delivery, may not have a measurable effect on the infant. However, some commonly used drugs, such as reserpine, may result in infant lethargy for twenty-four hours after birth. Morphine, although safe two hours before delivery, may cause breathing problems and anoxia at birth if used later in the labor process. Regional anesthetics such as the spinal block, while having no direct effect on the fetus, have been known to produce extreme hypotension in the mother. Thus, these also are not free of risk (Bowes, 1970; Vulliany, 1972).

Physicians long have known that drug effect is related directly to patient size. Even the large-sized newborn is affected by a given drug dosage much more than its mother. Since the fetus and newborn do not have well-developed mechanisms for elimination, drugs can be stored in infant tissues for many days (Kron et al., 1966).

Finally, the effect of medication is related to the labor process itself. In prolonged labor, medication may reduce oxygen intake of the mother and can dangerously deplete oxygen supply to an infant already in prolonged stress. The dangers of anoxia and resulting brain damage during long labors are high. In shorter labor, where less medication is likely, effects may not be so severe. However, onset of respiration still may be less prompt and less vigorous when sedative drugs are given than when they are withheld.

Examples of retarded development of drug-affected infants have been reported up to four weeks after delivery. Daily increases in sucking behavior in infants after medicated deliveries have been attributed to recovery from drug effects (Kron et al., 1963). Brazelton (1961) reported that mothers who used anesthetics during delivery needed to stimulate their infants far more to maintain sucking than did mothers who delivered without anesthetics. Some psychologists feel that these effects, even though they are temporary, may well affect feeding patterns and personal interrelationships in later life. Some researchers have suggested that "some of the psychological effects may be pervasive if not permanent" (Stone et al., 1973, p. 112).

Alternatives to Traditional Childbirth

With statistical data increasing on hazards of traditional childbirth methods both for babies and for mothers, many parents in recent years have elected alternative methods of having their children. Critics of traditional obstetrical methods have attacked a variety of procedures used routinely in American hospitals today. Excessive use of medication and forceps, artificial induction of labor, and impersonal care of mothers and infants have all come under fire (Arms, 1975).

Prepared childbirth One outgrowth of this criticism is an increasing trend toward more "natural" methods of childbirth in this country. Prepared childbirth involves a labor and delivery process with minimal or nonuse of anesthetics for the mother. Mothers electing this method prepare for it through special exercises during pregnancy, so as to develop muscles that will aid the body in labor and delivery. Proponents of this method suggest that if the mother is prepared psychologically and physically for labor, pain will be minimized. Many American doctors now agree to prepared childbirth, but point out that it is important to recognize that this is not an all-or-none method. The amount of anesthetic used, in the end, normally will depend on the mother's final desires as well as on the doctor's assessment of her physical state and that of the baby.

Family-centered childbirth Along with the trend toward prepared childbirth have come demands from many groups for increased participation of the father in the birth process. Proponents of father-present deliveries sugggest that the father can provide much needed psychological support. Associations such as the International Childbirth Education Association, the American Society for Psychoprophylaxis in Obstetrics, and the LaLeche League International have long supported father presence in the delivery room as part of the procedure for making childbirth more humane. Some hospitals in the United States today allow fathers to be present during the births of their children. Some doctors, opposed to fathers' presence, point out the dangers of increased possibility of infec-

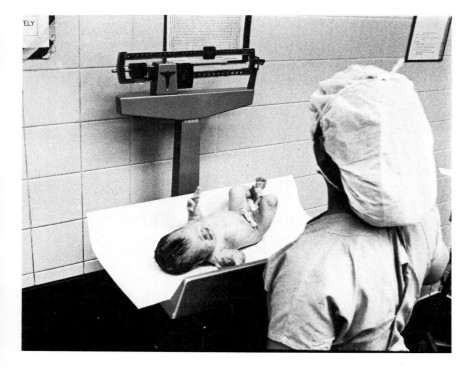

Weighing in.

tion and stress that the delivery room "is no place for sentimentality" (Shu, 1973). Parents also seem to be divided as to the desirability of father presence during childbirth. In 1968, when St. Mary's Hospital in Grand Rapids, Michigan first allowed fathers in the delivery room, only 9 percent of fathers chose to be present (Shu, 1973). In recent years, however, this percentage has increased considerably.

Nurse-midwifery Another major change in recent years in obstetrical procedures in the United States has to do with who actually delivers the baby. Because of increased requests for more attention and, at the same time, for lower costs, a new trend toward midwife delivery is occurring. In 1931, the first schools in the United States for nurse-midwives were reported to be ministering primarily to poor and rural American mothers. Sixteen schools were offering midwifery training programs. In a number of cities today, short-stay delivery units are available where midwives deliver babies, but where physicians and complete medical facilities are available in the event that birth complications develop. In normal deliveries, the stay of mother and child often is less than twelve hours, cutting expenses and allowing parents to assume more immediate responsibility for their children (Rawlings, 1973).

THE NEWBORN INFANT

Immediately after birth, the infant takes his or her first breath. Some infants do this themselves; others need assistance. The traditional picture of childbirth portrays the physician holding the baby upside down by the feet and slapping the baby's bottom so as to make the infant inhale air and cry. The so-called birth cry marks the infant's first breath.

The Neonate: A Description

The infant, for the first two weeks of life, is called a *neonate*. The neonate is tiny; average birth weight is seven-and-one-half pounds. He or she is red, wrinkled, and, at birth, wet with amniotic fluid. The skin is coated with a cheeeselike substance. The neonate is extremely vulnerable: the bones of the skull protecting the neonate's brain are soft and connected only by fibrous tissue. The skull contains six soft spots or openings called *fontanels*, where the bones have not yet grown together. The largest fontanel on the top of the head will not close until the baby is more than a year old. Neonates are extremely weak, unable even to hold their heads up unaided. But all body structures are present, if not yet matured. The infant now is ready to begin the life processes, including breathing, circulating oxygen through the blood, digesting food, and eliminating wastes.

The neonate spends most of the time sleeping. Regular sleep, with slow even breathing, is interspersed with irregular sleep, characterized by quick, uneven breathing. Both are normal. When the neonate is awake, he or she may cry vigorously and spasmodically. Thus far, no tears appear. Crying after birth usually means the infant is hungry, thirsty, or uncomfortable. It is unusual for an adequately fed baby who is given sufficient attention to cry for more than a total of two hours in a twenty-four-hour period (Vulliamy, 1972).

The neonate at birth is capable of making specific responses with some regularity to certain stimuli. For example, the rooting response, well known to mothers of newborn infants, occurs when the baby's mouth is stimulated. The baby responds by turning mouth and head toward the source of stimulation. If the stimulus is a milk-producing nipple, rooting behavior automatically will be followed by sucking, swallowing, and breathing. Finger and toe flexion can be elicited by pressure on the palms or the soles of the feet at the base of the toes. The neonate appears to grab the mother's finger when she places it in the infant's hand and touches the palm. If she strokes the middle of the baby's sole where the arch will be, she will get the opposite of the flexion response, called the Babinski response, in which the neonate's toes fan up and outward. This reflex occurs only at this early stage of development. The Moro or startle response is elicited by withdrawal of support and consists of a rapid flinging out and upward of the neonate's arms. The neonate also produces what is known as a reflexive smile. Interestingly, researchers have noted differences in both the startle response and the smiling response that apparently are dependent on the sex of the infant (Stone et al., 1973).

Care of the Neonate Immediately after Birth

Traditional obstetrics procedures include a rather abrupt entry into the outside world: the newborn infant is quickly picked up by the heels and slapped on the bottom. Immediately after breathing begins, the umbilical cord is clamped. Drops of silver-nitrate solution are placed in the eyes as protection against infection. The baby usually is given a physical examination, cleaned, labeled with the family name, and taken away to the nursery. Critics of these procedures have attacked what they call unnecessary separation of mother and infant in this process, delaying of first breast feeding, and restriction of infants afterwards to four-hour feeding schedules (Arms, 1975).

Many researchers have come forth with data to support many of the concerns of these critics, particularly as regards feeding patterns. Nutrition in newborn infants, particularly those who are premature, is critical. It now is known that malnutrition in neonates may result in permanent cellular deficit. It used to be pediatric practice to delay breastfeeding for several days. Researchers now believe that, in some cases, this practice could well have had detrimental effects on some babies. Restricting feeding during the first day because of hospital regimen, critics say, might be unwise.

Making happy babies?

A controversial new method for childbirth was recently described by a French obstetrician in a book that became a best-seller in the United States, *Birth Without Violence* (Leboyer, 1975). Leboyer, concerned with the emotional impact of childbirth on the neonate, questions the harshness of traditional childbirth practices. Leboyer's method includes dimming delivery room lights, so that the baby will not be startled unduly by bright lights. Immediately after birth, the newborn infant is placed on the mother's warm abdomen and allowed to retain as long as possible the prenatal curved spinal position. The umbilical cord is not cut until the baby's respiratory system is well established. The baby continues, for up until six minutes after birth in some cases, to receive oxygen through its prenatal respiratory system. After the cord is cut, the baby receives a warm, comfortable bath, often to soft music.

Critics of the Leboyer method point out that these procedures might in some cases be dangerous. Bright light is necessary to see facial color, they point out. The cord should be cut as quickly as possible so as not to risk infection. The doctor needs to hear the scream of the baby to be sure of forceful breathing. Leboyer has answered that all of these precautionary measures can be used with his method, when necessary, but they are not needed routinely. His advocates point out that follow-up studies at the Sorbonne of French babies born by the Leboyer method seem to show that these children are spared the usual infancy psychopathologies and are noticeably active, exhibiting avid interest in the world about them (Englund, 1974).

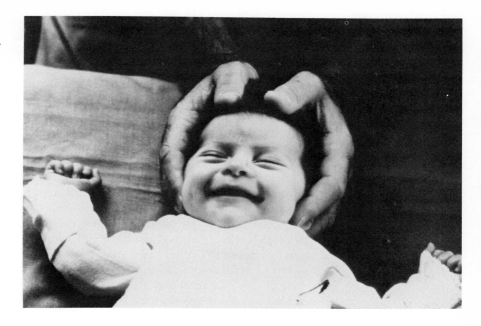

Another Leboyer baby smiles at the world. (Courtesy of New Yorker films)

Rooming-in Because of concerns both for feeding of the neonate and for increased mother-infant interaction, many mothers today select hospitals that allow for "rooming-in"—that is, keeping the infant in the same room with the mother. In rooming-in arrangements, fathers also have more opportunity to touch and to become acquainted with their children. Feeding schedules more easily can be arranged according to mother's and baby's needs rather than according to hospital schedule. Parents deciding to use such arrangements often report stronger feelings of closeness with their infants.

S ociety is on the threshold of creating life by means other than those described in this chapter—methods that today may sound like science fiction, but tomorrow may have a major impact on the world. Thus, many problems related both to development of the fetus in utero and to the birth process itself might be solved. Researchers already have found, for example, that it is possible to fertilize and develop rabbit eggs in solution outside of the uterus (Brackett, 1973; Gould, 1973). Researchers also have been able to transplant a blastocyst from its mother into the uterus of a different woman (Watson, 1971). Women in the future who are unable to carry their own babies safely or comfortably through nine months

PRENATAL DEVELOPMENT: IMPLICATIONS FOR THE FUTURE

of prenatal development may be able to use a "host mother" for this purpose. The development of an artificial placenta that would provide exactly the proper nutrients at the proper times already has been discussed by scientists (Schroeder, 1974).

Biological research may well change the entire developmental process. Until that time, however, it will be necessary for us to deal with the potential hazards to development discussed in this chapter. Retarded fetal development, defective fetuses, and mortality all have been shown to be related to improper nourishment, poor health, drugs and cigarette use, and inadequate prenatal care.

Is the United States doing anything about it? Government-sponsored programs in recent years have included maternity clinics, public-health nursing, immunization and screening clinics, and referral programs, all designed to help the poor. Maternity benefits have increased; pregnant women fortunate enough to have full insurance coverage receive up to ten full days of hospital care for mother and child, with up to 120 days in event of birth complications. Maternity leaves without pay for up to six months are guaranteed in many professions. To date, the American track record has been less than excellent, however. As an affluent nation, we rate considerably lower than we should in both the incidence of birth mortality and birth disorders. Of particular concern is an increasing number of young mothers under sixteen years of age giving birth without adequate nutrition, prenatal information, or care. Recently, the Committee on Maternal Nutrition of the National Research Council (Public Health Reports, 1970) suggested that all adolescents receive education in sound health, nutrition, and family planning as part of their public-school programs. Further, it suggested that social agencies must help with information on prenatal care and family planning and that all social agencies include on their staffs professionals trained specifically to deal with adolescents.

SUMMARY

The period of development from conception to birth is commonly referred to as the prenatal period. During the three basic stages of this period—the period of the ovum, the embryonic period, and the fetal period—the organism develops both in physical size and in complexity, and also in terms of its ability to function. The normal course of development during these periods and after birth is affected by many factors associated with pregnancy. These include nutrition of the mother and fetus, maternal age, spacing of births, disease, smoking, drug and alcohol use, radiation, Rh factor, and even the emotional state of the mother.

Birth of the infant, usually forty weeks after conception, marks the end of the prenatal period. Labor is a normal event in the life of the mother. Nevertheless, potential dangers exist, including anoxia, hemorrhaging, and prematurity. Alternatives to traditional childbirth procedures have been developed in recent years in order to reduce medication during labor and delivery, thought to be of possible harm to the infant, and to reduce other potential hazards. Prepared childbirth, family-centered childbirth, and the use of nurse-midwives are becoming increasingly popular. New methods of care of the newborn infant also are being developed to reduce further the potential hazards to the developing child.

1 What are the three principle stages of prenatal development? Describe the changes that should be expected of the developing organism at each of these stages. (For review, see pages 141–148.)

2 List what you consider to be two major sources of danger to the developing fetus. Explain why these are important to development. Propose a procedure by which society might remove this potential threat to its children. (For review, see pages 148–157.)

3 Traditional childbirth as it occurs in the United States has been under attack from various sources. Why? Do you feel that the alternative methods that have been proposed are beneficial to the mother and the newborn child? Justify your answer. (See pages 158–164 for review.)

4 What major changes do you foresee in the not-too-distant future which might make prenatal development a safer and more secure period for both mother and developing child? Be specific. (For review, see pages 162–170.)

Avery, G., *Neonatology*. Philadelphia: Lippincott 1975. This up-to-date anthology was prepared by medical experts. It discusses how the pregnant women should be cared for before the birth of her child, and what special care should be given the newborn infant. The special problems of high-risk infants are fully explored.

Babson, S., and R. Benson. *Management of High Risk Pregnancy and Intensive Care of the Neonate*. St. Louis: The C. V. Mosby Co., 1971. This book deals with issues discussed in this chapter. Factors that affect the development of the baby are discussed in detail, together with methods to eliminate adverse effects. The book is written in a particularly clear and easy-to-understand style.

Flanagan, G. *The First Nine Months of Life*. New York: Simon and Schuster, 1962. This is an excellent, informally presented but comprehensive, day-by-day description of prenatal development. Photographs are used throughout to show the changes that take place in the developing organism. This book is recommended for students particularly interested in normal prenatal development.

Pan American Health Organization. *Perinatal Factors Affecting Human Development*. Washington, D.C.: World Health Organization, 1969. This is the report of a symposium in which public-health, medical, and research scientists participated. The topic discussed is the health of the fetus and neonate. Diseases specific to this period of development are described.

Stone, L., H. Smith, and L. Murphy, eds. *The Competent Infant*. New York: Basic Books, 1973. This book of readings describes all aspects of prenatal and neonatal development. The editors' introductions and summary remarks are particularly clear and informative. The text contains summaries and sections of articles, rather than entire works, so as to review the largest number of issues possible.

REFERENCES

Alcoholic Inheritance. *Science Digest* 77 (June 1975): 17.

Altman, J. Nutritional deprivation and neural development. In M. Sterman, D. McGinty, and A. Adinolf, *Brain Development and Behavior*. New York: Academic Press, 1971.

Arms, S. *Immaculate Deception*. New York: Houghton Mifflin, 1975.

Babson, S., and R. Benson. *Management of High Risk Pregnancy and Intensive Care of the Neonate*. St. Louis: The C. V. Mosby Co., 1971.

Behrman, R. Birthweight, gestation age, and neonatal risk. In R. Behrman, ed., *Neonatology*. St. Louis: The C. V. Mosby Co., 1973, pp. 45–50.

Bowes, W., Jr. The effects of obstetrical medication on fetus and infants. *Monographs of the Society for Research in Child Development*, 1970, 137, 35, no. 4.

Brackett, B. Mammalian fertilization in vitro. *Federation Proceedings* 32 (1973): 2065–2068.

Braine, M., C. Heimer, H. Wortis, and A. Freedman. Factors associated with impairment of the early development of prematures. *Monographs of the Society for Research in Child Development* 31 (1966): 139.

Brazelton, T. Effect of maternal medication on the neonate and his behavior. *Journal of Pediatrics* 58 (1961): 513.

Brewer, T. Human pregnancy and nutrition: an examination of traditional assumptions, New Zealand. *Journal of Obstetrics and Gynecology* 10 (1970): 87.

Butler, N., and D. Alberman. High risk predictors at booking and in pregnancy. *Second Report of the British Perinatal Mortality Survey, Perinatal Problems*. London: E. and S. Livingstone, Ltd., 1969.

Cragg, B. Plasticity of synapses. *British Medical Bulletin* 30, no. 2 (May 1974): 141–144.

Dishotsky, N., R. Loughman, R. Mogar, and W. Lipscomb. LSD and genetic damage. *Science*, April 30, 1971, pp. 431–440.

Dobbing, J., and J. Smart. Vulnerability of the developing brain and behavior. *British Medical Bulletin* 30, no. 2 (May 1974): 164–168.

Driscoll, J., Jr. Infants of addicted mothers. In R. Behrman, ed., *Neonatology*. St. Louis: The C. V. Mosby Co., 1973, pp. 450–452.

Englund, S. Birth without violence. *New York Times Magazine*, 8 December 1974.

Flanagan, G. *The First Nine Months of Life*. New York: Simon and Schuster, 1962.

Fletcher, A. The infant of the diabetic mother. In G. Avery, ed., *Neonatology*. Philadelphia: Lippincott, 1975.

Giacoia, G., and S. Yaffee. Drugs and the perinatal patient. In G. Avery, ed., *Neonatalogy*. Philadelphia: Lippincott, 1975.

Goldenson, R. *The Encyclopedia of Human Behavior*. Garden City, New York: Doubleday, 1970.

Gorsuch, R., and M. Key. Abnormalities of pregnancy as a function of anxiety and life stress. *Psychosomatic Medicine* 36 (July–August 1974).

Gould, K. Application of in vitro fertilization. *Federation Proceedings* 32 (1973): 2069–2074.

Graham, F., R. Matarazzo, and B. Caldwell. Behavioral differences between normal and traumatized newborns. *Psychological Monographs* 70, no. 5 (1956).

Holley, W., A. Rosenbaum, and J. Churchill. Effects of rapid succession of pregnancy. In Pan American Health Organization, *Perinatal Factors Affecting Human Development*. Washington, D.C.: World Health Organization, 1969.

Hulka, J., and J. Schaaf. Obstetrics in adolescents: a controlled study of deliveries by mothers 15 years of age and under. *Obstetrics and Gynecology* 23 (1964): 678–685.

Iorio, J. *Principles of Obstetrics and Gynecology for Nurses*. St. Louis: The C. V. Mosby Co., 1967.

Iorio, J. *Childbirth*. St. Louis: The C. V. Mosby Co., 1975.

Keay, A., and D. Morgan. *Craig's Care of the Newly Born Infant*. London: Churchill-Ligninston, 1974.

Kornetsky, C. Psychoactive drugs in the immature organism. *Psychopharmacologia*, 1970, pp. 105–136.

Kron, R., M. Stein, and K. Goddard. A method of measuring sucking behavior of newborn infants. *Psychosomatic Medicine* 25 (1963): 181.

Kron, R., M. Stein, and K. Goddard. Newborn sucking behavior affected by obstetric sedation. *Pediatrics* 37 (1966): 1012–1016.

Leboyer, F. *Birth Without Violence*. New York: Knopf, 1975.

Lewin, R. Starved brains. In *Psychology Today* 9, no. 4 (September 1975).

Lewis, M., A. Martels, H. Campbell, and S. Goldberg. Individual differences in attention. *American Journal of Diseases of Children* 113 (1967): 461–465.

Marx, J. Drugs during pregnancy: do they affect the unborn child? *Science 180* (April 13, 1973): 174–175.

National Institute on Drug Abuse. *Report of Interviews of 2510 U.S. Men Collected from October 1974 to May 1975*, February 1976.

Nortman, D. Parental age as a factor in pregnancy outcome and child development. *Reports on Population/Family Planning*, No. 16, August 1974.

Novy, M. Evaluation and treatment of the fetus at risk. In R. Behrman, ed., *Neonatology*. St. Louis: The C. V. Mosby Co., 1973, pp. 1–45.

Ounsted, M. Familial factors affecting fetal growth. In Pan Amercian Health Organization, *Perinatal Factors Affecting Human Development*. Washington, D.C.: World Health Organization, 1969.

Plummer, G. Anomalies occurring in children exposed in utero to the atomic bomb in Hiroshima. *Pediatrics* 10 (1952): 687.

Public Health Reports. *Dangers of Adolescent Pregnancies* 85 (November 1970): 11.

Rawlings, E. A general practitioner short-stay delivery unit. *The Practitioner* 211 (1973): 329–334.

Schmeck, H. Brain harm in U.S. laid to food lack. *The New York Times Magazine*, 2 November 1975, A-32.

Schroeder, L. New life: person or property? *American Journal of Psychiatry* 131 (1974): 541–544.

Scrimshaw, N., C. Taylor, and J. Gordon. Interactions of nutrition and infection. *American Journal of Medical Science*, 1959: 237–367.

Shank, R. A chink in our armor. *Nutrition Today* 5, no. 2 (1975): 2–11.

Shu, C. Husband-father in delivery room? *Hospitals* 41 (1973): 90–94.

Siegel, E., and N. Morris. The epidemiology of human reproductive casualites. In *Maternal Nutrition and the Course of Pregnancy*. Washington, D.C.: National Academy of Sciences, 1970, pp. 5–40.

Simkin, J. Proper diet during pregnancy. Unpublished paper, September 1976.

Sterman, M., D. McGinty, and A. Adinolf. *Brain Development and Behavior*. New York: Academic Press, 1971.

Stone, L., H. Smith, and L. Murphy. *The Competent Infant*. New York: Basic Books, 1973.

United States Department of Health, Education and Welfare. *The Health of Children*. Washington, D.C.: U.S. Government Printing Office, 1970.

Usher, R. The special problems of the premature infant. In G. Avery, ed., *Neonatology*. Philadelphia: Lippincott, 1975.

Vulliamy, D. *The Newborn Child*. Baltimore: The Williams and Wilkins Co., 1972.

Watson, J. Moving toward the clonal man. *Atlantic Monthly*, March 1971, pp. 50–53.

Wishik, S., and N. Lichtblau. The physical development of breast-fed young children as related to close birth spacing, high parity and maternal undernutrition. Paper presented at the annual meeting of the American Academy of Pediatrics, San Francisco, California, October 1974.

Infancy: The First Two Years

After completing this chapter, you should be able to:

1
describe some of the major changes that take place during the first two years of life in the infant's ability to perceive the environment through the developing sensory systems, and in the abilities to manipulate the environment through prehension, locomotion, and communication;

2
explain how Piaget describes the period of sensorimotor development; use the terms equilibration, assimilation, and accommodation to explain what takes place during each of the separate stages of this period;

3
explain how social-emotional behavior develops; relate this developing behavior to sensorimotor development during the same period;

4
give some of the reasons why children differ in their development and list the variables most important to the appearance of individual differences.

Chapter 5 described the development of the individual from conception through the birth process. We left the newborn right after delivery into the outside world—a tiny, red, wrinkled creature, still wet with amniotic fluid and caked with a cheeselike substance.

Neonatal behavior is described in terms of the infant's state of activity. Together, these states form a continuum of consciousness or alertness, ranging from vigorous activity to regular sleep. Newborns, when left alone and unstimulated, spend most of the time sleeping. But they switch states regularly at extremely short intervals. The exhausted mother of a newborn often reports that her baby stayed awake "the entire night." What probably happened was that the baby woke up, cried loudly, and fell asleep again long before the mother was able to fall asleep herself. The baby then woke up again just moments after the mother finally drifted off, leading her to believe that they both stayed awake most of the night. It is extremely difficult to convince a tired mother that her baby ever sleeps at night!

Changes from state to state in the neonate occur often, apparently triggered by internal changes. Parents' inability to regulate their babies' sleep-wake cycles by keeping them up longer in the daytime attests to the fact that the regulatory mechanism cannot be controlled by external manipulation. Frustrated mothers often report that their infants cry all night long and then sleep all afternoon, just when friends and relatives want to see them. Nothing these mothers do seems to change the behavior of these babies.

Some changes in state are produced by changes in the level of ongoing stimulation. Loud noises, for example, make a new baby cry. Touching babies while they sleep may wake them up. Interestingly, swaddling, a

THE NEONATE: A BEHAVIORAL DESCRIPTION

Neonatal States of Activity

Neonatal states of activity

Psychologists have described different infant states in various ways. The following categories were used by Wolff (1966) in describing sleeping infants:

Regular sleep: closed eyes; slow, even breathing; relaxed facial features.

Irregular sleep: closed eyes; quick, uneven breathing; variable body movements.

Drowsiness: eyes open and shut intermittently; breathing regular; relatively slow body movements.

Alert inactivity: eyes open; relatively inactive body movement; relaxed facial features.

Waking activity: eyes open; diffuse motor activity involving whole body; irregular respiration.

Crying: vocalization associated with vigorous motor activity.

procedure in which babies are kept motionless and free from physical contact with their mothers by cloths wrapped firmly about their bodies, has been found to soothe infants rather than enrage them, as once was thought (Lipton et al., 1965). The quiet behavior of swaddled infants probably accounts for the fact that snug swaddling continues to be practiced in many countries today.

Neonates spend most of their time sleeping. Wolf (1966) reports that, during the first two weeks, many spontaneous behaviors—for example, smiles, random startle responses, penis erections, and reflex sucking responses—appear. Wolf attributes these behaviors, which are not clearly related to any external stimulation, to spontaneous discharge of central neural activity in the neonate—almost as if the infant were totally "wound up and ready to go." The awakened neonate may appear relaxed or may cry vigorously and spasmodically. During the awake state, the neonate, even though lacking a mature nervous system, is capable of learning.

THE DEVELOPMENT OF INFANT BEHAVIOR

The nervous system of the neonate is not fully mature. One of the most striking characteristics of the neonatal brain is the relative absence of *myelin*, the soft, white material that eventually forms sheaths around the nerve fibers (Reese and Lipsett, 1970). Because of this immaturity, studies that reported neonatal learning were regarded, until recently, with skepticism by many developmental psychologists. We know now, however, that, regardless of immaturity, the neonate is capable of receiving a great deal of input from the outside world, and is also capable of making many complex responses to this input. With each day of life, the infant increases these capabilities.

Infant Sensory Systems and Perception

What is the difference between sensation and perception? Infant *sensation* is awareness that results from stimulation of one of the infant receptor organs—for example, the skin or the ears. *Perception* involves the infant's abstracting of information from sensory experiences. The newborn infant *senses* touch and sound, and *perceives* mother's presence when he or she learns to associate certain touch and voice sensations with mother being there. Perception involves the infant's ability progressively to detect properties of stimuli not previously responded to, and to reduce uncertainty about the world (E. Gibson, 1969, 1970). Perception is altered by experience and can create for the infant new experiences. Sensation is not affected by experience at all.

Our knowledge of infantile senory and perceptual abilities has grown considerably in recent years. In this section, we examine two important sensory systems, audition and vision, as well as other developing systems.

Audition We know that, even before birth, the fetus is anatomically equipped to hear. At twenty-four weeks in utero, the fetus already moves to loud noises. Because of immaturity of the cortex, however, integration of sound from the two ears may be limited for the first several months after birth. It is not until about four to five months of age that infants are able to localize sounds. At this point, they will begin to look in the correct direction for a rattle that has been shaken and then hidden from sight. There is growing evidence that infants can discriminate between different sounds as early as five to six weeks of age (Appleton et al., 1975).

Different sounds have very different effects on babies. Some sounds are soothing. Low-frequency, rhythmic sounds, as, for example, a mother's crooning lullaby, are known to be especially calming. Infants show particular attention to and preference for human voices. One- to two-month-old infants, for example, sometimes show distress in response to ranges in their mothers' tone of voice. Sudden or loud sounds also produce distress.

Vision The neonatal visual system is immature. Pupillary reflexes are sluggish. Newborn infants are not able to focus their eyes easily in bright light, although they seem able to distinguish light and dark contrasts. Infants as young as five days old will stop sucking and watch bright lights moving in their visual fields. The ciliary muscles that control the neonatal lens are weak; newborn infants maintain relatively short focus length. For the first month of life, they are unable to focus on distant objects.

The visual system develops rapidly. Binocular convergence of the two eyes allows infants to fixate on objects placed in front of them. This

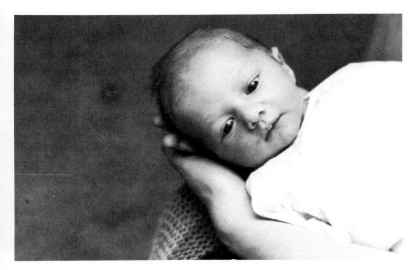

This six-week-old infant clearly responds with alert behavior to his mother's voice.

ability is developed by seven to eight weeks. Infants prefer moderate lighting at this age and are uncomfortable in brightly lit rooms. They can discriminate colors and seem to prefer (that is, pay more attention to) clear reds and blues. (Apparently, pink and powder-blue nurseries are for mothers rather than babies!) They watch moving objects and usually are able to track a toy moving across their visual field by the time they are three months old. It is at this age that a mobile hanging over the crib becomes an exciting toy. The visual system approximates adult capability by the time the infant is about four months old.

Vision is extremely important to development. Most babies explore the world first through their eyes. In the first month of life, they spend approximately 10 percent of their time just scanning their surroundings with rapid eye movements and frequent changes of direction. Most of the rest of their time, of course, is spent sleeping. Vision provides the bases for both sensorimotor and cognitive functioning. Complex patterns of responding, as, for example, crawling toward and picking up interesting objects, are achieved through coordination of vision with developing motor ability. (Of course, some babies do not have the opportunity to use vision in this way. These babies show different patterns of development. We will discuss blind children and children with other sensory impairments in Chapter 13.)

Earlier, we pointed out that infants show particular interest in human voices. The human face also is a potent stimulus for the baby from the very beginning. Three- to five-week-old infants pay much more attention to human faces than to other stimuli they see (Fantz, 1961). By two months of age, the faces of their mothers (or caretakers) are especially attractive and evoke the greatest attention. At this age, babies stare continuously at the faces around them. By four months, interest in faces intensifies still further. Babies now prefer to watch all stimuli resembling faces, even line drawings of faces. Apparently, drawings of other objects are not nearly so fascinating, for attention to these objects is much shorter.

The developing visual system is apparent in the attention babies give to objects outside their reach.

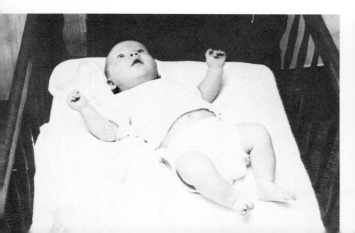
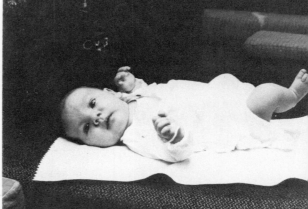

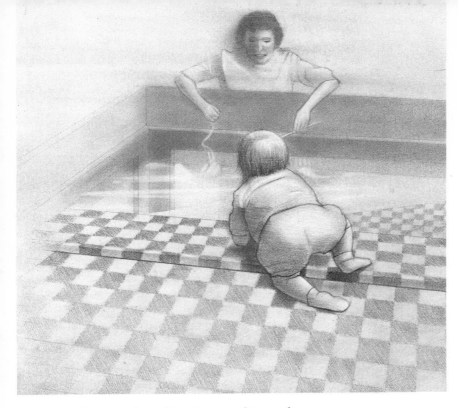

Infants in Gibson's study could not be coaxed to crawl
over a "visual cliff."

Babies seem also to prefer complexity in the stimuli they watch. Studies
have shown that infants attend longer to patterned stimuli that exhibit
color, angularity, and variations in brightness. Interest in complexity increases with age.

Babies apparently are capable of depth perception by two months of
age. Binocular convergence of the eyes now is possible. At two months,
babies will watch a sculpture of a human head much longer than they
will watch a line drawing of a head.

Some extremely interesting research was conducted by Eleanor Gibson
with what she called the "visual cliff" (E. Gibson, 1970). In Gibson's
research, infants were placed on a surface that appeared to end in a
cliff with a large drop to the floor; actually, the "drop-off" was covered
with transparent glass that allowed them to see the floor below. Six-
month-old infants could not be coaxed by Gibson or her colleagues to
crawl across the glass surface. Apparently, human infants perceive depth
and avoid such a visual cliff as soon as they are able to crawl. Gibson
has hypothesized that these avoidance responses might occur at earlier
ages, as they do with animals lower on the phylogenetic scale, if motor
development allowed human babies to make the necessary movements.

Other sensory systems Other sensory systems mature during the infancy period and are critical to early development. The *tactile sense*, used throughout life as a major source of information about the outside world, clearly begins to function during this stage. A mother's touch, for example, is capable of changing the neonatal state from sleep to wakeful activity. As we discuss in later chapters, touch is important also to the development of both social and cognitive functioning.

Pain receptors are present at birth, although sensitivity to pain is only slight in the neonate. Newborn infants are relatively insensitive to pain; mothers can pinch them without getting much of a response. But sensitivity to pain increases rapidly with age. In one study, as neonates increased in age from birth to one week, the number of slight pinpricks needed to make them move decreased rapidly (Sherman and Sherman, 1925).

The *olfactory senses* also are present at birth and develop with age. Newborns turn their heads away from extremely unpleasant odors. Infants a few months older are likely to exhibit more strenuous avoidance responses, squirming or crying when they come in contact with extremely unpleasant smells.

Clearly, the various sensory systems develop in relationship to one another and to learned perceptual ability in the developing infant. The *vestibular sense*, concerned with perception of body position and movement, is mediated through the inner ear and is stimulated by the starting and stopping of head movements. This complex sense provides a good example of sensory interrelationship. The development of both vestibular and tactile orientation to the outside world is related in many ways to visual perceptual ability. When mothers touch their babies and hold them in vertical positions, the infants are noticeably more visually alert (Korner and Thoman, 1970).

Sensorimotor Behavior and Cognition

Piaget (1952) described the first two years of life as the sensorimotor period. It is during this period that the abilities to sense and to perceive the outside world and to develop motor behaviors appropriate to these perceptions are developed. During the first two years, according to Piaget, sensorimotor development causes the beginning of truly intelligent behavior. Increase in the baby's ability to respond occurs largely through coordination of sensory and motor functioning. Large muscle activities (usually referred to as gross motor behavior) related to posture and locomotion develop. Small muscle activities (referred to often as fine-motor-adaptive activities) coordinate sensory input with muscle movement. A good example is the baby's increasing abilities to sense and manipulate objects in the environment. The infant first learns to shake a rattle to make noise, later to find blocks hidden under a blanket. When older, the baby will learn to use a knife, fork, and spoon. By learning to control his or her body and the objects in the world around, the infant evolves from a helpless individual with limited mobility and communication skills to an alert, verbally and socially adept person. The central nervous system has gone through an explosive growth process. Brain weight alone increases 350 percent by two years of age.

Three trends can be noted in the development of sensorimotor and cognitive activity. Development in the first two years progresses in cephalocaudal (from head to foot) and proximodistal (from near to the central nervous system to the body peripheries) directions. There is, in addition, a continued combination and integration of simple acts into more complex behaviors.

Prehension: ability to reach for and grasp objects Neonates are born with what Pavlov (1927) called "orienting" responses. They are capable of turning their sensory receptors toward particular stimuli. They also are born with ability to produce change in the environment. For example, newborns can turn their heads, changing the visual and kinesthetic stimuli surrounding them. They can cry, creating new sounds. They seem at this early age to be looking at the world almost as if it were a continuous panorama of fleeting images. The world of infants has no permanence. Young infants are unable to control arm and hand muscles, and thus are prohibited from reaching out and stopping the objects passing before them. However, their grasping reflexes develop rapidly into reaching responses. Soon they will be able to reach out, grasp, and stop these objects. At this point, they begin to create permanence in their world.

Parents can usually take their three-month-olds with them when they go out. Fear of strange people and places is not yet a concern.

The first step toward the development of *prehension* (ability to reach for and grasp objects) occurs with control of arm movements. Control of arm muscles develops gradually. Arm movements are coordinated with already-present responses to produce successful grasping behavior. This occurs through a series of steps. The two-week-old infant can reach for objects (Bower et al., 1970). With gradual development of depth perception and sequential and temporal organization of movements, reaching becomes a successful venture.

Until eight weeks, infants prefer familiar stimuli. Even at this extremely early age, memory of some sort exists. One evidence of infant memory is that before ten weeks of age, infants *habituate*. That is, infants stop paying attention to objects that do not produce change—for example, objects that do not move or change color or change sound (Pavlov, 1927, p. 147).

At three months, the infant's world still has no permanence; "out of sight, out of mind" is an apt description of this stage. If the mother of a three-month-old leans over the crib to play and then leaves, the baby won't look around for her.. At this age, parents usually can take their baby with them when they go to a friend's for an evening. Fear of strange people and places won't be a concern until much later.

At three to four months of age, infants learn to control their heads and arms separately. They develop the abilities to search, reach, and grasp. At about six months, practice at eye-hand coordination has reached the point where infants are able to reach successfully for objects while looking in another direction.

This two-month-old baby holds his head up ahead of schedule.

At about six months, babies begin to demonstrate some understanding of the notion of permanence. Gradually, they begin to search for hidden objects. When mother displays a rattle, then hides it from sight, the six-month-old will look around for it. At first, the infant doesn't remember easily where the rattle last appeared; he or she searches in the wrong places. Later, the infant develops the ability to remember where hidden objects were put.

Grasping behavior changes with age from an early "raking" movement of the entire hand to a movement that involves use of the opposable thumb. When this ability is developed, babies can hold objects firmly. Now it is difficult to take a rattle from a baby who wants to keep it. Fine muscles of the fingers develop; grasp becomes more secure. Bilateral reaching (reaching with either hand) changes to reaching with a preferred hand. Some infants have been reported to change from 50 percent use of each hand in the fifth month to 70 percent use of a preferred hand by the end of the first year (Landreth, 1967).

By seven to eight months, American babies usually develop fear of new faces and places. At this age, they exhibit surprise when objects differ in some way from their usual appearance. For example, babies of this age usually will be startled by a teddy bear with an upside-down head. The fact that they have expectations and are surprised when these expectations are not met is another indication that they have the ability to remember. Later, by eighteen months, this memory will be exhibited through lengthy searches for missing objects.

During this period, the young child becomes capable of what Bruner calls *volition*—voluntary control of the body to obtain what is wanted (Bruner, 1968). Children now are in control of their grasping and reaching behavior. They can pick up objects and place them one after another in a container or throw them out of the playpen onto the floor, whichever is preferred. They can reach out and touch other people. They are capable of eye-to-eye contact. They can communicate through smiling, crying, and other vocalizations. By eighteen months, young children usually are able to hold toys in such a way as to allow another person to take them.

Locomotion: ability to move about in the environment Sensorimotor development proceeds in a cephalocaudal direction. Development of the upper part of the body (including arms and hands) proceeds earlier and at a more rapid rate than development of lower parts of the body. Locomotion begins with development first of the muscles of the neck and then of the back, enabling the infant to sit. At three or four months of age, infants usually can sit for several minutes with support. Later, at about seven or eight months, they will be able to sit for several minutes without support—a major step toward ability to move in the environment. By about nine months old, they will be able to sit alone for ten minutes (Gesell and Amatruda, 1941).

Crawling takes place when the infant gains command of legs, trunk, and arms.

Can motor skills be taught?

What can mothers or caretakers do to foster motor coordination in their babies? One of the rules of learning motor skills is that ability is increased through practice. Consider the following two situations in which a fifteen-month-old baby plays after napping. Which situation provides the greatest opportunity for practicing and increasing motor skills?

Situation 1: It is two o'clock in the afternoon and a group of mothers is sitting in the backyard chatting. Their conversation is interrupted by a cry from the fifteen-month-old son of one of the mothers. He has just awakened from his nap. His mother excuses herself, goes into the house, and emerges a few minutes later with a freshly diapered baby. She places him on the grass at her feet. He is happily lurching from chair to chair with an occasional clutch at the furniture when coffee is brought in. At this point, his mother jumps up, briskly picks up the baby, and places him in a 4 × 4 portable playpen. The baby begins to cry. His mother reaches over and pops a pacifier into his mouth. He relaxes, sucks contentedly at his pacifier, and sits observing the coffee klatch. "What a darling baby!" exclaims

one of the women. "He's so well behaved! You'd hardly know he's there!"

Situation 2: It is two o'clock in the afternoon and a group of mothers is sitting in the backyard chatting. Their conversation is interrupted by a cry from the fifteen-month-old son of one of the mothers. He has just awakened from his nap. His mother excuses herself, goes into the house, and emerges a few minutes later with a freshly diapered baby. She places him on the grass at her feet. Soon he is happily lurching from chair to chair. When it is time to bring in the coffee, the baby's mother comes out with a box of toys. Some are mobiles hung on strong stands too heavy for the baby to tip over. Others can be moved if they are pushed. She carefully surrounds the baby with these toys. As an afterthought, she brings out a number of pots and pans and places them nearby. Then she serves the coffee. It is difficult at times for the ladies to continue their conversation without shouting, because the baby is busily engaged in banging pots and pans together. After about fifteen minutes, he begins to crawl away, but turns back to the toys when his mother rolls a large ball across the lawn toward him.

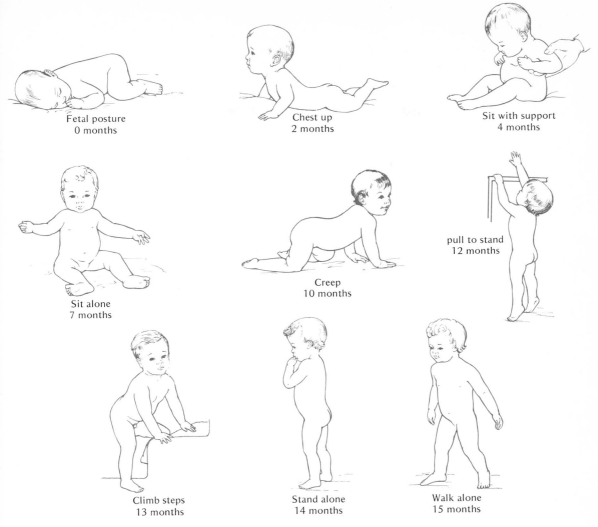

Fig. 6.1 The sequence of motor development. (Adapted from M. M. Shirley, *The First Two Years: A Study of 25 Babies*, Vol. 2, Institute of Child Welfare Monograph Series No. 7, University of Minnesota, Minneapolis. Copyright 1933.)

Most infants begin to crawl at about seven months and are quite mobile on hands and knees by eight-and-a-half months. All babies progress from sitting to crawling to walking stages in the same order, although it is possible for some babies to skip one or more of the intermediate steps.

At the end of the first year, many babies begin pulling themselves to standing positions. The average age for walking without support is fifteen months for babies in the United States (Shirley, 1933). Walking adds a new dimension to the infant's control of the physical and social environment. Psychologists have reported that, during this period, children demonstrate new feelings of "competence," accompanied by attempts to "assert themselves." Assertion is exhibited in a number of ways; one-year-old behavior is characterized by a large number of negative responses. Although mothers rarely mention it, the first word of a twelve- to fifteen-month-old baby often is "No!"

Walking is important not only because it allows the baby to move about more quickly and easily, but also because it frees infant hands to perform other acts. At eighteen months of age, the baby is filling cups with water, building towers of blocks, and learning how to use the objects in the environment in many new ways.

Vocalization: the beginning of language We noted earlier that the newborn infant cries and creates new sounds in his or her world. Noncrying vocalization has been reported in infants as young as three weeks old. The three-week-old baby makes fussing sounds. Later, he or she will begin to chuckle and laugh. Vowel sounds gradually increase in the infant's response repertoire from 4.5 sounds at two months to 11.4 sounds at thirty months. Consonants increase from 2.7 sounds at two months to 15.8 sounds at thirty months (Chen and Irwin, 1946).

Babbling is the result of combining vowel and consonant sounds. From three to six months, the baby babbles when excited. The amount of

The fostering of infant speech

The fostering of speech begins in the cradle with the encouraging affectionate sounds and gestures made by a mother as she bends over her baby, feeding and bathing him and making him comfortable. With his eyes on her face, he hears the sounds she makes and sees the movements that accompany them. Speech thus becomes recognized as a means of identification and communication, an accompaniment of comforting care.

Later, accompanying actions by words—"pat-a-cake," "bye-bye," "all gone," "up and off" inventing naming games involving baby's nose, toes, feet, hands, and mouth; singing to him and repeating nursery rhymes can all help to make heard speech interesting and pleasant, as long as this is kept at an entertaining rather than a

coaching level. A home that provides some variety of occasional sounds—a cuckoo clock, a music box, or chirping birds—without a confusing blare of background noise helps too in making an infant aware of different sound qualities. Adult response to his vocalizing, if only a smile and a word or two, rewards early efforts. Repeating after him his attempts at new words helps him to learn correct articulation, always provided the repetition is friendly and not argumentative.

Reprinted with permission from C. Landreth, *Early Childhood Behavior and Learning* (New York: Knopf, 1967), p. 122. Copyright © 1967 by Alfred A. Knopf, Inc.

babbling is associated with the amount of attention given the infant. Three-month-olds have been found to babble more when their mothers responded to this babbling with smiles and touching (Rheingold, Gewirtz, and Ross, 1959).

At six months, babies babble socially and use their increasing repertoire of sounds to attract and respond to adult vocalizations. Through imitation, infant sounds increasingly resemble adult speech. Finally, at twelve to fifteen months of age, the young child begins to utter his or her first simple words.

Infant understanding precedes speech. Understanding of simple adult speech has been reported in infants eight and nine months old (Church, 1966). Eight- or nine-month-old babies often understand what their mothers mean when they say, "No!" But they will not begin to say "No!" themselves until three to six months later.

At about a year, the first linguistic utterances occur. Earliest speech is made up of reduplicated syllables formed from sounds heard and imitated by the baby. Examples are typical baby words: "bye-bye"; "Mama"; "Dada"; "no." This early speech, referred to as *holophrastic speech*, includes single-word utterances used to express whole ideas (Dale, 1972). When children say, "No!" they may mean a variety of things. For example, they may use the same word to say that they don't want to go to bed, or that they don't want to take a toy, or that they aren't hungry. At this age, nouns are seldom used as names. When year-old children say "milk," they might mean that they want milk. Or, they might mean that they want the listener to look at the glass of milk on the table. Both context and intonation can help the listener understand what a child's holophrastic speech means.

During the first half of the second year, the young child builds a vocabulary from a beginning average of three words to fifty words. By two years, holophrastic speech decreases. Two-word phrases and short sentences are common in two-year-old speech.

Language development is related directly to the child's growing motor ability. Indeed, language development is even more directly correlated with motor development than it is with chronological age. Of course, children who have little or no opportunity to hear spoken language will develop language deficits, regardless of their motor development. We explore some of the reasons for this in Chapter 7.

All of the developing behaviors discussed in this chapter are accounted for in Piaget's theory of development (see Chapter 2). According to Piagetian theory, sensorimotor development accounts for future cognitive functioning. The changes that characterize the developing child during the first two years are described by Piaget as a series of discrete and qualitatively different substages. These stages allow the child progressively to respond to the environment in increasingly complex fashion, and eventually to think and solve problems in mature ways.

Piaget's Theory of Sensorimotor Development

following conversation between a father who has just come home from work and is changing clothes:

"Hi Daddy."
"Hi Johnny. Did Mommy buy this truck?"
"This truck."
"Can you make it go fast?"
"Go fast. Hat off. Shirt off. Pants off. That blue."
"Yes, my pants are blue."
"Sweater on. Chair."
"Where's the kitty?"
"Kitty all gone. Here is. See Mummy. There Mummy."
"Yes, here comes Mommy."
"Here Mummy."
"I'll go out and help her carry in the groceries."
"Groceries. Bye bye. Two bag. Chicken, That red. Here kitty.
"Bag fall. Close it."
"I can't close the box, so we'll have pizza for dinner."

"John dinner."
"We'll make your dinner now."
"Baby dinner."
"Yes, we'll make dinner for the baby too."
"Pick glove."
"I'll pick up my glove. Say, how did your knees get so dirty?"
"Knee dirty. See knee."
"Let's wash you off before dinner."
"Wash off."
"Where's the washcloth?"
"Wash cloth. Here is. Two cloth. Dirty. Dirty allgone."

While this conversation is fictitious, most of the child's utterances have been taken from those recorded by developmental psychologists. These are the kinds of things we might hear from a child who has begun to put words together into pairs at about eighteen to twenty-four months of age.

Reprinted with permission from H. Reese and L. Lipsitt, *Experimental Child Psychology* (New York: Academic Press, 1970), p. 437.

Basic to Piaget's theory is the concept of cognitive structure. We learned earlier (p. 60) that the cognitive structure of the child is a "well-balanced set of ideas organized into a coherent mental system." According to Piaget, in the first two years, the cognitive structure develops through increasing sensorimotor abilities. Infants respond to the world around them through their senses. Their increasing ability to respond to perceived stimuli allows them to progress from simpler to more advanced stages of development. As they progress from one stage to the next, they go from periods in which they are at first unable to make use of objects (disequilibrium) to later periods in which they become capable of using these objects in useful ways (equilibrium). This equilibrium, in turn, allows them to extend their environments. This extension creates new disequilibrium. The young baby in the playpen has not yet developed sufficient muscular strength to use the playpen bars as a way to pull himself to a standing position (disequilibrium). As soon as he is strong enough, he will use the bars in optimal fashion (equilibrium). Once in a standing position, he will have access to a great many new objects, most of which he is not quite ready to make use of (disequilibrium).

As we discussed in Chapter 2, equilibration, Piaget's name for this continuous process, assumes the interplay of two processes, assimilation and accommodation. Assimilation occurs when infants use a new object to perform activities they already know how to do. A good example of assimilation by young babies is adjusting to sucking bottle nipples after having been exclusively breastfed. Accommodation occurs when new activities are added to the infant's repertoire of responses. As infants increase the number of stimuli to which they respond (assimilate), they simultaneously increase the number of new responses they are able to make (accommodate).

Reflexive stage During the first month of life, the infant proceeds through what Piaget calls the reflexive stage of development. During this time, innate responses, such as sucking and grasping, become efficient. The infant also develops new abilities to reach for objects. These accommodative responses allow the infant, in turn, to assimilate the objects grasped into his or her cognitive structure.

Circular reaction stages After one month, infants begin to perform more and more complex behaviors. They do this through what Piaget described as a series of circular (repetitive) reactions to the environment—active behaviors that gradually accommodate to the experiences around them. At first, they wilfully repeat new actions over and over again, apparently for the sake of performing them. Piaget is careful to point out that, at this stage, babies lack apparent intention. That is, "even when the child grasps a new object to suck or look at it one cannot infer that there is a conscious purpose" (Piaget, 1952, p. 143). Infants wave their hands over their heads over and over again or kick the side of the crib repeatedly with the same motion. Piaget called this the *primary circular reaction stage*.

New behaviors develop at about four-and-one-half months of age, with coordination of vision and prehension. The baby might reach for a string of rattles hanging over the crib, for example, shake them, and exhibit surprise at the result. Now babies begin to repeat the action in order to observe the results.

The *secondary circular reaction stage* occurs when infant behaviors give the appearance of being "almost intentional." According to Piaget, infants at this stage are reproducing a series of new movements learned by chance through interacting with the world. In *The Origins of Intelligence in Children* (1952), Piaget cited examples of his own daughter Jacqueline's behavior at this stage. When, for example, he held her cheek in his hand, she took his hand in her own two small hands and pressed it back against her cheek.

According to Piaget, babies in the primary circular reaction stage may grasp or study objects without any conscious purpose to their actions.

The period of development from eight or nine months of age through the first year is characterized by what Piaget termed *tertiary circular reactions*. At this stage, babies begin to apply what they have already learned to new situations. They still repeat behaviors again and again, and may repeat the same one- or two-syllable word repeatedly, this time to draw attention to themselves. They have learned to move about by crawling and use this new power of locomotion to explore the world. They will touch, taste, and throw again and again whatever they can reach with their own hands.

Trial and error stage The first half of the second year marks what Piaget termed the trial and error stage. We noted earlier that the developing infant has been learning gradually that objects can be identified and are permanent—they don't vanish from the universe when removed from sight. Major achievements of this period are the infant's understanding of the notion of *causality* and the concepts of *object identity* and *object permanence*.

By eighteen months of age, the young child has learned that objects can be hidden and also that he or she can move about to find them. Now when mother removes a teddy bear from the crib to be cleaned in the washing machine, the baby will hunt for it. This period of development is a period of exploring the environment. Children are more mobile than ever before and use this mobility to seek out new objects. At this age, children require careful watching. Taste exploration can be a major hazard for an unsupervised eighteen-month-old, particularly if household bleach or medications have been left within reach. In response to public concern, the government now requires safety caps on bottles containing potentially harmful ingredients.

Mental combinations stage The second half of the second year marks what Piaget termed the mental combinations stage of development. The cognitive structure now enables children to think before they act. They spend less time in searching out items they can't find and use their memories to help locate what they want. Piaget described a situation in which his daughter Jacqueline was playing with a number of toys: a fish, a swan, and a frog. Later, while putting all of the toys in a box, Jacqueline noticed that the frog was missing. She then carefully took the toys out, put them together in a group, and only then began systematically to hunt for the frog. Careful planning was used in her search (Piaget, 1952, p. 356).

In the first two years, the developing infant is capable of many different types of learning. Each of the learning-environmental explanations of behavior described in Chapter 3 is in some way applicable to infant activity during this period.

Infant Learning

Taste exploration can be a hazard for an unsupervised eighteen-month-old.

Newborn infants are capable of learning through both classical and operant procedures. Neonates, for example, can learn classically conditioned sucking responses when signals such as sounds or lights are paired with milk (Brackbill and Koltsova, 1967; Lipsitt and Kaye, 1964). Ten-day-old infants also have been classically conditioned to blink when a tone signaled a puff of air to the eye (Little, 1971). Sucking responses of newborns have been conditioned by operant procedures as well (Siqueland and Lipsitt, 1966; Stone et al., 1973).

Infant learning has been explained also by motivation theory. One response studied frequently by motivation theorists is the sucking response of infants. In Chapter 3, we discussed how the motivation theorist interprets infant sucking behavior. The example given involved a newborn baby who, a few hours after birth, has developed a strong need for food. At this age, we cannot assume that babies know that feeding will reduce their need for food; they have not yet been fed through their mouths. According to the motivation theorist, babies' hunger drives compel them to activity. The hunger drive accounts for much of the infant's early crying behavior. The longer babies go hungry, the longer they can be expected to cry. When they are fed, the motivation theorist assumes, drive reduction takes place; crying behavior ceases. As babies get older, they experience drive reduction through their mothers' breast many times and come to learn that breast-feeding reduces hunger drive. Now, according to the motivation theorist, motivated behavior occurs: the babies have learned to direct their activities toward obtaining a very particular goal, the breast. At this point, many mothers report that their babies have learned also to communicate their needs. Mothers now can tell by the particular sound of their babies' voices that they are hungry.

Another drive often discussed by motivation theorists is the *exploratory drive*. According to some psychologists, infants have a need to explore their environments. This need is manifested through a variety of exploratory activities: throwing toys, putting objects in their mouths, touching things with their hands. Exploratory play is thought by many psychologists to be a necessary part of learning.

Much of babies' learning comes through imitation of adult behavior. Early imitative responses involve immediate repetition of what the baby sees and hears. Familiar gestures and sounds are copied. In the beginning, babies are not able to reproduce what they see and hear with much accuracy. They have very short memory spans, so are able to imitate only what has most recently occurred. As they get older, however, imitative responses become more and more accurate. Toward the end of the second year, young children imitate sounds with great accuracy and may deliberately imitate behavior they have seen or heard hours or even days earlier (Piaget, 1951). Parents of babies can learn a lot about their offsprings' developing verbal behavior by doing just what developmental researchers do: listen in on the baby when he or she is alone in the crib.

Much of the information gathered by psychologists on infant vocalization has been obtained from tape recordings made in the nursery while the baby imitated sounds heard during the day.

The infant also is capable of learning simple intellectual skills and cognitive strategies. Quite early, infants develop their own strategies for responding to the environment. Operant-conditioning studies using five-month-old babies have shown that infants at this age can learn to make certain responses in order to obtain the maximum amount of reinforcement possible (Papousek, 1967). However, once babies have learned to make specific responses in specific situations, it is very difficult for them to change their behavior. This is true even when these responses are no longer useful to them (Appleton et al., 1975). This inability to change behavior when it is no longer helpful may be the reason babies develop the concept of permanence so very slowly. It takes eighteen months of development for the young child to learn that his teddy bear has not vanished from the universe when his mother takes it away to wash it and, further, to learn that he should look for the teddy bear in the laundry room where he last saw his mother taking it, rather than on the toy shelf where it sits each morning.

Emotional behavior—that is, behavior expressive of the infant's feelings —apparently is not present at birth (Landreth, 1967). Even though the baby cries, this crying seems to be a reflexive response rather than an emotional one. Watson (1919) first described what he called "response systems" present in the neonate at birth. He identified three major ones: (1) love—characterized by a calm demeanor elicited in the neonate by gently stroking; (2) fear—an outgrowth of the startle response elicited by sudden movements, loss of support, or loud sudden noise; and (3) rage—crying, excited movement, and a flushing color of the face, caused primarily by preventing movement of the infant's arms and legs. We know now that Watson's early description of the neonate is not an accurate one. For one thing, as noted earlier, swaddled babies usually exhibit quiet behavior and not rage.

Bridges (1932) gave a somewhat more accurate picture of developing emotional behavior in the infant. She suggested that neonatal behavior is expressive of one emotion only: excitement. According to Bridges, other emotions develop gradually and are characterized by an increasing number of responses as the infant gets older. For example, noticeable fear responses first became apparent at about one month, noticeable delight at two months. Later, anger, fear, disgust, jealousy, and other emotions gradually make their appearance.

Why do different emotional behaviors appear at different ages? Some psychologists, as Bridges, assume simply that emotional behavior ma-

Social-Emotional Behavior

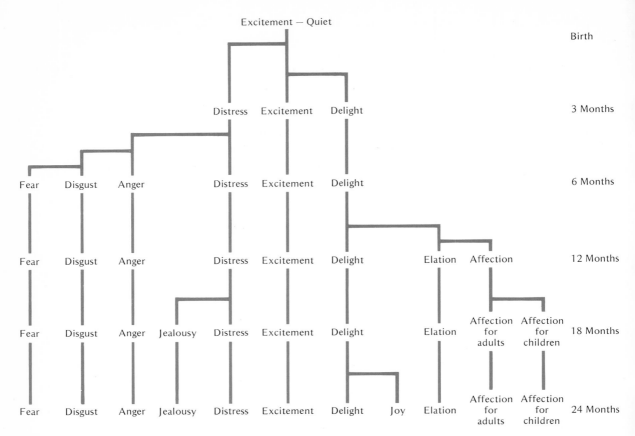

Fig. 6.2 Bridges' theory of emotional development. (From K. M. Bridges, Emotional development in early infancy, *Child Development* 3 (1932): 324–342. Reprinted by permission of The Society for Research in Child Development, Inc. Copyright © 1932.)

tures. Others theorize that interaction with the environment significantly affects the developing emotional response. At any rate, it is clear that the ability of objects in the environment to affect emotional responding increases with the age of the child. In addition, the range of objects that can produce excitation and, later, distress is greater than the range of those that elicit calm behavior (Reese and Lipsitt, 1970).

Fear responses and attachment Loud noises, sharp movements, lack of support, and pain all can produce what psychologists call "fear" in a one-month-old baby. The response used to express this fear usually is crying. Mothers of very young infants generally can soothe their babies with soft noise, gentle movement, and gentle contact. Mothers of young infants often hold their babies when they want them to sleep, cooing softly and rocking them.

Later, when babies reach seven to eight months, they develop feelings of attachment to their mothers or caretakers. Stranger anxiety—i.e., fear of strange people—first appears in babies at about this age and reaches a peak at about eight months. The typical response of the fearful baby to a new face is low whimpering and clinging to the mother.

According to some psychologists, attachment is the natural result of the infant's associating his or her mother with drive reduction (satisfaction of needs). Attachment affects the baby's development of affectional responses and also triggers development of a strong fear of separation from the mother. Separation anxiety occurs most frequently at about ten to twelve months (Bowlby, 1951, 1958, 1969). Learning theorists suggest that separation and stranger anxiety are a result of the baby's inability at this age to develop appropriate responses in unexpected situations with unfamiliar people (Bronson, 1972). The baby has learned which responses are appropriate in interactions with his or her mother, but has not yet learned what responses are appropriate in interactions with others. A good example of fear caused by not knowing how to respond is the baby who sees a stranger, watches him for some time without moving or changing facial expression, and then suddenly bursts into tears. The initial presence of the stranger did not produce the tears; rather, in this case, the tears appear to be the result of the infant not knowing just what to do.

Many acquired fears—that is, those that are learned—appear after about nine months of age. In Chapter 3, we discussed the case of Baby Albert who was classically conditioned to fear white rats and other soft, furry animals. Fear responses to many other stimuli are learned through conditioning processes. Fear responses also are learned through modeling. Mothers who scream when they see mice in the kitchen are likely to have children who also scream at the sight of mice.

Social smiling Smiling is another response that has received attention from child psychologists. Reflexive smiling occurs at birth. It appears in bursts and occurs more frequently in premature babies than in full-term infants. After two-and-a-half to three months, babies smile in response to many objects in their environment. By far, the stimulus that produces the greatest amount of smiling is the human face. At four months, infants will smile at faces that smile back (Brackbill, 1967). They even will smile at a photograph of a human face (Ende and Harmon, 1972). By seven months, babies learn not only to smile at faces, but to respond differently to different facial expressions (Ahrens, 1954). Wolff (1963) charted the course of babies' smiles in response to human faces. In Wolff's study, the age at which smiling behavior peaked was somewhere between sixteen and twenty weeks.

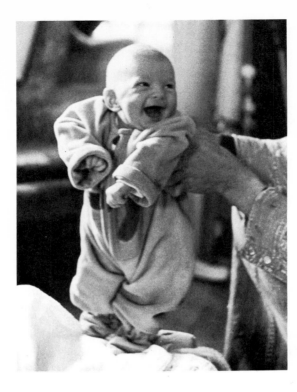

Delight responses first become apparent at two months.

Developmental Tests   A number of tests have been designed to measure the infant's developmental state, so that any one infant can be meaningfully compared with other infants of the same age. Because children under two years of age cannot solve complex cognitive problems, most scales make use of sensorimotor perceptual tasks for this age level. Gross motor behavior, vocalization and language behavior, fine motor behaviors, and social behaviors are studied in relation to sensorimotor abilities. Fig. 6.3 shows some of the tasks that appear on a typical and popular developmental test, the Denver Developmental Screening Test.

Psychologists generally agree that the developmental state of an infant in the first year, as measured by these tests, is a poor predictor of later development. Data seems to suggest, however, that cognitive and perceptual-motor development are related. For example, items on the California First Year Mental Scale that measure perceptual-motor ability have the greatest predictive value for estimating later cognitive ability. Such items include problems requiring eyehand coordination, attention, and ability to continue searching for an oject after it is hidden (Stone et al., 1973).

Fig. 6.3 The Denver Developmental Screening Test. ▶

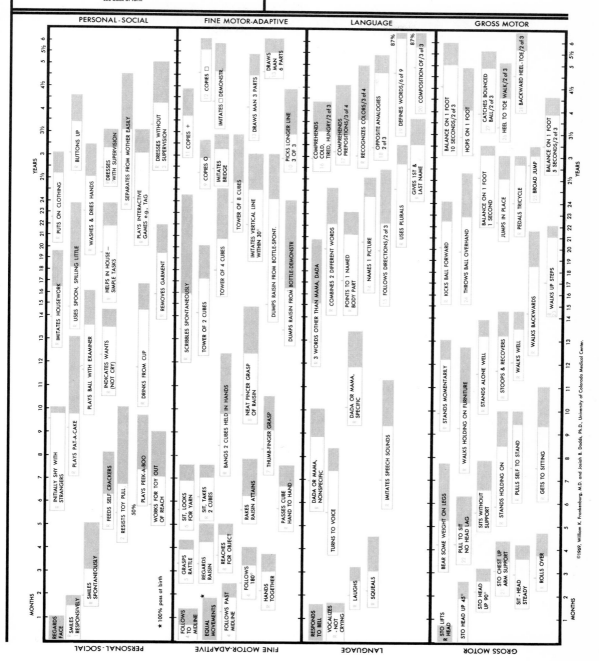

DENVER DEVELOPMENTAL SCREENING TEST

1. Try to get child to smile by smiling, talking or waving to him. Do not touch him.
2. When child is playing with toy, pull it away from him. Pass if he resists.
3. Child does not have to be able to tie shoes or button in the back.
4. Move yarn slowly in an arc from one side to the other, about 6" above child's face. Pass if eyes follow 90° to midline. (Past midline; 180°)
5. Pass if child grasps rattle when it is touched to the backs or tips of fingers.
6. Pass if child continues to look where yarn disappeared or tries to see where it went. Yarn should be dropped quickly from sight from tester's hand without arm movement.
7. Pass if child picks up raisin with any part of thumb and a finger.
8. Pass if child picks up raisin with the ends of thumb and index finger using an over hand approach.

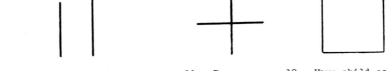

9. Pass any enclosed form. Fail continuous round motions.
10. Which line is longer? (Not bigger.) Turn paper upside down and repeat. (3/3 or 5/6)
11. Pass any crossing lines.
12. Have child copy first. If failed, demonstrate

When giving items 9, 11 and 12, do not name the forms. Do not demonstrate 9 and 11.

13. When scoring, each pair (2 arms, 2 legs, etc.) counts as one part.
14. Point to picture and have child name it. (No credit is given for sounds only.)

15. Tell child to: Give block to Mommie; put block on table; put block on floor. Pass 2 of 3. (Do not help child by pointing, moving head or eyes.)
16. Ask child: What do you do when you are cold? ..hungry? ..tired? Pass 2 of 3.
17. Tell child to: Put block on table; under table; in front of chair, behind chair. Pass 3 of 4. (Do not help child by pointing, moving head or eyes.)
18. Ask child: If fire is hot, ice is ?; Mother is a woman, Dad is a ?; a horse is big, a mouse is ?. Pass 2 of 3.
19. Ask child: What is a ball? ..lake? ..desk? ..house? ..banana? ..curtain? ..ceiling? ..hedge? ..pavement? Pass if defined in terms of use, shape, what it is made of or general category (such as banana is fruit, not just yellow). Pass 6 of 9.
20. Ask child: What is a spoon made of? ..a shoe made of? ..a door made of? (No other objects may be substituted.) Pass 3 of 3.
21. When placed on stomach, child lifts chest off table with support of forearms and/or hands.
22. When child is on back, grasp his hands and pull him to sitting. Pass if head does not hang back.
23. Child may use wall or rail only, not person. May not crawl.
24. Child must throw ball overhand 3 feet to within arm's reach of tester.
25. Child must perform standing broad jump over width of test sheet. (8-1/2 inches)
26. Tell child to walk forward, ⟫⟫⟫⟫➤ heel within 1 inch of toe. Tester may demonstrate. Child must walk 4 consecutive steps, 2 out of 3 trials.
27. Bounce ball to child who should stand 3 feet away from tester. Child must catch ball with hands, not arms, 2 out of 3 trials.
28. Tell child to walk backward, ◀⟫⟫⟫⟫ toe within 1 inch of heel. Tester may demonstrate. Child must walk 4 consecutive steps, 2 out of 3 trials.

DATE AND BEHAVIORAL OBSERVATIONS (how child feels at time of test, relation to tester, attention span, verbal behavior, self-confidence, etc,):

Fig. 6.3 (Cont.)

Studies using the Bayley Scale, another popular scale of development, show that, before fifteen months, no differences in developmental scores can be determined for babies of different races, sexes, birth orders, geographical locations, or parent educations (Bayley, 1965). This seems to suggest that many of the ability differences we observe in older children are related to their experiences.

Thus far, our discussion of development has focused on the so-called average child during the first two years of life. Age norms have been given for many different aspects of development to provide as broad a picture as possible of the various ways children can be expected to change with chronological age. But the ranges and rates of human development actually are highly variable. Although most babies develop according to the patterns described, the "average" classification is extremely wide and comprises an enormous number of describable individual differences. Shirley (1933) reported that the average child walks alone at fifteen months. But many babies walk alone before fifteen months, while many others first walk after this age. Why the difference?

Psychologists agree that many different hereditary factors control the individual development of each child (see Chapter 4). In addition, many individual differences are the result of environmental factors. The uterine environment has a tremendous effect on the infant even before birth and, in many ways, affects all later development. Newborns exhibit a variety of individual differences in behavior. For example, some newborn infants demonstrate states of activity and sensitivity to stimulation much more clearly than do others (Stone and Smith, 1973).

In this section, we examine how the postnatal environment affects developmental trends. Two important variables are given consideration: the amount and type of sensory stimulation given the infant and the nutrition provided. Later, in Chapter 7, we discuss these same variables once again in relation to specific child-rearing practices and socialization processes.

INDIVIDUAL DIFFERENCES IN DEVELOPMENT

Effects of Sensory Stimulation

Sensory stimulation is necessary to development. Some psychologists, while not particularly concerned about the specific *kinds* of stimulation provided, do assert that stimulation *per se* is critically important to overall development. They further state that there is a minimum amount of stimulation necessary. Children receiving less than this amount can be expected to be developmentally impaired (Brossard and Decarie, 1971).

Other psychologists believe that certain types of stimulation are necessary to development. Harlow's classic study of infant monkeys discussed in Chapter 1 demonstrated the need for tactile contact from a live monkey mother in order for normal development to occur. Harlow compared the behavior of monkeys reared with their own mothers with that of baby monkeys kept in isolation with monkey-mother surrogates (Harlow, 1962). He noted that all babies raised with their own mothers eventually developed normal adult sexual behavior and, in the case of females, maternal responses to their offspring. Monkeys raised with surrogate mothers and, therefore, deprived of the same touch contact did not develop normally in respect to either of these behaviors.

Concern about the amount of stimulation provided a child is based, in part, on evidence accumulated over a number of years and from many different societies. Infants institutionalized in orphanages or hospitals long have been known to display retarded physical and psychological development. In addition, some studies have shown them to exhibit far less exploratory behavior (Collard, 1971). Many studies comparing infants reared in institutions with infants of similar background reared in their own homes have indicated that institutionalized children are more often retarded. Psychologists have suggested that a primary cause of this retardation is the relatively unstimulating institutional environment (Casler, 1965, 1968). Rheingold (1960) reported that infants in typical institutions receive less verbal stimulation than infants reared in situations where there is more opportunity to interact with a caretaker. It has been suggested that another cause of retardation in institutionalized infants is lack of tactile stimulation and less holding of these infants by their caretakers. When babies cry and are picked up by their mothers, they become more visually alert and begin to scan their environments (Korner, 1964). Conversely, Soviet psychologists have reported that babies who are *not* picked up frequently receive less vestibular and kinesthetic feedback. The development of these babies often is retarded (Kistiakovskaia, 1960). Soviet belief in the importance of handling babies has resulted in large numbers of caretakers being provided in the state nurseries.

In some situations, lack of attention and stimulation in infancy can cause serious retardation. Rheingold and Bayley (1959) studied sixteen babies living in a state institution for the first nine months of their lives. Half of the babies in the study were provided extra attention by one caretaker from the sixth to the eighth month. Tested after a year, these babies were more socially responsive than the babies who had not received this special attention. However, they did no better on tests of developmental progress than did babies who had received much less attention. The authors suggested that this was an example of too little attention provided too late. Their hypothesis was confirmed by another study conducted ten years later on children reared in their own homes by low-income mothers (Gordon, 1969). In this two-year study, low-income mothers were specially trained in ways to stimulate their infants. At the end of the first twelve months, the stimulated infants did far better on developmental tests than did their nonstimulated counterparts. After the experiment had been discontinued for twelve months, however, differences in development between the two groups of babies disappeared. Adequate stimulation, to be effective, must begin early and continue.

Just as studies have shown that not holding babies is related to developmental retardation, picking up of babies clearly is related to advanced rates of development. Advanced development of infants in Uganda and other African countries frequently has been reported (Ainsworth, 1967). Babies in these countries usually are carried upright on their mothers' backs. They are in constant skin contact with their mothers and also are handled frequently. Many Ugandan infants can hold up their heads and straighten their backs when pulled to a sitting position in the first days of life. Also, they can follow moving objects with their eyes. This advanced rate continues, apparently for many months. In one study (Geber, 1958), some babies were reported to sit unsupported for a few seconds at three months. By five months, all babies studied could sit unsupported for thirty minutes. Apparently, rapid development is related to the particular style of handling. When Ugandan infants are reared in the European tradition of a horizontal crib position and more rigid feeding schedule, they do not exhibit this advanced development. Similarly, Soviet psychologists have shown that babies who are handled continuously increase their rates of development dramatically. Some babies, they report, learned to turn themselves over "four months ahead of schedule" with proper exercise and handling.

All of this information has led to a variety of experimental programs designed to increase stimulation for children in the first few years of life. One such program, begun in the United States in 1964, was the Children's Center Program at Upstate Medical Center in Syracuse, New York (Caldwell, 1968). Caldwell's program was an educationally oriented day-care center for children aged six months to three years. The program emphasized areas of development involving sensory, perceptual, and cognitive functioning, including motor agility, fine muscle coordination, ability to attend and to discriminate, classification and evaluation, formation of learning sets, problem solution, memory, attention span, and communication abilities. Sensory-stimulation aspects of the program resulted in significant gains in developmental progress. Caldwell often provided stimulation for the infants in her program by encouraging exploratory play, reported earlier in the text as important for development.

Psychologists, biologists, and physicians agree that proper nutrition is necessary for optimal growth and development. Nutrition and stimulation often go hand in hand. It is thought that the reason some babies in our society do not thrive is a lack of both (Ramey et al., 1975).

In Chapter 5, we learned that early malnutrition produces detrimental and often irreversible effects on the development of the skeletal system,

Effects of Nutritional Status

bodily organs, brain, and other parts of the central nervous system. In the prenatal period of development, the brain develops faster than other parts of the body and is particularly vulnerable to damage. This rapid growth rate and consequent vulnerability continues through the first two years of postnatal life (Altman, 1971). Malnutrition during these two years can stunt both ability to learn and memory (Keppel, 1968). Nutritional defects have been cited as the cause of fundamental attentional deficit (as measured by the inability of one-year-olds to make orienting responses) (Lester, 1975). Protein deficiency has been related to apathy as well as to abnormalities in electroencephalographic records of infants (Eichenwald and Fry, 1969). Abnormally slow growth in height and weight, anemia, and emotional problems all have been associated with malnutrition of infants in the United States, as well as elsewhere (*Hunger, U.S.A.*, 1968).

More than half the children in the world are suffering from the effects of early malnutrition. The National Nutrition Survey (1965) indicated alarming dietary deficiency in the poverty population of the United States. Of course, high income alone does not ensure good diet. According to the survey, the affluent spend far more on nonnutritive potato chips, soft drinks, and liquor than do the poor. The nutritional adequacy of the average American diet has decreased considerably over the past two decades.

This Guatemalan infant shows the effects of malnutrition during the prenatal and postnatal periods.

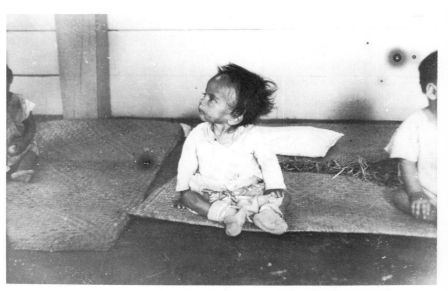

Direct and indirect effects of nutrition on the developing child

Nutrition begins to affect the life of a baby both directly and indirectly long before the child is born. Directly, as we learned in Chapter 5, the baby's health and future development is affected by the adequacy of prenatal nutrition, particularly during periods of rapid growth. Indirectly, the nutrition of the baby's ancestors can affect its development through effects on the uterine environment.

After a baby is born, he or she is still vulnerable to the stress of nutritional deficiencies. Nutritional deprivation can damage the developing brain and thereby impede mental development. Learning difficulties or, in extreme cases, mental deficiencies can result. Nutritional deficiency can also indirectly affect mental capability. One researcher (Cravioto, 1969) has pointed out three ways in which this can happen: (1) Children who are undernourished become ill more often than properly nourished children, and thus miss out on many opportunities to learn. (2) Hungry, undernourished children frequently have low levels of concentration and low motivation in school. (3) Malnutrition is linked to poverty and lack of food. The undernourished child often is deprived of the social learning situations associated with mealtime in middle-class families, for they do not have the opportunity to participate in dinner-table conversation.

Infant Mortality

In spite of the decline in infant mortality in recent years, the United States now ranks only thirteenth in the world in terms of birth risks. That is, babies born in twelve other countries have a lower probability of dying during infancy than do babies born in America. Infant mortality has been related to a large number of factors, among them poor nutritional status. Income, race, education of the infant's parents, and mother's age all are correlated to rate of infant mortality. Almost twice as many nonwhite as white babies die each year in the United States (U.S. Department of Health, Education and Welfare, 1970).

Clearly, education in child care and nutrition, as well as increased medical facilities for the poor, would go a long way toward helping to change these statistics. In point of fact, the federal government has taken steps in a number of states to begin to wage battle against infant mortality. Chapter 5 discussed programs designed to assist pregnant women and their babies. In addition, comprehensive medical care for low-income infants and children now is provided in some areas. Federally subsidized maternal- and infant-care projects that provide maternity care as well as care for mother and child during the first year came into being in 1964. $43,000,000 in federal funds were contributed to this program in 1972. Federal subsidization of the Children and Youth Project, which provides comprehensive medical care for low-income children, was authorized in 1965. The total federal appropriation in 1972 was $47,000,000 (Robinson et al., 1973). Unfortunately, in more recent years, subsidies to these and other programs related to child welfare have been cut back because of lack of funds (See Vetoing Children, 1975).

Sudden death syndrome: the mysterious crib deaths One major cause of death for infants between three weeks and six months of age is the mysterious crib death known medically as sudden-infant-death syndrome (SIDS). It is believed that 10,000 babies in the United States die of this syndrome annually. SIDS babies apparently are healthy when they are put to sleep for the night or for a nap. They are later found dead in their cribs, with no clue as to cause of death. Parents of SIDS babies frequently report feelings of great guilt, together with fear that, somehow, insufficient attention has been the cause. One commonly accepted belief is that these infants somehow have suffocated in pillows or loose garments, a speculation that never has been verified as a cause of SIDS. Although physicians have not yet determined the origin of this syndrome, they have identified certain recurrent features. Crib death occurs

Clues to crib death

On the morning of December 12, 1973, a young housewife in Maplewood, New Jersey got up to give her six-week-old baby his early morning feeding. The baby was sound asleep, so his mother decided not to wake him up, but lay down on a couch nearby to wait for him to cry. Three hours later, she awoke with a start: the baby hadn't awakened at all. Lifting his blanket, she noted that he had squirmed to the foot of the crib. As soon as she lifted him up, she knew he was dead.

Autopsy showed that this baby, as some 10,000 others in the United States each year, died of sudden infant death syndrome, commonly known as SIDS. Doctors, as yet, have no complete understanding of the malady's cause. This baby, as other SIDS babies, had gone to sleep the night before with no apparent symptoms of illness: he seemed a perfectly happy, healthy, normal baby.

Not the least tragic side of SIDS is the crushing guilt parents of SIDS babies often feel. The mother of the baby just described was convinced at first that, if she had awakened her son when she first got up to feed him, he perhaps wouldn't have died. She wondered whether he had suffocated in the diapers lying at the foot of the crib. Doctors explained the peculiar syndrome to her and thereby relieved some of her anxieties. The cause of SIDS is unknown, although some evidence indicates that SIDS babies have, for some reason, respiratory difficulties. Researchers suspect neurologic problems, perhaps involving the respiratory centers of the brain.

For many parents, however, guilt persists. Marriages have been destroyed in the aftermath of SIDS. The National Foundation for Sudden Infant Death has been designed to promote medical research on the problem, as well as to help SIDS parents understand what is and what is not known about this baffling disease (*Newsweek*, 1976).

most frequently in winter. There is increased incidence of crib death among premature infants. These factors have led physicians to hypothesize a number of causes, including suffocation due to sudden respiratory infection, suffocation due to regurgitated food, and failure of the breathing mechanism during sleep. Autopsies of infants who have died from SIDS consistently show excessive red-blood-cell production and thickened arterial walls. The results of these autopsies are consistent with theories that suggest that the infant has suffered from lack of oxygen. The fact that premature babies more frequently die from crib death than do full-term babies further suggests the possibility that immature breathing mechanisms partly account for the respiratory failure.

SUMMARY

The development of behavior proceeds rapidly during the first two years of life, in both quantitative and qualitative fashion. Infant sensory and perceptual abilities improve and, as they do, the ability of the infant to function in his or her environment also increases. The infant gradually develops prehensile ability, as well as the ability to move about. Communication with others also increases.

The period encompassing the child's first two years was referred to by Piaget as the period of sensorimotor development. During this period, the most easily observable changes in infant behavior are related to sensory and motor abilities. Many other changes take place at this time as well. The relationship between sensorimotor and cognitive development during this period is extremely complex. The development also of social-emotional behavior is affected in many different ways by how young children learn to think and problem solve at this time.

Although children tend to be similar in many aspects of their development, individual differences are quite normal. Sensory stimulation and nutrition are examples of two variables that can lead to significant individual differences in ability, attention, and rate of development during the first two years.

QUESTIONS FOR THOUGHT AND REVIEW

1 How do sensorimotor abilities increasingly affect the ability of the developing child to manipulate his or her environment? Which sensorimotor abilities do you think are most important to this manipulation? Why? (For review, see pp. 176–191.)

2 Piaget has stated that the sensorimotor period is necessary for later intelligent functioning. Explain exactly what he meant by this statement. (For review, see pp. 187–191.)

3 Are separation anxiety and stranger anxiety learned? Explain. (For review, see pp. 193–195.)

4 The author of this text has identified sensory stimulation as a variable that affects development in major ways. What is the basis of this opinion? Do you agree? Why? (For review, see pp. 199–201.)

FOR FURTHER
READING

Appleton, T., R. Clifton, and S. Goldberg. The development of behavioral competence in infancy. In F. Horowitz, ed., *Review of Child Development Research*. Chicago: University of Chicago Press, 1974. This chapter is devoted to careful descriptions of the behavior expected of infants at each stage of development. The charts describing particular aspects of behavioral development month by month are particularly useful to students seeking detailed account of what to expect of infant behavior.

Corbin, C. *A Textbook of Motor Development*. Dubuque, Iowa: Brown, 1973. Corbin's text does for motor development what Appleton et al. have done for behavioral development. Particularly useful are the stage-by-stage charts describing in clear detail what to expect as the infant increases in age.

Gesell, A., and C. Amatruda. *Developmental Diagnosis: Normal and Abnormal, 2nd Edition*. New York: Hoeber, 1947. Gesell, the famous stage-dependent developmental psychologist, presents here a comparison of average development with development that deviates from the average. This classic text provides an excellent explanation of individual differences in development and the stage-dependent approach to understanding children.

Lehane, S. *Help Your Baby Learn: 100 Piaget-Based Activities for the First Two Years of Life*. New York: Prentice-Hall, 1976. In *Help Your Baby Learn*, Dr. Lehane shows how to recognize subtle developmental changes and explains Piaget-based activities parents can use to facilitate infant development as their babies become ready to learn.

Lipton, E., A. Steinschneider, and J. Richmond. Swaddling, a child care practice: historical, cultural, and experimental observations. *Pediatrics*, Part II, March 1965. This is an excellent article for anyone interested in swaddling. The variations and extent of swaddling of infants is examined not only historically, but cross-culturally as well.

REFERENCES

Ahrens, R. Beitrage zur entwicklung des physiogriomig und mimiker kennes. Cited in T. Appleton, R. Clifton, and S. Goldberg, Development of Behavioral Competence. In F. Horowitz, ed., *Review of Child Development Research*. Chicago: University of Chicago Press, 1975, p. 4.

Ainsworth, M. *Infancy in Uganda: Infant Care and the Growth of Love*. Baltimore: Johns Hopkins Press, 1967.

Altman, J. Nutritional deprivation and neural development. In M. Sterman, D. McGinty, and A. Adinolfi, eds., *Brain Development and Behavior*. New York: Academic Press, 1971.

Appleton, T., R. Clifton, and S. Goldberg. The development of behavioral competence in infancy. In F. Horowitz, ed. *Review of Child Development Research*. Chicago: University of Chicago Press, 1975, p. 4.

Bayley, N. Comparisons of mental and motor test scores for ages 1–15 months by sex, birth order, race, geographical location, and education of parents. *Child Development* 36 (1965): 379–412.

Bower, T., J. Broughton, and M. Moore. Demonstration of intention in the reaching behavior of neonate humans. *Nature* 228 (1970): 679–781.

Bowlby, J. Maternal care and mental health. *Bulletin of the World Health Organization* 3 (1951): 355–534.

Bowlby, J. The nature of the child's tie to his mother. *International Journal of Psychoanalysis* 39 (1958): 1–34.

Bowlby, J. *Attachment and Loss*. Attachment, vol. 6. New York: Basic Books, 1969.

Brackbill, Y. The use of social reinforcement in conditioning smiling. In Y. Brackbill and G. Thompson, eds., *Behavior in Infancy and Early Childhood*. New York: Free Press, 1967, pp. 616–625.

Brackbill, Y., and M. Koltsova. Conditioning and learning. In Y. Brackbill, ed., *Infancy and Early Childhood*. New York: Free Press, 1967, pp. 207–289.

Braine, M. The ontogeny of English phrase structure: the first phase. *Language* 39 (1963): 1–13.

Bridges, K. Emotional development in early infancy. *Child Development* 3 (1932): 324–342.

Bronson, G. Infants' reactions to unfamiliar persons and novel objects. *Monographs of the Society of Research in Child Development* 37 (3, Serial No. 148).

Brossard, M., and T. Decarie. The effects of three kinds of perceptual-social stimulation on the development of institutionalized infants. In *Early Child Development and Care*, vol. 1. Great Britain: Gordon and Breach Science Publishers, Ltd., 1971, pp. 111–130.

Brown, R., and C. Fraser. The acquisition of syntax. In U. Bellugi and R. Brown, eds. The acquisition of language. *Monographs of the Society for Research in Child Development*, 1964, 29 (1, Serial No. 92), pp. 43–79.

Bruner, J. *Processes of Cognitive Growth: Infancy*. Heinz Werner Lecture Series No. 3. Worcester, Mass.: Clark University Press with Barre Publishers, 1968, pp. 35–64.

Caldwell, B. The fourth dimension in early childhood education. In R. Hess and B. Bear, *Early Education*. Chicago: Aldine, 1968.

Casler, L. The effects of extra tactile stimulation on a group of institutionalized infants. *Genetic Psychology Monographs* 71 (1965): 137–175.

Casler, L. Perceptual deprivation in institutional settings. In G. Newton and S. Levine, eds., *Early Experience and Behavior*. Springfield, Ill.: Charles C Thomas, 1968.

Chen, H., and O. Irwin. Infant speech vowel and consonant types. *Journal of Speech Disorders* 11 (1946): 27–29.

Church, J. *Language and the Discovery of Reality*. New York: Vintage, 1966.

Collard, R. Exploratory and play behaviors of infants reared in an institution and in lower- and middle-class homes. *Child Development* 42 (1971): 1003–1015.

Cravioto, J. Symposium presented at the Meeting of the American Association for the Advancement of Science. Boston, December 1969.

Dale, D. *Language Development*. Hinsdale, Ill.: Dryden Press, 1972.

Eichenwald, H., and P. Fry. Nutrition and learning. *Science* 163 (1969): 644–648.

Ende, R., and R. Harmon. Endogenous and exogenous smiling systems in early infancy. *Journal of the American Academy of Child Psychiatry* 11 (1972): 177–200.

Fantz, R. A method for studying depth perception in infants under six months of age. *Psychological Record* 11 (1961): 27–32.

Frankenburg, W., and J. Dodds. *Denver Developmental Screening Test*. Boulder, Colorado: University of Colorado Medical Center, 1969.

Geber, M. The psycho-motor development of African children in the first year, and the influence of maternal behavior. *Journal of Social Psychology* 47 (1958): 185–195.

Gesell, A., and C. Amatruda. *Developmental Diagnosis: Normal and Abnormal Child Development*. 2d ed. New York: Hoeber, 1947.

Gibson, E. *Principles of Perceptual Learning and Development*. New York: Appleton-Century-Crofts, 1969.

Gibson, E. The development of perception as an adaptive process. *American Scientist* 58 (1970): 98–107.

Gibson, E. The ontogeny of reading. *American Psychologist* 25 (1970): 136–143.

Gordon, I. *Early Child Stimulation Through Parent Education. Final Report to the Children's Bureau for Development of Human Resources*. Gainesville, Fla.: College of Education, University of Florida, 1969.

Harlow, H. The heterosexual affectional system in monkeys. *American Psychologist* 17 (1962): 1–9.

Hunger, U.S.A. A Report by the Citizens' Board of Inquiry into Hunger and Malnutrition in the United States. Boston: Beacon Press, 1968.

Hursh, D., and J. Sherman. The effects of parent-presented models and praise on the vocal behavior of their children. *Journal of Child Psychology* 15 (1973): 328–339.

Kagan, J. Continuity in cognitive development during the first year. *Merrill-Palmer Quarterly* 15 (1969): 101–119.

Kagan, J. Attention and psychological change in the young child. *Science* (1970): 826–832.

Kaplan, B. Malnutrition and mental deficiency. *Psychological Bulletin* 78 (1972): 321–334.

Kellaghan, J., and J. MacNamara. Family correlates of verbal reasoning ability. *Developmental Psychology* 7 (1972): 49–53.

Keppel, F. Food for thought. In N. Scrimshaw and J. Gordon, eds., *Malnutrition, Learning, and Behavior*. Cambridge, Mass.: M.I.T. Press, 1968.

Kistiakovskaia, M. Cited by I. London. A Russian report on the post-operative newly seeing. *American Journal of Psychology* 73 (1960): 478–482.

Korner, A. Some hypotheses regarding the significance of the individual differences at birth for later development. *The Psychoanalytic Study of the Child*. Vol. 19. New York: International Universities Press, 1964, pp. 58–82.

Korner, A., and E. Thoman. Visual alertness in neonates as evoked by maternal care. *Journal of Experimental Child Psychology* 10 (1970): 67–78.

Landreth, C. *Early Childhood Behavior and Learning*. New York: Knopf, 1967.

Lenneberg, E. Predictability of language development. *Science* 164 (1969): 635–644.

Lester B. Cardiac habituation of the orienting response to an auditory signal in infants of varying nutritional status. *Developmental Psychology* 11 (1975): 432–442.

Lipsitt, L., and H. Kaye. Conditioned sucking in the human newborn. *Psychonomic Science* 1 (1964): 29–30.

Lipton, E., A. Steinschneider, and J. Richmond. Swaddling, a child care practice. *Pediatrics* 35 (1965): 521–567.

Little, A. Eyelid conditioning in the human infant as a function of the ISI. Paper presented at meeting of the Society for Research in Child Development, Minneapolis, Minnesota, 1971.

Miller, W., and S. Ervin. The development of grammar in child language. In U. Bellugi and R. Brown, eds. The acquisition of language. *Monographs of the Society for Research in Child Development*, 1964, 29 (1, Whole No. 92), pp. 9–34.

Nelson, K. Structure and strategy in learning to talk. *Monographs of the Society for Research in Child Development*, 1973, 38 (1, Serial Number 149), pp. 1–2.

Newsweek. Medicine: clues to crib death, 5 January, 1976, p. 53.

Papousek, H. Experimental studies of appetitional behavior in human newborns and infants. In H. Stevenson, E. Hess, and H. Rheingold, eds., *Early Behavior: Comparative and Developmental Approaches*. New York: Wiley, 1967.

Piaget, J. *Dreams and Imitation*. New York: Norton, 1951.

Piaget, J. *The Origins of Intelligence in Children*. New York: Norton, 1952.

Piaget, J. *Psychology of Intelligence*. Totowa, N.J.: Littlefield, Adams, and Co., 1973. (Piaget's French edition, 1947)

Ramey, C., R. Starr, J. Pallas, C. Whitten, and V. Reed. Nutrition, response-contingent stimulation, and the maternal deprivation syndrome: results of an early deprivation program. *Merrill-Palmer Quarterly*, 1975: 45–53.

Reese, H., and L. Lipsitt. *Experimental Child Psychology*. New York: Academic Press, 1970.

Rheingold, H., and N. Bayley. The later effects of an experimental modification of mothering. *Child Development* 30 (1959): 363–372.

Rheingold, H., J. Gewirtz, and H. Ross. Social conditioning of vocalizations in the infant. *Journal of Comparative and Physiological Psychology* 52 (1959): 68–73.

Robinson, H., N. Robinson, M. Wolins, U. Bronfenbrenner, and J. Richmond. Early child care in the United States of America. *Early Child Development and Care* 2, no. 4 (1973).

Salapatek, P., and W. Kessen. Visual scanning of triangles by the human newborn. *Journal of Experimental Child Psychology* 3 (1966): 113–122.

Sherman, M., and I. Sherman. Sensorimotor responses in infants. *Journal of Comparative Psychology* 5 (1925): 53–68.

Shirley, M. *The First Two Years: A Study of Twenty-five Babies*. Institute of Child Welfare Monographs, No. 7. Minneapolis: University of Minnesota Press, 1933.

Siqueland, E., and L. Lipsitt. Conditioned head turning in human newborns. *Journal of Experimental Child Psychology* 3 (1966): 356–376.

Stone, L., H. Smith, and L. Murphy. *The Competent Infant*. New York: Basic Books, 1973.

U.S. Dept. of Health, Education and Welfare. *The Health of Children*. Washington, D.C.: U.S. Government Printing Office, 1970.

Vetoing Children. *New York Times*, 5 October 1975, E-7.

Watson, J. *Psychology from the Standpoint of a Behaviorist*. Philadelphia: Lippincott, 1919.

Watson, J., and R. Raynor. Conditioned emotional reactions. *Journal of Experimental Psychology* 3 (1920): 1-14.

Wolff, P. Observations on the early development of smiling. In B. Foss, ed., *Determinants of Infant Behavior II*. New York: Wiley, 1963, pp. 113–138.

Wolff, P. The causes, controls and organization of behavior in the neonate. *Psychological Issues* 5, no. 1 (1966): 17.

Infant Care

bjectives

After completing this chapter, you should be able to:

1

explain how the caretaker-infant relationship affects the developing infant and young child;

2

describe what can be expected to happen if adequate caretaker attention is not provided in the first two years of life;

3

describe how caretaking methods in other societies differ from ours, and select those methods that seem to have the greatest potential use in the United States;

4

list factors to consider in selecting a day-care arrangement for children under age two in the United States; advise a working mother or single parent on where and how to look for adequate day-care programs.

C hapter 6 focused on the general course of development during the first two years of an infant's life. What each infant becomes depends on this natural course, and also on environmental factors after birth. We have already discussed the effects of two such environmental factors, sensory stimulation and nutrition. In Chapter 7, we consider another major environmental factor: infant-caretaker interactions. Only recently have psychologists come to realize the importance of this factor in the development of infant responses, as well as in the socialization process and the shaping of personality.

INFANT CARE: AN EXTREMELY IMPORTANT OCCUPATION

From birth, infants are capable of processing information and responding to sensory input. They play active roles in their relationships with the environment. Since infant survival itself is dependent on the attention provided by caretakers, it is not at all surprising that the infant's earliest adaptive responses are made toward these caretakers.

Importance of the Infant-Caretaker Relationship

The relationship between infant and caretaker is mutual. Just as the infant's behavior is affected by the caretaker, the caretaker, in turn, is affected by the infant. The continuous feedback between the two has important consequences for each (Thoman, 1974). The behavior even of a newborn can exert a powerful influence, shaping the reaction of the nursing mother even before she brings her baby home from the hospital. For example, the mother of an infant who cries a great deal during feeding is likely to develop anxieties related to her ability (or inability) to care for her child. Unfortunately, the interaction is circular: the anxious mother, because of her anxiety, is more likely to have a baby who cries frequently. It's not surprising that researchers investigating the relationships between maternal needs and infant behavior report striking personality similarities between mothers and their infants (Caldwell et al., 1973; Murphy, 1971). It is important to remember, however, that these relationships, by themselves, do not prove causality. The mother-infant relationship is highly complex; both mother and infant affect one another in more and more complicated ways as the relationship grows.

Mothering Since the first caretaker in most societies usually is the mother, most psychologists refer to the earliest caretaking as "mothering." Kagan (1968) wrote, "The relationship between infant and mother is a ballet in which each partner responds to the steps of the other." To give a simple example from the earliest stage of this relationship, if the baby cries and the mother responds immediately by picking the baby up, she thereby increases the probability that her baby will cry in the future in order to be picked up. Similarly, the mother is more likely to go into the nursery if she hears her baby cry than if the baby lies quietly in the crib.

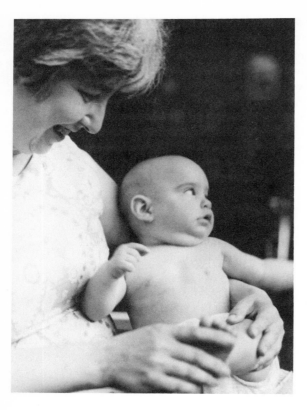

"Mothering."

The pattern of caretaking clearly is related to patterns of infant competence. The important factor appears not to be the specific rearing practice used—such as breast or bottle feeding or specific method of weaning or toilet training—but rather the interaction as measured by quality and amount of affection and stimulation given. Psychologists have shown that happy, loving mothers with positive accepting attitudes tend to provide warm physical handling. These same mothers tend to have affectionate, smiling babies, regardless of the specific rearing methods used. Mothers who provide a great deal of verbal stimulation tend to have babies with high levels of cognitive development (Clarke-Stewart, 1973). Conversely, mothers who feel they are unable to solve their day-to-day infant care problems satisfactorily tend to have infants who do not thrive. In one study of infants who were retarded both behaviorally and physically, even though they had no known organic dysfunction, researchers found that the mothers reported themselves "inadequate" (Leonard et al., 1966). Similarly, Carey (1968) found that mothers of colicky infants tended to be uncertain in their descriptions of their roles as mothers. These mothers gave attention to their infants, but often were inconsistent in their manners of responding to their offspring.

How much actual time is spent by most mothers interacting with their infants? In a provocative study of American families, Clarke-Stewart (1973) showed that, even though mothers of extremely young infants usually remain in close physical proximity to their offspring, actually a relatively short amount of time is spent interacting with them. The study made repeated observations in the homes of thirty-six American mothers and their first-born infants, from the time the infants were nine months old until they were eighteen months old. Only thirty-six percent of these infants' waking hours was spent in infant-mother interaction. The remainder of the time was spent in observing and interacting with other objects in the environment, such as toys, household objects, and, in some cases, other people. Between nine and eighteen months, the mothers

Mothering: a vastly underrated occupation

"Mothering" is the word usually used in this country to describe child rearing as well as the relationship that exists between the mother and her child. The reason for the term "mothering" is clear: until recently, at least in the United States, most infant care was done by mothers in their own homes.

Today, the increase in our country of working women, single-parent families, and communal child-rearing practices leads to many instances in which people other than the natural mothers are doing the actual caretaking. For this reason, many psychologists feel that the term "mothering" should be changed to "caretaking."

The following statement by White (1971), published by the Ontario Institute for Studies in Education, clearly expresses the importance of infant care, although the terms used in 1971 already are outmoded for many of today's modern families:

. . . the mother's direct and indirect actions with regard to her one- to three-year-old child are . . . the most powerful formative factors in the development of a preschool child. Further, I would guess that if a mother does a fine job

in the preschool years, subsequent educators such as teachers will find their chances for effectiveness maximized. Finally, I would expect that much of the basic quality of the entire life of an individual is determined by the mother's actions during these two years. Obviously, I could be very wrong about these declarative statements. I make them as very strong hunches that I have become committed to, as a kind of net result of all our inquiries into early development.

Let me quickly add that I believe most women are capable of doing a fine job with their one- to three-year-old children. Our study has convinced us that a mother need not necessarily have even a high school diploma, let alone a college education. Nor does she need to have very substantial economic assets. In addition, it is clear that a good job can be accomplished without a father in the home. In all of these statements I see considerable hope for future generations.*

* Reprinted with permission from B. White, Mothering, a vastly underrated occupation, *Interchange: A Journal of Educational Studies* 2, no. 2 (Toronto, Canada: The Ontario Institute for Studies in Education, 1971).

studied tended gradually to decrease both attention given and interactions with their offspring. At the same time, the infants developed reciprocal responses: they gradually spent less and less time showing interest in their mothers or responding directly to them, and they spent more and more time interacting with and displaying increasing interest in the outside world.

Fathering The roles of fathers in relation to infants and young children are similar across most cultures. Most societies relegate major responsibility of infant care to mothers, particularly when the infants are still extremely young. Fathers usually are assigned assisting roles. Only sometimes, when babies are bottle-fed, can fathers participate in the major task of feeding. (It is for this reason that many parents of today are choosing to bottle-feed rather than breast-feed their infants.) In situations in which mothers are not present, however, fathers play major roles in the infant-caretaker relationship. In at least one country, Sweden, the federal government has attempted legally to provide fathers opportunity to participate equally with their wives in the rearing of their infants. The expression "male emancipation" has been coined to denote the rights of husbands in Sweden to remain at home while their children are extremely young. At the time this book was being written, many Swedes were calling for legislation to provide fathers leaves of absence with pay to stay home with their newborn babies. This legislation would bring the rights of Swedish men in line with women who already have this right. A legislative study at the same time was seeking to find legal means to shorten the work shifts of *both* parents to give them more time at home.

Attachment Attachment, described earlier in Chapter 6, is an ongoing, durable, affectional tie between caretaker and infant. In other words, it describes what most people understand as "love." In infancy, attachment is manifested through clinging, following, smiling, and watching the caretaker, as well as crying and protesting at separation. Separation anxiety and fear of strangers were described in Chapter 6 as the natural result of caretaker-infant tie.

According to psychoanalytic thinkers, attachment is rooted in the natural makeup of the individual (Bowlby, 1969). Harlow, in his studies of infant monkeys, demonstrated that lower animals develop attachment at very early ages (see pp. 21–23 for a review of Harlow's research). Harlow called the monkeys' desire to cling to their soft, cloth mothers "attachment." When the baby monkeys were confronted with frightening stimuli, they ran to their soft mother surrogates and clung to them. According to this study, at least in monkeys, attachment seems to be related more to contact comfort than to feeding (Harlow, 1962; Harlow and Harlow, 1966; Harlow and Zimmerman, 1959).

Newborn infant with father.

Imprinting, discussed earlier, is another type of attachment that has been found to develop in some lower animals. If newly hatched goslings are presented within a short period after birth with a moving object other than the mother goose, they will continue to follow that object rather than their mother. In some sense, these babies are developing an attachment for the new object. Imprinting behavior has been noted in a number of animals, including goats, chickens, and sheep. Motherless lambs have been known to follow their human caretaker when their own mothers are not available (Lorenz, 1952, 1970, 1971).

Attachment behavior in humans ordinarily is learned and is oriented toward a specific person: the caretaker. Since the early caretaker in our society usually is the mother, this often is referred to as "maternal attachment." In a typical family setting, by four months of age, most infants already have developed an understanding of object permanence and are responding differently to their mothers than to other people. When they see their mothers, they usually smile and vocalize more readily. They also pay much more attention when their mothers are present. The rate of development of attachment varies greatly from infant to infant. Babies provided with the greatest amount of contact seem to develop the strongest attachments. However, no simple statement can be made about

Anaclitic identification begins when the infant is
physically and emotionally dependent on the mother.

progress during the first year. Not until two years of age can fairly typical attachment behavior be expected in most noninstitutionalized children
(Bowlby, 1969).

Identification Motivation theorists have pointed out that a primary
characteristic of human interaction is the forming of social bonds, first
for biological survival, later for psychological and cultural adaptation.
One such bond, identification, was defined in Chapter 3 as the process
by which individuals gradually adopt for themselves the behavior and
standards of another individual, who serves as a model by which they
can judge their own behaviors. Early or *anaclitic identification* first begins

in infancy and is a plausible explanation for attachment to the caretaker model (Sears et al., 1965).

Anaclitic identification begins when the infant is physically and emotionally dependent on the caretaker. In societies in which mothers usually are the first caretakers, identification usually is with them. At this stage, infants seek out their mothers' presence to satisfy their own basic needs. Later, according to motivation theorists, infants come to derive pleasure from mothers' presence alone. After babies are nine months of age or older, mothers gradually tend to spend less and less time interacting with them (Clarke-Stewart, 1973). Thus, as babies get older, they gradually are deprived of the pleasure of their mothers' presence. At this point, by "some mechanism not yet satisfactorily described," they begin to imitate their caretakers (Sears et al., 1965). Sounds and smiles are among the first imitated responses. Some psychologists hypothesize that babies use this early imitation as a substitute for the pleasure of their mothers' presence. Babies who learn quickly to imitate become less dependent on their mothers. They learn more easily to interact with other objects and people in the world around them. Later, children learn not only to copy maternal behaviors, but also to internalize them. The mothers' attributes gradually become part of the infants' "psychological organizations," so that they begin to react to events as their mothers would react (Kagan, 1958).

Anaclitic identification first involves imitation of the caretaker, and then identification of the perceived attributes. *Defensive identification*, in which children internalize the prohibitions of the caretaker-model, involves a similar process of imitation followed by identificaton. As an example, the baby's first word often is a prohibition: "No!" As children get older, they enjoy using this prohibition in situations in which they have seen their mothers use it.

According to motivation theorists, identification enables babies gradually to decrease their attachment to their caretakers. At the same time, it provides a primary vehicle through which acceptable and necessary responses for socialization are learned. Thus, factors necessary for identification are necessary also for the learning of socialization responses. Sears et al. (1965) listed these necessary factors as (1) high early dependency, (2) high adult nurturance, (3) high use of love-oriented discipline, and (4) clear presentation of models. All clearly require a caretaker who interacts frequently, consistently, and with warmth and affection.

Sex-role identification. Identification of sex role, in which individuals gradually internalize the role considered appropriate to a given sex and the reactions characteristic of that role, begins in infancy with caretaker identification. Since most caretakers in our society are mothers, most male and female infants identify first with women. In our own society, at least until the advent of the women's movement, female children have tended to continue this identification and usually have been rewarded for it. However, as male babies get older, they often learn through prohibition learning that imitation and identification of female sex-role behaviors are not appropriate. Boys thus learn appropriate sex-role responses through punishment and trial and error. If legislation permits Swedish fathers to remain at home to rear their infants, as we mentioned earlier, we will have new information regarding this identification process and the effects of father-infant relationships on sex-role identification.

Maternal deprivation   Care given infants is crucial to their development. What happens when the prime source of this care is removed abruptly? We know that brief separations, such as those caused by hospitalization, can produce disruptions in infant development. Disruption seems to be greater after six months than before (Landreth, 1967). Of course, many other potentially pertinent factors often accompany these disruptions—pain, illness, strange people and procedures, to name just a few. However, whatever the circumstances, maternal absence itself seems to be the key factor; infants tend to tolerate even surgery well as long as mothers stay with them in the hospital. For this reason, many hospital pediatric units now provide for "mother rooming-in."

Do parents perceive girl babies as different from boy babies?

When does sex stereotyping begin? A *Pittsburgh Press* article (Sex-typing, 1976) described two studies that seem to indicate this stereotyping begins in earliest infancy. According to the article, adjectives that parents use to describe their babies are related more to the sex of the babies than to their actual characteristics. Parents of newborn infants were asked within twenty-four hours after delivery whether their babies were boys or girls, and also what they were like. Daughters were rated as significantly softer, finer featured, smaller, and more inattentive, even though there was no difference in actual size or weight of male and female babies. Fathers tended to engage in more of this sex-typing than did mothers.

The expectations of these parents are in no way unusual. Expectations of sex-typed attributes and behaviors occur regularly in our society. A second study cited required college students to examine pictures of a week-old infant named Sandy and then to describe the baby. The subjects in this study exhibited sex-typing similar to that in the study just reported. Students who were told that Sandy was female proceeded to describe the baby as smaller, weaker, and more cuddly than did students who were told Sandy was a male.

As more fathers become primary caretakers, more information on father-infant
sex-role identification should become available.

Institutionalization. The effects of sensory deprivation on institutionalized infants were discussed in some detail in Chapter 6. The studies cited involved infants deprived not only of sensory stimuli, but also of maternal contact. Most studies of institutionalization have focused on children separated from their parents at early ages. Researchers have shown that these children display disrupted behavior ranging from listlessness, loss of appetite, and retardation of normal development to a general wasting away that can continue even to the point of death. Terms used by researchers to describe such gradual wasting away are hospitalism, or sometimes *marasmus*. Spitz (1945) reported that, during this century, one of the major orphanages in Germany had a mortality rate for children during the first year of life of over 70 percent. Spitz attributed this excessive rate to lack of mothering.

Other studies of institutionalization report similar developmental disruption. In a study of one hundred Lebanese orphan babies institutionalized in a Beirut orphanage, Dennis and Najarian (1957) reported that these babies exhibited continual listlessness. Toward the end of their first year, they showed significantly decreased abilities to perform, as measured by developmental scales, when compared with Lebanese infants of comparable backgrounds who were reared with their own families.

The caretakers in the Beirut orphanage in which Dennis and Najarian conducted their investigation provided for the physical needs of the babies in indifferent and apathetic ways. In addition, they appeared to be unresponsive to signs of interest or affection from the infants. Because of a large infant-caretaker ratio of 10:1, bottles often were propped by pillows during feeding and any contact during feeding was quite limited. Individual caretakers were not assigned to individual children, so that attachments to particular caretakers were not developed. Few toys were provided. Infants spent most of their time in cribs, later in playpens. Cribs were equipped with canvas sides, so that infants could not see out of them.

Skeels (1966) reported a twenty-year study of subjects who, as infants, had resided in a similarly impoverished orphanage. At the outset of the study, all were classified as mentally retarded. Skeels arranged for thirteen of these babies, all under two years of age, to be transferred from the orphanage to a resident institution for the mentally retarded. This institution, paradoxically, was able to provide more mothering and stimulation for the babies than the orphanage. Babies received individual attention from older retarded inmates who enjoyed serving as mother-figures. The babies played often with others and joined in group activities. Unlike the IQs of control subjects left in the original orphanage, the IQs of all thirteen of these babies increased sufficiently to permit later adoption. Skeel's twenty-year follow-up study reported finally that all thirteen subjects, when adults, were self-supporting, had gained economic independence, and exhibited no antisocial behavior. Control subjects, left in the unstimulating orphanage, had completed lower levels of education and were employed in considerably lower-level occupations. Only seven were employed at all and four remained institutionalized at adulthood.

It has been shown in a number of studies that the rate of infant and child development is increased in foster homes where one mother-figure is available to provide attention and stimulation. Skodak and Skeels (1945, 1949) wrote a series of reports describing 139 children placed in foster homes when they were less than six months old. In a longitudinal study that followed these children through adolescence, Skodak and Skeels found that their development continued to be above average. Further, their IQs were higher than would have been predicted on the basis of the IQs and backgrounds of their natural parents alone.

One versus many caretakers in institutionalized settings. We know today that institutions that do not provide rich interaction experiences, no matter how well they provide for other needs, will have developmentally impaired children. Spitz (1945) found similar apathy and retarded development in homeless and neglected World War II children. Although Spitz related this developmental impairment to lack of a single mothering figure, psychologists are by no means agreed as to the primary cause of the developmental damage. Institutionalized infants studied by Spitz, as well as by Dennis, Najarian, and Skeels, all were deprived of more than primary caretakers—they were deprived of environmental stimulation of *all* sorts. Many researchers have suggested that this lack of environmental stimulation was a much more important cause of retardation than lack of close association with any single caretaker figure (Casler, 1961; Gardner et al., 1961; Rheingold and Bayley, 1959).

In what ways did the few apathetic caretakers affect the development of the institutionalized infants studied by Dennis and Najarian? Clearly, they affected the infants both by their lack of presence and by their inability to interact directly with them. Even the presence of a caretaker's face is known to affect infant development. We learned in Chapter 6, for example, that babies show interest in human faces at early ages. Fantz (1961) showed that young babies show more interest even in line drawings of human faces than in other pattern types. But this interest is restricted to babies who see faces regularly. Fantz and Nevis (1967) showed that socially isolated infants show no more interest in human faces than in any other patterns presented them. Institutionalized Israeli infants were observed to smile less frequently at the presentation of a human face than do either family- or kibbutz-reared infants (Wolff, 1963). It is not surprising, therefore, that institutionalized babies who rarely have the opportunity even to see a human face are disrupted in their development.

Landreth (1967, p. 98) listed the following caretaker attributes as critical to optimal infant development: "amount of physical contact,

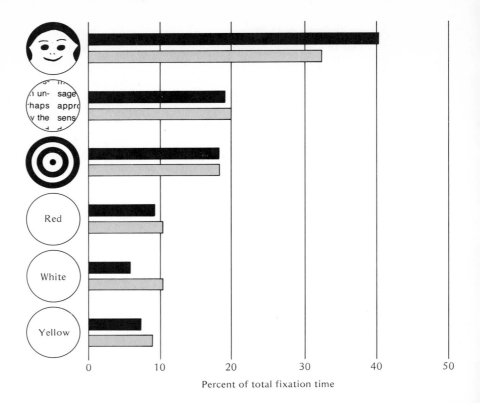

Fig. 7.1 Importance of pattern rather than color or brightness illustrated by infants' response to a face, a piece of newsprint, a bull's-eye, and plain red, white, and yellow disks. Black bars show the results for infants from two to three months old, gray bars for infants more than three months old. (From Robert L. Fantz, The origin of form perception, in *Scientific American*, Vol. 204. Copyright © 1961 by Scientific American, Inc. All rights reserved.)

speed of response, soothing, physical closeness, achievement stimulation, social stimulation, communication stimulation, stimulus adaptation, positive-affective expression, consistency, emotional involvement, acceptance-rejection, and individualization of care." Also cited were: "time spent looking at baby, looking at baby's face, talking, talking to infant, patting, showing affection, playing, holding, diapering, bathing, feeding, dressing, adjusting position, and rocking." These attributes could be contained in multiple as well as single caretaker figures.

In studies of multiple mothering in institutions, it is, of course, difficult to determine whether deficits are due to lack of one single maternal caretaker or to lack of other maternal behaviors. Chapter 6 described a study by Rheingold and Bayley (1959) of babies institutionalized for the first nine months of their lives. Of the sixteen babies studied, eight received attentive care by one person during the sixth through the eighth month. The other eight were provided the same amount of care, but by randomly selected caretakers. The eight babies assigned to single caretakers were reported to be socially more responsive than their peers. They did not score better on tests of developmental progress. One year later, however, no differences either in social responsiveness or in developmental progress were reported between the two groups. Rheingold and Bayley's conclusion was that if attentive mothering by a single caretaker *does* affect infant development, it does so only if provided for periods of time longer than the three-month duration of this study.

Stimulation, exploration, and play The importance of sensory stimulation as it relates to perceptual responding was described earlier in this chapter and also in Chapter 6. How does caretaker stimulation affect infant ability to explore and play with objects in the environment?

Nurseries in the jailhouse: a case of beneficial mutual interaction

The German government recently demonstrated its belief that babies should all be provided ample opportunity to interact with those individuals who will give them the greatest attention. In West Germany, mothers jailed for serious crimes are being given the chance to provide their children with love and support. The theory is that if preschool children are allowed to remain with these mothers, the children, the mothers, and, ultimately, society will benefit.

In the West German town of Preungesheimin, in a high-walled century-old prison, is the prison Kinderheim or "children's home." Completed in the spring of 1975 at a cost of $800,000, the Kinderheim is capable of housing twenty women prisoners and up to twenty-five of their children. The prisoners have been convicted of many crimes, including shoplifting, burglary, drug addiction, and prostitution.

What attention do the children in the Kinderheim receive? Their mothers live with them in a special section of the prison. Their cells are brightly painted and contain windows and modern furniture. Except for the forty hours per week that each mother is required to work in the prison, mothers are free to spend all of their time playing with their children, engaging in activities in the Kinderheim, or watching TV with them. Every three months, mothers are allowed to leave the prison to shop. With good behavior, each mother is allowed a brief vacation home with her child after six months.

Critics of the Kinderheim program make many of the same points that critics of prison reform in the United States have made. They suggest that the Kinderheim "coddles" its inmates so much that their return to the outside world may provide a rude shock. But of the fifty prison inmates who have thus far lived in Kinderheim and returned to the outside world, only one has been returned to prison. It appears that the mutual interaction of preschooler and mother, even in the confines of a prison, can be a highly beneficial one (Sheils and Agrest, 1976).

Many theorists, including Piaget, have argued that infant exploration of the objects in the immediate environment is the single most important learning experience of the child. Infant behavior during what Piaget called the circular reaction stages, in which babies repetitively hit their rattles or throw toys out of their playpens, is crucial in learning how the world works. As infants come in contact with increasing numbers of objects, they explore them tactilely. They learn their shapes, dimensions, slopes, edges and textures. They finger, grasp, push, pull, and learn the physical properties of the objects. Only then do they learn to use these objects in novel and creative ways.

In reviewing early studies of human infants, McCall (1974) reported that these studies suggested little relationship between types of mothering and exploratory behavior. Later studies comparing five- to seven-month-old infants related caretaker attentiveness and stimulation to a greater amount of visual exploration, tactile manipulation, and vocalization (Rubenstein, 1967). Infants tend to explore more when mothers are present. Home rearing, however, is not a necessary prerequisite for adequate stimulation. Caldwell (1968) showed in her preschool program that babies as young as six months can increase their cognitive, sensory, and perceptual functioning when wide and varied stimulation by many caretakers is provided.

Clearly, nonstimulating home environments provide less-than-adequate places for child development. Often, mothers who are passive rather than active in their interactions with their infants have children who sit apathetically in their playpens. Children whose mothers do not talk regularly to them tend to be retarded in their speech. The impact of verbal deprivation is most noticeable after eighteen months, and seems to be related both to the verbalizations of the mother and her socioeconomic background (Golden and Birns, 1971). Tulin (1971) found differences in working-class and middle-class ten-month-old infants in both the amount and ways they responded to their mothers' voices. Poverty children tend to score lower on tests of psychological development and respond less actively and with less interest to objects in their environments. Two variables related to this slowed development seem important: (1) intensity of the stimulation provided; and (2) the opportunity to hear vocal signs for specific objects, actions, and relationships. Retarded development, of course, is not always extreme. The impact of less extreme environmental variations has less effect on the developing infant.

ALTERNATIVE METHODS OF INFANT AND CHILD REARING

We have talked thus far about rearing of infants in situations where there is a ratio of one caretaker to one infant. We have also examined situations in which infants were removed from their caretakers and placed in environments that did not provide adequate caretaker-infant contact. Insufficient caretaker attention has been linked to retarded development. However, retardation of children raised in group situations certainly is not universal. In many tribal societies, children are raised in group settings without any noticeable detrimental effects. In addition, in many socialist countries today, as well as on Israeli kibbutzim, group infant and child rearing is practiced. In our own country, the increasing number of working mothers has led to new interest in day-care programs for infants as well as for young children. The decision by many young people to pursue alternate life-styles has resulted in a variety of types of communal child-rearing techniques. The evidence supplied thus far by psychologists seems to show that the children raised in these new settings, if given adequate amounts of attention, do not suffer the problems of the institutionalized children reported earlier. Communally raised children, in fact, exhibit a number of interesting and adaptive behavioral characteristics that are well worth examining.

Margaret Mead and other anthropologists have studied a variety of non-literate societies to determine, among other things, how child rearing and infant rearing affect development. Mead noted in a number of now-famous studies that, in societies in which infants and children are reared in groups by a number of caretakers, children do not develop attachment responses to one single person. However, these children also fail to develop separation anxiety and fear of strangers. Both failures, she asserted, are important assets in a society where change of companions is frequent. Mead concluded that attachment to a single caretaker is not necessary for all healthy, interpersonal relationships (Mead, 1935). These findings are extremely relevant in light of the current studies of communal and infant child rearing that we next discuss.

Anthropological Studies of Infant and Child Rearing

Nursery programs in the USSR Communal rearing in the Soviet Union begins usually at three months of age, when the Soviet mother first is able to bring her infant to the all-day center. Working mothers in the Soviet Union are given three months leave from their jobs with full pay after the birth of each child. After three months, large numbers of Soviet women bring their children to the state day-care program for rearing. Day-care centers are open during working hours and provide facilities for nutritional, medical, physical, and social care of infants and small children at nominal fees.

The Soviets have long known the importance of attention in the development of infants. As noted earlier, they have gone to great lengths to ensure that caretaker-infant ratios are kept low, particularly for the youngest infants. The caretaker-infant ratio in Soviet infant programs is reported to be 1:4. Attention is provided through continual visual and auditory stimulation, through exercise of muscles, and through constant physical contact. Brightly colored objects are available at all times for play and exploration. When babies are placed in playpens in Soviet preschools, they are never alone: Soviet playpens hold several babies at the

Communal Infant and Child Rearing in Modern Societies

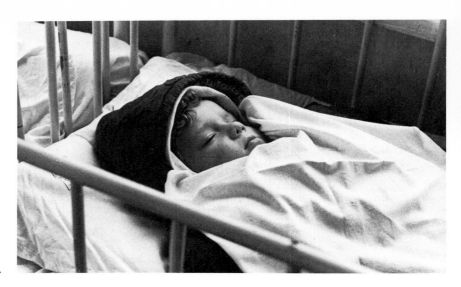

Child in a Soviet nursery naps on an open veranda.

same time. The use of group playpens marks the beginning of very systematic teaching of *vospitanie* (communist morality and upbringing). Soviet preschools are designed specifically to teach Soviet children to live in a communal society.

Group playpens also are a major source of human stimulation, deemed necessary for rapid development of perceptual and social-emotional responding. Many Soviet babies are able to make perceptual discriminations at earlier ages than can most American babies. Motor coordination develops also at an early age. The photograph on page 229 shows one of the infants observed in a visit to a preschool in Uzbekistan in August 1975. The infant pictured is nine months of age and already is able to use his hands to place the different colored spools in front of him in the proper places. Certainly these infants, attending nursery upwards of eight hours per day, show no signs of marasmus!

Nursery programs in Cuba Cuba, a country with many political ties to the USSR, has developed many of the same general guidelines for educating and caring for infants and young children. A new maternity law gives all working women four-and-a-half months leave at full pay, some six weeks longer than that given Soviet women. In addition, Cuban law requires that women stop work six weeks prior to expected delivery and allows them three months leave of absence after their babies are born. Day-care centers (*circulos infantiles*) are free. Children can enter as young as forty-five days and stay until they are old enough to enter public school. The programs and goals of the day-care centers are similar to those in the Soviet Union (Steffens, 1975).

Soviet infant plays with brightly colored spools.

Nursery programs in the People's Republic of China Children in the People's Republic of China also are reared in programs similar in many respects to those of the Soviet Union. Infants in China begin their nursery training at fifty-six days of age. Like Soviet infants, they are reared in communal settings. When they are not being held or played with by their caretakers, they are placed in communal playpens. Like the Soviets, the Chinese are well aware of the importance of physical contact. The nursemaid-infant ratio in Chinese preschools is 1:4. Visitors to China who have observed infants report that they tend to be happy, healthy, alert youngsters (Alston, 1975).

Infants' homes on Israeli kibbutzim Kibbutzim are characterized by co-operative partnership and shared responsibility; each member contributes to the vitality and productivity of the Kibbutz as a whole. Kibbutz infant and child rearing is designed to develop children well adapted to communal living. The methods used to accomplish this are in some ways similar to those used in the USSR and the People's Republic of China. There are, however, striking differences between kibbutzim educational programs and nurseries in either the USSR or China. Perhaps most important is the fact that there is no single national plan for kibbutz education, as there is in each of these other countries. Instead, a number of major kibbutz movements, each characterized by different political-philosophical approaches, exist. Unlike educational programs in the USSR and China, the kibbutz programs differ in philosophy and methods of infant and child rearing, as well as in family patterning. What is true of one kibbutz's infant home may not be true of another.

In most kibbutzim, infants enter infant homes to be reared communally at very young ages—usually, when they are four to seven days old. On some kibbutzim, infants remain overnight; on others, they return to their parents' rooms at the end of each day. (In 1971, I spent two months visiting several kibbutzim, each of which followed a different procedure regarding nighttime arrangements for young children.) At this early stage, mothers remain for most of the day to feed, wash, and care for their infants. Only gradually do mothers turn these activities over to

A typical daily schedule in a kibbutz infant house

Following is an hourly schedule of activities of both parents and metapelet, to illustrate a typical day in the infant house:

Morning

5:00–6:00   Mother comes for first feeding, changes diapers. Metapelet arrives, helps prepare bottles, assists nursing mothers, changes bedding, etc.

6:00–9:00   Infants nap, supervised by metapelet.

9:00–13:00   Mother comes, gives second feeding, bathes her child, plays. Metapelet takes children outdoors in pens.

Afternoon

13:00–13:30   Mother comes for third feeding.

14:00–16:00   Infants nap, supervised by metapelet.

16:00–18:00   Parents change infant's clothes, take child to their room.

18:00–19:00   Parents return infant for fourth feeding and put to sleep.

Evening

19:00–22:00   One set of parents watches over all infants until the nightwatch comes.

Following are observations reported by a psychologist to illustrate aspects of this day:

Several mothers come in to feed and care for their infants. Two mothers share a table as their infants are three and three-and-a-half months old and are eating solid food. One mother talks constantly to her baby as she feeds him. The other mother has trouble with her baby who has just recovered from an illness and keeps spitting up food. She continues the feeding, and one sees her controlled concern. The first mother reassures her that less food was coming up than during the previous day and that the infant seems to be better. The first mother is gay and tries to engage the second mother in conversation—and before long the second mother discontinues her gentle forced feeding of the infant, begins to imitate the first mother and to sing and talk to her infant. The metapelet then joins them, and also comments reassuringly to the mother about the child's improved condition. During the period of this observation, two fathers dropped by and visited their babies, playing with them a few minutes.

From J. Marcus, Early child development in kibbutz group care, *Early Child Development and Care*, Vol. 1. Great Britain: Gordon & Breach Science Publishers, 1971, pp. 67–98. Reprinted by permission.

the nurses or *metapelot*. The influence of psychoanalytic thinkers like Bowlby and Spitz is apparent in most infant homes: most kibbutzim have arranged for small metapelet-infant ratios. One researcher (Marcus, 1971) estimated this ratio to be one metapelet for every three to five infants.

The metapelet, according to kibbutz educators, provides a constant caretaker figure who, together with the infant peers, helps to provide constancy in the life of the infant. Kibbutzniks attempt whenever possible to keep the same metapelet or, at the least, to allow her to spend transition time with babies when they move to the next nursery, called the toddler home. Life in both the infant home and the toddler home is characterized by much contact both with the mother who visits frequently and the metapelet who provides constant stimulation in the mother's absence.

Observations of kibbutz children have shown that they have warm, close relationships with their peers. What about their relationships with their parents? Most experts agree that affectional ties between kibbutz children and their parents are not upset by communal child rearing, and that kibbutz children develop the same affectional ties as those not raised on kibbutzim (Bronfenbrenner, 1969). One study (Rheingold, 1956) showed that kibbutz children display the same separation anxiety when their mothers leave them in a room alone with a stranger as do American children reared in nuclear families. Quite possibly, communal child rearing, when warm, loving, attentive caretakers are used, has much less effect on the development of attachment than we are accustomed to thinking.

Full-day centers in Sweden Communal child-rearing programs are not found exclusively in communist and socialist societies; they exist in Western societies as well. In Sweden, for example, a total national commitment to the well being of young children has led to the establishment of full-day centers that provide programs at nominal fees for infants and young children beginning as young as six months. The hours of full-days centers are from 7:30 A.M. to 7:00 P.M weekdays and mornings on Saturdays, in order to accommodate children of working parents. Swedish educators and psychologists are aware of the potential hazards of unstimulating institutionalized care for children between the ages of six months and three years. Therefore, the programs provide ample caretaker attention and contact, as well as stimulating objects for the children to explore. In general, the Swedish programs attempt to nurture and develop attitudes of open expression, individuality, and freedom from repression. They surround the children in the center with objects that exist for their use and learning. They avoid excessive prohibition and supervision, so as to avoid thwarting emotional development and natural curiosity (Passantino, 1971).

Day Care in the United States In the United States, as in other countries discussed here, increasing numbers of mothers are entering the work force. By the mid 1970s, over 30 percent of mothers of children under six years of age were employed. Today, the number of working mothers is significantly larger.

The United States provides federal, state, and local public as well as private day-care programs for infants and young children. The most common arrangement is the family day-care home, in which children are cared for in private homes. The reported advantage of this arrangement is that the homes usually are located in the immediate neighborhoods; working mothers do not have to transport their children long distances. Many states license day-care homes. However, most arrangements, in fact, are made privately between working mothers and day-care mothers. Most facilities are privately run and are not state inspected (Robinson et al., 1973).

A second type of day-care facility in the United States is the day-care center. Day-care centers can be found in churches, settlement houses, social centers, public housing units, or, in some cases, specially constructed facilities. Most centers take children beginning at three years. However, some facilities take infants as well. Day-care centers can be privately or publically operated, and either profit or nonprofit.

From 1965–1970, numerous government-sponsored programs to help the poor were organized under the provisions of the 1967 and 1970 amended Social Security Act. Another series of programs, included Head Start and Parent and Child Centers, were organized as major components of the War on Poverty of the Office of Economic Opportunity.

In recognition of the extreme importance of stimulation to the child, new federal standards in 1974 required that all licensed federally funded programs provide, among other things, at least one adult attendant for each infant under six weeks old, and one adult for every four children under three years of age. In 1970, the actual annual cost of day care run

Rest hour in a United States preschool.

Rest time in a state day-care center in the Soviet Union.

by state welfare was $1,140 per child, less than half the amount paid for each child in Soviet programs (Robinson et al., 1973). These new standards, however, increased considerably the costs of running many then-existing programs, which, up until that time, had provided larger ratios. Unfortunately, by 1976, at the time this book was being prepared, many programs were closing their doors rather than decreasing caretaker-infant ratios, because of lack of necessary funding.

Current day-care facilities in the United States vary considerably, both in quality of programming and in the centers' efforts to involve or inform parents. Although some programs clearly are adequate for proper development, others have been found to be seriously lacking. Keyserling (1972) reported, in a survey of day-care facilities in the United States, that approximately two-thirds of the centers observed provided only custodial care. One in seven was rated either as "poor" or "very poor." Some of the poorer centers, which "can be found in virtually every city in the country" were described by observers (Keyserling, 1972, p. 64). One example follows:

> The proprietor is not interested in child care but only in making a profit. She wants to get out of the business and will sell to anyone who wants to buy it. Back in a dark room, a baby was strapped in an infant's seat inside a crib and was crying pitifully.

Another observer noted:

> One worker washed every child's face with a cloth dropped in a bucket of water one-tenth full. No decent toys. The center was run by high-school girls without any adults present. The children were not allowed to talk.

Currently, what are the options for American working mothers of infants and young children who cannot find adequate day-care centers? The options are small in number and each has its own dangers. Women with fairly high incomes can afford to hire caretakers to come into their own homes. Or, mothers may leave their children with neighbors or relatives. In some situations, working mothers have pooled resources and developed their own programs.

In comparing efforts in this country to provide care for children of working mothers with efforts of other countries, it appears the United States trails far behind. Why? One obvious reason is the low priority of day-care in the United States, as evidenced by the lack of government appropriations for programming. Chapter 1 mentioned the low priority American children seem to have in our society. But it is not as simple as all that. The United States, with its highly diverse population and its many different educational goals, has had difficulty in determining what constitutes the "best" program for all, or even most, of its children. We, as a nation, have no single superordinate goal for child development, no single agreed-on ideology to teach our children, as in many of the other countries we have examined.

Day care in America is not in as depressing a state as the above information would suggest, however. Working mothers need not anticipate that their children will suffer retarded development as a consequence of their decision to work. With careful planning, knowledge of what to look for, and sufficient resources, American working mothers can provide stimulating and beneficial environments for their children. Keyserling's report showed that 25 percent of the programs observed provided superior quality "developmental care." Numbers of experimental programs, as, for example, the Caldwell program mentioned earlier, also are providing stimulating environments that can increase considerably the cognitive and social growth of infants and young children. Caldwell's center enrolled infants six months old to three years old, and kept them from six to nine hours daily. The center systematically programmed teacher behavior, supplied materials in the environment related to cognitive development, and presented culturally relevant information to older children. After seven months, IQs of children in the Caldwell program increased an average of 5.6 points, a clear indication that day care for these children did not retard development.

Another successful experimental intervention program for infants at the University of Wisconsin Infant Education Center used a different but equally successful strategy (Strickland, 1971). This program, instead of providing initial infant care in day-care centers, developed initial enrichment programs at home for mothers or caretakers of the infants. The program called for daily home visits of several hours duration from shortly after birth until the infants were three months old. After three months, the infants began spending several hours daily at the Child Center, where they were exposed to stimulation on a one-to-one basis with trained adult caretakers. After age two, they spent all day in the centers, in small groups with caretaker-children ratios of 1:5. Striking differences were found in the developmental progress of these children as compared to children of similar background who had not participated in the program. By the age of three-and-one-half years, IQ differences between the two groups of children averaged 33 points.

Youth experiments in communal living and infant rearing Within the past ten years, a significant number of young, often middle-class Americans have made the decision to try communal living. Communes have appeared in all states of the United States, many growing out of the counterculture movements of the sixties and early seventies. Present-day communes are found in both urban and rural areas. They vary widely in both structure and interest, ranging from anarchist to highly organized groups with explicit philosophical systems. Concerning infant-family

Fathers raising their children in communal settings often
spend more time in child rearing than do fathers raising their
children in nuclear families.

relationships, communes range from those that maintain nuclear parental
units within the communal families to those that regard children as "belonging" to the commune. In some communes in the United States
all commune members, including the children, may be present at the
birth of the baby. The father is encouraged to assist in delivery, on the
assumption that this will encourage a deep attachment relationship.
Breast-feeding is commonly practiced. Babies frequently are carried on
their mothers' backs and accompany them most of the time, so there is
almost constant physical proximity between mother and child. Intense
mother-child relationships between birth and two years are common. In
addition, there often is an attempt to develop in the infant generalized
feelings of trust. This may be accomplished in some communes by providing multiple caretakers or, in some cases, by switching infants among
mothers for breast-feeding (Eiduson et al., 1973). In many communes,
there is no clear distinction between the roles of the parents and those of
other commune members. The dominant child-rearing ideology often is
to allow for maximum free expression and creativity. It remains to be
seen whether children reared in these settings will follow in their parents'

footsteps, or, as frequently has occurred in this country, will reject communal values and return to the middle-class value system from which most of their parents came.

Single-Parent Families Together with the increasing number of women in the work force and the increasing number of divorces in our country, more and more single parents are raising children. Today, thousands of single men and women raise their children without the help of another parent. Evidence presented in this chapter makes it clear that the single parent faces a number of obstacles in caring for the young child that the two-parent family does not face. It simply is more difficult for one person to supply easily the same individual attention and affection that two parents can provide. It isn't impossible, however. In spite of the financial and personal setbacks that have resulted from the loss of mate through divorce or death, many single parents report that they have made good adjustments and are suc-

One single parent who "made it"

"I was widowed when I was twenty-six, and left with three children. Kevin was two months old, Joanne was three, and Shirley had just started school and was six. We'd just moved to Chicago a month before my husband died, and I didn't know anyone. I was lonely, depressed, and felt sorry for myself. For the first few months, I moped around the house—barely paid any attention to the kids except to go through the motions of feeding them and taking care of them. I just couldn't seem to get myself together. Here I was in a strange city, with three small children, and the little money my husband left was running out fast.

"Well, one day I was down at the laundromat, sitting there waiting for the wash to dry and thinking about how it had been before Bob died, and how on earth I was going to raise those kids by myself. I felt I just couldn't face the future, and was almost on the verge of tears. Then this woman came over and asked me if I had some change for the machines. She was real nice and

friendly, and I guess she could see I was at the end of my rope. We got to talking and somehow it came out about Bob's death and all. Then she told me her husband had run off and left her with six kids a couple of years ago, and I thought, "Wow, she's worse off than I am," and I really felt sorry for her. But, she didn't feel that way. She felt she had made a pretty good job of handling things without him. So I asked her how she did it. Maybe what worked for her could work for me.

"It didn't sound easy, but I knew I had to do something soon, so I decided to take her advice. Like she said, keep smiling and go to everybody who might help. Well, I didn't always smile. At first I was scared, but I forced myself to go to lots of agencies and talk to a lot of people. Some places, they told me I didn't qualify for their services, because I hadn't been in the area long enough, but finally the Public Assistance helped me to get ADC (Aid to Dependent Children), and a church nearby took my two youngest ones cessfully coping with many of the problems of being one-parent families. Psychologists recognize that the loss of a mate seldom occurs without some degree of shock or emotional upheaval. They suggest that, at the time of the change to single-parent life, single parents should begin seeking help. Relatives and friends often can provide emotional support at times of emotional upheaval. Many institutions also are available for assistance in solving the problems unique to single parents. Family help institutes, such as the Community Chest or Red Feather Agencies, the city social services or welfare agencies, mental-health agencies, and veteran administrations are a few of the public agencies that provide professional family counselors to listen and advise. Private agencies often offer these services as well. Parents Without Partners, a national organization of single parents, was established to meet the unique needs of the single parent trying to provide a stimulating environment for his or her child and, at the same time, develop a meaningful personal life.

into their day-care center. That was a big help because, with the kids taken care of, I could go look for a job. I wasn't trained to do anything, but the employment office found a job for me waiting tables. The tips were good, and so were the hours. I could be with my children when they were home from school, and I started to take more interest in them. I guess I just hadn't realized before how rough it was on them without their father, and with a mother who could only think about how much she was suffering. I gave them a lot of love and attention, and tried to comfort them about losing their dad.

"Things were going pretty good for us, but I was still lonely for companionship. I talked to the woman I worked for at the restaurant about it, and she invited me to join her bowling team. I'm still not much of a bowler, but I have fun, and I've made some good friends.

"I've even joined the PTA at Shirley's school because she wanted her teachers to meet me. At first I went just to please her, but I really enjoy it now. And, would you believe it, last week I was elected chairman of the Ways and Means Committee.

"It seems that the happier I am with myself and my life, the happier my children are. When I look back to four years ago, I'm amazed at how much I have accomplished for myself and for my children. The kids are doing well in school, and the future is looking brighter all the time. Oh, we have our ups and downs, but the older the kids get, the more they realize that we all have to work together. And we've become a very close family because of that.

"I'd say there are several things you have to do when you are left to raise your children alone. First, try to stop feeling sorry for yourself, and that things are hopeless. Realize that the children need you more now than ever before. Make yourself get out and talk with people. Ask for their advice and help. And get help from any agency you can find. Most of all, don't give up. Keep working at it, and anyone can raise kids by themselves if they have to, and do a good job, and have some fun, too."

From *One Parent Families*, case history #1, U.S. Dept. of HEW, Office of Human Development Children's Bureau, 1974, pp. 2–3. DHEW Publication No. (OHD) 74–44.

SUMMARY

Infant care, a vastly underrated occupation, clearly and critically affects the developing infant and child. Apparently, the variable most critical to development is not the specific technique used (e.g., breast- versus bottle-feeding), but the general quality and amount of interaction provided the infant by the caretaker. Mothers who are warm and affectionate tend to have happy, smiling babies. Babies whose caretakers spend a great deal of time interacting with them and handling them develop stronger attachments to their caretakers than do babies whose caretakers spend less time with them. Attachment appears to be a necessary precursor of identification, the process whereby the baby gradually adopts not only the behavior but the standards of the caretaker. The identification process is the basis for the learning of most socialized behaviors. Deprivation of caretaker attention, as in unstimulating institutional settings, leads to lack of attachment and identification, and corresponding retarded development.

The question of whether infant care is provided most effectively by one or many caretakers has been argued by psychologists and psychoanalytic researchers. Anthropological studies have shown few ill effects on children reared in tribal societies. In modern societies, many communal child-rearing programs have shown that, with attentive caretakers and small caretaker-infant ratios, development can progress rapidly. Countries such as the USSR, Cuba, and the People's Republic of China have developed programs in which infant development is conscientiously nurtured in communal settings while mothers work. Similar programs have been developed on kibbutzim in Israel, and in western countries such as Sweden. In the United States, the need for day-care programs grows as more and more women enter the work force. Concern for the quality of existing programs mounts as information increases on the importance of these early years to all of later development.

Not only are day-care programs needed for the increasing number of working mothers, they often are needed to provide assistance to the growing number of single parents—both mothers and fathers. Single parents today, as well as parents who have made the decision to try communal living, are developing new lifestyles and methods of raising their children. The real effects of these new methods will be observed as the children reach adulthood.

QUESTIONS FOR THOUGHT AND REVIEW

1 Swedish men have requested equal opportunity with women to stay home after the births of their children in order to interact extensively with their infants. In the United States, men also are requesting equal time to interact with their infants. In a few situations, husbands and wives have shared full-time jobs, each staying home half of the time to be with their young children and working the other half. What do you think will be the effects of this additional father interaction on attach-

Single parents face a number of obstacles in caring for their young children.

ment, identification, and other aspects of the development of young children? (For review, see pages 216–220.)

2 Do you think it is preferable today for a working mother to leave her infant at home with a single mother-surrogate housekeeper or to send her young child off to a day-care center where he/she will have the opportunity to interact with many mother surrogates and many other children? Give the reasons for your answer. (For review, see pages 223–226 and 232–234.)

3 Consider the different communal infant and child-rearing practices of other societies that we have discussed. Which do you think would work most effectively with children in the United States? What aspects of these programs would be difficult to implement in the United States? Why? (For review, see pages 227–231 and 234–235.)

4 Imagine that you are a single parent (either male or female) of two children under the age of two. List the procedure you would follow in deciding what arrangements to make for them while you go out to work. Justify your decision on the basis of what you know about the effects of caretaker-infant interactions in the first two years of life. (For review, see pages 236–237.)

FOR FURTHER
READING

Bowlby, J. *Attachment and Loss.* Vols. 1 and 2. New York: Basic Books, 1969, 1973. Bowlby's masterwork in two volumes considers the issue of attachment from a psychoanalytic position. Bowlby's deep concern for the presence of a single caretaker is highly controversial and his views are essential reading for those concerned with early child development.

Day Care in Your Home. Dept. HEW Pub. No. (OHD) 74–217. Washington, D.C.: U.S. Government Printing Office, 1975. This short booklet provides guidelines for the working mother who is selecting day-care arrangements for her children. It describes the two main sources of day-care in the United States and offers advice on what to look for in choosing a day-care facility. Equally important, the book includes some practical information on what to do when no adequate facilities are available in the community.

Early Child Development and Care: A Multidisciplinary Periodical and Book Series. New York: Gordon and Breach Science Publishers. This series contains articles describing child rearing and child development in a number of different societies. Social, educational, and medical research are reported.

Kagan, J. *Personality Development.* New York: Harcourt, Brace, Jovanovich, 1971. This short book summarizes much of the research on the process of identification. Kagan reports much of his own work here and ties his findings to those of other researchers.

Robinson, H., N. Robinson, M. Wolins, U. Bronfenbrenner, and J. Richmond. Early child care in the United States of America. *Early Child Development and Care* 2, no. 4 (1973). 3rd special monograph issue.

Childrearing in the United States, including upbringing, role of the family, and current childhood programs are described. (Other monographs in the same series examine child and infant rearing in other countries, including Great Britain, Israel, and Sweden.)

Alston, F. Early childhood rearing practices in the People's Republic of China. Paper delivered at the annual meeting of the American Educational Research Association, San Francisco, April 1976.

Bowlby, J. *Attachment*. New York: Tavistock Institute of Human Relations, Basic Books, 1969.

Brazelton, T. Effect of maternal expectations on early infant behavior. *Early Child Development and Care*. Vol. 2. Northern Ireland: Gordon and Breach Science Publishers, 1973, pp. 259–273.

Bronfenbrenner, U. The dream of the kibbutz. *Saturday Review*, September 20, 1969, pp. 72–73.

Caldwell, B. The fourth dimension in early childhood education. In R. Hess and R. Baer, *Early Education*. Chicago: Aldine, 1968.

Caldwell, B., L. Hersher, E. Lipton, J. Richmond, G. Stern, E. Eddy, R. Drachman, and A. Rothman. Mother-infant interaction in monomatric and polymatric families. *American Journal of Orthopsychiatry* 33, no. 4 (1973), 653–664.

Carey, W. Maternal anxiety and infantile colic: is there a relationship? *Clinical Pediatrics* 7 (1968): 590–595.

Casler, L. Maternal deprivation: a critical review of the literature. *Monographs of the Society for Research in Child Development*, 1961, 26 (2, Whole Number 80).

Clarke-Stewart, K. Interactions between mothers and their young children: characteristics and consequences. *Monographs of the Society for Research in Child Development*, 1973, 38 (1, Serial Number 153).

Dennis, W., and P. Najarian. Infant development under environmental handicap. *Psychological Monographs* 71, no. 7 (1957): 1–13.

Eiduson, B., J. Cohen, and J. Alexander. Alternatives in child rearing in the 1970's. *American Journal of Orthopsychiatry* 43, no. 5 (October 1973): 720–728.

Fantz, R. The origin of form perception. *Scientific American* 204 (1961).

Fantz, R., and S. Nevis. The predictive value of changes in visual preferences in early infancy. In J. Hellmuth, ed., *Exceptional Infant*. Vol. I. *The Normal Infant*. New York: Brunner/Mazel, 1967, pp. 351–414.

Fein, G., and K. Clarke-Stewart. *Day Care in Context*. New York: Wiley-Interscience, 1973.

Gardner, D., G. Hawkes, and L. Burchinal. Noncontinuous mothering in infancy and development in later childhood. *Child Development* 32 (1961): 225–234.

Golden, M., and B. Birns. Social class, intelligence, and cognitive style in infancy. *Child Development* 42 (1971): 2114–2116.

Harlow, H. The heterosexual affectional system in monkeys. *American Psychologist* 17 (1962): 1–9.

Harlow, H., and M. Harlow. Learning to love. *American Scientist* 54, no. 3 (1966): 244–272.

Harlow, H., and R. Zimmerman. Affectional responses in the infant monkey. *Science* 130 (1959): 421–432.

Hoffman, L., and F. Nye. *Working Mothers*. San Francisco: Jossey-Bass, 1974.

Kagan, J. The child: his struggle for identity. *Saturday Review*, December 7, 1968.

Kagan, J. The concept of identification. *Psychological Review* 65 (1958): 296–305.

Keyserling, M. *Windows on Day Care*. New York: National Council of Jewish Women, 1972.

Landreth, C. *Early Childhood Behavior and Learning*. New York: Knopf, 1967.

Leonard, M., J. Rhymes, and A. Solnit. Failure to thrive in infants. *American Journal of Disabled Children* 8 (1966): 600–612.

Lorenz, K. *Studies in Animal and Human Behavior*. Vol. II. Cambridge, Mass.: Harvard University Press, 1971.

Lorenz, K. *Studies in Animal and Human Behavior*. Vol. I. Cambridge, Mass.: Harvard University Press, 1970.

Lorenz, K. *King Solomon's Ring*. New York: Crowell, 1952.

McCall, R. Exploratory manipulation and play in the human infant. *Monographs of the Society for Research in Child Development*, 1973, 39 (2, Serial No. 155).

Marcus, J. Early child development in kibbutz group care. *Early Child Development and Care*. Vol. 1 Great Britain: Gordon and Breach Science Publisher, 1971, pp. 67–98.

Mead, M. *Sex and Temperament in Three Primitive Societies*. New York: Morrow, 1935.

Murphy, L. Later outcomes of early infant and mother relations. Paper read at the annual meeting of the American Orthopsychiatric Association, Washington, D.C., March 1971.

Passantino, R. Swedish preschools: environments of sensitivity. *Childhood Education*, May 1971, pp. 406–411.

Rheingold, H. The modification of social responsiveness in institutional babies. *Monographs of the Society for Research in Child Development*, 1956, 22 (2, Serial No. 63).

Rheingold, H., and N. Bayley. *Child Development* 30 (1959): 363–372.

Robinson, H., N. Robinson, M. Wolins, U. Bronfenbrenner, and J. Richmond. Early child care in the United States of America. *Early Child Development and Care* 2, no. 4 (1973). 3rd special monograph issue.

Rubenstein, J. Maternal attentiveness and subsequent exploratory behavior in the infant. *Child Development* 38 (1967): 1089–1100.

Sears, R., L. Rav, and R. Alpert. *Identification and Child Rearing*. Stanford, Cal.: Stanford University Press, 1965, pp. 1–8.

Sex-typing. *Pittsburgh Press*, 22 February 1976.

Sheils, M., and S. Agrest. Nurseries in the jailhouse. *Newsweek*, January 12, 1976.

Skeels, H. Adult status of children with contrasting life experiences: a follow-up study. *Monographs of the Society for Research in Child Development*, 1966, 31 (3, Serial No. 105).

Skodak, M., and H. Skeels. A final follow-up study of one hundred adopted children. *The Journal of Genetic Psychology* 75 (1949): 85–125.

Skodak, M., and H. Skeels. A follow-up of children in adoptive homes. *The Journal of Genetic Psychology* 66 (1945): 21–58.

Spitz, R. Hospitalism: an inquiry into the genesis of psychiatric conditions in early childhood. In A. Freed, ed., *The Psychoanalytic Study of the Child*. Vol. I. New York: International Universities Press, 1945, pp. 53–74.

Steffens, H. Cuba: the day women took over Havana. *Ms Magazine*, April 1975.

Stone, L., H. Smith, and L. Murphy. *The Competent Infant*. New York: Basic Books, 1973.

Strickland, S. Can slum children learn? *American Education*. Washington, D.C.: U.S. Dept. of Health, Education and Welfare, Office of Education, July 1971, pp. 3–7.

Thoman, E. Some consequences of early infant-mother interaction. *Early Child Development and Care* 3 (1974): 249–261.

Tulin, S. Infants' reactions to mothers' voice and stranger's voice: social class differences in the first year of life. Paper presented at the biennial meeting of the Society for Research in Child Development, Minneapolis, Minnesota, April 1971.

Vincze, M. The social contacts of infants and young children reared together. *Early Child Development and Care*. Vol. 1. Great Britain: Gordon and Breach Science Publishers, 1971, pp. 99–109.

Wachs, T., I. Uzgiris, and J. McV. Hunt. Cognitive development in infants of different age levels and from different environmental backgrounds: an exploratory investigation. *Merrill-Palmer Quarterly* 17 (1971): 283–317.

White, B. Mothering, a vastly underrated occupation. *Interchange: A Journal of Educational Studies* 2, no. 2 (1971). Toronto, Canada: The Ontario Institute for Studies in Education.

Wolff, P. Observations on the early development of smiling. In B. Foss, ed., *Determinants of Infant Behavior II*. New York: Wiley, 1963, pp. 113–138.

Yarrow, L., J. Rubenstein, F. Pederson, and J. Jankowski. Dimensions of early stimulation and their differential effects on infant development. *Merrill-Palmer Quarterly* 18 (1972): 205–218.

PART 3

Early Childhood

8

Socialization
and the Family

Learning objectives

After completing this chapter, you should be able to:

1
explain how the maintenance system of our society affects the learning of socialized behaviors;

2
discuss how child-rearing practices affect child development and list some of the most important attributes of "successful" parents;

3
describe and evaluate ways of disciplining young children; discuss how emotional responses may be channeled into socially acceptable behavior;

4
describe some of the important effects of changing family styles on the socialization process; provide suggestions to parents in crisis situations on how to help their children.

As children increase in age, they increase also in their ability to move about actively and communicate with others. They develop increasingly unique interests, attitudes, values, and behaviors, all shaped by their diverse past experiences.

While children each develop in individual ways, they also learn behaviors that make them similar to other people who live around them. These behaviors help them to meet the expectations of the cultures in which they live. In our society, for example, young children learn to reduce their hunger drives in a specific way: they learn to eat three meals a day. They also learn to eliminate body wastes at appropriate times and places, and to walk, talk, dress, and behave in ways considered acceptable in the United States. The process by which all of these behaviors are learned is called *socialization*.

A Cultural-Anthropological View of Socialization

Socialization differs from society to society. In the United States, children learn to eat with spoons, forks, and knives. In Japan, they learn to eat with chopsticks. How does the society in which we live determine which behaviors are learned?

Cultural anthropologists have long suggested that the basis of socialized behavior in any society is the *maintenance system* (Harrington and Whiting, 1972; Whiting, 1963; Whiting and Child, 1953). The maintenance system of a society is comprised of all the economic, social, and political structures that serve to preserve and perpetuate the society. Some societies—for example, the kibbutzim described earlier—collectively arrange family life and labor and collectively distribute the re-

Socialization in the United States involves learning to eat with proper utensils.

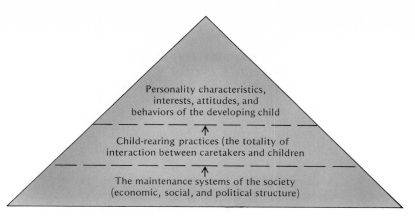

Fig. 8.1 A model of the socialization process. (Adapted from Harrington and Whiting, in F. L. Hsu, *Psychological Anthropology*, 2d ed. Used with permission of Schenkman Publishing Co., Inc. © 1972.)

sources of the group. In other societies, as, for example, the United States, the maintenance system prescribes individual rather than collective labor and ownership; family life usually involves sharing only within a small family unit rather than within a larger, organized group.

The maintenance system is important, according to Harrington and Whiting, because it is the basis for the establishment of a society's child-rearing practices. As we learned in Chapter 7, different societies approach the task of raising children in quite different ways. To give just one example, young kibbutz children, raised communally by multiple caretakers in infant and toddler homes, are taught at early ages to share the toys of the group. Young American children, on the other hand, usually have less opportunity to interact with other children. Therefore, sharing is learned in America much later than on the kibbutz. Psychologists agree that child-rearing practices directly affect the personality characteristics, interests, attitudes, and behaviors of the developing child.

THE FAMILY: TRANSMITTER OF SOCIALIZATION IN WESTERN SOCIETIES

The maintenance system of a society affects child-rearing practices first by determining the unit within which children are raised. In many socialist societies, as we learned earlier, children often are raised in groups in governmentally controlled programs. Parents play relatively small roles in determining day-to-day practices. The maintenance systems of most western societies, on the other hand, require that children be raised within much smaller units, usually composed of family members. Within

A society's maintenance system affects its child-rearing practices. These Greek children have both a mother and grandmother available in their extended family for affection and attention.

these units, parents generally function as the primary caretakers and teachers. They determine what behaviors will be reinforced, what methods of discipline will be used, and so on. Even in situations in which the parents themselves do not do the actual caretaking (as when children are placed in day-care arrangements while both parents work), the parents still have a major impact on the socialization process. Attitudes, values, and interests of working parents are reflected in the specific type of day-care they select. Attitudes, values, and interests also are reflected in the time and quality of attention working parents give their children during nonworking hours.

Within the family unit, of course, mothers and fathers are not the only influencers of young children. Brothers and sisters, as well as other adults living in the home, can also be transmitters of socialized behavior. As the size of the American family tends to decrease, however, this potential additional influence becomes less prevalent. When children are older and spend more time outside the home, peers and teachers become important factors in determining socialized behavior (Kagan, 1971).

Child-rearing practices, as described by psychologists, do not refer to any one specific caretaker practice. Rather, the term refers to what Harrington and Whiting called the totality of caretaker-child interactions. This includes both caretaking (feeding, cleaning, and protecting the child) and socialization training (teaching behaviors both common and acceptable to society). It also includes the many different ways that caretakers communicate affection, aggression, values, interests, attitudes, and beliefs to children. Kagan (1971) referred to these as the overall

A Description of American Child-Rearing Practices

attitude toward caretaking, and said that it is this attitude that is of prime importance to socialization. Do American parents display certain characteristic attitudes toward child rearing? Are American parent-child interactions of a specific type? If so, how do these attitudes and interactions affect our children? How are they affected by our maintenance system?

The classic descriptive study of child rearing in the United States was conducted two decades ago at the Harvard University Laboratory of Human Development. Although there have been major changes in family patterning since that time, the study is still pertinent, because it describes many practices widely accepted and suggests some important trends in child rearing in this country.

Sears et al. (1957) interviewed American mothers and asked them to describe their day-to-day interactions with their children. They asked the mothers how they took care of their young children, what sorts of play activities they engaged in, what they considered "good" and "bad" behavior, how they disciplined their children, and, generally, how they enjoyed their roles as mothers. From the mothers' answers, the authors developed a list of dimensions of maternal behavior that they considered important to child rearing and to socialization. They then rated the mothers on the bases of these dimensions. The Sears et al. study was limited to include only second-generation middle- or upper-working-class mothers who lived with their husbands and were not employed outside the home. Poor families or single-parent families were not included in the study.

The important dimensions of maternal behavior determined by Sears et al. were as follows:

1 *maternal permissiveness versus strictness* in dealing with behaviors related to sex play, modesty, table manners, noise, toilet training, orderliness, and neatness;
2 *maternal self-esteem and happiness with her status in the family;*
3 *warmth of the mother-child relationship* as measured by demonstrable affectional responses such as hugging, patting, and smiling;
4 *maternal tolerance for child aggression in play* and day-to-day activities both with peers and with the mother;
5 *types of rewards and punishments* used in disciplining the child.

The findings were very interesting. Ratings of maternal behaviors along these dimensions revealed generally strict, punitive caretaking methods. Compared to mothers in many tribal societies described in other studies, the mothers in the Sears study required their children to behave in specific, socially prescribed behaviors at earlier ages. For example, children in the Sears study were toilet trained earlier than were children in many tribal societies. Inappropriate behavior was more frequently punished. In teaching manners, methods of playing with other children, or ways to interact with adults, American mothers tended to be more strict, more punitive, and often more rigid. At the same time, they reported more personal dissatisfaction and unhappiness with their own statuses in their own families (Gibson, 1976; Harrington and Whiting, 1972; Sears et al., 1957).

One explanation for what appear to be harsh child-rearing practices, as described by Sears et al., is the small unit responsible for caretaking. Mothers in the Sears study all were unemployed outside the home and lived with husbands who were employed. In the sample population studies, only a few families included adults other than the mother and father. Mothers served as single, full-time caretakers for their children. The less strict mothers in the tribal societies described above, on the other hand, generally came from societies that reared their children communally, with many full-time caretakers sharing the responsibility. (In some societies, the major child rearers were adult women; in others, they were older children.) It can be assumed, therefore, that mothers in the Sears study had more child-care responsibility for longer periods of time. They were more concerned than were tribal mothers that their children be toilet trained early and not soil their clothing, clean up after themselves, and, generally, not "cause a fuss" around the home. It might be assumed that the American mothers described by Sears were more burdened by their chores and, therefore, used child-rearing methods designed to ease these burdens more often than did tribal mothers.

Since the Sears et al. study, there has been more than a 30 percent increase in single-parent families in this country. In single-parent families, usually only one adult is responsible for child rearing and all other activities associated with maintaining a home. In addition, a large number of families now have two working parents. For caretakers in these families, the individual attention necessary for teaching socialization is even more difficult to arrange than it was for mothers in the Sears study.

The results of a rapidly changing maintenance system and a decreasing family size in the United States have included not only harsh child-rearing methods designed to decrease parent labor, but greater permissiveness coupled with decreased attention to child rearing. Psychologists, educators, and parents all have voiced concern over the potential effects of such trends on our children. What we know of these effects will be discussed in this and later chapters.

Social-class differences and child-rearing practices Sears et al. studied child rearing in middle-class and upper-working-class American homes. Psychologists who have compared the child-rearing practices of poor and middle-class parents in this country have found a number of differences in the ways parents of different social classes interact with their children. According to several studies, methods of disciplining children vary according to social class. For example, working-class mothers more often control their children by appeal to parental authority. Discipline frequently includes remarks like: "Don't talk to your mother like that!" or "Wait till your father comes home! He'll make you do it right!" Middle-class mothers more frequently appeal to guilt feelings with remarks like: "Do you want me to feel bad?" or "Don't you want Daddy to be proud?" (Hess and Shipman, 1967; Kamii and Radin, 1967)

Studies report that working-class mothers tend to be more strict and to demand more conformity from their young preschool children than do middle-class mothers. At the same time, they provide older children with greater freedom. Masland et al. (1959) reported that working-class children often are "turned loose" by busy caretakers at earlier ages than are middle-class children. Less assistance is provided them by caretakers once they are able to care for their own physical needs. From that time on, a great deal of learning comes from peer interactions.

Psychologists more recently have related social class to the type of verbal stimulation given young children (Robinson et al., 1973). Bernstein (1960), in a detailed analysis of working-class and middle-class language styles, showed that middle-class mothers use more complex and abstract language in their verbalizations to their offspring than do working-class mothers. Middle-class mothers, according to Bernstein, also make more use of verbal problem-solving activities with their children than do working-class mothers.

Studies have shown that middle-class mothers give more verbal stimulation to their children than do working-class mothers.

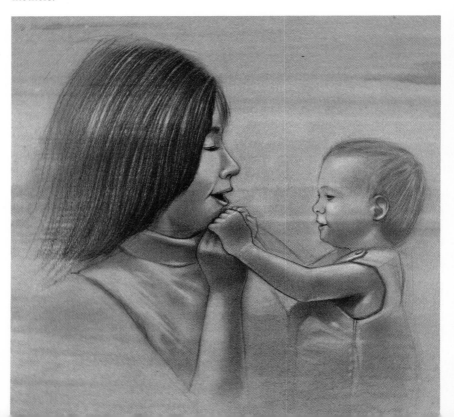

Recent trends in child-rearing practices Since 1957, when Sears et al. did their classic study, psychologists have noted a number of new trends in child-rearing practices.

Through the mass media, educational materials related to child care and child rearing are now easily accessible. Newspapers, magazines, and television, as well as paperback books available in drugstores and supermarkets, all provide professional advice on how to raise children. For example, virtually all American parents today are at least aware of Dr. Spock, and many have relied on his child-rearing advice. One result of this widespread dissemination of information has been generally to decrease social-class differences in child-rearing practices.

Psychologists report that this new availability of professional advice also has led to greater permissiveness in all social classes (Bronfenbrenner, 1970). Today, American parents are more apt to accept behaviors in their children that, in the past, they considered unacceptable. For example, American parents often used to tell their children that it was "not nice" to be jealous of a baby brother or sister, or even to express anger or jealousy overtly. Today, psychological advice provided through the mass media helps parents to realize that these feelings are quite normal and that the best thing they can do is help their children find socially acceptable ways to express them.

Parenting: a how-to-do-it approach

We've come a long way from the time when all our information needs were taken care of within the family. Today, American parents with complex problems can learn how to behave toward their children not by copying what they have seen their own parents do, but by finding out what the experts have to say.

"Parenthood is the most important role we assume in life, but it's the role we're given the least amount of preparation for," complained Dr. Lee Salk in *Newsweek* (September 22, 1975, p. 50). The mass media are trying diligently to correct this problem. American parents are turning more and more to the expertise provided by the media when seeking answers to their child-care questions. The market for how-to-parent books is booming. Books such as *Father Power* (Biller and Meredith, 1976) and *Black Child*

Care (Comer and Poussaint, 1976) advise parents on how to deal with day-to-day problems. Dr. Spock's famous series of child care now focuses on many modern social issues (Spock, 1976). Newspapers and popular magazines contain regular "how-to" columns on child rearing.

For some parents, however, how-to-do-it books are not adequate, especially when help is needed to solve urgent problems. *Newsweek* reports that in major cities today community help is a must. Networks of "Hot Lines," "Tot Lines," and Parents Anonymous have been made available for parents in crises. One longer-term program, Parent Effectiveness Training, provides a more formalized eight-week course in parenting methods for parents who seek professional assistance in dealing with their youngsters.

Psychologists also report disturbing trends. One prime concern is a decrease in attention given children by parents increasingly concerned with other interests (Bronfenbrenner, 1970). Studies at the Russell Sage Foundation showed that many American mothers spend as little as fifteen minutes daily in face-to-face interactions with their preschoolers (Kagan, 1975). Robinson et al. (1973) reported that the average amount of time fathers spend interacting with their children varies from twenty minutes to thirty-eight seconds daily.

At the same time that American parents are being exposed to more and more advice on how to raise their children, increasing numbers of parents report high levels of anxiety associated with child rearing. They feel "less sure about the right thing to do." In their uncertainty, they tend to switch from one approach to another, never confident that they are acting properly.

One fundamental cause of this anxiety, according to Kagan (1975), is "a lack of consensus on values." Parenting, says Kagan, means "implementing a series of decisions about the socialization of your child—what you do when he cries, when he's aggressive, when he lies, or when

---

Dr. Spock's 1976 advice to parents

It is estimated that Dr. Spock's book, *Baby and Child Care*, has been read by 300 million American parents. In his 1976 revision of the famous text, Spock added a major new component, the "psychological side of child rearing." Issues in the world today, such as racism, sexism, poverty, and hunger, affect parents the world over. Spock reports in his new book that all of these issues need to be taken into consideration by parents in child rearing. According to Spock, people who have strong feelings about the condition of other people generally are happier and psychologically more healthy.

The role of fathers is discussed at length in the 1976 edition. In particular, Spock suggests ways that fathers can contribute to the rearing of their children. In regard to sex-typing, he specifically advises that boys be given dolls to play with when they're about three years old. "Most boys at that age request dolls," he re-

ports. There's nothing sissyish about it. "It's playing parents and we should encourage parentalness."

In an interview with *Pittsburgh Press* reporter Franklynn Peterson, Spock suggested a number of changes for the family system (Peterson, 1976). He attacked as particularly dangerous to the family unit our current high mobility rate, caused, in part, by the frequent employee transfers typical of corporate life. Spock urges American parents to say "No!" to corporate demands to move on—their families are more important than the materialistic gains offered by moving.

Above all, Spock calls for a return to relaxed and happy family life, something he thinks is the exception to the rule in America. In most cases, he reports, "families are in-grown and full of tensions"—the result of a complex maintenance system.

he doesn't do well in school." According to Kagan, child-rearing decisions are harder to make today than fifty years ago, even though experts are ready and willing to give advice on childcare, because "there is no consensus in America today as to what a child should be like when he is a young adult."

One way that children learn socialized behavior is by imitating the behavior of those around them. We noted earlier that infants first learn to imitate the behavior of their caretakers and later learn to identify with them. Imitation and identification both are used to teach socialization. Studies have long shown that warm, affectionate parents generate more imitative responses than do parents who are cold and unresponsive (Bandura and Huston, 1961). Warm parents thus tend to be more effective at socializing their children.

Modeling and Socialization

Learning sex-typed behavior Socialization includes learning behaviors considered acceptable for one's sex; these are called sex-typed behaviors. Chapter 7 showed that mothers tend to teach sex-typed behaviors to their sons through punishment, while they teach their daughters more often through reward. In general, fathers and mothers are more indulgent and protective with girls than with boys. When four-year-old Mary falls down and scrapes her knee, her mother is likely to pick her up and kiss her. When Johnny hurts himself, his mother is more likely to tell him to be "a big boy" or to be more careful. Parents expect their sons to be more aggressive than their daughters. They expect and accept greater aggression in most interactions—in play with peers, with parents, and even with playthings.

When does sex-typed behavior begin? As noted in Chapter 7, it often begins immediately after a baby is born. Parents of newborns actually respond differently to boy and girl infants. In one study, young mothers were permitted to play with a six-month-old baby (Wills et al., 1976). Sometimes this baby was dressed in "girl" clothes, sometimes in "boy" clothes. The mothers treated the same baby differently depending on what the infant was wearing. They selected dolls to give to the baby wearing a dress, trains or trucks to the baby wearing pants. They tended even to smile more at the baby wearing a dress!

Not only do parents behave differently toward boys and girls, they provide them with entirely different environments. Rheingold and Cook (1975) studied the bedrooms of boys and girls under age six. They found striking differences both in the furnishings and the toys selected by parents. Boys' rooms tended to be decorated in "masculine" colors and designs, girls in "feminine" decor. Boys' toys were more often vehicles, educational materials, sports equipment, machines, and military toys. Girls were provided with more dolls, doll houses, and domestic toys.

Today, with the advent of the feminist movement in this country, sex-typed clothing and toys are gradually becoming less prevalent. For

Girls are often given dolls to play with.

example, it's harder to guess, simply from watching a group of preschool-aged children on a playground, which are boys and which are girls. Both are likely to be clad in dungarees. It's more usual now to see girls playing with trucks or boys with dolls (Margolin, 1974). However, stereotyped behavior changes slowly. Today, parents still tend to provide harsher models for young boys to imitate. Similarly, they tend to expect and condone more aggressive behavior from their sons than from their daughters.

Sex-typed behavior and adjustment in father-absent homes. In families where both mothers and fathers are present and available, children imitate the behavior of both parents. Babies as young as eighteen months show strong signs of attachment to fathers who interact regularly with them (Lamb, 1975). However, by the age of two, boys and girls begin to display differences in imitative and attachment behavior toward mothers and fathers. Although they may interact extensively with both parents, two-year-old boys learn to imitate their fathers' behaviors rather than their mothers' (Lamb, 1974, 1975).

What happens, then, when a father is away from the home temporarily because of job requirements, or permanently because of divorce or death? Extended father absence has been shown to influence identification, mental functioning, and psychological adjustment of young children. Researchers have shown that father absence may affect children in a variety of complex and often indirect ways, the most important of which has to do with the child's total environment. Father absence may influence, for example, maternal attitude toward child rearing, which can, in turn, affect the child in many different ways. Mothers who adjust well to father absence tend to have more positive attitudes than mothers who remain depressed or angry (Biller, 1969).

Specific methods of discipline used by parents have different effects on children. "Discipline," as we use the term here, is not necessarily punitive. "To discipline" means to teach. Parents discipline their children to behave in ways that are socially desirable and will allow the children to adapt satisfactorily to the world in which they will live. We know that the degree to which mothers and fathers are supportive, controlling, hostile, or reasoning in their daily parent-child interactions has a significant impact on their children's overall development. Is the fact that American mothers generally tend to be strict and punitive in their disciplining important to the development of American children?

Sears et al. distinguished in their 1957 study between two types of discipline. Love-oriented discipline involves personal behaviors such as praising, kissing, hugging, or withdrawing affection. Object-oriented discipline involves less personal interaction with the child. Giving candy or sending the child to his room are examples. Love-oriented discipline

Discipline and Socialization

was used more often by mothers in the Sears study than was object-oriented discipline.

Becker (1964) suggests two dimensions of discipline that he considers critical to the development of child personality. According to Becker, both these dimensions relate not so much to specific parental behaviors as to parental attitudes toward child rearing.

Becker's first dimension is love-oriented versus power-assertive discipline. Becker's love-oriented discipline includes praise and reasoning, and tends to be used by warm, supportive parents who provide the child with models of appropriate behavior. Power-assertive discipline involves the use of parental power and authority to control. This type of discipline tends to be used by cold, hostile parents. Power-assertive discipline promotes child aggression.

The second dimension suggested by Becker is restrictive versus permissive discipline. Parents using restrictive discipline tend to dominate their children's behaviors, plan excessively for their needs, and control through frequent criticism. Restrictive discipline leads to inhibited behavior. Children of restrictive parents tend to be more obedient than those of parents using more permissive methods. As they get older, they tend also to be more courteous, neat, and polite. Permissive discipline, in which more freedom is afforded the young child, tends to lead to uninhibited, disorderly, and expressive behavior.

Other differences in methods of discipline have been noted. For example, in the American middle-class family, the mother is more likely to discpline the young child verbally, while the father is more likely to discipline physically (Gecas and Nye, 1974). Both these forms of discipline may be punitive. Ironically, studies of two-and-a-half-year-old children whose parents are punitive have shown that these children are much less likely to exhibit the behaviors desired by their parents than are children of nonpunitive parents (Lytton and Zwirner, 1975).

There is no direct link, of course, between specific behaviors and method of discipline. Other factors must be taken into consideration. Becker, for example, noted that the effects of discipline can be changed by the overall warmth of the parent. Punishment by a warm, loving parent has a very different effect than punishment by a cold, unaffectionate parent. Table 8.1 describes a number of behavioral outcomes revealed by discipline studies.

All of these findings may be interpreted according to learning models of child behavior. In Chapter 3, we learned that negative reinforcement of all kinds often has an effect quite different from what one might expect. Punitive disciplinary techniques used by hostile parents frequently lead to an increase of other unexpected and often unwanted behaviors. Inconsistent parents are more likely to have children who learn socialized behaviors more slowly. According to Fritz Redl, the psychoanalytic theorist, the effects of punishment on the developing

TABLE 8.1 Consequences of different kinds of parental discipline: results of interactions among warmth and hostility, restrictiveness and permissiveness

	RESTRICTIVENESS	PERMISSIVENESS
WARMTH	Submissive, dependent, obedient Minimal aggression Maximum rule enforcement, boys Dependent, not friendly, not creative Maximal compliance	Active, socially outgoing, creative Minimal rule enforcement, boys Minimal self-aggression, boys Independent, friendly, creative, low projective hostility
HOSTILITY	"Neurotic" problems More quarreling and shyness with peers Socially withdrawn Maximal self-aggression, boys	Noncompliance Maximal aggression

Source: Adapted from W. C. Becker, Consequences of different kinds of parental discipline, in **Review of Child Development Research,** Vol. 1, ed. by Martin L. Hoffman & Lois W. Hoffman. Copyright © 1964 by Russell Sage Foundation. Used with permission.

child are extremely complex (Redl, 1959). Among the many outcomes possible are upsurges of anger, often directed by the child toward himself or herself. Effects may vary, particularly if the child being disciplined has any sort of emotional problem.

Parents and other caretakers are not the only people who contribute to the socialization of young children. Although the trend today is toward smaller families, most American families still have more than one child. How do siblings affect socialization?

Siblings and Socialization

Greeting the birth of a new baby Let's begin with the arrival of a new baby sister or brother. In the United States, we customarily talk about rivalry among siblings for the mother's attention. In small American families, the amount of attention and warmth given to young children decreases significantly when a new baby comes into the home. Many mothers without assistance find that there simply doesn't seem to be enough time and energy to go around. From the positions of older children in the family, their affection and desire for approval now are focused on a mother who is less capable of reinforcing this affection. It is not surprising that researchers have found a decrease in warmth of children toward their mothers after the arrival of a new baby (Taylor and Kogan, 1973).

The birth of a new baby, when dealt with carefully by parents, can be greeted with joy and affection by older siblings.

American preschool children tend to exhibit two types of unwanted behavior when confronted with a new baby brother or sister. Often, they exhibit regressive socialized responses in their feeding, eating, or toileting activities. Children who have been eating with spoons may request a bottle now and wish to nurse just as they see their baby sisters or brothers doing. Children who have been toilet trained for some time may begin wetting their pants. Another typical unwanted behavior is aggression toward the new infant. This may exhibit itself verbally ("I don't like the new baby—He's ugly and dumb!") or, occasionally, even physically —as, for example, when the young child actually slaps the baby. Henchie (1963), in a study of the reactions of preschool-aged children to new babies in the family, found that at least 15 percent exhibited markedly unfavorable responses to the new infants. Another 27 percent exhibited what the authors called "slight disfavor," either verbally or physically.

Another fairly common reaction of preschool children to the decreased attention of their mothers at the arrival of a new baby is the invention of imaginary playmates. Imaginary playmates can have all the positive characteristics of the desired caretaker: they are loyal under all conditions, are available whenever wanted, and, in general, provide the reinforcement lost when the mothers of the newborns took on their new duties (Legg et al., 1974).

Of course, not all children exhibit regressive or aggressive behavior at the arrival of a new baby. Generally, the older the child when the younger sibling arrives, the less the disruptive behavior. In Henchie's study, 89 percent of children under the age of three exhibited unwanted behavior, while only 11 percent of children over the age of six were so affected.

An important variable affecting child behavior at the arrival of a new offspring, of course, is maternal attitude. Mothers who want to have a new baby and look forward happily to its arrival tend to encourage this attitude in their other children (Legg et al., 1974).

Birth order and modeling Young children imitate and identify both with parent and older-sibling models. The strength of identification depends on the amount and type of affection given by the prospective models and on the strength they exhibit.

Birth order is an important factor here: the modeling behavior of older children, particularly firstborns, differs from that of younger children. Older children frequently react with some undesirable behavior at the arrival of younger siblings. Later, instead of imitating and identifying with them, older children tend to react by identifying more strongly with their parents. (Alice, three years old when her baby sister was born, is identifying with her father when she plays on the floor next to the crib and chants, "No! No! You're a very bad girl for wetting your diapers! No one will like you when you wet your diapers! I'm too too busy playing with my truck to change you!" In this particular case, the modeled behavior represents prohibition learning and verbal aggression.)

The sex of younger brothers or sisters also affects modeling behavior. Koch (1956) reported that older children often assume sex-role characteristics of the parent whose sex is opposite that of the younger sibling. (Alice, for example, reacts to her infant sister by playing with her toy trucks rather than her dolls. Later, she might exhibit her identification with her father by showing preference for a toy lawn mower rather than a doll carriage.)

Love, attachment, and dependence Love, or attachment, as defined in Chapter 7, is an ongoing affectional tie between child and caretaker. In infancy, it is manifested by clinging, following, smiling, and watching the caretaker. Dependent behavior includes crying or protesting at separation and, when the child is older, seeking help, attention, and approval constantly from others. Love and dependency both are influenced by the attitude and behavior of the caretaker. Mother caretakers who are happy

Channeling Emotional Responses into Socially Acceptable Behavior

Development of trust comes
gradually.

with their own family statuses and are warm and affectionate toward
their offspring tend to have children who are loving and happy. Aggressive, strict, and punitive mothers, on the other hand, tend to have children who exhibit many unwanted behaviors, such as fighting, aggressiveness, and intolerance of others. Warm, restrictive mothers tend to
have dependent children (Becker, 1964).

Trust Another type of behavior learned in the first several years is trust,
the expression of confidence in the environment. Overprotective parents
tend to interfere with the development of trust in their youngsters (Gibson, 1976). Children who are not allowed to do anything by themselves
come to believe that they are not capable and eventually lack trust even
in themselves. Physical abuse also leads to lack of trust.

Altruism and cooperation Apparently unselfish behavior that has no
observable reward is called altruism. Truly altruistic behavior is not
exhibited by preschool children. However, altruism has its roots in the
early parent-child relationship in the presentation of altruistic models
with whom the young child can identify. The young child begins to
learn altruism first by identifying with an altruistic model and later by

practicing and being rewarded for altruistic behavior (Hartup, 1970; Hoffman, 1970).

Cooperation Unlike altruism, cooperation can be learned at very early ages. Toddlers in kibbutzim and in Soviet preschools learn to cooperate and share even in playpens. Like altruism, cooperation can be fostered through provision of cooperating models, opportunities to practice cooperation, and reward for that behavior.

Jealousy and rivalry Two socially undesirable behaviors common to preschool children are jealousy and rivalry. Older children frequently are jealous of attention given a new infant; when they compete with the new baby for this attention, we call their behavior sibling rivalry. "Let's send the baby back to the hospital" is a typical remark of preschoolers exhibiting sibling rivalry.

Anger and aggression Anger and aggression are two emotions often expressed together with jealousy and rivalry. Anger is a feeling of distress that surfaces when the child is restrained. Aggression is the behavior usually exhibited with this feeling. The child whose parents are highly aggressive in disciplining is likely to be aggressive in return. Aggression also can occur as a result of frustration. Parents can teach their children to control unwanted aggression by giving them as much assistance as

Preparing for the new baby

Smart and Smart (1973, p. 224) point out that behaviors expressive of jealousy and rivalry are to be expected in our society. However, they suggest procedures by which unwanted expressions can be minimized:

1 Prepare young children carefully for the birth of a new baby. Children who are prepared for the changes that will come in the family react less negatively than do children who are taken by surprise. Tell them that the baby is coming; teach what babies are like; help them to understand their own infancies. Above all, assure them of parental affection, even though parents may be busier than before.

2 Understand and accept children's expressions of jealousy and rivalry. Allow them outlets for their feelings, as long as they do not hurt anyone else.

3 Above all, find time to continue accepting and appreciating all children in the family, treating them consistently with affection and interest.*

* Adapted from M. Smart and R. Smart, *Preschool Children: Develoment and Relationships* (New York: Macmillan, 1973). Copyright © 1973 by Macmillan Publishing Co., Inc. Used by permission of the publisher.

Different types of fear appear
in children at different ages.

possible, so that they are not unduly frustrated. They also can reduce
aggression by providing models for more appropriate behavior.

Fear Fear responses can appear in babies as young as one month. Different types of fears appear at different ages. Infant fears are related primarily to needs for food, protection, and other basic wants. Later, young children develop fear of losing their main source of reinforcement, usually the mother caretaker. At the same time, they develop fear responses associated with strangers and strange situations.

Preschool children develop many fears through conditioning. Sometimes even one frightening experience, such as a large dog knocking down a small child, is sufficient to establish long-term fear. Other times, parents unknowingly teach fear to young children through imitation. The father who trembles during a thunderstorm is likely to have a child who also fears thunderstorms.

The majority of children's fears are learned and are common to their culture. Table 8.2 lists some of the most common fears of American children.

Children do not fear things they haven't heard much about, such as nuclear power or disease. They do fear being alone, seeing strange things, or hearing strange sounds. They also fear animals they have heard discussed, even if they have never actually seen the animals (Maurer, 1965).

TABLE 8.2 Fears shown by children age two to six in several experimental situations

SITUATION	PERCENTAGE OF CHILDREN SHOWING FEAR			
	24–35 MONTHS	36–47 MONTHS	48–59 MONTHS	60–71 MONTHS
1. Being left alone	12.1	15.6	7.0	0
2. Falling boards	24.2	8.9	0	0
3. Dark room	46.9	51.1	35.7	0
4. Strange person	31.3	22.2	7.1	0
5. High boards	35.5	35.6	7.1	0
6. Loud sound	22.6	20.0	14.3	0
7. Snake	34.8	55.6	42.9	30.8
8. Large dog	61.9	42.9	42.9	0
Total	32.0	30.2	18.1	4.5

Source: Reprinted by permission of the publisher from Arthur T. Jersild and Frances B. Holmes, **Children's Fears** (New York: Teachers College Press, copyright 1935 by Teachers College, Columbia University), Table 14, p. 237.

E arlier in this chapter, we discussed the recent trend toward greater permissiveness in child rearing and the decrease in amount of attention given children in our society. In this section, a number of specific changes that have taken place during the past decade in American family patterns are discussed in relation to their effects on child rearing and socialization.

Together with the increased mobility of American families has come a decrease in the size of the family unit. Both have had a major impact on socialization of the American child. As we noted in Chapter 7, the trend toward single-parent families in this country has increased in momentum over the past decade. Almost six million families in the United States today are headed by only one parent, because of divorce, separation, death, or other causes? What are the effects?

Divorce and separation The United States today has the highest divorce rate among Western nations, and the figures continue to increase. In 1975, there was nearly one divorce for every two marriages. Parents of more than one million American children were divorced in that year, more than twice the number of a decade earlier (Kagan, 1975). An equal number of parents live apart, although not legally divorced or separated.

Most single-parent families today are headed by mothers. However, judges gradually are moving away from the assumption that children need mothers more than fathers. In an increasing number of cases, judges are awarding child custody to fathers. According to 1974 statistics, there was a 10 percent increase between 1970 and 1974 in the number of children living with fathers after a divorce. One Chicago law firm reported that in 65 percent of its divorce cases, fathers are seeking custody and are winning 75 percent of the time ("New Divorce Laws," *Newsweek,* September 22, 1975, p. 54).

Obviously, it is necessary to know the particular situation before the effects of divorce or separation can be understood. Research shows that divorce per se need not necessarily cause children serious emotional problems; children of divorce generally are *not* more disturbed than their counterparts coming from intact two-parent families. However, the period of divorce can produce many different types of stress for all family members. Such stress can cause socialization problems, for, oftentimes, children blame themselves for the difficulties they see around them.

Some children believe in the domino theory: "If Daddy goes, why not Mommy?" Many children become overly dependent on the remaining parent. They are likely to resist losing sight of that parent—even by going into another room—for fear the parent might be gone when they come back. They might regress in their toilet training or become possessive of things. In cases where children are particularly vulnerable, crisis intervention from family groups, friends, or psychologists can be helpful. Whatever the therapeutic approach used during crisis intervention, it is important to remember that adjustment comes through reduction of family stress, with or without divorce. Age of children at the time of divorce seems to be correlated to ease of adjustment. Family tensions apparently have greater detrimental effects on older children than on younger ones. Preschool children whose parents divorce are less aware of family conflicts, tend to feel more secure, and exhibit fewer feelings of inadequacy than do children whose parents divorce when they are older (Landis, 1960).

Studies of divorced parents show that they enjoy certain advantages that those in two-parent households do not share. Divorced heads of families do not have to engage in mutual decision making with partners who might not agree with their child-rearing strategies. Some authors have pointed out that this is a clearly stated advantage for many divorced mothers (Goode, 1956). The parental partner can be of great help when both parents agree on how their children should be reared. However, when this is not the case, one parent can probably do a better job going it alone.

The period of divorce can be very stressful for children.

Desertion Desertion in our society is typically a male phenomenon: fathers are usually pictured leaving behind destitute mothers and help-less children. However, it is possible also for a woman to desert her family, an increasingly frequent occurrence today. Desertion often has been characterized as "the poor man's divorce." Kephart (1955) dis-covered however, that 43.6 percent of the desertions in one major city involved individuals from the upper half of the socioeconomic ladder.

Desertion, in many cases, produces more stressful family situations than does divorce, partly because the decision to desert usually is uni-lateral and may not be expected by other family members. Financial as well as social problems complicate the lives of the deserted parents and inevitably affect in some way their interactions with their offspring.

Widowing The widowed parent shares the problems of the single par-ents described above. However, the widow or widower generally has one major advantage over other single parents: strong emotional support from family, friends, and community immediately following the loss of the spouse. After the period of bereavement, however, the widow or widower must confront and resolve the same day-to-day child-rearing problems other single parents face.

Unmarried mothers as family heads Unmarried mothers who keep their children are increasing in number in the United States. In the past, the unmarried mother and her child had one dubious advantage over the divorced, deserted, and separated: she did not have to deal with the ambivalent feelings her status aroused in others, for she *knew* that society disapproved almost unanimously.

Studies have shown that many unmarried mothers are capable of providing satisfactory home environments for their young children. Wright (1965), for example, reported on a follow-up study of eighty unmarried mothers who decided to keep their babies after first going to adoption agencies for help. Children were judged to be receiving ade-quate care in the majority of cases. One significant finding was that relatively few problems were noted concerning adverse community attitude. Apparently, it is now possible for many unmarried mothers and their children to establish satisafctory lives and become accepted community members.

Teenage Mothers

Together with an increasing number of single-parent families, the 1970s have brought an increase in young, school-aged mothers. A 1973 study showed that one in ten teenaged girls in the United States can be expected to become a mother before the completion of high school. Forty percent of these will be unmarried. Problems abound in the relationships between these young mothers and their offspring. Frequently, young mothers report ambivalent feelings about their children. Maternal behaviors are affected by insecurity, which many times leads to inconsistent behaviors and attitudes toward the children. Young mothers often seem less able to view their children as integral parts of their lives. In addition, they report a general lack of confidence in their mothering ability (Williams, 1974).

Working Mothers

Much has been said in this chapter and earlier chapters about the increasing number of mothers in the work force. Today, in American families with preschool children, one mother in three holds an outside job. The vast majority of working mothers are employed for economic reasons. However, more and more women are pursuing careers to achieve personal fulfillment or for other noneconomic objectives. Whatever their reasons for working, many mothers report feeling guilty about the time spent away from their young children.

One factor that clearly affects child socialization when the prime caretaker works outside the home is the quality of the substitute care provided. Chapter 7 discussed in detail a variety of substitute-care programs currently available. In the United States, the difference in quality from program to program is considerable. Preschool children raised in unstable substitute-care programs give evidence often of being insecure. However, studies have shown no increase in unwanted behaviors—e.g., poor eating, bedwetting, aggression—when children are placed in high quality, stable day-care programs. The strength of attachment to the mothers has been found to be related to the amount of stimulation provided in the day-care center, rather than to whether or not the mothers worked (Etaugh, 1974).

Another factor affecting children of working mothers is the mother's attitude toward working. Early studies of overworked mothers who did not want to leave their homes, or who were ashamed about their economic statuses, revealed that children of such mothers generally felt neglected. Career-minded mothers with strong guilt about working often pass their anxieties on to their young children. Professional women, on the other hand, who enjoy their work and are proud of their accomplishments communicate this pride to their children.

The process of adoption is not new in our society. However, in recent years, there has been new interest in the effect of adoption on young children. Psychologists have been concerned particularly with the harmful effects of maternal separation, especially on children from six to twelve months of age. They strongly suggest that adoption, whenever possible, take place prior to this period.

Telling adopted children about their unique status is sometimes troublesome for adoptive parents. Disagreement exists concerning the most favorable age for discussing adoption with a child. Most psychologists encourage parents to introduce the topic early, preferably by the time their children are two to three years old.

Studies of parental ability to discuss adoption with adopted children indicate that, in our society at least, many parents find it difficult to be candid and frank (Jaffe and Fanshel, 1970). Poor handling of the issue can lead to behavior problems, particularly as the adopted children approach adolescence.

Mech (1973) developed the following guidelines for achieving what he termed "positive identity" between adoptive parents and their children:

1. *It is critical that parents share with children the fact of adoption. "One-shot" telling is insufficient—interpretation of adoption is a developmental process.*
2. *Adoptees report that comprehension of adoption comes gradually with genuine comprehension not attained until adolescence or young adulthood.*
3. *Questions about biological parents should not be perceived as threatening by the adoptive parents. Adoptees report asking such questions out of curiosity, with most having little or no interest in seeking out the biological parents.*
4. *Adoptees tend to see adoptive parents as the "real" parents, particularly so if the couple is comfortable about adoption and has accepted the child.*
5. *Adoptees report wanting general factual information about their natural parents and about their origins. Few, however, seem inclined to seek out the biological parents.*
6. *Adoptive children report hesitancy in initiating questions about adoption. Despite their curiosity, adoptees felt reluctant to raise questions, inferring that information should be volunteered by the adoptive parents.**

Interracial adoption In the last decade, interracial adoption has become common in the United States. In most situations, adoptees have been hard-to-place children of minority-group background. Children of

---

* From E. Mech, Adoption: a policy perspective, in *Review of Child Development Research*, ed. by B. Caldwell and H. Ricciuti (Chicago: University of Chicago Press, 1973). Copyright © 1973 by the University of Chicago Press. Reprinted by permission.

American black and Indian backgrounds, Korean children, and Vietnamese children are among those adopted by American families. Regrettably, families choosing interracial adoption today sometimes must still contend with societal disapproval. Despite increased willingness on the part of society to accept these children and their families, and increased willingness on the part of families to make such adoptions, the number of minority children needing adoption exceeds by a wide margin the number of applicants.

Child Abuse

In very recent years, public attention has been called to a new "national epidemic": child abuse. Child abuse, of course, is as old as human society. However, since such abuse is rarely reported and easily covered up, it has been difficult to assess its frequency until recently. Now, with the advent of medical technology that allows physicians to measure the extent of old healed fractures and other wounds, it has become increasinly apparent that physical abuse of children is far more prevalent in our society than most of us had imagined (Rosenheim, 1973).

It is estimated that, in the United States today, 1.6 million children per year are victims of child abuse or serious neglect. More than half of these are children under the age of six (Cohen and Sussman, 1975). According to statistics gathered for the United States Department of Health, Education and Welfare, at the very least 2,000 children die annually from abuse, including beatings, burnings, sexual molestings, and inadequate feeding and care ("Child Abuse Called National Epidemic, *APA Monitor*, 1976). Some of the abuse begins even before birth. In a study of violence between husbands and wives in this country, Gelles (1975) found that many attacks by fathers begin on mothers during pregnancy.

Diagnosis of child abuse poses many difficulties for physicians, psychologists, and social workers, even with new laws that establish procedures for reporting such cases. For one thing, it often is difficult to distinguish between abuse and neglect. For another, there is a noted scarcity of verified reports (Holmes et al., 1975).

Even so, practitioners have been able to describe the sorts of family situations and parental characteristics most likely to be found in verified or suspected abuse. Roth (1975) has distinguished between three sorts of abuse cases seen by physicians. The first, *situational abuse*, is the least serious from the point of view of the child. It occurs as the immediate parental reaction to stressful family situations and disappears when the stress passes. *Behavior-patterned abuse* includes scapegoating and role reversal. The abusing parent is unable to cope with his or her feelings of inadequacy and punishes the child for them. *Chronic abuse*, the most serious, occurs when the parent has deep psychological problems. The parent may be acting out rage toward society by way of continual attacks on the child. In some cases, the abused child provides an au-

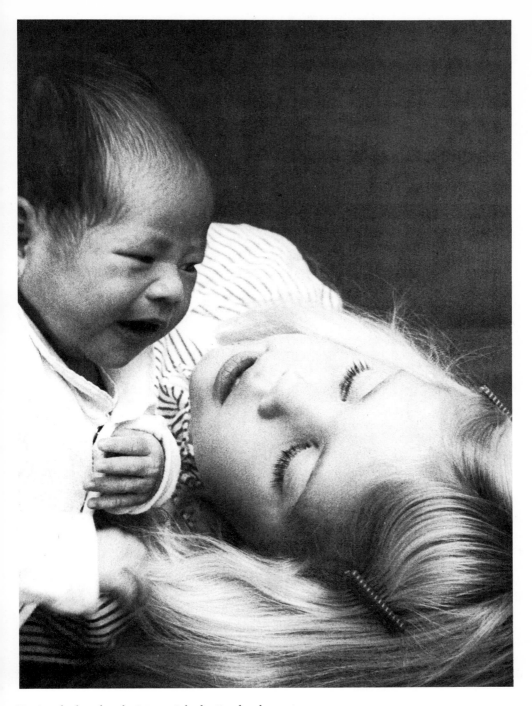

During the last decade, interracial adoption has become more common in the United States.

thority symbol against which the abusing parent fights. Such a battle cannot be won by the abusing parent until the child is totally vanquished.

Abusive parents come from all socioeconomic and cultural backgrounds. Parental characteristics common to all three types of abuse include a variety of psychological diagnoses, such as low self-esteem, personal-social isolation within the family and community, fear of rejection, and low frustration tolerance. Abused children often have some characteristic (for example, a physical deformity) that sets them off from their siblings and causes them to be selected for scapegoating.

Treatment of child abuse usually takes two directions. The first, of course, is treatment of the young child. Decisions must be made concerning the physical safety of the child as well as his or her psychological well-being. In many cases, when help can be given simultaneously to the abusing parent and when the child's physical safety is not in danger, psychologists think it best for parent and child to work out their problems together. In some large cities today, hospital staffs, including physi-

Parents anonymous: dealing with child abuse

The Parents Anonymous group described below consisted of six mothers of small children and a caseworker.

Mrs. P. was angry with her one-year-old daughter because she kept dropping food from her high chair onto the carpeted diningroom floor. Eating had become intolerable both to mother and child. Mrs. P. reported to Parents Anonymous that she often felt as if she would like "just to slap her, and keep on slapping her until she kept still and didn't cause any more trouble." When she expressed her concern about this feeling to the group, one of the other mothers pointed out that dropping food is common with year-old children. Someone else remarked that the mother's feelings of frustration and anger also was common. Other group members spoke of similar experiences with their own babies. One mother reported, "I always feel that my son *knows* I want the kitchen to be neat. He

knows that I hate the mess and does it just to get me!" The caseworker explained that babies learn about distance by watching things go away from them and that, by dropping food, babies actually are learning about gravity. The worker pointed out that if the mothers gave their babies toys to drop from the high chair, it would be less tiresome and messy. She suggested leaving the babies in their high chairs only to eat and suggested that they spend more playtime in playpens, where they might be able to pick up their toys themselves after they threw or dropped them.

When the mothers understood that dropping things actually was a valuable learning experience for their babies, they felt that they might be able to tolerate this behavior more easily, possibly even enjoying the interaction with their babies.

cians, psychologists, and social workers, use team approaches. Group therapy, in which parents can discuss their problems openly with others who share these same problems, is often recommended. Parents Anonymous, found today in most large cities, is a voluntary group of abusing parents who have come together to try to resolve their mutual problems. Group therapy, usually led by a caseworker, is provided by the program. The group also provides crisis intervention and, when necessary, placement for the abused child.

SUMMARY

Through the socialization process, young children learn to make responses that are both common and acceptable in the world in which they live. Socialization is controlled by the maintenance system of the society, which, in turn, affects the specific child-rearing practices used within each family.

The family, parents, and siblings all are important to the socialization of the developing child. Different types of parent-child interactions and different methods of discipline also affect socialization in important ways. Siblings also can play major roles in socialization, in some cases by providing actual caretaking services, in some cases by providing stimulation for rivalry.

One common way that children learn socialized behavior is by imitating the behavior of those around them. Adults in the family as well as older children serve usually as models. Sex-typed behaviors often are taught through modeling.

Socialization involves the learning of many types of responses, including the channeling of emotional responses into socially acceptable behavior. Love, attachment, trust, altruism, and cooperation are fostered in American society; anger, aggression, and fear are minimized whenever possible.

Changing family styles in the United States have affected interactions between parents and children in varieties of ways. Significant trends include the increase in teenage mothers and working mothers, the increase in single-parent families, and the increase in public awareness of and concern over child abuse.

QUESTIONS FOR THOUGHT AND REVIEW

1 American children are said to be highly competitive in their play activities with other children. Soviet children tend not to develop these same behaviors. Explain how the different maintenance systems and child-rearing techniques of the two societies might contribute to very different behaviors. (For review, see pages 249–256 of this chapter, and also pages 227–228 of Chapter 7.)

2 The mass media frequently provides parents with advice on how to teach young children socialized behaviors. Can you design some projects that could be used to teach sex-typed behavior? If you do not believe that sex-typed behavior is appropriate for today's children, suggest ways to teach unisex-typed behavior. (See pages 257–259 for a review of sextyping.)

3 Is aggression a necessary behavior that should be expected of all young children? What are some reasons it occurs? What should the caretaker do about it? (For review, see pages 259–272 of this chapter. Review also Chapter 3.)

4 Child abuse is considered a major problem in the United States today. Parents Anonymous is a group designed to help abusive parents work together to reduce the damage they do to their children. Design a program that might solve the problem *before* it becomes a problem—that is, before child abuse takes place. In formulating your response, consider all of the factors that contribute to child abuse in our changing society. (For review, see pages 272–274.)

FOR FURTHER READING

Caldwell, B., and H. Ricciuti, eds. *Review of Child Development Research*. Chicago: University of Chicago Press, 1973. This anthology contains a series of articles dealing with modeling, parent-child communication, divorce, child abuse, and adoption. Each article is written by an expert in the field. Good summaries of the research literature are provided.

Child Development in the Home. Washington, D.C.: U.S. Department of Health, Education and Welfare, Office of Human Development, Office of Child Development. Children's Bureau, 1974, Publication No. (OHD) 74-42. This government pamphlet provides practical, down-to-earth advice for mothers on developing healthy self-images, a sense of responsibility, resourcefulness, and problem-solving skills. It is a useful teaching aide, especially for mothers with little background in psychology.

Patterson, G. *Applications of Social Learning to Family Life.* Champaign, Ill.: Research Press, 1976. Another practical manual for families to use in working out day-to-day child-rearing problems. Material deals with adult-child negotiations and child management. Behavior problems—for example, bedwetting and teasing—are discussed.

Roberts, A., ed. *Childhood Deprivation.* Springfield, Ill.: Charles Thomas, 1974. Child-parent relationships are the focus of attention in this collection of articles. Various problems, including divorce, death of one or both parents, and child abuse, are discussed from several perspectives.

Robinson, H., N. Robinson, M. Wolins, U. Bronfenbrenner, and J. Richmond. Early child care in the United States of America. *Early Child*

Development and Care, Monograph Issue 2, 1973. This monograph is more difficult to read than the other references listed, and should be used by the advanced student. Social, medical, psychological and emotional care of young children in this country is discussed in some detail.

REFERENCES

Anthony, E. Children at risk from divorce. In E. Anthony and C. Koupernik, *The Child in His Family*. New York: Wiley, 1974.

Bandura, A., and A. Huston. Identification as a process of incidental learning. *Journal of Abnormal and Social Psychology* 63 (1961): 311–318.

Becker, W. Consequences of different kinds of parental discipline. In M. Hoffman and L. Hoffman, eds., *Review of Child Development Research*. New York: Russell Sage Foundation, 1964.

Bernstein, B. Language and social class. *British Journal of Sociology* 11 (1960): 271–276.

Biller, H. Father absence, maternal encouragement, and sex-role development in kindergarten-age boys. *Child Development* 40 (1969): 539–546.

Biller, H., and D. Meredith. *Father Power*. New York: McKay, 1976.

Bronfenbrenner, U. Socialization and social class through time and space. In E. Maccoby, T. Newcomb, and E. Hartley, eds., *Readings in Social Psychology*. New York: Holt, 1958.

Bronfenbrenner, U. *Two Worlds of Childhood: U.S. and U.S.S.R.* New York: Russell Sage Foundation, 1970.

Child abuse called national epidemic. *APA Monitor* 7, no. 1 (January 1976): 8.

Cohen, S., and A. Sussman. The incidence of child abuse in the United States. *Child Welfare* 54 (1975): 432–443.

Comer, J., and A. Poussaint. *Black Child Care*. New York: Simon and Schuster, 1976.

Etaugh, C. Effects of maternal employment on children: a review of recent research. *Merrill-Palmer Quarterly* 20 (1974): 71–98.

Frank, G. The role of the family and development of psychopathology. Psychological Bulletin 64 (1965): 191–205.

Gecas, V., and F. Nye. Sex and class differences in parent-child interactions: a test of Kohn's hypothesis. *Journal of Marriage and the Family* 36 (November 1974): 742–749.

Gelles, R. Violence and pregnancy: a note on the extent of the problem and needed services. *The Family Coordinator* 24 (January 1975): 81–86.

Gibson, J. *Psychology for the Classroom*. Englewood Cliffs, N.J.: Prentice-Hall, 1976.

Goode, W. *After Divorce*. Glencoe, Ill.: Free Press, 1956.

Harrington, C., and J. Whiting. Socialization process and personality. In F. Hsu, ed., *Psychological Anthropology*. 2d ed. Cambridge, Mass.: Schenkman, 1972.

Hartup, W. Peer interaction and social organization. In P. Mussen, ed., *Carmichael's Manual of Child Psychology*. 3d ed. New York: Wiley, 1970.

Henchie, V. Children's reactions to the birth of a new baby. Unpublished child development report, University of London Institute of Education, 1963.

Hess, R., and V. Shipman. Cognitive elements in maternal behavior. *Minnesota Symposia on Child Psychology*. Vol. 1. Minneapolis: University of Minnesota Press, 1967.

Hoffman, M. Moral development. In P. Mussen, ed., *Carmichael's Manual of Child Development*. 3d ed. New York: Wiley, 1970.

Hoffman, M. Moral internalization, parental power, and the nature of parent-child interaction. *Developmental Psychology* 11, no. 2 (1975): 228–239.

Holmes, S., C. Barnhart, L. Cantoni, and E. Reymer. Working with the parent in child abuse cases. *Social Casework* 56 (January 1975): 3–12.

Jaffe, B., and D. Fanshel. *How They Fared in Adoption: A Follow-up Study*. New York: Columbia University Press, 1970.

Kagan, J. *Personality Development*. New York: Harcourt Brace Jovanovich, 1971.

Kagan, J. Parent anxiety. *Newsweek*, September 22, 1975, p. 48.

Kamii, R., and L. Radin. Class differences in the socialization practices of Negro mothers. *Journal of Marriage and the Family* 29 (1967): 302–310.

Kephart, W. Occupational level and marital disruption. *American Sociological Review*, August 1955, pp. 173–180.

Koch, H. Some emotional attitudes of the young child in relationship to characteristics of his sibling. *Child Development* 27 (1956): 393–426.

Kotelchuck, M. The nature of the child's tie to the father. Ph.D. dissertation, Harvard University, 1971.

Lamb, M. Interaction between two-year-olds and their mothers and fathers. Unpublished paper, Yale University, 1974.

Lamb, M. The sociability of two-year-olds with their mothers and fathers. *Child Psychiatry and Human Development*, Spring 1975, pp. 182–188.

Landis, J. The trauma of children when parents divorce. *Marriage and Family Living* 22 (1960): 7–13.

Legg, C., I. Sherrick, and W. Wadland. Reaction of preschool children to the birth of a sibling. *Child Psychiatry and Human Development* 5, no. 1 (Fall 1974): 3–39.

Lytton, H., and W. Zwirner. Compliance and its controlling stimuli observed in a natural setting. *Developmental Psychology* 11, no. 6 (1975): 769–779.

Margolin, E. *Sociocultural Elements in Early Childhood Education.* New York: Macmillan, 1974.

Marsella, A., R. Dubanoski, and K. Mohs. The effects of father presence and absence upon maternal attitudes. *The Journal of Genetic Psychology* 125 (1974): 257–263.

Masland, R., S. Sarason, and R. Galdwin. *Mental Subnormality: Biological, Psychological, and Cultural Factors.* New York: Basic Books, 1959.

Maurer, A. What children fear. *Journal of Genetic Psychology* 106 (1965): 265–277.

Mech, E. Adoption: a policy perspective. In B. Caldwell and H. Ricciuti, eds., *Review of Child Development Research.* Chicago: University of Chicago Press, 1973.

Peterson, F., Postscript, Dr. Spock. *Pittsburgh Press Roto*, 23 May 1976, p. 24.

Radpoff, L. Sex differences in mental health: the effects of marital and occupational status. Paper presented at the American Public Health Association, Washington, D.C., October 1974.

Redl, F. The concept of punishment. Paper presented at the meeting of the American Orthopsychiatric Association, 1959.

Rheingold, H., and K. Cook. The content of boys' and girls' rooms as an index of parents' behavior. *Child Development* 46 (1975): 459–463.

Robinson, H., N. Robinson, M. Wolins, U. Bronfenbrenner, and J. Richmond. Early child care in the United States of America. *Early Child Development and Care*, Monograph Issue 2, 1973.

Rosenheim, M. The child and the law. In B. Caldwell and H. Ricciuti, eds., *Review of Child Development Research.* Chicago: University of Chicago Press, 1973.

Roth, F. A practice regimen for diagnosis and treatment of child abuse. *Child Welfare* 55 (1975): 268–273.

Sears, R., E. Maccoby, and H. Lewin. *Patterns of Child Rearing.* Evanston, Ill.: Row, Peterson, 1957.

Smart, M., and R. Smart. *Preschool Children: Development and Relationships.* New York: Macmillan, 1973.

Sorosky, A., A. Baran, R. Pannor. Identity conflicts in adoptees. *American Journal of Orthopsychiatry* 45 (January 1975): 18–25.

Spock, B. *Raising Children in a Difficult Time.* New York: Norton, 1976.

Taylor, M., and K. Kogan. Effects of birth of a sibling on mother-child interactions. *Child Psychiatry and Human Development* 4 (1973): 53–58.

Thomas, A., H. G. Birch, S. Chess et al. Individuality in responses of children to similar environmental situations. *American Journal of Psychiatry* 117 (1961).

Thompson, S. Gender labels and early sex role development. *Child Development* 46 (1975): 339–347.

Whiting, B., and I. Child. *Child Training and Personality.* New Haven: Yale University Press, 1953.

Whiting, B. *Six Cultures.* New York: Wiley, 1963.

Wills, J., P. Self, and N. Datan. Maternal behavior and perceived sex of infant. *American Journal of Orthopsychiatry* 46, no. 1 (January 1976): 135–139.

Williams, T. Childrearing practices of young mothers: what we know, how it matters, why it's so little. *American Journal of Orthopsychiatry* 44, no. 1 (January 1974): 70–75.

Wright, H. *Eighty Unmarried Mothers Who Kept Their Babies.* Sacramento: State of California Department of Social Welfare. Los Angeles: Children's Home Society of California and Los Angeles County Bureau of Adoptions, 1965.

9

**The Young
Child
and the
Outside World**

Learning objectives

After completing this chapter, you should be able to:

1

describe how peer playmates and others help to socialize young children;
describe how peers can affect the socialization process in the absence of adult models;

2

describe preschoolers' understanding of social and moral rules, and their abilities to cooperate, share, and control their aggressions;

3

describe common defense mechanisms employed by children to deal with anxiety;

4

design some play activities to help socialize preschool children and to reduce shy and aggressive behavior.

C hapters 7 and 8 focused primarily on caretaker-child interactions and their effects on early development. In Chapter 9, we turn to other factors that affect development and, particularly, the socialization process. Peer and other extraparental influences are playing an increasingly major role in the socialization of children growing up in our society today.

Young children, as they get older and have more opportunity to interact with others, are affected increasingly by factors outside their immediate family environments. Some societies, as, for example, socialist societies with mass day-care programs, arrange formally for peer interaction at early ages. Most of these societies place prime emphasis on peer interaction in teaching socialization. Other societies, such as our own, place prime responsibility for child rearing on the nuclear family, giving much less emphasis to peers and outside influences. Papers delivered at a recent symposium on social factors in personality development at an International Congress of Psychology clearly reflected this difference in emphasis: papers presented by Soviet and Eastern European psychologists dealt exclusively with the influence of the peer group, that is, the children's collective; papers from western European countries, on the other hand, dealt with parent-child interactions (Bronfenbrenner, 1970, pp. 108–109).

The impact of peers on child socialization, of course, varies enormously from culture to culture. Children raised in the United States today obviously are not influenced by peer interaction to the extent that Soviet children are. However, as day-care programs continue to enroll more and more American children, and as American children reared in nuclear families extend their activities to playgrounds, nursery schools, and neighborhood backyards, the influence of peers can be expected to increase correspondingly.

PEERS AND SOCIALIZATION

As children increase in age, they interact more frequently with peers.

**The Compensatory
Role of Peer Contact**

How do peers influence child behavior? Most American studies of the peer influence have used lower animals as experimental subjects. Harlow and Harlow (1965) showed, for example, that baby monkeys reared for the first four months of life with their mothers in the absence of other baby monkeys later were more wary of and aggressive toward their peers than monkeys who had not been deprived of peer contact. Apparently, peer interaction at this very early stage of monkey development affects ability to interact later with others.

Harlow and Harlow found also that peer contact can play a compensatory role when the mother caretaker is absent. As already noted (see Chapter 1), baby monkeys raised in total isolation from all other monkeys later developed abnormal adult mating and maternal behaviors. However, baby monkeys raised with these same surrogate mothers but who had the opportunity to play with other baby monkeys did not develop these abnormal behaviors.

One poignant study of the compensatory role of peer contact in human development when normal caretakers are removed was reported by Freud and Dann (1951). These authors studied orphaned children reared in concentration camps during World War II. Hartup (1970) described and interpreted the study as follows:

> These children had arrived at the same camp when they were a few months old and were always in close contact with one another after that. When the children were between three and four years of age, they were taken to live in England. At this time, their behavior toward adults was bizarre in many ways: They showed no pleasure in the arrangements which had been made for them and behaved in a wild, restless, and uncontrollably noisy manner. During the first days after arrival, they destroyed all the toys and damaged much of the furniture. Toward the staff they behaved either with cold indifference or with active hostility, making no exception for the young assistant Maureen who had accompanied them from Windermere and was their only link with the immediate past. At times they ignored the adults so completely that they would not look up when one of them entered the room (p. 130).

> But their extensive contact with each other during their early years had produced a high degree of mutual attachment. This attachment was similar in many respects to the peer attachment shown by infant monkeys who have been reared with peers even though deprived of contact with a mother-figure: The children's positive feelings were centered exclusively in their own group. It was evident that they cared greatly for each other and not at all for anybody or anything else. They had no other wish than to be together and became upset when they were separated from each other, even for short moments. No child would consent to remain upstairs while the others were downstairs, or vice versa, and no child would be taken for a walk or on an errand without the others. If anything of the kind happened, the single child would constantly ask for the other children while the group would fret for the missing child (p. 131).

The group as a whole was closely knit, there were no clear leaders, and there was almost none of the jealousy, rivalry, or competition shown between siblings in normal families. Sharing was spontaneous; there was much evidence of mutual support. The whole concentration camp experience, in spite of maintaining an opportunity for the development of social attachments, had effects on behavior that persisted through a year of residence in the therapeutic nursery. At the close of the study, the children were still "hypersensitive, restless, aggressive, and difficult to handle. They showed a heightened autoerotism and some of them the beginning of neurotic symptoms." The major significance of this study, however, is contained in the following words: "But they were neither deficient, delinquent nor psychotic. They had found an alternative placement for their libido and, on the strength of this, had mastered some of their anxieties, and developed social attitudes. That they were able to acquire a new language in the midst of their upheavals, bears witness to a basically unharmed contact with their environment" (p. 168).

This study obviously furnished only limited evidence concerning the variance contributed by peer relations to the social development of the child. Early deprivation and separation were confounded with the unusual peer experiences in this experiment of nature. When combined with data emerging from comparative studies, however, this study persuasively supports the conclusion that early contact with peers contributes significantly to the social development of the human child.*

American children between two and five years of age change both quantitatively and qualitatively in the manner in which they interact with their peers. As they get older, the number of day-to-day interactions with others increases. Children participate more frequently in activities with peers and at the same time, they gradually increase the complexity of the responses they are able to make toward one another. Similarly, they decrease in the amount of idleness and solidarity play.

Developing Peer Relationships

Developing social rules The ways that children change both in their responsiveness towards one another and also in the rules they use to govern their interactions have been studied extensively by stage-dependent theorists. Two theorists concerned with the development of social rules are Jean Piaget and Lawrence Kohlberg, whose theories were described in Chapter 2.

Piaget's stages of social and moral development. Piaget, in *The Moral Judgment of the Child* (1932), discussed the development of social and moral rules. Much of his theory was based on his observations of children playing marbles in the environs of his laboratory at Geneva. He

* From W. Hartup, Peer interaction and social organization, in P. Mussen, ed., *Carmichael's Manual of Child Psychology* (New York: Wiley, 1970). Reprinted by permission of Wiley & Sons, Inc.

noted what he called clear developmental changes in the ways that children of different ages played and also in the ways that they viewed the rules of the game.

According to Piaget, the development of social rules occurs in a stage sequence essentially similar to that observed in cognitive development. The first stage, which he called the *presocial egocentric stage*, is characteristic of children in the preschool years, until approximately age six. Preschool children, according to Piaget, consider any rules they follow "as made by God—unchanging and unchangeable." Instead of concerning themselves with learning rules, Piaget's preschool subjects were preoccupied with learning control of their bodies and how to manipulate the marbles. "Who won?" was a common question at the end of a game.

According to Piaget, the only rules and regulations that govern preschool social activity are those set for them by adult caretakers. Thus, three year olds who refrain from biting their playmates behave in this manner most probably because their mothers have told them not to bite —not because they understand that their friends will feel pain if they are bitten.

Preschool children take great pleasure in imitating the ordered doings of their elders and in identifying with them. However, according to Piaget, they neither know nor care why they are behaving this way. When they play, it is strictly for themselves. As they get older, they begin gradually to absorb rules by imitating others. Piaget's school-aged subjects slowly increased their social conformity and the importance they placed on the judgments of their peers during the games.

After middle childhood, children first begin to perceive clear social rules governing human interactions. In this more advanced stage, the ability to respond without conforming becomes possible.

Kohlberg's stages of social and moral development. Lawrence Kohlberg (1969), also a stage-dependent theorist, extended and refined the stages described by Piaget. Like Piaget, Kohlberg found a positive relationship between age and stage. Kohlberg, however, was more detailed: he described two stages typical of Piaget's "presocial" young children. Kohlberg's first stage, *orientation to punishment and reward, and to physical and material power*, is descriptive of the behavior of extremely young preschool children, whose guiding purpose is either to receive rewards or to avoid punishments.

A second more advanced stage follows this very early stage: *hedonistic orientation with an instrumental view of human relations.* Young children are learning at this time that their peers are capable of responding in many ways similar to adult caretakers. That is, peers and other outsiders are capable also of providing reinforcers. Children at this stage of development respond to many reinforcers other than physical power. They may respond positively, for example, to praise or to sharing toys

Kohlberg's theory of moral development stresses that the best way to help a child reach the next stage of moral development is to use methods of correcting wrong behavior that appeal to that higher stage. Caretakers of young children are warned not to equate obeying rules with moral development. When Jimmy doesn't hit his sister with a shovel, this doesn't necessarily mean that he knows it's "wrong" to behave that way. Jimmy may be responding at a primitive Stage 1 level (obedience and punishment) and may not be hitting his sister because of fear of retribution. Or, he may be responding at a Stage 2 level (hedonistic) and may not be hitting her because he expects a reward from his mother for this behavior.

In order to determine children's levels of moral development, caretakers must be attentive; they must pay close attention to why children make the responses they do. When neces-

sary, they must ask the reasons for behavior. Only then can they respond by appealing to the next stage.

Let's assume the following conversation between Jimmy and his nursery school teacher.

Teacher: Jimmy, who knocked down Annie's sand house on the playground?
Jimmy: I don't know.
Teacher: Jimmy, did you knock it down?
Jimmy: No, that's bad to do.
Teacher: Why?
Jimmy: You mad at me. Tommy broke the house. I didn't. Tommy's bad.

At what level of Kohlberg's stages of moral development is Jimmy operating? How can you tell? What should the teacher do to teach Jimmy to take care of the property of his playmates? Why?

with their peers. They learn at this stage that, if they respond in certain ways to their peers, their behaviors will be rewarded. The five-year-old child may bring a favorite toy to nursery school to share with a best friend. According to Kohlberg, most nursery-school children share not because sharing is intrinsically good, but because they have the beginning notions of reciprocity, with emphasis on the exchange of favors. They fully expect to receive a favored toy in return.

We learned in Chapter 8 that socialization involves channelling emotional expression into behaviors that are acceptable to society. Learning to relate socially and emotionally to others is one of the developmental tasks listed by Havighurst (1952) for the first six years of life. (See Chapter 2 for a detailed review of Havighurst's tasks.)

Emotional Expression and Peer Interaction

Cooperation, sharing, and generosity Relating satisfactorily to others requires, in our society, cooperation, sharing and generosity. In addition, it sometimes requires inhibiting expression of socially unwanted emo-

Learning to relate socially and emotionally to others is one of Havighurst's developmental tasks.

tions, such as jealousy. Of course, both cooperation and sharing are fostered when caretakers reward children for those behaviors.

In societies making use of communal preschools, children often learn to cooperate and share while still in the playpen. In this country, generosity in peer interactions often is exhibited in very young children. Developmental studies, with rare exceptions, indicate that the incidence of generosity increases with age (Rosenham, 1969).

Jealousy Jealousy, an emotion *not* conducive to successful peer interaction, occurs when one child desires the attention or other reinforcement given to a peer. Children who have been provided with consistent loving attention are less likely to exhibit jealousy.

Aggression Very young preschool children in the United States exhibit a variety of aggressive behaviors that are incompatible with socially acceptable peer interactions. In interactions with peers, preschool aggression can include such antisocial behavior as punching, kicking, biting, verbal abuse, taking away toys, breaking toys, and destroying property. Older preschool children tend more often to be verbally rather than physically aggressive when dealing with younger children. Younger children, on the other hand, are more prone to physically aggressive acts, such as taking away toys, especially when they are dealing with age-mates or younger children.

Why do preschool children exhibit aggressive behavior? Researchers have found that the degree and type of aggression displayed in peer interaction is related only very tenuously to aggression displayed by children in home situations (Korner, 1937). However, as we learned in Chapter 8, aggression in young children can be fostered by harsh or restrictive parents who provide aggressive model figures with whom children identify. In studies of aggression exhibited by preschool children in doll play, severe punishment by parents appeared to correspond directly to preschool children's aggression against the dolls (Lewin and Sears, 1953). Children who are afraid to aggress against their parents may well aggress instead against their own age-mates.

Hostile versus instrumental aggression. Psychologists have distinguished between two basic types of aggressive behavior in preschool children (Bandura and Walters, 1963; Feshbach, 1970). The first, called *angry* or *hostile aggression,* seems to occur for its own sake and is its own goal. The preschool bully who calls a smaller child "sissy" in order to make that child cry is exhibiting hostile aggression. The same bully might grab away a toy or break it to achieve the same end. In both these examples,

If all else fails, a preschool child may grab for a desired toy.
Psychologists call such behavior instrumental aggression.

the crying or unhappiness of the smaller child serves to reinforce the bullying child. Reinforcement of hostile aggression may also come from the social approval of other children, or through vicarious means, such as identifying with a bullying model-figure parent.

A second type of preschool aggression identified by psychologists is *instrumental aggression*. In this case, the child's behavior is directed toward the achievement of what actually is a nonaggressive goal. For example, a preschool child who wants a toy held by a playmate may first try a variety of nonaggressive responses to get that toy. The child may ask for the toy, offer to trade another toy for it, or cry. If all of these fail, the child may finally resort to the aggressive behavior of grabbing the toy. Frequently, antisocial behaviors such as grabbing, punching, or verbal abuse are designed to obtain a goal unobtainable by other methods. Reinforcement (in this case, obtaining the desired toy) increases the behavior.

Instrumental aggression can be learned through identification with parents who daily exhibit instrumental aggression in their interactions with their children. The mother who grabs a teacup roughly and angrily away from her child to keep it from getting broken is likely to have a child who grabs other objects away from other children in a similar rough manner.

Sex and aggression. We have discussed earlier the fact that boys tend to be more aggressive than girls. This difference in behavior between boys and girls has been measured as early as eighteen months and in varieties of situations (Maccoby, 1974; Wallers et al., 1957). Chapters 7 and 8 suggested a number of possible reasons: Boys in our society learn to identify with their fathers primarily through punishment, while girls learn to identify with their mothers primarily through reward. Model figures presented to boys tend to be more aggressive than model figures presented to girls. In addition, aggressive behavior is reinforced more regularly in our society for boys.

Cultural and socioeconomic differences and aggression. Children reared in different cultural or socioeconomic backgrounds tend to express aggression in different ways. Children reared in communal preschools often learn to cooperate and share at very early ages. These same children only infrequently exhibit either hostile or instrumental aggression. Bellack and Antell (1974), in a study of German, Italian, and Danish preschool playground activity, found that children raised in a country where parents tend generally to act aggressively toward their children (Germany) tend to exhibit much more aggression in playground activities than do children raised where parents tend to be more affectionate (Italy and Denmark).

Aggression also has been linked by some authors to socioeconomic status. We noted earlier that child-rearing techniques exhibited by par-

What should we do about disobedient children?

Each day, parents and caretakers must respond to young children who exhibit disobedient behavior. A child of, say, four, left to play in the sandbox, takes a handful of sand and throws it in the face of another child. Another three-year-old knocks down her playmate, grabs her toy, and takes it for herself, leaving the playmate crying. What should a parent do?

Susan Isaacs (1968), in a popular manual for parents, provides simple directions. First, parents should realize that it is necessary to establish rules for behavior. Rules for preschoolers should be simple, easy to understand and easy to follow. Next, parents need to teach preschoolers what they must do to obey the rules. According to Isaacs, parents should fully expect the little child to obey—in some things and for some purposes. But the careful caretaker needs to decide specifically what obedient behavior is important—and why. Obedience, she cautions, should never become an end in itself.

Children need to have freedom and choice as well as to be obedient, if they are to develop socially desirable independence and responsibility when they are older. Even the very little child needs some measure of real responsibility. Where do we draw the line? What behaviors are important? Isaacs divides the activities of preschoolers into three basic categories: (1) behaviors essential for health and socialization; (2) behaviors that are interesting to the child, but not damaging either to health or proper socialization; and (3) contingent behaviors not falling into either of the above categories. Let's look carefully at each, and decide what to do about them:

Behaviors essential for health and socialization. These include such behaviors as going to bed at certain hours, eating proper foods, not eating certain foods, washing hands before meals, and behaving in play activities in ways that do not hurt playmates. Isaacs suggests that these activities be regulated by rules established by parents and caretakers. They are sufficiently important not to be left to chance. But rules should be clear and consistent! For example, rules for play should be the same, regardless of the playmate. It may be necessary to establish special rules for playing with little playmates, like much smaller siblings. But these new rules apply to *all* babies —not just to the one in your house. This should be made clear to the preschooler.

Behaviors interesting to the child and not damaging to health or socialization. This category includes very different sorts of behavior than those included in the first grouping. These behaviors don't require either rules or obedience, according to Isaacs. Even three-year-olds are capable of arranging toys on the toy shelf in the manner that is "nicest" for them. Selecting toy arrangements hurts neither health nor ability to interact with others, even if the arrangement is not aesthetically appealing to the mother. This particular activity may, in fact, provide useful learning experiences that will help in later decision making and object selection.

Contingent behaviors. This category also should never be made part of rules or obedience prescriptions, according to Isaacs. Into this category Isaacs places friendly and generous behaviors, pleasant activities that are taught not through rules, but rather through long-term imitation and modeling of adults. Other, less desirable behavior, like nailbiting and stammering, are behaviors often symptomatic of other problems. Nailbiting and stammering, Isaacs cautions, are far best left alone until psychological help can be obtained. They are not reduced by the development of rules.

ents from middle and lower socioeconomic backgrounds in the United States differ in several ways (see Chapter 8). Poor children generally are more aggressive toward their parents than are children from higher socioeconomic backgrounds. Similarly, McKee and Leader (1955) found that three- and four-year-old children from lower socioeconomic backgrounds tend to be considerably more aggressive, as well as more competitive, in their peer interactions than are children from higher socioeconomic backgrounds.

Age and aggression. Even though it is generally considered to be socially undesirable, peer interaction involving physical aggression tends to increase as children get older. This increase seems to be related primarily to time available to learn aggressive responses. As children get older, they move from solitary to cooperative play; this cooperative play affords them greater opportunity to aggress against their peers. Since language use and vocabulary also increase with chronological age, it is not at all surprising that verbal aggression increases at the same time as physical aggression.

TV watching and aggression. TV can be an important tool for learning. Indeed, as we shall see in Chapter 10, public educational TV has played a significant role in increasing cognitive development. However, in some instances, researchers have shown that TV has the potential of increasing some socially undesirable behavior. Ever since Bandura et al. (1963) reported that filmed violence increases the probability that viewers will exhibit aggressive behavior in stressful situations, Americans have been concerned about the effects of TV watching on children's behaviors. The concern is a real one: surveys taken in the 1950s indicated that American preschool children then were watching TV an average of one to two hours daily. Systematic content analysis of prime-time TV in the late 1960s, when children were watching for even longer periods of time daily, indicated that violent episodes appeared in 80 percent of the programs. During children's cartoons, violent episodes average 25.1 appearances per hour (Friedrich and Stein, 1973).

Just what effect does watching televised violence have on children's behavior? Friedrich and Stein (1973) studied a group of ninety-three children who watched TV daily for four consecutive weeks as part of a nursery-school program. Each child was exposed to one of three different types of programs: "aggressive" programs in which cartoon characters (Batman and Superman) committed violent acts regularly; "prosocial" programs in which the models purposefully taught acceptable social responses (*Mr. Roger's Neighborhood*); and "neutral" programs in which neither aggression nor socially desirable behavior specifically were taught. The results of the study were striking. Preschool children who initially tended to be more aggressive toward their peers than the average of their group exhibited significantly more aggression after the four-

Television can have significant modeling effects, even on preschool children.

week period than before. TV aggression, however, had no such effect on initially nonaggressive children. Similarly, the prosocial program had significant effects on its viewers: children watching *Mr. Roger's Neighborhood* increased their prosocial behaviors. (Interestingly, *Mr. Roger's Neighborhood* had greater positive effects on higher-IQ children than on lower-IQ children.) The study seems clearly to indicate that television can produce significant modeling effects, even on preschool-age children. At a time when TV is used more and more frequently as a baby sitter for young children, it is vital that acceptable model figures be provided in the programming.

Dependency and independency Behavior that is designed to obtain or maintain the attention of the adult caretaker is called dependent behavior. The dependency of infants and very young children on their adult caretakers was discussed in earlier chapters. Chapter 7, for example, described the development of dependency through attachment. In infancy, dependency is manifested usually through clinging, following, smiling, or watching the caretaker, as well as through crying and protesting at separation. Reinforcement is provided young children through imitating and identifying with parent caretakers. This behavior helps them later to interact more easily with other people, and also to be less dependent on their own mothers for reinforcement. With preschool children, dependency on the adult caretaker is related also to the type of child rearing and childcare given. Restrictive discipline (described in Chapter 8), for example, is related to dependency in preschool children; more permissive caretaker behavior seems to lead to greater independence.

Instrumental versus emotional dependency. Two basic types of dependent behaviors have been studied in preschool children (Goggin, 1974). *Instrumental dependency* includes behaviors initiated by children that directly reflect their desire for attention. The instrumentally dependent child asks directly for help or approval. For example, the three-year-old who stops the nursery-school teacher every few minutes to ask, "Am I making my drawing right?" or "Is this the right way to put the blocks?" probably is seeking feedback.

Emotional dependency includes behaviors that do not directly appeal for help. These behaviors are designed to obtain attention indirectly by asking for social approval. Emotionally dependent children will be less likely to ask whether their drawings or blockpiles are what the teacher wanted. Instead, they might ask if they are loved. Or, they might demand that the teacher demonstrate this love by asking, "Let me sit on your lap." Negative-attention getting also is a reflection of emotional dependency. Even a spanking, since it requires attention of the caretaker, can provide reinforcement for the emotionally dependent negative-attention getter.

Children with high dependency needs exhibit many behaviors evidencing these needs. Situations that do not present opportunities for reinforcement will be perceived by these children as highly stressful.

Dependence, age, and peer interaction. Infants gradually decrease their dependence on adult caretakers as they receive more and more reinforcement from imitating and identifying with them. Preschoolers continue to decrease their dependence as they increase their interactions with other

Preschoolers become less and less dependent on adult caretakers as they increase their contacts with other people.

people. Psychologists studying preschoolers have found a marked decrease in instrumental dependence on adult caretakers, as well as a corresponding decrease in interest in the nonliving objects around them (Scholtz and Ellis, 1975). At the same time, other sorts of contacts with adults increase—for example, helpful contacts in which children give assistance, presents, or information to adults, instead of seeking aid. The five-year-old child who brings home a Valentine's Day present for Mommy and Daddy is making a helpful contact.

Independence. Children, as they get older, learn more ways to provide helpful contacts both to adult caretakers and to peers. At the same time, they learn new ways to seek and receive help from other people. Similarly, as they develop new skills, young children gradually learn new ways to help themselves and to manipulate the environment to meet their personal needs. We say that they are developing independence.

Independence: learning about the environment

Independence develops as children learn new skills and develop new capacities to interact with their environments. But skills and capacities are not enough. Children also must learn what their environments have to offer them.

Following are a few suggestions for trips parents or caretakers can easily make in their immediate neighborhoods to teach their children about the environment and how it works:

1 *Visit the firehouse* Learn about the tools firemen use to put out fires. See the fire trucks. Find out how firemen know where to go to put out fires. Ask what each fireman does at a fire.
2 *Visit a construction site* Go often to see what progress has been made. See how many different machines are used. Watch one worker at a time and try to guess what his or her job is.
3 *Visit the post office* Take a self-addressed letter and find out what happens when you mail it. Look for it in your mailbox the next day.
4 *Visit the zoo or the pet shop* Go at feeding time, if possible. Listen to the many different sounds animals make. Find out what different animals and birds eat. Watch the different ways they eat. Do they use their claws, teeth, beaks?
5 *Visit the florist* Watch the florist make floral arrangements. How many different flowers can you see? Smell the flowers. Take a flower home.
6 *Visit the library* Look at all those books! Talk to the librarian and ask him/her to show you how to take out a book. Pick out a book together.

From *Child Development in the Home* (Washington, D.C.: Office of Child Development, Children's Bureau, DHEW Publication, No. (HO) 74-42, 1974).

Children become more and more independent with age. They gradually come to require less intimate and less frequent expressions of affection from their caretakers. They play for longer periods of time on their own and enjoy their own accomplishments without having to turn to others for approval. Increasing independence also is demonstrated through adopting more assertive roles in peer interaction.

Defense mechanisms Sometimes young children, no matter how hard they try, have difficulty expressing their emotions in socially desirable ways. Such children are likely frequently to be punished or ignored by others. As a result, asocial children often experience high anxiety. According to motivation theory, highly anxious children are likely to develop defense mechanisms designed to reduce the anxiety. Many different mechanisms have been described by psychologists. One mechanism commonly used by preschoolers involves substituting acceptable behavior for unacceptable behavior. This mechanism is called *sublimation*. The young preschool bully discussed earlier may learn gradually that aggressive behavior will not lead to desired goals. Such a child may learn to redirect this behavior by becoming best in the class at block building, thereby regaining social approval and attention.

Another defense mechanism, *denial*, involves explaining away or refusing to acknowledge the existence of anxiety-producing stimuli. Children whose parents are in the process of a stressful divorce may reduce the anxiety they feel by denying that they care about their parents, or even by denying that these parents exist.

Projection, another defense mechanism, reduces anxiety by permitting a child to attribute his or her own unacceptable behavior to the outside world. Some preschoolers constantly initiate fights with other children, then accuse these victims of their own bad behavior. When this happens, we say that these children are projecting.

Sometimes young children feel hostile toward an adult or toward another perceived powerful individual. Since they are afraid to act aggressively toward this person, they sometimes displace their aggression to a weaker person. A preschooler whose teacher has just been highly punitive may immediately turn around and knock down a smaller child. Such behavior is an example of *displacement*.

A defense mechanism closely associated with denial is *repression*. Repression is purposeful but unrecognized forgetting. Consider the child who is overtly aggressive toward a new baby brother. The child's mother may have placed excessive demands on the child to love this infant and, in response, the older child may have learned to exhibit outwardly love and affection, while, at the same time, repressing inwardly deeply hostile feelings. According to psychoanalytic theory, if this repression is sufficiently severe, all memories associated with this event also may be blocked out. Excessive use of repression or denial can lead to later refusal to acknowledge the real world (Blackham, 1967; Fenichel, 1965; Hall, 1954). By the same token, excessive use of any of these defense mechanisms can lead eventually to some of the problem behaviors of older children discussed in Chapter 13.

As children get older, they involve themselves more and more frequently in different types of play. Play, a behavior engaged in for the child's amusement, can assume many different forms, including games, behavior imitative of adult models, dramatic play in which animals or objects are imitated, and "make-believe" acting out of socially unacceptable behavior.

Anthropologists long have used the play activities characteristic of different societies to describe those societies. Some anthropologists have distinguished societies according to the type of games their members play, as, for example, games of chance (bingo), games of competition (sports), or games of strategy (chess or bridge). Anthropologists and psychologists both have noted relationships between the child-rearing practices of societies and the games they engage in. Roberts and Sutton-Smith (1962) pointed out that games of strategy are more common to societies in which caretakers are concerned with developing obedience, mastery, and independence in their offspring.

Play recently has become a source of major interest to developmental psychologists who view it both as a mechanism of socialization and as an activity related to later creative output (see Chapter 10). Bruner

Games of strategy can involve varieties of behavior. This game is being played in a Siberian day-care center.

(1972) noted that there is a tendency among all young higher-level primates to imitate the purposeful behavior of their elders. In play, young primates actually are rehearsing for later adult activities. At the same time, they are learning to explore their bodies and their environments while minimizing the consequences of their behaviors. In preschool-age children, play serves a number of functions: it gives children an opportunity to imitate and to identify with adult models. It allows them also to practice what they have learned and develop skills necessary for later life. Children often use play as an outlet for expression of socially unacceptable behaviors and for working out social problems.

Role Playing and
Socialization

Play among preschoolers often takes the form of role playing, in which children "try out" the roles of adult-model figures. A favorite game is "playing house," in which small children often assume the roles of "Mommy" and "Daddy."

As children get older, role-play situations gradually increase in complexity. For example, the role play of two- and three-year-old children often takes the form of activities with which they are familiar—for example, taking care of baby, shopping, or visiting the doctor. As children expand their environments, they are expected in real life to take on ever-increasing responsibility; they may be expected to clean up their rooms or keep themselves neat. These experiences are reflected in their play

Playkits

Children love to imitate grownups. And, as they do, they learn about roles, jobs, and how it feels to be an important person with special tasks to perform. Encourage your youngsters to try out new roles and new activities. You supply the props—they'll do the pretending, if you put the right things in their hands.

1 *Kitchen kit*
 Pots, pans, bowls, egg beater, spoons, measuring cups, measuring spoons, cookie sheets, cake pans, a cardboard carton turned upside down for a stove.
2 *Dress-up kit*
 Fancy hats, dresses, jewelry, pocketbooks; shirts, ties, shoes, coats, hats.

3 *School kit*
 Paper, pencils, crayons, chalk, small blackboard, books.

4 *Supermarket kit*
 Toy cash register, play money, price tags, sales pad, unopened canned goods, empty food containers, used cake-mix boxes, wax fruit.

From *Child Development in the Home*
(Washington, D.C.:
Office of Child Development,
Children's Bureau,
DHEW Publication,
No. (OHO) 74-42, 1974).

In role playing, children try out the roles of adult models.

activities, which involve increasing competence and interaction with others.

Erikson (1963) pointed out that role playing is important to the development of identity and self-esteem. According to Erikson, role playing allows children to gain "reflected views of themselves" and helps them to understand that they are "different from but related to" others. In addition, role playing gives them an opportunity to practice and perfect new behaviors.

Group norms also can be expressed through role-playing activities. In societies where group roles are reinforced, understanding of group norms can develop as early as two years of age. Studies of kibbutz children have shown that two-year-olds already have a clear understanding of the difference between "we" and "they" (Faigin, 1958).

Another popular form of preschool play is dramatic play, in which children pretend to be animals, objects, or other people. Interestingly, the ability of children to get along with their peers is related to their ability to indulge in different forms of dramatic play. The greater the child's initiative at this activity, the greater the probability of social acceptance among peers.

Fantasy and Socialization	Play often involves fantasy, in which children "make believe." This fantasy is firmly grounded in social reality and in what has already been learned. For example, children who pretend that the "bogeyman" will eat them up if they go out in the dark have probably been taught by their mothers that it is dangerous to go out at night without an adult protector.

Fantasy is used often as a socially acceptable outlet for socially unacceptable behaviors. Children who are jealous of the arrival of a new baby brother or sister would be severely punished if they were physically to act out this jealousy with the new baby. However, no such punishment will be meted out if a dollbaby is used in fantasy play as a substitute for the unwanted sibling. Consider, for example, the following description by an observational researcher of the free play activity of Alice, a four-year-old girl whose mother gave birth last month to a new baby boy:

> *Alice played for awhile with a set of blocks, first building them into towers and then knocking them down to the floor. After awhile, she wandered to the other side of the room where there was a baby doll and some kitchen toys. She found a baby bottle and began to "feed" the doll. Then she threw the bottle in the corner and said, "No, Tommy, you can't have any more milk! You threw the bottle away. Too bad!" She threw the doll to the floor and left it there. Next, Alice begin to play with the pots and pans on the toy stove. She mixed some pebbles in one pan and then set them on the toy table. She sat down on a chair, and arranged another chair facing her. She said to an imaginery playmate sitting there, "Let's have these nice cookies. Two for me and two for you. That's because you are a good friend, and you like me. No cookies for Tommy because he didn't drink his milk."*

The Development of Social Play

Early play of preschool children usually involves *solitary play*—play that does not require peer interaction. Play in these early years usually centers around objects rather than people. Toddlers often enjoy playing by themselves with blocks. Role-playing toddlers may play "Mommy" or "Daddy" to toy "families" of doll babies. Later, as children learn to interact with others, their play more and more frequently includes other people. By the time they reach four or five years old, children in free play situations usually exhibit much more interest in their peers than they do in toys (Scholtz and Ellis, 1975).

Social play, which involves human peers rather than toy objects, has its beginnings at about two or two-and-a-half years of age in what is called *parallel play*. Children engaged in parallel play do not directly involve themselves with others. Instead, they may play side by side with their peers, observing them, obviously enjoying the fact that they are present, but not directly interacting with them.

Early play of preschool children is solitary play.

The next step after parallel play is *associative play*, in which children not only observe their playmates, but imitate their behaviors as well (Hurlock, 1971). This imitation occurs most often when the children playing together differ in age or ability. Younger children tend to imitate the behaviors of older children.

Cooperative play develops after age three, when children learn to interact cooperatively with each other. Cooperative play involves learning how to use peers for help and also how to provide help for others. Children may take turns at different activities—for example, pushing each other on the swings. In cooperative play involving role playing, one child usually plays a central model figure while others play satellite roles. Children playing "school," for example, often play teacher and students. The child who plays the teacher in this game is likely also to play the Mommy or Daddy when the children play "house."

In comparing the play of children of different ages, psychologists have noted that the amount of reinforcement children give each other increases with their ages. Charlesworth and Hartup (1967) noted that four-year-olds, as compared with three-year-olds, exhibit much more positive attention, social approval, and affection toward one another. Other not-so-positive behaviors, including peer rivalry, also increase in frequency with age.

Sex differences and social play. We learned earlier that boys in our society tend to choose, and also have selected for them, toys different from those selected for girls. This occurs even in infancy. Boys, as early as age three, have learned to be aware of sex-typed behaviors and objects. They often are rewarded for behaving in ways that are "male" and for playing with objects that are considered "male." Thompson and McCandless (1970) pointed out that *sex-role preference* (preferring "male" toys or "male" games) precedes *sex-role adoption* (identification with the male sex in all situations). Girls are usually rewarded for different activities and different play objects. It therefore is not surprising that boys and girls often behave differently in play situations.

By age four or five, children understand the difference in body structure and capacity of males and females. By age five, they understand the concept of permanent sexual identity as well (Hartup and Zook, 1960; Kagan, Hosken, and Watson, 1961).

Children of both sexes tend to associate sexuality with degree of strength and power. Interestingly, sex-role preference of girls is more variable than that of boys, until the age of nine or ten. This had led some psychologists to question whether our society's emphasis on the strength and power of "maleness" has led small girls to be more ambivalent in their desires to play female roles (Kagan, 1964).

By age three, boys in our culture tend to exhibit significantly more aggressive behavior at play than do girls. They also engage in play activities involving the large muscles more often than do girls. Boys spend much of their play time involved in sports, such as ball playing, while young girls tend more often to play games involving observed household activities or work roles. When raised at home, they also respond in ways that reflect significantly more dependence on their mothers than do boys (Cornelius and Denny, 1975).

Sex-role identification and social play. We talked a great deal in earlier chapters about the ways in which sex-role identification is initiated by the early infant-caretaker interaction. Early in life, young children imitate and identify with adult models more than they do with peer models (Bandura and Kupers, 1964; Hicks, 1965). However, as children get older and have more and more opportunity to interact with other children, peers play increasingly important roles in sex-role identification. One vehicle through which this takes place for the preschool child is the social play situation. Later, of course, when children reach the school years, sex-role identification will take place in a variety of ways, as determined by the school setting.

For the preschool child, sex-role identification is a complex process. As we have learned, it can lead to behaviors unique to each child. Children ordinarily are exposed to many different model figures. They may selectively adopt certain behavioral components from each of these models, and thereby develop for their own behavioral repertoires responses that represent a composite of all behaviors observed (Bandura, Ross, and Ross, 1963). Studies of sex-role identification of children in families containing two female siblings, as opposed to children in families containing both male and female siblings, show very different sets of composite behaviors. Female children without male siblings are likely to demonstrate many more female characteristics than do female children with male siblings (Rosenberg and Sutton-Smith, 1968).

PRESCHOOLS AND SOCIALIZATION

In earlier chapters, we examined the behavioral effects of maternal separation and multiple mothering in day-care programs. In this section, we focus on the ways in which preschool and day-care programs affect the development of socialized responding.

What Day-Care and Preschools Accomplish

Preschool and day-care programs for young children in the United States differ both in terms of origin and purpose. Preschools or, as they are sometimes called, nursery schools, in this country reflect the desire of middle-class parents to teach their children social skills and help them develop physically and emotionally. Day-care programs, on the other

Children, like these in a Siberian day-care center, who spend most of their day in the company of other children learn to use peers to help meet their own needs.

hand, arose out of a need to provide basic caretaking for the children of working parents. Preschools or nurseries usually keep children for a half-day learning session; day-care programs provide full-day care, including meals and rest periods.

Chapter 7 discussed the effects on young children of full day-care programs, both in the United States and in other societies. It was pointed out that the effects vary, depending on the type and quality of day-care provided. Regardless of the program, however, psychologists have shown that children who spend the vast proportion of each day together in the company of other children learn to use their peers to help meet their own needs. In countries such as Israel that use full day-care extensively, the peer group plays a major role in socialization. Except for a few hours in the late afternoon, children spend their entire day in the company of the same small group of peers. Together, they eat, sleep, go to classes, and engage in recreational activities. The children learn of necessity to cooperate and get along with others. On the kibbutz, all of this seems to happen quite naturally, without the more formal structures of peer government and indoctrination employed in children's collectives in the Soviet Union and China (Devereaux et al., 1974).

Playing and learning in the Soviet preschool

The Soviet educational system emphasizes a long-term goal called *vospitanie*, which translates roughly as "communist upbringing and morality." The preschool program lays the groundwork for this general principle. Rewards are meted out on group bases to children who behave "properly." Children learn at very young ages to cooperate with one another. If they cooperate, their group will be rewarded; if they don't, their entire group will receive no reward at all.

Learning by imitation is stressed in the Soviet preschool. With very young preschool children, the teacher who serves as model, exhibits the behavior she wants the children to imitate. When they get older, Soviet children learn by imitating older children.

Activities organized by teachers often take the form of role playing, in which real-life situations are enacted. Soviet preschool children "play at work." Through their play, they learn to identify with the Soviet laborer, doctor, or teacher. The photograph on page 305 shows Siberian preschool children observed by the author in 1975 role playing doctor and nurse. The same scene might well have been enacted that summer in preschools in each republic of the USSR.

Soviet children also learn to identify with various occupations through their own work activities. Even the youngest children help to tend the preschool garden. These same children are responsible for such tasks as caring for their clothes and clearing the table after meals.

Soviet children play doctor and nurse in a Siberian preschool.

The American preschool or nursery, with its typical three-hour program, certainly does not as extensively affect the socialization of the young child as does full day-care. Exactly what does it accomplish? The American preschool was designed to facilitate socialization, as well as physical and emotional development. There is, however, little evidence to support the notion that simply sending children who have not already learned how to play with others to preschool will increase their abilities in this area. The teaching technique selected by the preschool teacher apparently is one factor critical to whether or not children develop the ability to interact effectively with others. One study found that teachers who helped children whenever they "thought it advisable" were far more effective than teachers who helped only when children specifically asked for assistance (Thompson, 1944). Apparently, waiting for children to ask for help is not a satisfactory teaching strategy with preschoolers. Shy, withdrawn children, as well as overly aggressive children, may never ask.

Children develop ability to interact with others only gradually. As noted earlier, they progress in their play activities from solitary to parallel to cooperative interactions. The degree to which children are able to initiate physical and verbal interactions with others, to participate in group games, and to develop independence from their adult caretakers increases with age. Shy, withdrawn children who prefer solitary to cooperative play will require more assistance from the teacher as well as help from peers in order to develop the ability to socialize with others.

Teachers and peers as social reinforcers Even though simply attending preschool program may not change the abilities of young children to interact with others, the day-to-day presence of teachers and other children certainly affects learning in many ways. Children, particularly highly dependent children, receive a great deal of reinforcement from teacher attention and approval. The teacher in this situation plays the role of mother-substitute. Children who spend a great deal of time in the company of other children learn also that peers can be used as sources of reinforcement. Caldwell et al. (1970) pointed out that children in high-quality day-care programs (as described in Chapter 6) were more dependent on peers for this reinforcement than were children who remained at home. Even overly shy or aggressive children who have not learned to play in socially acceptable ways can be reinforced by the attention of peers.

Pupil-teacher ratio and social responding In nursery school or preschool, as well as in the full day-care programs discussed in Chapter 7, the ratio of children to teacher-caretaker is important in the development of social responding. O'Connor (1975), in a study of nursery schools that differed in pupil-teacher ratio, noted that different types of social interactions develop in programs with different ratios. When the pupil-teacher ratio is large, children interact more frequently with peers and make fewer bids for adult interactions. With lower pupil-teacher ratios and more opportunity to interact with teachers, children make increasing bids for adult attention.

Helping preschool children reduce unwanted behavior Two main types of behaviors seem to affect preschool children adversely in their social interactions: extreme shyness and excessive aggression.

Overcoming shyness. Shy children are uncomfortable in social situations. Some shy preschool children limit their social interactions with peers and prefer the companionship of the teacher. Others prefer peer interactions and exclude the teacher. Some extremely shy children limit social interactions with everyone in the preschool class. Goetz et al. (1975) suggests four ways in which caretakers of preschool children can affect the behavior of shy children: using direct and indirect reinforcers, and using direct and indirect primes. An example of a *direct reinforcer* is praise given directly to the shy child. For example, the caretaker might say, "Mary, you have done a beautiful job making your bed!" An example of an *indirect reinforcer* is praise given the entire group without singling out the shy child. In this case, the caretaker might say, "Alice, you and Mary both did a good job in cleaning up the room!"

Primes are suggestions on what to do or how to behave. An example of a *direct prime* to a shy child might be a suggestion to play with other children: "Tommy, why don't you select a helper and go feed the rabbits today?" An example of an *indirect prime* is a suggestion given to two children: "Today, let's have Sean and Tommy feed the rabbits." Instead of singling out Tommy, the shy child, the caretaker in this case uses the indirect prime to draw attention to the group.

Goetz et al. suggest that of the four ways to affect the behavior of shy children, indirect reinforcers and primes seem to be most beneficial.

Overcoming aggression. We discussed earlier many of the causes of aggression in preschool children. Aggressive children, for a variety of reasons, have not learned to play in socially acceptable ways. They tend to alienate their peers through constant aggressive attention-getting behaviors. The caretaker needs carefully to shape the behavior of these children; they need to learn acceptable ways to respond in order to receive their much desired attention. Aggressive children can be helped considerably by a caretaker who realizes that both the caretaker and the peer group serve as major sources of reinforcement. The understanding caretaker will use both sources to help. He or she will point out to the class or play group desirable behavior whenever it occurs, so that they may reinforce the shy child as well. When Teddy, who has been roughly pushing down his playmates, stops this undesirable behavior and goes off to build a tall block castle, the caretaker will notice, applaud this work, and point it out to the entire group for their approval.

SUMMARY

As children get older, they increase both in their mobility and in their ability to interact with others. The two abilities together allow them increasingly to be affected by adults and children both within and outside their immediate families.

Psychologists concerned with the development of peer relationships have described the ways children change in their responsiveness towards one another and also in the rules they use to govern their interactions. According to Piaget and Kohlberg, the development of social rules occurs in a stage sequence similar to that observed in cognitive development. The only rules that govern preschool social activity are those set by adult caretakers. Only after middle childhood do children begin to perceive clear social rules governing interactions.

Peer relations important to social development are governed by the development of the child's control of emotional expression: children who learn to cooperate, share, and control their aggressive impulses find it easier to interact in socially acceptable ways with others. As children learn to seek and receive help from their peers and then from themselves, they gradually become more independent and require less feedback from others for each behavior.

Play, a behavior engaged in for the amusement of the child, fulfills an important role in the socialization process. It allows children the opportunity to imitate and identify with adult models. It also permits them to practice and develop skills necessary for later life. At the same time, it often serves as an outlet for "working out" problem behaviors.

As children increase in age, they advance from simple, solitary play to parallel play, in which they observe others without interacting with them. Eventually, through socialization, they begin to engage in cooperative play, in which they not only interact with others, but also help one another meet more complex goals.

In our own culture, boys and girls often behave differently in play situations. For example, by age three, boys tend to exhibit significantly more aggression at play than do girls. They also engage in play activities involving the large muscles more often than do girls. Much of the social play of both boys and girls reinforces sex-role identification.

Preschool and day-care programs give children the opportunity to interact with peers more frequently than would be possible within the nuclear family. Preschool and day-care programs, by themselves, do not necessarily reinforce socialized behavior. However, understanding caretakers working with children in small groups are often able to reinforce social responding in such a way that interaction is facilitated.

QUESTIONS FOR
THOUGHT AND
REVIEW

1 Describe a way that a preschool teacher could teach a "presocial" child to share toys in a play situation. On what basis should the teacher try to convince the child that sharing is a good idea? Why? (For review, see pages 285–288.)

2 Why are small children often aggressive in social situations? Should we expect boys and girls in our society to behave differently? Why? (For review, see pages 288–293.)

3 To what uses can role playing be put in the preschool? Design a role-playing activity to teach small children non–sex-typed behavior. (For review, see pages 297–299 and 302–303.)

FOR FURTHER
READING

Aldis, O. *Play Fighting.* Menlo Park, Cal.: Behavioral Science Research Fund, 1975. This text offers perhaps the first detailed analysis of two important types of play behavior: play fighting (chasing, wrestling, mock biting, etc.) and play-fear or thrill-seeking behavior (rides on swings, slides, etc.). It explores the implications of such behavior for child rearing. The author also attempts to distinguish clearly between play and exploratory, manipulative, and immature sexual behavior. A thorough review of the literature is included.

Duska, R., and M. Whelan. *Moral Development: A Guide to Piaget and Kohlberg.* New York: Paulist Press, 1975. This brief text provides a straightforward introduction to the psychology of moral development. It includes a selection of moral-dilemma stories that parents can use, hints on how to apply moral stages to religious education, and sound advice for parents who want to make use of moral-education theory at home.

Hoffman, L., and L. Hoffman. *Review of Child Development Research.* Vol. 1. New York: Russell Sage Foundation, 1964. Volume 1 of this series is relevant to issues discussed in this chapter. Articles describe effects of separation from parents during the early years, sexual curiosity, sexual interest, and sex-typing. The effects of early group experiences are discussed, as are a number of other topics of interest to the student of socialization.

Keyserling, M. *Windows on Day Care.* New York: National Council of Jewish Women, 1972. This manual is a comprehensive study of daycare in the United States in the early 1970s. The variations in type of care provided across the nation are described in relation to their effects on the development of preschool children.

Mussen, P., *Carmichael's Manual of Child Psychology.* 3d ed. New York: Wiley, 1970. The second volume of this two-volume set devotes considerable attention to socialization of the young child. Articles focus on such topics as sex-typing and socialization, attachment and dependency, aggression, and peer interaction.

REFERENCES

Bandura, A., and C. Kupers. Transmission of patterns of self-reinforcement through modeling. *Journal of Abnormal and Social Psychology* 69 (1964): 1–9.

Bandura, A., D. Ross, and S. Ross. Imitation of film-mediated aggressive models. *Journal of Abnormal and Social Psychology* 66 (1963): 3–11.

Bandura, A., and R. Walters. Reinforcement patterns and social behavior. In A. Bandura and R. Walters, *Social Learning and Personality Development.* New York: Holt, Rinehart and Winston, 1963.

Bellack, L., and M. Antell. An intercultural study of aggressive behavior on children's playgrounds. *American Journal of Orthopsychiatry* 44, no. 4 (July 1974): 503–508.

Blackham, G. *The Deviant Child in the Classroom.* Belmont, Cal.: Wadsworth, 1967.

Bronfenbrenner, U. *Two Worlds of Childhood.* New York: Russell Sage Foundation, 1970.

Bruner, J. Nature and uses of immaturity. *American Psychologist* 27, no. 8 (1972): 687–708.

Caldwell, B., C. Wright, A. Honig, and J. Tannenbaum. Infant daycare and attachment. *American Journal of Orthopsychiatry* 40 (1970): 397–412.

Charlesworth, R., and W. Hartup. Positive social reinforcement in the nursery school peer group. *Child Development* 38 (1967): 993–1002.

Cornelius, S., and N. Denney. Dependency in daycare and homecare children. *Developmental Psychology* 11, no. 5 (1975): 575–582.

Devereaux, E., R. Shouval, U. Bronfenbrenner, R. Rodgers, S. Venaki, E. Kiely, and E. Karson. Socialization practices of parents, teachers, and peers in Israel: the kibbutz versus the city. *Child Development* 45 (1974): 269–281.

Erikson, E. *Childhood and Society*. New York: Norton, 1963.

Faigin, H. Social behavior of young children in the kibbutz. *Journal of Abnormal and Social Psychology* 56 (1958): 117–129.

Feingold, B. *Why Your Child is Hyperactive*. New York: Random House, 1975.

Fenichel, O. *The Psychoanalytic Theory of Neurosis*. New York: Norton, 1965.

Feshbach, S. Aggression. In P. Mussen, ed., *Carmichael's Manual of Child Psychology*. 3d ed. New York: Wiley, 1970.

Freud, A., and S. Dann. An experiment in group upbringing. In R. Eisler et al., eds., *The Psychoanalytic Study of the Child*. Vol. 6. New York: International Universities Press, 1951.

Friedrich, L., and A. Stein. Aggressive and prosocial television programs and the natural behavior of preschool children. *Monographs of the Society for Research in Child Development* 38, 1973 (4, Serial No. 151).

Goetz, E., C. Thomson, and B. Etzel. An analysis of direct and indirect teacher attention and primes in the modification of child social behavior: a case study. *Merrill-Palmer Quarterly* 21, no. 1 (1975): 55–65.

Goggin, J. Dependency, imitation learning, and the process of identification. *Journal of Genetic Psychology* 125 (1974): 207–217.

Hall, C. *A Primer of Freudian Psychology*. New York: Mentor Books, 1954.

Harlow, H., and M. Harlow. The affectional systems. In A. Schrier, H. Harlow, and S. Stollnitz, eds., *Behavior of Nonhuman Primates*. Vol. 2. New York: Academic Press, 1965, pp. 287–334.

Hartup, W. Peer interaction and social organization. In P. Mussen, ed., *Carmichael's Manual of Child Psychology*. 3d ed. New York: Wiley, 1970.

Hartup, W., and E. Zook. Sex role preferences in three- and four-year-old children. *Journal of Consulting Psychology* 24 (1960): 420–426.

Havighurst, P. *Developmental Tasks and Education*. 2d ed. New York: Longmans-Green, 1952.

Hicks, D. Imitation and retention of film-mediated aggressive peer and adult models. *Journal of Personality and Social Psychology* 2 (1965): 97–100.

Hurlock, E. Experimental investigations of childhood play. In R. Herron and B. Sutton-Smith, ed., *Child's Play*. New York: Wiley, 1971, pp. 51–70.

Isaacs, S. *The Nursery Years*. New York: Schocken Books, 1968.

Kagan, J., B. Hosken, and S. Watson. The child's symbolic conceptualization of the parents. *Child Development* 32 (1961): 625–636.

Kohlberg, L. Stage and sequence: the cognitive developmental approach to socialization. In D. Goslin, ed., *Handbook of Socialization Theory and Research*. Chicago, Ill.: Rand McNally, 1969.

Korner, A. *Some Aspects of Hostility in Young Children*. New York: Grune and Stratton, 1949.

Lewin, H., and R. Sears. Identification with parents as a determinant of doll play aggression. *Child Development* 27, no. 2 (June 1956): 135–153.

McKee, J., and F. Leader. The relation of socioeconomic status and aggression to the competitive behavior of preschool children. *Child Development* 26, no. 2 (June 1955): 135–143.

Maccoby, E. Sex differences revisited: myth and reality. Address given at annual meeting of the American Educational Research Association, Chicago, Ill.: 1974.

O'Connor, M. The nursery school environment. *Developmental Psychology* 11 (1975): 556–561.

Piaget, J. *The Moral Judgement of the Child*. Glencoe, Ill.: Free Press, 1932.

Roberts, J., and B. Sutton-Smith. Child training and game involvement. *Ethnology* 1 (1962): 166–182.

Rosenberg, B., and B. Sutton-Smith. Family interaction effects on masculinity-femininity. *Journal of Personality and Social Psychology* 8 (1968): 117–120.

Rosenham, D. The kindnesses of children. *Young Children* 15, no. 1 (1969).

Scholtz, G., and M. Ellis. Repeated exposure to objects and peers in a play setting. *Journal of Experimental Child Psychology* 19 (1975): 448–455.

Thompson, J. The social and emotional development of preschool children under two types of educational programs. *Psychological Monographs* 56, no. 5, 1944 (Whole # 258).

Thompson, N., and B. McCandless. IT score variations by instructional style. *Child Development* 41 (1970): 425–436.

Walker, S., III. Drugging the American child: we're too cavalier about hyperactivity. *Psychology Today*, December 1974, pp. 43–48.

Wallers, J., D. Pearce, and L. Dahms. Affectional and aggressive behavior of preschool children. *Child Development* 28: 15–26.

10

The Language and Thinking of Young Children

Learning objectives

After completing this chapter, you should be able to:

1

describe how language develops during the preschool years;

2

explain cognitive development during these years, and discuss how language and thinking affect one another;

3

give examples of ways that caretakers can facilitate the development of both language and thinking;

4

describe some of the early-intervention programs currently being used in this country; evaluate them in terms of their effects on the development of language, thinking, and creativity of preschool children;

5

explain what is meant by IQ; describe what abilities IQ tests for preschool children measure.

The learning of socialized behavior, as described in Chapters 8 and 9, assumes basic language, thinking, and problem-solving abilities. Without these, it would be impossible for young children to get along in the outside world, to solve day-to-day problems, or, in fact, to accomplish any of the developmental tasks set for this age group.

Linguists and psycholinguists have shown that the learning of language is remarkably similar for children throughout the world, regardless of the particular language learned. Language abilities increase both quantitatively and qualitatively with age. As children get older, they increase the number of words they can speak. At the same time, they use these words in increasingly complex ways.

According to Piaget, cognition, the ability to think and solve problems, also increases in remarkably similar fashion from child to child. We learned in Chapter 6 that, in infancy, children solve problems primarily through learning to manipulate and control their bodies. (Piaget called this the sensorimotor stage of development.) Later, from ages two to six, the thinking and problem solving of children are characterized by their learning to use signs, symbols, and more effective ways of communicating ideas and feelings.

Since language and thinking abilities are interrelated, we examine them together in this chapter. Later, in Chapter 12, we refer to them again, particularly in relation to their effects on school-age children.

As infants increase in age, the number of sounds they are able to make also increases.

The Relationship between Language and Thinking

Because language is the basic medium of communication for humans, it is impossible to talk about thinking and problem solving without discussing verbal ability. Theorists have argued for years, however, as to the specific manner in which language and cognition are related.

Piaget believed that the early sounds made by infants and young children are linked to the ways they think and solve problems. He stressed, however, that these utterances are *reflections* rather than *causes* of children's thinking. He therefore interpreted these early words as an indication of the stage of development at which a child was operating.

Many psycholinguists have disagreed with Piaget's interpretation. They suggest that the words children use actually affect the thinking process and the ways they interpret the world around them (Carroll and Carroll, 1956). According to these theorists, slowed speech development will cause children to have difficulty solving certain kinds of problems. Evidence supporting this position was provided by Bernstein (1958),

Teaching Helen Keller's first word

The Miracle Worker, the story of the education of Helen Keller (Gibson, 1957), illustrates dramatically how the abilities to speak and to think relate to each other. Helen Keller, a deaf and blind child, was first assumed to be unable to learn. Her parents tried unsuccessfully for years to teach her simple communication and socialization skills. When they failed, they considered sending her to an institution for the mentally retarded. Helen, at that point, appeared retarded: she could not interact with others. With very little information reaching her through her senses, she was learning almost nothing about the world.

Before sending Helen away, her family made one last attempt: they hired Annie Sullivan, a teacher of deaf children, to work with Helen. Annie Sullivan believed that Helen was capable of learning, if she could just find the key. She began by making use of Helen's ability to imitate and thereby learn the hand movements used in the language of the deaf. Annie provided reinforcements of both material reward and

love. Lacking vision, however, Helen still could not associate the new signs she had learned with objects in her world.

Annie Sullivan persevered. Helen's first insight came after many trials. She suddenly associated the sign word "water" with real water when it was poured over her hand. With great excitement, she tried out other words and concepts. Associations with objects followed one after the other. Now Helen had names for objects and could communicate her thoughts to others. Using sign language, her family could communicate back. Development of thinking for Helen Keller from that time forth proceeded rapidly, in a normal developmental sequence.

We all know the rest: Helen Keller grew to be a famous, literate, and extremely intelligent adult. The book, *The Miracle Worker*, suggested that the ability to communicate was the key to learning to think. Or do you think it was Helen's thinking ability that allowed her to speak?

who showed that children whose parents did not teach them complex language had difficulty dealing with problems requiring abstract thought.

Whatever the relationship between language and thinking, it is clear that young children can use their language abilities not only to communicate, but also to manipulate their environments in complex fashion. It has been shown, for example, that preschool children use language communication not only to obtain answers, but also as a means of maintaining social contact and gaining attention (Endsley and Clarey, 1975).

Even newborn infants are able to create new sounds. As infants get older, their abilities increase. So do the number of different sounds they can make. By the time young children reach their thirtieth month, their repertoires average eleven different vowel sounds and sixteen different consonant sounds. At one year, young children are ready to make their first *linguistic utterances,* sounds used to tell the rest of the world what they are thinking. Earliest speech is called holophrastic speech (described in Chapter 6) and contains single-word utterances only. An example is the cry of "Hot!" made by the small child touching a warm bowl of soup. Another is that word used so commonly by babies, "No!" Both utterances are meant to convey full thoughts.

During the period from twelve to eighteen months, vocabularies build from a beginning average of three words to fifty words. Later, by the end of their second year, children learn to put two words together and make their first simple sentences. Now they often say, "Bye bye, Daddy!" as their fathers go off to work. Then, they turn to whomever is with them in the house and say, "Daddy gone!"

Later, in the third year, children learn relationships between words. They also learn to use words in more complex ways and begin mastering the fundamentals of grammar. By five years, they know many grammatical rules and are beginning to utter complex sentences and use language in sophisticated ways.

A number of generalizations can be made about the ways that young children speak. For one thing, the number of linguistic utterances (the number of different sounds made in a given verbal communication) increases with age (Reese and Lipsitt, 1970). *Nouns* and *content words* (consisting of verbs and adjectives) occur most often when children first begin to speak. Later, *function words* appear regularly in their vocabularies. Now children begin to talk about how action is carried out.

At first, children tend to *overgeneralize* when they use words. Two-year-olds, for example, often refer to all animals as "doggy." Later, they learn to *discriminate* between different categories of words. Four-year-olds will not only be able to differentiate among the different animals they see, but they will probably refer to each by its proper name.

A Description of Preschool Language

Birth order, sex, and language development It is now generally accepted that birth order is an important component of the child's environment and affects both personality and behavior. In general, younger siblings speak later than do older siblings. Psychologists attribute delayed speech in younger siblings to a lack of parental attention at early ages; parents with more than one child are likely to have less time to devote to each child. The fact that singletons (children with no siblings at all) speak earlier than do children raised in larger families provides evidence for this position.

The sex of a child also is related to language acquisition: girls tend to speak earlier than do boys. The mean age for speaking fifty words for girls is eighteen months; for boys, it is twenty-two months.

Interests and language development Children's speech reflects their interests. We learned in Chapter 6 that by two years of age, children usually reach what Piaget called the trial-and-error stage of development. They begin to understand the concepts of permanence and causality. Later, in the second year, they develop the ability to plan ahead in their problem solving. Piaget called this the mental combination stage.

Before age three, children appear to use language primarily for the purpose of satisfying their own needs. Typical early sentences might be "Want cookie!" or "Want ball!" or "Want Mommy!" Children at this age seem to "want" constantly! When they are not "wanting," they are reporting on events that affect them personally. They might say, for example, "Tommy hit [me]" or "Daddy come" (Schachter et al., 1974). Piaget and Erikson both refer to the age before three and to the speech of that age as *egocentric*—reflecting an inability to separate the self from actions and from the rest of the world (Erikson, 1963; Piaget and Inhelder, 1969).

Somewhere about three years of age, children first begin to understand themselves as entities separate from the rest of the world. Erikson called this period of the stage of *ego differentiation* or *self-other differentiation*. Three-year-olds develop what is called *socialized speech*—speech that communicates to others what the child is doing as well as what other people are doing. "Me poo! poo!" and "Donny bad boy" are typical three-year-old sentences.

Piaget assumed that the reason young children use egocentric speech before socialized speech is simply that they have not learned yet how to socialize or to communicate, and therefore are not interested in the rest of the world. Vygotsky, a Soviet neuropsychologist, disagreed with Piaget. Vygotsky suggested that egocentric speech has a function different from that of socialized speech, and that the use of egocentric speech does not indicate lack of interest in communicating. According to Vygotsky, egocentric speech is used by young children as a method of guiding behavior: they tell out loud what is happening or what should happen. Later, this *overt speech* disappears and is replaced by what Vygotsky (1962) called nonverbalized or *inner speech*. Four-year-old children need not tell themselves out loud what they are doing or how they should behave; their inner speech communicates these messages without being apparent to others.

Children eighteen to twenty months old exhibit their first understanding of syntax (sentence structure). Their first sentences are simple two-word utterances. Later, they are able to use a greater number of words and increase the length of their utterances.

Psychologists have isolated two types of words at this stage of development. *Pivot-class words* constitute a small class of words used very frequently by the child. Children tend to use pivot words in fixed positions in their sentences. Young children all over the world, regardless of their native languages, use similar pivot words at this stage (Dale, 1972). According to some psycholinguists, children's speech develops when they attach the second type, *open-class words*, to these pivots in order to create new sentences:

"Bye-bye Daddy"	"See baby!"	"No candy!"
"Bye-bye car!"	"See doggy!"	"No bad!"
"Bye-bye house!"	"See red!"	"No cake!"
"Bye-bye doggy!"	"See book!"	"No kitty!"
"Bye-bye cold!"	"See pretty!"	"No bite!"

Some researchers note that, even at this early stage, children appear to know more about grammar—that is, more about inherent relationships between words in syntactic structure—than is represented by pivot-class–open-class analysis (Bloom, 1971).

Following the development of pivot-class and open-class words, noun phrases or three-word combinations appear; modifiers are added; sentences become more complex. "Doggy stop!" becomes "Bad doggy stop!" Finally, it becomes "Bad doggy eat ice cream! Go way!" As the number of words and word combinations increases, inflections of speech begin to develop. Before children are old enough to go to school, they are speaking in complex sentences with almost infinite variations of word combinations. They use inflections similar to those used by the adult models around them.

So far we have described changes that can be expected to occur in the language of children as they get older. Why does language develop in the manner that it does?

In earlier chapters, we learned that very early language develops when the baby imitates caretaker speech and then is reinforced for this imitation. Six-month-old babies already babble socially—that is, they use their increasing repertoires of sounds to attract adults. Gradually, through imitation and reinforcement, they become more able to make sounds that resemble adult speech.

How Language
Develops

A random vocalization that sounds like "Mama" is likely to get a positive response from the baby's mother.

But how do children, if they learn only by imitating, learn grammatical structure, the proper positioning of words into sentences? Psychologists and psycholinguistics have not yet agreed on an answer. Some say that language, including grammatical structure, is a learned behavior; others say that, although human language is learned, innate and highly complex biological mechanisms permit human beings to acquire language and govern the course of language development.

Language as a type of learning B. F. Skinner, the famous learning theorist, maintains that language, as other behaviors, is learned through operant conditioning. According to Skinner's theory (described in Chapter 2), infant vocalizations that sound like adult words first are reinforced selectively by parental attention. For example, a random vocalization that sounds like "Mama" is likely to cause mother to react with pleasure and encouragement. Later, Skinner theorizes, the process changes and becomes more complex. Not only do parents continue to reinforce more complex speech responses, but reinforcement comes also from the child's own increasing ability to obtain desired objects through verbal communication.

Some learning theorists agree with Skinner that caretakers who want their charges to learn to speak need to praise and give attention to their children's verbalizations. Others feel, however, that reinforcement, by itself, is not sufficient. Bandura, for example, places major emphasis in language learning on the ability of infants and young children to imitate their caretakers' speech (Bandura and Harris, 1966). Thus, caretakers who want their charges to learn to speak should spend a great deal of time talking to them. Children do tend to imitate the verbal behavior of their caretakers; this is true even when their imitations are not overtly or noticeably reinforced.

Some learning theorists use imitation to explain why function words appear later in the language repertoires of children than do nouns or content words. These theorists offer an interesting explanation for "baby talk." They note that parents who use baby talk with their children tend to have children whose first words also are baby talk. They therefore suggest that parent models probably stress nouns and content words rather than function words in their verbal interactions with their children.

Another learning theorist, Jerome Bruner, suggests that we consider language in the context of the everyday needs and activities of children. Unlike stage-dependent theorists such as Piaget, Bruner believes that language development is primarily culturally determined. Day-to-day cultural activities such as games can be used to teach children to "signal and recognize certain expectancies. . . ." In this way, "they learn to

What does grammar do?

What are children learning when they learn grammar? One way to answer this question is to take a series of words and arrange them in various ways. Following are three examples taken from Slobin (1971):*

1 pie little blue mud make eye girl was

2 the little pie with mud eyes was making a blue girl

3 the little girl with blue eyes was making a mud pie

* From *Psycholinguistics* by Dan I. Slobin. Copyright © 1971 by Scott, Foresman and Co. Reprinted by permission of the publisher.

Most people would agree that the first string of words is not a sentence. This is one way of saying it has no grammar. The second and third are sentences, even though the second doesn't make any sense.

Read these three strings of words. Now try to repeat them back in the order in which they appear. Which is the easiest? Which is the hardest? Most people remember the two sentences much more easily than the nonsentence.

Children learn quickly to make meaning from the words they speak. They develop rules for putting words together, so that sentences result. According to Chomsky, we are almost never asked to create new words. Yet, the number of novel sentences we can produce is endless.

manipulate features of language that they must later put together in complex ways" (Bruner, 1975, p. 83).

Bruner provides an example of a nine-month-old child, Nan, to explain how syntax develops. An abbreviated description of Nan's activities follows: First, Nan plays "give and take back" with her mother. She gives a toy to her mother. Then her mother gives it back. At this age, Nan has not yet learned the adult expression for giving and taking back. When she gives her mother a toy, she says "Kew," her version of "thank-you." Later, when she is a year old, Nan will learn to place "Kew" in its proper position in the giving-taking interaction. When this happens, she will say "Kew" only after her mother gives her a toy, not when Nan gives it back. According to Bruner, children use the order of steps in such games to sort out the proper order for language.

Luria, a Soviet psycholinguist, takes Bruner's argument one step further. According to Luria (1974), social conditions play a tremendously important role in speech development. For this reason, he believes that a structured pedagogical approach emphasizing social learning, as used in Soviet education programs, is the most effective way to teach language.

Noam Chomsky, the famous linguist, disagrees with all the theorists described above. He feels that each of these approaches to learning is an oversimplification of a much more complex developmental process. Chomsky (1958), in reviewing Skinner's *Verbal Behavior*, suggested that learning theory, by itself, does not adequately explain the young child's extremely rapid development of complex language and mastery of grammatical rules. He cited as an example the extremely rapid learning of English language by young immigrant children in this country.

Chomsky theorizes that language learning involves early learning of what he called *kernel* or *elementary grammar*. This grammar contains the main parts of speech and rules for creating simple sentences (Chomsky, 1957). Later, according to Chomsky, children learn more advanced grammatical rules. Using these rules, they are able to create an infinite number of complex sentences from simple ones.

Chomsky agrees that imitation and reinforcement are necessary to language learning, and that caretakers should provide opportunity for both. However, he feels that these processes cannot fully explain what happens when children learn to speak. In order to explain the infinitely large number of sentences that even young children are able to construct, Chomsky suggests that the human nervous system contains innate mechanisms which enable children to process language, construct language rules, and understand complex speech.

Stage-dependent approaches to language development Chomsky's theory is used by many stage-dependent theorists to explain how children learn to speak. These theorists present a number of generalizations to back up their arguments. First, children all over the world produce new language sounds and develop syntax in essentially the same way. The order of development, from simple to complex forms of speech, also is constant across cultures. Although the number of words spoken at a given age varies from child to child, the order in which each type of word appears is constant.

Many other stage-dependent theorists, including Piaget, view language development primarily as a maturational process. To support their view, they cite the many cross-cultural similarities in language development noted above. In addition, they point out that similarities occur in the kinds of meanings expressed in children's language, regardless of the individual language learned (Slobin, 1972). Finally, they note that these similarities occur even though the usual rewards effective in other learning situations have little effect on the teaching of grammar to young children (Brown et al., 1969). Lenneberg (1967) suggested that the best explanation of language development is that it is unrelated to the learning of any single, specific articulatory skill; rather, it is related to the "cognitive maturity" of the child.

Children around the world produce new sounds and develop syntax in essentially the same way.

Piaget, in describing the thinking of young children, outlined characteristics common to this age level. Earlier in the chapter, we talked about the egocentricity of preschool children and their language. According to Piaget, young children talk in terms of themselves and exclude all of the rest of the world from their speech. Their thinking processes, he says, are characterized by the same inner direction.

Piaget suggests that preschool children increase their abilities to think and to understand by characterizing all new experiences in terms of past experience. For example, young Susie might pick up a new red ball and bounce it on the floor because she knows her old red ball used to bounce when she threw it that way. Young children assimilate new objects into their cognitive structures when these new objects are similar to others they have encountered previously.

Young children have less ability to generalize from past experience than do older children. Although the preschool child just described has learned that her new red ball bounces when she throws it on the floor, she has not yet learned to associate the concept of "ball" with the concept of "bouncing." When presented with a new yellow ball, for example, Susie may, at first, need to experiment with it to learn that it also bounces. Only later, as she learns both the concept "ball" and the concept "bouncing," will she associate the two. Susie will then be able to respond to all types and sizes of balls in the same way.

According to Piaget, preschool children tend to concentrate on one aspect of an event to the exclusion of all others. The preschooler, for example, when asked which of two containers holds the larger amount of water, is apt to decide on the taller of the two containers, regardless of their relative widths. This tendency to concentrate on one single aspect of the event during problem solving extends through the early school years.

Another characteristic of preschool thinking is that it is visual-action oriented. Very young children solve problems by actively and physically manipulating the environment. Bruner (1964, 1966) called this an *enactive mode* of responding. Very young children using this mode characteristically use only one habitual active response—for example, a motor response—to interact with objects in their worlds.

Thinking for very young children also is characterized by trial-and-error learning. As they get older, children gradually replace this early responding with directed trials. Two- and three-year-olds can search for lost objects without having to look in places where they know already the object won't be found.

Piaget's Stages of Preconceptual Thought

Piaget described a number of specific changes that take place in thinking during the preschool years.

The preschool years are marked by an increase in image-based thinking.

The early stage: symbolic representation The preschool years are marked by an increasing interest in and ability to use signs and symbols to represent objects in the outside world. During these years, for example, the young child first learns to treat a doll as a baby and plays at feeding and dressing it. Piaget called this *symbolic representation* or *image-based thinking*, and referred to this period of development as the *early stage of preoperational thought*. Since children at this stage are not yet quite prepared to deal with conceptual problems, the period is also referred to as the *stage of preconceptual thought*.

Bruner referred to the problem solving of children at the preoperational stage of development as *iconic* (image representation) *responding*. Children using the iconic mode of responding, according to Bruner, actually are describing the outside world to themselves by using images related to the real world by particular sensory correspondences, such as smell or taste (Bruner, 1966). Objects now develop meaning without the necessity of active and physical manipulation by the child, a step up from the enactive mode of responding.

Children using the iconic mode of responding do not define concepts fully and make many errors in learning new concepts. They can, however, understand concretely how their responses affect their own worlds. Preschool children usually choose proper behavior because they don't want to be punished, not because they understand the concepts of "right" or "wrong."

Piaget's theory of cognitive development stresses the importance of matching the complexity of objects presented to the child with his or her cognitive structure. Bruner's modes of responding stress matching also,

Making practical use of Piaget

A good understanding of Piagetian principles can be very useful to the busy caretaker. With the current glut of popular books packed with hints on how to raise children properly, it's often difficult to separate the useful suggestions from those that just won't work. The following child-rearing hints have appeared in popular parenting manuals and are said to be accepted in common practice. Do you agree or disagree with them? Why? Can you come up with any other suggestions that might be more useful to caretakers?

1 In the past few years, a number of child-rearing manuals have reminded parents that "there is no such thing as a bad child, only bad behavior." These manuals warn caretakers that, when disciplining their children, they should be careful to punish "only the behavior, not the child."

   The preschool years, according to Piaget, are characterized by egocentricity. Children under three have difficulty separating themselves from their actions. In light of this fact, what do you think is accomplished by the caretaker who carefully punishes action rather than the child? What would you suggest as an alternative method of disciplining? Why?

2 In recent years, Americans have become more and more concerned about the apparent increase in dishonesty and immoral behavior among our children and young people. Many child-rearing manuals have suggested that one reason for this increased unwanted behavior is a lack of appropriate adult models —adults who present examples of moral behavior for children to imitate. Some manuals

stress the importance of teaching morality through "appeal to children's innate reasoning."

It is well known that children understand concrete symbols long before they understand abstract symbols. Considering what we know about the preschool child's level of reasoning ability, do you agree that preschool children should be taught morality through appeal to reason? What do you think, specifically, would be the most effective way to teach a three-year-old child appropriate behavior toward others in the sandbox?

3 Many parenting manuals suggest appealing to children's pride and using the secondary reinforcement of social approval. They suggest that busy caretakers of preschool children use social approval as reinforcers—for example, by saying, "Your mother really will be proud when she comes home later and sees the nice drawing." When bad behavior is exhibited, some of these manuals portray harried caretakers saying, "Wait till your mother comes home! Then you'll get it!"

It is true that learning theorists suggest that a most effective way to teach young children to behave in desired ways is to reinforce them for desired behavior. But, according to Piaget, young children, before they enter school, still have only a hazy understanding of the concept of time. Long-term goals are meaningless. What do you think will be accomplished by the caretaker who uses delayed reinforcers of the sort described above? What would you suggest as the most effective method of reinforcing?

Playing "dolls" is an example of what Piaget calls symbolic play. These dolls are provided by a nursery school in central Asia specifically to enable preschoolers to engage in doll play.

both in order to evoke interest on the part of the child and to facilitate developmental progress (Hunt, 1973).

The later stage: intuitive responding Young children learn gradually to use signs and symbols representing objects in the outside world to test new methods of dealing with these objects. At the same time, they learn to think and problem solve in increasingly complex fashion, and to communicate to others about what they see around them. Children, by the time they are four years old, reach what Piaget calls the *intuitive stage of preconceptual responding*. At this age, although they begin to be able to solve more complex problems, they still have trouble in many instances arriving at solutions based on logic. Logic must wait until a later stage of conceptual thinking.

By the time children are four, they use symbols to represent objects in their world. They use dolls to represent babies and stuffed animals to represent live pets. If they want to play with a drum, for example, and none is available, they may use the tabletop for a drum and beat on it with their hands.

We discussed in Chapter 9 the importance of play in developing thinking and in understanding the world. As children begin to use symbols to represent objects, they learn also that they can use symbols to imitate what they see happening around them. For example, a child who has watched someone in the house cooking might make mud pies on a make-believe stove. Piaget (1962) called this *symbolic play*.

Preconceptual Thought and Symbolic Play

Sometimes symbolic play takes the form of *fantasy play*, in which children's imaginations allow them to go beyond the limits of immediately perceived events and objects. Children "take apart reality" in this process, scrutinize the parts closely, and reconstruct a new order from them.

Symbolic and fantasy play clearly are important to more complex thinking. Such play permits the child to practice responses that will be useful in later problem solving. In Piagetian terms, symbolic play increases the child's ability to assimilate objects in the environment when these objects are not readily obtainable, and to find increasingly complex ways to accommodate to these new objects. Researchers have found that fantasy play helps children learn language skills, achieve integration of their experiences, and develop creative thought (Freyberg, 1975).

| THINKING AND THE IQ | Although we can readily observe young children's increasing abilities to think, to understand, and to solve problems, it's far more difficult to measure these and other abilities quantitatively. In order to do so, psychologists have developed IQ or intelligence tests. |

Although we can readily observe young children's increasing abilities to think, to understand, and to solve problems, it's far more difficult to measure these and other abilities quantitatively. In order to do so, psychologists have developed IQ or intelligence tests.

Just what is IQ and what is its relationship to thinking? The answer is not simple. Psychologists have for years been debating the meaning of intelligence, as well as the best way to measure it. To date, there are almost as many definitions of intelligence as there are psychologists studying it. Definitions run the gamut from the general ("ability to adjust to the environment") to the specific ("ability to perform school-type learning tasks"). Different tests have been developed to measure different types of intelligence.

Most tests of intelligence used today include both cognitive and verbal tasks, the rationale being that, for most people in our society, both cognitive and verbal abilities are important to successful functioning. To measure intelligence of small children with limited language and problem-solving abilities, however, different types of tests have been designed.

Measurement of infant intelligence is primarily limited to testing the infant's ability to respond to sensorimotor-type tasks. Later, when children are about two years old and have developed the rudiments of language, intelligence tests measure their ability to solve more complex cognitive and verbal problems. The Stanford Binet Scale, for example, in measuring intelligence of two-year-olds, asks children to name the different body parts of a doll (arm, legs, head, etc.) and also to describe the uses of everyday household items, such as cups or spoons. Later, for four-year-olds, the Binet Scale places more emphasis on verbal ability. Among the questions asked of four-year-olds are the names of objects they can remember from pictures shown to them, the definitions of commonly used words, and the number of blocks placed on a table in front of them and then removed.

Infant scales, as, for example, the Denver Developmental Screening Test and the Bayley Scale discussed in Chapter 6, are useful in comparing the developmental progress of individual preschoolers with the progress of their average-ability peers. Particularly when children are progressing at rates much slower than average, it is important to discover this lag early and determine its cause. Most of these scales have limited use, however, in predicting adult intelligence. This isn't surprising, since infant and adult tests measure such very different types of abilities.

We learned in Chapter 8 that mothers of different sociocultural backgrounds use different amounts and types of verbal stimulation with their children. Studies have shown that mothers of different backgrounds also teach their children to solve problems in different ways (Bernstein, 1960). Does sociocultural background affect preschool thinking and IQ?

Some theorists have proposed that many economically poor children are deprived not only of material goods, but also of the stimulation necessary for proper cognitive growth. They have suggested that, for these children, lack of adequate attention, little guidance in goal seeking and problem solving, and little emphasis on positive reinforcement all lead to decreased cognitive abilities and lowered IQs (Hess and Shipman, 1965; Schoggen, 1969; Smilansky, 1968). This view is known as the *deficit interpretation* of sociocultural differences.

Many psychologists have voiced strong disagreement with the deficit interpretation. They point out that IQ tests often have a significant cultural bias; in other words, one's ability to answer questions correctly may be determined largely by cultural knowledge. Thus, such tests are unfair to cultural groups different from those on whom the tests were standardized. For example, in order to tell what a "cup" is, a child needs to have seen or used a cup. Psychologists who take into account the environmental factor when explaining differences in IQ scores are called *environmentalists*.

Environmentalists use what is called the *difference interpretation* of sociocultural differences to explain differences in test scores of children from varying sociocultural backgrounds. They suggest that all differences found between groups are related directly to differences in the children's types of learning, particularly learning that occurs after they have begun to speak. To support this position, environmentalists point out that no differences in results exist in preschool IQ tests administered to different racial groups. Only later, when children have interacted more fully with their environments, and when the culturally determined verbal content of test items increases, do score differences appear (Reese and Lipsitt, 1970, p. 558).

Sociocultural Differences, Thinking, and IQ

Some psychologists suggest that
many economically poor children do
not receive the stimulation needed
for proper cognitive growth.

Many psychologists have expressed doubt "as to whether any non-superficial differences exist among different cultural groups" at all (Cole and Bruner, 1972). Advocates of the difference interpretation suggest, instead, that children of different sociocultural backgrounds learn to deal in particular cultural contexts with specific learning objects, languages, and concepts. Tests currently used in the United States to measure intelligence rely heavily on responses, concepts, and words taught in middle-class homes. Lack of knowledge of any one of these particular concepts or words does not imply a deficit in thinking ability. Rather, it demonstrates the tests' inability to measure words and concepts these children do know. As this book was going to press, a U.S. district court in San Francisco was grappling with the question of whether, because of biases inherent in IQ testing, standardized IQ tests should be banned from our public schools. Although the case specifically involves only the placement of black children in classes for the mentally retarded, the decision might swiftly affect other children in other states.

The difference interpretation has, of course, many other implications for our educational system as well. Environmentalists point out that conventional educational methods using middle-class concepts and dialects often force ghetto children to function in what are, to them, foreign linguistic and conceptual systems. It is because of their different early learning experiences that urban ghetto children make errors in speaking, problem solving, and, later, in reading, as well as score lower on IQ tests. One solution proposed by educators is to design separate early-education programs based on the specific language and concepts learned in the home.

Ⓞ ver the past fifteen years, increasing public concern has been expressed for the problems of poor people. Governmental interest was shown first by the Office of Economic Opportunity (OEO) and, later, by the Office of Child Development (OCD) (see Chapter 2). Programs have been sponsored to intervene positively in the development of children.

Intervention programs differ in a number of respects from the day-care programs described earlier. Unlike day-care, which simply provides essential care for children of working mothers, intervention programs are designed specifically to *change* the course of cognitive development. Advocates of both the deficit and the difference interpretations have developed intervention programs for poor children. Programs vary according to the theoretical approaches of their designers. Different goals and curricula are used; different age groups are served. Programs have been developed in special early-education centers, in public buildings, and in the children's own homes.

The most widespread governmental early-intervention program for poor children in the United States was begun in the summer of 1964. It served, at that time, some 560,000 youngsters. By 1971, the federal government had expended a total of $2.5 billion on the program throughout the country; it was estimated that one in every ten children in elementary schools in the United States was a Head Start graduate (Spicker, 1971). Initially, the program was planned as an eight-week, introductory summer course, taken just prior to public school.

Since Head Start was one of the first early-intervention programs in this country, it had no specific model on which to base its curriculum. Learning experiences for children in the various Head Start programs were modeled to some extent on existing nursery programs. Activities such as unstructured free play, field trips, music, dramatics, arts and crafts, story telling, and games were used to provide new learning experiences for children. It was assumed that poor children who had never had the opportunity to visit zoos, handle books, or play with toys and games would profit from these experiences. Head Start also provided assistance to poor children in the form of nutritional and medical aid.

Did Head Start succeed? Success of any program depends, of course, on one's expectations. The effects of Head Start were variable. The programs clearly increased the physical health of children enrolled. The original summer programs, however, did not produce academic achieve-

INCREASING COGNITIVE AND LANGUAGE DEVELOPMENT: EARLY-INTERVENTION PROGRAMS

Governmental Early Intervention: Head Start

Early-intervention programs are designed specifically to change the course of cognitive development.

ment gains that lasted into the school years (Cicirelli, 1969). Subsequent Head Start programs provided for longer daily sessions and lasted for a full year. These new programs seemed, at first, to produce more positive results, at least as measured by increased IQ and achievement scores in the first grade. However, longitudinal studies showed that Head Start graduates did not maintain their gains over time (Spicker, 1971). Some researchers criticizing Head Start suggest that the reason scores were not maintained was not the curriculum, but the lack of any satisfactory follow-through program for these children during the school years. According to these critics, it was a matter of too short an exposure to the intervention experience. Others feel the intervention was far too late: most of the children involved were already five years of age. Unfortunately, although in recent years a number of follow-through programs have been researched and instituted, they remain few in number.

Experimental Early-Intervention Programs

Head Start was produced on a mass scale in the United States in order to provide as quickly as possible programs for large numbers of poor children. At the same time, many agencies, universities, and colleges were developing smaller-scale programs to test the effectiveness of specific methods of instruction on children of different ages.

The Caldwell Program Chapter 7 (pp. 226 and 234) described one experimental program that demonstrated that children as young as three months could profit by an early-intervention program. By the end of seven months, children who attended the Caldwell Program six to nine hours daily had significantly increased IQ scores.

The Bereiter-Engelmann Program Another extremely controversial experimental program was developed by two educational psychologists, both advocates of the deficit interpretation. The Bereiter-Engelmann Program is based on two beliefs: (1) language development is critical to the development of thinking; and (2) children who are not taught language skills at home are deficient in these and cognitive skills as well (Bereiter and Engelmann, 1966). The best remedy for this deficit, according to Bereiter and Engelmann, is direct language teaching. The program provides for a highly structured two-and-a-half-hour day for three- and four-year-olds who, according to the authors, are deficient in language ability. Included in the daily activities are three twenty-minute lessons in language, reading, and arithmetic, taught in small groups. Each lesson makes heavy use of structured drill and pattern practice. Each new pattern is introduced in the same way. Children imitate the teacher in presenting their answers. Each child then is given the opportunity to give the response independently, and then to use that response in proper context.

In a typical language lesson, the teacher might present to the group a series of objects. For each object, the teacher voices a positive or negative response, such as, "This *is* a cup" or "This is *not* a cup." In order to learn the concept "cup," the children will repeat the exercise in unison with each of a series of objects. Then, they will repeat the exercise themselves. The pace is rapid.

Some critics have attacked the Bereiter and Engelmann program on the grounds that so much of the learning is by rote. Others, proponents of the difference interpretation, have attacked Bereiter's and Engelmann's assumption that the children initially are deficient. These critics question the logic of teaching a vocabulary that meets the needs of a middle-class society without taking into consideration the needs of the society from which the children come. Bereiter's and Engelmann's response is pragmatic and unhesitating: their goal is to teach children the concepts with which, realistically, they will have to deal in the middle-class world.

In terms of short-term success, as measured by test scores, the Bereiter-Engelmann program reportedly has produced some of the largest increases in scores obtained in any experimental intervention program. Reading performance in kindergarten and first grade of children previously enrolled two years in the program was well above the expected level (Osborn, 1968). Bereiter and Engelmann (1967) reported that their graduates entered first grade with grade levels of 2.6 in reading, 2.5 in arithmetic, and 1.9 in spelling (Wide Range Achievement Test—WRAT). However, like Head Start, the Bereiter-Engelmann program does not provide follow-through programs for its graduates. This may explain why longitudinal studies have indicated that the higher preformance was not maintained (Karnes, 1969).

Operation Upgrade In July 1968, a community-based intervention program to teach reading was begun by an advocate of the difference interpretation of sociocultural differences. The locale was a low-income neighborhood in Kansas City, Missouri. To teach reading, Operation Upgrade used stories written by the children themselves, rather than standard reading texts (Johnson, 1973). The stories proved to be exciting to the children, for they were based on experiences related directly to the ways the children played and interacted with others in their own homes. The method stimulated varieties of creative responses, in addition to improving reading skills. The stories were enjoyable and interesting for teachers as well as pupils. Interestingly, children were able, by means of story games, not only to learn to read in their own home dialects, but to transfer this early reading ability to reading of standard middle-class dialect as well.

Parent intervention programs Many psychologists, dissatisfied with the results of early-intervention programs that begin at three or four years of age, suggest that, for optimal results, intervention should begin in infancy. According to them, the problem for so-called disadvantaged children is "too little, too late." These psychologists point out that programs such as the Caldwell program, as well as the preschool programs established in many eastern European countries, show excellent results when they begin in infancy.

Very early intervention, which usually involves sending children away from home for long periods each day, thus far has not proved popular in the United States. Parents generally prefer to raise their children in their own homes. One alternative suggested by psychologists that allows intervention in infancy at home is parent-training programs.

A number of parent-training programs already are operative in the United States. Chapter 7 discussed one experimental program for training parents, the University of Wisconsin Infant Education Center. Another program, developed by Karnes (1969), provided for eleven two-hour training sessions for mothers, held on a weekly basis. In these training sessions, mothers were taught how to use inexpensive home-built toys to stimulate their children to learn. Karnes reported that children of mothers enrolled in the program increased their IQ scores. These results, however, were limited to children who did not have additional experience in preschool settings.

Nimnicht and Brown (1972) produced a slightly different model for home intervention. Their Parent-Child Toy Library Programme provided mothers with instruction on the use of educational toys, and then provided the toys for the children's use through their own library. Nimnicht and Brown reported that, in addition to helping their children increase their cognitive abilities, parents learned a great deal about the capabilities of their children and thus became better caretakers. They suggested also that parents in the program often increased in "personal" regard for their children.

According to the *New York Times,* for the first time in the United States "a public school system has become an active partner in bringing up babies" (Pines, 1975). Beginning in 1972, the public school system in Brookline, Massachusetts, in an experimental program called the Brookline Early Education Project (BEEP), provided a continuous educational program for children from birth to the age of five.

More than one-third of the children born in Brookline since 1972 had entered the project by the time this book was being written. The following services were provided by BEEP for each child: Shortly after the birth of each new baby, a BEEP teacher visited the home to answer questions about the feeding, sleeping, and crying habits of the babies, or about whatever else the new parents want to know. From then on, teachers made visits every month or six weeks. In each case, the purpose was to help parents figure out why their children were behaving as they were. BEEP teachers paid special attention to the first eighteen months, which are thought by many psychologists to be most critical for emotional, social, and cognitive development.

BEEP teachers also taught parents how to design and organize their children's physical environments, how to act as authorities to set limits to dangerous and annoying behavior, and how to act as consultants in brief episodes, according to their children's needs. Parents learned, for example, how to teach important skills through informal pauses in day-to-day activities, and were encouraged to pay close attention to the learning of their children.

BEEP also provided educational pediatric services to children. The program identified many children with special needs through medical examinations and psychological tests provided by the center. Parents also were asked how their children respond to cognitive tasks, whether or not their children suck their thumbs, what their sleep patterns are like, whether they rock in bed, bang their heads, or ever act as if they are "driven by a motor."

Some of the psychological tests given by BEEP have uncovered physical problems, even though all the families involved have had regular medical care of their own. One small boy who "seemed apathetic and did poorly on tests of mental development" turned out simply to be anemic.

Developmental sessions and meetings in the BEEP program between parents and BEEP experts were held in a relaxed atmosphere on regular bases. Children were cared for in a day nursery while their parents met. Day-to-day questions were answered with practical, well-reasoned advice.

The results of the program? BEEP, at the time of writing, was still too new to permit a thorough evaluation, for the oldest children were but three years old. Reports of parents who have learned how to interact with their children and to stimulate them, however, were promising. One parent, seemingly typical of the BEEP population, reported that she was tired of reading in how-to-raise-your-child manuals that her child's behavior was "what happens at that age." She wanted to know *why* it happened. Moreover, she wanted to do something about it if she could. She called her BEEP teacher who gave her a suggestion. "Write down every time he does it. Plot a curve. If you keep putting him back to bed firmly and consistently each time, it will peak and you won't have a problem." According to the mother who followed this advice, the teacher was right.

BEEP clearly has built the foundations of a totally new type of public school system for babies and young children—a system in which parents do the actual teaching, but receive extraordinary support: masses of information, home visits, training, consultants, evaluations, and, perhaps as important as all the other services, advocacy.

Montessori Education

The Montessori method of teaching is one of the oldest and most successful methods of increasing cognitive development in preschool children. In this country today, Montessori methods are used primarily in private nursery programs. Curricula used in these programs are based on the curricula used successfully by Montessori with young, working-class Italian children in the early 1900s. Maria Montessori believed that all preschool children have the ability, as well as an almost insatiable desire, to learn words. She believed that children at this age can learn most easily if they are taught words that relate directly to objects and experiences in their own home environments. She felt also that children ought not to be segregated by age for the purpose of learning, and that children of different ages can learn effectively from each other. A typical Montessori classroom includes children three to six years old (Montessori, 1964, 1967).

Montessori education emphasizes motor and sensory training, as well as cognitive and social skills. Montessori herself often used teaching methods that combined skills. For example, to teach reading, she cut out letters from brightly colored sandpaper. Children were invited to come to a table on which all the letters were laid out, and to trace the pattern of the letters with their fingers. At that time, they were told the names and sounds of the letters and were encouraged to repeat them. A game often developed between teacher and students, in which students tried to name sounds of letters before the teacher could announce them. Often, older children played at these games with younger

Children in a Montessori school, Berlin 1932, learn about the world through play with real objects.

Maria Montessori.

children. According to Montessori (1967), four-year-olds learned to read by this method, often in only a month and a half.

The success of the Montessori program is not surprising, given what we know of learning theory and the use of immediate feedback, and also given what we know of children's cognitive abilities during the preschool years. Montessori carefully selected teaching stimuli to match the cognitive levels of the children. Letters were brightly colored, so as to attract attention. Montessori used older children to help younger children in the classroom, a method that has proved successful in other preschool programs. The Soviets, for example, teach *vospitanie* (communist upbringing) by giving older children and high achievers the responsibility of helping younger children and low achievers. (Observers in the Soviet Union have been amazed to see four-year-olds helping to prepare the noontime meal for two- and three-year-olds, while three-year-olds have cleared the table after lunch.)

Preschool children in the United States spend an enormous amount of time watching television. In recent years, public educational television (ETV) has developed a number of programs specifically designed to increase the cognitive development of preschool children. Of all ETV

Public Educational Television for Preschool Audiences

programs, the best known is *Sesame Street. Sesame Street* presentations utilize stimuli designed to attract young children. Entertaining cartoons, music, and electronic effects are generously used. Animated figures and puppets also play major roles in the program. Through modeling, various behaviors are taught: models on ETV may clap their hands, snap their fingers, or give the names of letters in the alphabet, and then ask the audience to imitate them. Special care is taken to select models with whom poor children can identify. Repetition is used to develop habitual responses. Thus, the Cookie Monster or Kermit the Frog may repeat the same lesson over and over again over a period of several weeks, until it becomes habitual for the audience.

A second program developed by ETV to upgrade cognitive skills is *The Electric Company.* Like *Sesame Street, The Electric Company* gains children's attention through the use of stimuli carefully matched to their cognitive level. The program's primary purpose is to teach reading skills to children in the first through the fourth grades (Cazden, 1972).

CREATIVITY

Thus far, we have explored the development of language and the ability to think, and have discussed various ways to foster this development. Creativity, the ability to solve new and different problems in new and innovative ways, is another commonly sought goal for children in our society.

Most parents say they would like their children to be creative. But what does this really mean? It is simple enough to describe creative authors or creative artists: they are able to produce new works that are exciting or interesting to us, creations that stimulate our imaginations or stir us emotionally. What about the creative preschool child? The creative child usually has not yet developed the ability to create entirely new works matching in quality those of adults. Creative children can, however, be quite innovative, producing works often expressive of their interests and desires. The artwork of preschool children evidences this creativity, as do their imaginative songs, games, and fantasy play. Creativity can be expressed simply in language, as illustrated by these examples from the speech of two-year-olds (Chukovsky, 1968):

"Can't you see? I'm barefoot all over."
"I'll get up so early that it'll still be late."
"Isn't there something to eat in the cupboard? There's only a small piece of cake, but it's middle-aged."*

Creative children share certain common characteristics. They are open to suggestions for revision in problem solving; they are flexible in deci-

---

* Copyright © 1963 by Miriam Morton. Reprinted by permission of the University of California Press.

sion making; they tend to trust their own abilities to solve problems; and they are not afraid to use their own experiences in deciding on new courses of action. The creative child frequently "plays" with ideas, words, and, later, with concepts and human relationships. Signs of creativity include playfulness, little need for orderliness, and unconventional responses (Rogers, 1966).

Guilford (1950) pointed out that a number of different thinking abilities appear in what we normally consider creative thinking. Included in Guilford's list are sensitivity to certain types of problems, fluency of ideas, flexibility, originality, and ability to redefine problems according to the evidence. Even so, creativity is only slightly related to measures of IQ (Torrance, 1960). It seems to be more strongly related to personality characteristics than to many of the thinking processes we have been discussing in this chapter. Interestingly, many emotional and behavioral disturbances tend to be related to low creativity.

Unfortunately, preschool creativity seems generally to decrease with chronological age. Many authors relate this decrease to learning experiences during the school years. They point out, for example, that creative children often antagonize or intimidate teachers, and therefore receive primarily punishment for their creative behavior. In addition, many creative children are "turned off" by uncreative assignments and learning by rote. We discuss this problem more fully in Chapter 12.

Helping your child to be creative

The preschool years provide some of the best opportunity for caretakers to foster creativity in their children. Psychologists point out that, in our affluent society, with educational TV, nursery programs, and ready-made toys, much of the spontaneity of learning situations has vanished. Children no longer need to devise toys or make up games to play, for they are all there, frequently accompanied by rigid sets of rules or elaborate instructions.

Caretakers who would enjoy seeing their charges solve challenging problems and develop trust in their decision-making abilities might consider the following:

1 Give your children more time to engage in activities that are not organized fully, supervised continually, or prescribed fully. This does *not* mean that you should leave preschool children alone for long periods of time. Rather, you should watch them at activities *they* select and provide stimulation and assistance when *they* call for it.

2 Provide your children with some household utensils, instead of ready-made toys. Pots and pans are safe and nonbreakable, and can be used in all sorts of fantasy play. Often, they spark more spontaneous, creative play than the most expensive store-purchased toy.

3 Be available when needed to provide stimulation. Question your children about their products—not derogatorily, but with interest in what they've created. Remember, the child's creative product should match no other in the world.

The artwork of preschool children reflects their creativity.

SUMMARY

The preschool years are marked by major changes in the ways children observe and interpret the world, and also in the ways that they are able to communicate to others about what they have learned. The development of thinking and the development of communication abilities are interrelated in such a way that it is impossible to talk about one without the other.

Language changes during the preschool years from simple holophrastic (single-word utterance) speech to highly complex speech and grammar. Many factors are related to this change, including birth order, sex, and both personal and cultural interests.

The development of language has been described by both learning and stage-dependent theorists. B. F. Skinner maintains that language, as other behavior, is learned through operant conditioning. Other learning theorists feel that reinforcement alone is not sufficient to explain language development. Imitation is used by some theorists to more fully explain the process of language learning. Noam Chomsky, the psycholinguist, suggests that most learning theories by themselves provide simplistic descriptions of the highly complex process that takes place when children learn to speak. He hypothesizes, as an alternative explanation, that an "innate mechanism" exists in all human beings that allows them to develop the ability to think.

The development of the abilities to think and to problem solve, according to Piaget, takes place in a series of stages. Piaget's early stage of preconceptual thought is characterized by inner direction, by a tendency to concentrate on one aspect of a problem to the exclusion of all others, and, most important, by increasing ability to use signs and symbols to represent objects in the outside world. Later, during what Piaget called the intuitive stage of preconceptual thought, the use of image-based thinking allows children to expand their worlds to include objects that are not always physically present. Children begin to use symbols to imitate what they see happening around them. Piaget called this symbolic play.

Although we can readily observe your children increasing problem-solving abilities in these years, it is far more difficult to measure these and other abilities quantitatively. In order to do so, psychologists have developed IQ or intelligence tests. Most tests of intelligence used today include both cognitive and verbal tasks, the rationale being that, for most people in our society, both abilities are necessary to successful adjustment. Since differences in cultural background are known to affect ability to perform these tasks, many psychologists are concerned that IQ tests are unfair to children from cultural groups different from those on which the IQ tests were standardized.

Verbal interaction and stimulation of all sorts are important to the development of language and cognitive abilities. When stimulation is decreased, the rate of development is slowed. Intervention programs have been developed in the United States to provide stimulating environments for children who otherwise might not have opportunity to receive adequate stimulation. Some programs, based on deficit interpretations of cognitive development, assume that slow-learning children all have received inadequate stimulation in early life. Others, those based on difference interpretations, assume instead that slow-learning children may not have received the same type of learning that middle-class children have received.

Creativity, the ability to solve new and different problems in new and different ways, is not related directly to intelligence, at least as measured by IQ tests. Creativity is increased by providing children opportunity to try out new responses in new ways. Rote learning does not foster creativity. Unfortunately, creativity seems to decline with age after the preschool years. Most probably, this decline is related to the types of academic programs frequently used in the elementary-school years.

1 Do you believe that problem-solving ability is the "innate mechanism" that allows children to learn to speak? Or do you think that speech, itself, is the vehicle by which children learn to solve problems? Use the example of Helen Keller's education (p. 316) to explain your answer. (Hint: In answering this question, it would be helpful to consider the theories of both Piaget and Chomsky). (For review, see pages 319–327.)

2 Does IQ measure problem-solving ability? Is there any way that psychologists can use IQ scores to describe the development of cognition? If not, of what use are IQ tests for preschool children? Explain your answer. (For review, see pages 328–330.)

3 Review each of the early-intervention programs described in this chapter. Which presupposes a deficit interpretation of cognitive development and which a difference interpretation? If you planned to implement one of these programs on a mass scale in this country (and had ample funding to do whatever you wanted) which program would you select? What changes would you make? Why? (For review, see pages 331–338.)

4 Do you think that it's possible to foster language development, cognitive development, and creativity all at the same time in preschool children? How might you go about doing this? (For review, see pages 338–339.)

Cazden, C. *Child Language and Education*. New York: Holt, Rinehart and Winston, 1972. Cazden's book deals with the nature of language as well as with the development of language in young children. The theories of Chomsky are discussed in some detail.

Cole, M., and S. Scribner. *Culture and Thought: A Psychological Introduction*. New York: Wiley, 1974. The relationship between language, thought, and culture is given careful consideration in this text. Effects of different types of environments on cognitive and language abilities are described. Excellent examples from a variety of cultures provide interesting reading.

Dale, P. *Language Development, Structure, and Function*. Hinsdale, Ill.: Dryden Press, 1972. Theories of language development are described in detail together with programs to foster language development in disadvantaged youngsters.

Gibson, W. *The Miracle Worker: The Story of Helen Keller*. New York: Knopf, 1957. This story of the education of Helen Keller is written in biographical form. It is intriguing reading for anyone interested in how children learn to speak. The question of the complex relationship between language and cognitive development is discussed. The examples provided should prompt all readers to think seriously about their own educations.

Moore, T., ed. *Cognitive Development and the Acquisition of Language.* New York: Academic Press, 1973. This volume contains a series of articles written by both psychologists and psycholinguists to explain the relationship between cognition and language. The introductions to each section are especially helpful to readers who are interested in a general understanding of the theories, but have little background in the subject area.

REFERENCES

Bandura, A., and M. Harris. Modification of syntactic style. *Journal of Experimental Child Psychology* 4 (1966): 341–352.

Bereiter, C., and S. Engelmann. The effectiveness of direct verbal instruction on IQ performance and achievement in reading and arithmetic. Unpublished manuscript, University of Illinois. Urbana, Ill., 1967.

Bereiter, C., and S. Engelmann. *Teaching Disadvantaged Children in the Preschool.* Englewood Cliffs, N.J.: Prentice-Hall, 1966.

Bernstein, B. Language and social class. *British Journal of Sociology* 11 (1960): 271–276.

Bernstein, B. Some sociological determinants of perception: an inquiry into subcultural differences. *British Journal of Sociology* 9 (1958): 159–174.

Bloom, L. Why not pivot grammar? *Journal of Speech and Hearing Disorders* 36 (1971): 40–50.

Brown, R., C. Cazden, and U. Bellugi-Klima. The child's grammar from one to three. In J. Hill, ed., Minnesota Symposia on Child Psychology. Vol. 2, Minneapolis: University of Minnesota Press, 1969, pp. 28–73.

Bruner, J. Child development: play is serious business. *Psychology Today* January, 1975, pp. 81–83.

Bruner, J. *Toward a Theory of Instruction.* Cambridge, Mass.: Harvard University Press, 1966.

Bruner, J. The course of cognitive growth. *American Psychologist* 19 (1964): 1–15.

Bruner, J., R. Olver, and P. Greenfield. *Studies in Cognitive Growth.* New York: Wiley, 1956.

Carroll, J., and J. Carroll, eds., *Language, Thought, and Reality: Selected Writings of Benjamin Lee Whorf.* Cambridge, Mass.: MIT Press, 1956.

Cazden, C. The Electric Company turns-on to reading. *Harvard Graduate School of Education Bulletin* 16 (Spring 1972): 2–3.

Chomsky, N. A review of verbal behavior by B. F. Skinner. *Language* 35 (1959): 26–58.

Chomsky, N. *Syntactic Structures.* The Hague, Netherlands: Mouton, 1957.

Chukovsky, K. *From Two to Five.* Translated by M. Morton. Berkeley: University of California Press, 1968.

Cicirelli, V. *The Impact of Head Start: An Evaluation of the Effects of Head Start on Children's Cognitive and Affective Development.* Springfield, Va.: U.S. Dept. of Commerce Clearinghouse, PB184 328, 1969.

Cole, M., and J. Bruner. Cultural differences and inferences about psychological processes. *National Society for the Study of Education Yearbook on Early Childhood Education,* 1972.

Dale, P. *Language Development.* Hinsdale, Ill.: Dryden Press, 1972.

Endsley, R., and S. Clarey. Answering young children's questions as a determinant of their subsequent question-asking behavior. *Developmental Psychology* II, no. 6 (1975): 863.

Erikson, E. *Childhood and Society.* New York: Norton, 1963.

Freyberg, J. Hold high the cardboard sword. *Psychology Today,* February 1975, pp. 63–64.

Gibson, W. *The Miracle Worker: The Story of Helen Keller.* New York: Knopf, 1957.

Guilford, J. Creativity. *American Psychologist* 9 (1950): 444-454.

Hess, R., and V. Shipman. Early experience and socialization of cognitive modes in children. *Child Development 36* (1965): 869–886.

Hunt, J. McV. Development and the educational enterprise. Paper delivered at the College of Education at Hofstra University, November 15, 1973.

Jenkins, J., and D. Palermo. Mediation processes and the acquisition of linguistic structure. In V. Bellugi and R. Brown, eds. *The Acquisition of Language. Monographs of the Society for Research in Child Development* 29, 1964 (1 Whole No. 92).

Johnson, N. Four steps to precision teaching. Unpublished manuscript, Western Illinois University, 1973.

Karnes, M. *Research and Development Program on Preschool Disadvantaged Children.* Final Report. Vol. 1. University of Illinois, Contract NO. OE-6-10-235, U.S. Office of Education, 1969.

Lenneberg, E. *Biological Foundations of Language.* New York: Wiley, 1967.

Luria, A. A child's speech responses and the social environment. *Soviet Psychology* 13 (1974): 7–39.

Montessori, M. *The Absorbent Mind.* Translated by C. Claremont. New York: Holt, Rinehart and Winston, 1967.

Montessori, M. *The Montessori Method.* Rev. ed. New York: Schocken Books, 1964 (originally published, 1909).

Nimnicht, G., and E. Brown. The parent-child-toy library programme. *British Journal of Educational Technology* (1972), 3: 75–81.

Osborn, J. Teaching a language to disadvantaged children. In M. Brottman, ed., Language remediation for the disadvantaged preschool child. *Monographs of the Society for Research in Child Development,* 1968 (Serial No. 124).

Piaget, J., and B. Inhelder. *The Psychology of the Child.* New York: Basic Books, 1969.

Pines, M. Head head start. *New York Times Magazine,* 26 October 1975.

Proscura, E. The role of teaching in the foundation of seriation actions in preschool children. *Voprosy Psychologee* 15 (1969): 37–45.

Reese, H., and L. Lipsitt. *Experimental Child Psychology.* New York: Academic Press, 1970.

Rogers, C. A theory of therapy as developed in the client-centered framework. In B. Art, Jr., ed., *Counseling and Psychotherapy.* Palo Alto: Science and Behavior Books, 1966.

Schachter, F., K. Kirshner, B. Klips, M. Friedricks, and K. Sanders. Everyday preschool interpersonal speech usage: methodological, developmental, and sociolinguistic studies. *Monographs of the Society for Research in Child Development,* 1974, *39* (3, Serial No. 156).

Schoggen, M. An ecological study of three-year-olds at home. Paper delivered at George Peabody College for Teachers, November 7, 1969.

Slobin, D. Seven questions about language development. In P. Dodwell, ed., New Horizons in Psychology. No. 2. Baltimore: Penguin, 1972, pp. 197–215.

Slobin, D. *Psycholinguistics.* Glenview, Ill.: Scott, Foresman, 1971.

Smilansky, S. The effect of certain learning conditions on the progress of disadvantaged children of kindergarten age. *Journal of School Psychology* 4, no. 3 (1968): 68–81.

Spicker, H. Intellectual development through early childhood education. *Exceptional Children* 37 (1971): 629–640.

Torrance, E. Explorations in creative thinking. *Education.* Indianapolis, Indiana: Bobbs-Merrill, 1960.

Vygotsky, L. *Thought and Language.* Trans. by E. Hanfmann and G. Vakar. Cambridge, Mass.: MIT Press, 1962.

PART 4

Middle Childhood

11

**Personal-Social
Behavior
During the
School Years**

Learning objectives

After completing this chapter, you should be able to:

1

describe the development of attitudes and values during the school years;

2

explain how trends in living styles in the United States have affected developing attitudes and values;

3

suggest several ways in which friendship groups affect American school children; explain why children, during the school years, tend to conform to the behavior of other children;

4

explain how discipline affects self-esteem; describe various ways in which teachers and caretakers can increase the self-esteem and learning of school children.

Since most studies by child psychologists have involved children under the age of six, much more is known about the early years than about the school years of middle childhood. The school years, however, are critical ones in the development of personal-social behavior. During this period, interests, attitudes, and capabilities develop; the child's environment expands dramatically and increases opportunities for socialization and other new learning. During middle childhood, children develop new ways of interacting with family members, peers, and teachers. School exerts an increasingly strong influence on the attitudes and values of children, on the ways children perceive themselves, and on their abilities to interact with others.

A definition of terms In order fully to appreciate attitude and value development, it is important to understand just what these terms mean, both in the context of concepts discussed earlier in this book and in terms of their roles in the socialization process.

Attitude and Value
Development during
the School Years

Attitudes. Fairly consistent orientations toward different aspects of the environment and toward oneself are called attitudes (Yarrow, 1970). Attitudes develop through and reflect the individual problem-solving activities, emotions, and perceptions of each child. Different learning experiences produce different attitudes. A child constantly exposed to

One way to study how social values and attitudes are learned and expressed is to observe children at play.

ridicule in the classroom, for example, may develop an attitude toward school that includes apathy or disinterest at best; a child who receives constant praise in school is likely to develop a more joyous attitude toward learning.

Values. Dimensions of acceptability or unacceptability are called values. Values are the criteria by which children judge their own responses and their environments; on the basis of values, they decide what is "good" or "bad," what should be desired, and what sorts of actions to take. Values, like attitudes, are consistent. The child who is apathetic toward school may well have learned at home that school learning is to be highly valued. Such a child can be expected to be very unhappy in school, for he or she is caught in a value-attitude clash.

School-age children perceive attitudes and values quickly and tend to develop attitudes and values similar to those of people they encounter in their play and other activities. In our own society, attitudes, values, and behaviors toward others change somewhat with age. As children progress through the elementary grades, they gradually develop accepted and socialized responding: they become less selfish, less domineering, less approving of asocial behavior, and more inclined to value large numbers of friends (Guilford, 1974).

Cross-cultural researchers have noted that attitude and value development is related to the pervasive attitudes and values expressed by the larger society. Communist societies, for example, place high value on conformity to conventional rules. Children growing up in these societies clearly exhibit behavior that conforms more to those around them than do their same-age counterparts in Western nations (Shouval et al., 1975). This holds true of child behavior in school, at camp, and on the playground.

Self-concept. An individual's attitude toward himself or herself as a person is called self-concept. Self-concept often is expressed in terms of learned roles or prescribed patterns of behavior. As we learned earlier, preschool children have little or no understanding of "self." That is, they do not yet perceive themselves as entities separate from their environments; they are not ready to develop self-concepts. It is only later, during the school years, that children first express interest in who they are and what they can do.

Children's self-concepts are a complex blend of attitudes shaped gradually by each child's individual learning experiences. Very young children, of course, do not view themselves in terms of any specific role behaviors. As they get older and learn from their interactions with others, they gradually develop more clearly defined pictures of their abilities and limits. Children who have learned, for example, that they can manipulate their environments successfully by adopting socially accepted sex-role behaviors are likely to maintain those behaviors and to perceive themselves most easily in terms of these sex roles. Children who have not been reinforced for particular sex-typed behaviors are not so likely to develop these perceptions

Finally, preschool children characteristically lack empathy—that is, they are not readily able to perceive or understand the feelings of others. With the development of self-concept, children begin to understand how they are both similar to and different from others—a prerequisite, of course, to empathetic responding.

Social attitudes and values One way to study social attitudes and values as they are learned and then expressed in social interactions is to observe children at play.

Piaget's studies of the development of social rules. We discussed earlier the importance of play in socialization. Piaget, you will recall, studied the social rules involved in the children's game of marbles. According to Piaget, preschoolers playing marbles are interested primarily in learning how to use their arms and hands to shoot the marbles, rather than in establishing social rules for group play. At this age, children believe that the rules of the game should be determined by authority figures and accepted unquestioningly. By the time they are seven years old, however, children consider "winning the game" to be a major reward. Now, for the first time, they are interested in learning rules for the purpose of winning. Piaget called this the *stage of incipient cooperation.*

By eleven or twelve years of age, most children are interested in rules for their own sakes. Children at this stage spend a great deal of time codifying rules and using them as the basis of play (Piaget, 1932). It is at this age that secret clubs with "club rules" known only to the members become very popular.

Piaget's studies of the development of moral reasoning. In another series of experiments aimed at measuring the development of moral reasoning, Piaget told stories to young children in which other model children performed morality-relevant acts. Piaget's subjects then were asked to judge these acts on the basis of their acceptability. Preschool children tended to regard as unacceptable acts that had the most serious consequences. For example, models who broke fifteen cups accidentally were judged "naughtier" than models who very deliberately broke one cup. Only children nine years or older, who had already developed the ability to empathize, were likely to take motive into consideration and judge as more serious deliberately performed actions.

Piaget got similar results when he studied children's attitudes toward lying. He discovered in these studies that what preschool children felt to be most unacceptable were words their parents disapproved of. By the time they reached schoolage, children disapproved also of clearly falsified statements. It was not until they reached nine or ten years old, however, that they consistently disapproved not so much of untruths, but of untrue statements made with specific intent to deceive (Berndt and Berndt, 1975; Flavell, 1963).

THE FAMILY

The family was described in earlier chapters as an important influencer of child development and socialization. During middle childhood, children spend increasing amounts of time away from home. At the same time, when they are home, parents spend less and less time interacting directly with them, and more and more time at their own adult pursuits. According to one critic of child rearing in the United States, television appears to be taking over as a "flickering blue parent" that occupies more of the waking hours of American children than any other single influence (Kenniston, 1975).

Bronfenbrenner (1970), another critic of American child rearing, points out that busy American parents tend to reward their children with material goods rather than with attention. Bronfenbrenner suggests that American families today tend increasingly to be age segregated. That is, activities within the family are organized by age in such a way that members of different ages have less and less time to interact with one another. School children tend to eat dinners only infrequently with adults, for example. Family chores are generally performed on age-segregated bases: children clean their own rooms, parents take care of the shopping and meal preparation, and so on. Age segregation is perpetuated physically as well. Middle-class homes often include "game rooms," where school-age children can play and not "bother" others in the house. Similarly, in apartment complexes, architects design separate playgrounds for different ages, all situated so as not to disturb the adults of the community.

Does the fact that children spend more and more time away from home with their peers and that adults exert less and less influence in the time still spent at home affect the family's role in fostering personal-social development of school-age children?

The family affects child development both directly and indirectly. Earlier, we talked about certain effects—for example, the family's influence on role development. Indirect effects also are numerous. For example, the decreasing attention given to child rearing by parents increases the influence of peers. School-age children are measurably more dependent on attention from their friends now than they were even two decades ago (Condry and Simon, 1968). Decreasing attention given by parents coupled with increasing time spent in front of the television set seems also to be related to a decrease in communication-skills development (Robinson et al., 1973). This latter finding should not be surprising: one study showed that 78 percent of families watching TV report that they do not speak at all when the TV set is on (Garbarino, 1972).

Child-rearing methods and parental behaviors are related in more direct ways to self-esteem. Self-concept, you will remember, is the individual's perception of himself or herself as a person. When this perception is given a value judgment, we call it self-esteem. Coopersmith (1967) found that he could predict the self-esteem of school-age boys more accurately by the behaviors and attributes of their parents than by factors more commonly assumed to be related to self-esteem in school children, such as physical attractiveness, intelligence, or motor ability.

In Coopersmith's longitudinal study of middle-class school-age boys, those rated high in self-esteem described themselves as "worthy human beings." These boys tended to be more secure and less anxious than lower–self-esteem boys. In addition, they tended to be more inquisitive, more interested in activities around them, less afraid to question the teacher, and more creative than lower–self-esteem boys. They also tended to be less physically aggressive toward their peers. Lower–self-esteem boys either reported that they were unsure of their self-worth or, more sadly, that they were unworthy.

The Family, Self-Concept, and Self-Esteem

Seventy-eight percent of the families that watch TV report that they do not speak at all when the television set is on.

Parents of high–self-esteem boys interviewed by Coopersmith tended to rate higher in self-esteem and emotional stability than did other parents. Mothers tended to be happier in their parental roles and both parents tended to be significantly more attentive to their children. Although there were two working parents in many of the homes, these parents, when they were at home, consistently devoted their free time to their children.

Parental behavior clearly serves as a model for the behavior of children. It is well known, for example, that aggressive models teach aggression and that highly aggressive parents tend to have aggressive children (Eron et al., 1974). Coopersmith suggested that parents of the high–self-esteem boys in his study served successfully as models for behaviors associated with high self-esteem.

What behaviors did these parents teach? High–self-esteem parents tended to be more strict than were the parents of lower–self-esteem boys. They were, at the same time, less punitive—that is, they established clear-cut rules of behavior for themselves and for their children, and administered these rules consistently. High–self-esteem boys disobeyed infrequently. Parents rarely administered punishment; when administered, punishment was consistent and not harsh. One way to interpret these findings is that parents of high–self-esteem boys taught their children by rules consistent with operant approaches to behavior. As a result, they were highly efficient at teaching desired behavior. Parents of high–self-esteem boys tended also to use reasoning in their disciplinary methods, an approach consistent with nonauthoritarian methods of upbringing discussed earlier in this book.

The development of self-esteem has been studied by a number of researchers. Their results, for the most part, complement those of Coopersmith. Miller (1975), for example, reported that self-esteem is related to the educational level and profession of the mother. Miller found, interestingly, that whether or not both parents are employed seems to be related to self-esteem. Low-income and low-educational-level mothers who were employed out of necessity tended to have lower–self-esteem children than did mothers who were more highly educated and who were employed by choice. In this study self-esteem of mothers probably is the factor most important to the self-esteem of children.

Woods (1972) found that the effect on school-age children of working mothers is dependent to a great extent on what substitute supervision is provided. Supervised children in Wood's study were more self-reliant and more independent; children left unsupervised tended to develop cognitive and social problems.

Divorce There is a tendency in the United States to relate juvenile delinquency to broken homes. Studies show, however, that the dynamics of divorce are far too complicated to permit such generalizations. (Herzog and Sudia, 1973). Too often, conclusions are drawn from studies in which all types of broken homes were considered without regard to other factors, such as the quality of child rearing provided (Bachman, 1970). Researchers have found that broken homes, when the quality of child rearing remains high, are unrelated either to child behavior or to academic problems (Robins, 1966).

How do school-age children perceive themselves and the situation at the time of divorce? Generally, children seven to eight years old are the most vulnerable (Kelly and Wallerstein, 1976). Common child reactions include strong feelings of sadness and a longing for the absent parent; crying is not uncommon. Children often express fear of not being wanted or guilt at being the cause of divorce. Frequently, they express considerable anger toward the custodial parent. School-age children

Helping single parents and their children

The needs of single parents and their children in this country do not differ significantly from those of other societies. In a report to governmental agencies in Canada concerned with helping single-parent families and with reducing social problems (Guyatt, 1971), the following recommendations were made.

1 Because the greatest common problem of one-parent families is financial need, more adequate public support is recommended, in the form of a guaranteed annual income, a greatly increased family allowance to single mothers with dependent children, and a revision of tax laws to permit the cost of supplementary child care to be deducted from taxable income.
2 Single parents tend frequently to be subject to social isolation because of their status. It is recommended, therefore, that the public be educated to recognize the importance of keeping single parents and their children in the mainstream of social life.
3 In order to keep single parents and their children in the social mainstream, it is important

that the same social agencies that deal with other families deal also with them.
4 Subsidized day-care services are needed by most one-parent families with small children if they are to become self-supporting. These should be provided.
5 Counseling services and additional volunteer programs to bring casework services to needy families are very important, and are recommended to help prevent further family breakdown.
6 Since increasing numbers of unmarried women are keeping their children, it is recommended that accommodative, counseling, and rehabilitative services in this area be provided.
7 Rehabilitation services to assist single parents who wish to become self-supporting should be more realistic and helpful.

Do you think the United States already has taken steps to deal with any of these issues? If so, which ones? Can you make additional recommendations?

often are bitterly realistic about their situations: "I wish my Mommy and Daddy were married. I wouldn't mind so much that they're not if I just could see my Daddy more." The following response of a first grader to her therapist, when asked what she would tell another child whose parents were getting divorced, is also not an uncommon one: "I would never say it will be good because it just won't." There is apparently no straightforward relationship between the intensity of a child's suffering at home and his or her reaction to divorce as observed in the school setting. Sometimes children who exhibit serious problem behavior at home may appear totally happy in school, where no painful associations are present.

The Family and Moral Behavior

Psychologists agree that child-rearing methods have important effects on the ways children solve problems related to moral issues. They have long been aware, however, that morality is not taught directly through lessons on "how to be moral." Hartshorne and May (1928) reported some fifty years ago that simply teaching "right" or "wrong" behavior in school in no way guarantees how children will behave later. The situation clearly is complex: children who will cheat in one situation may well be honest in another. Hartshorne and May's data is quite logical when considered in the light of Kohlberg's theory of moral reasoning (see Chapter 2 for review). If moral judgments are based at early ages on hedonistic principles, as Kohlberg suggests, there is no reason to expect a child's behavior to reflect principled types of ethics, regardless of whether or not schools teach such ethics.

Since the Hartshorne and May studies, many researchers have shown that the behavior and attitudes of parents toward moral issues are a much better indicator of what to expect of children than is simple knowledge of "right" and "wrong" (Devereux, 1972). Parents can teach moral reasoning in a variety of ways. Perhaps most importantly, they serve as effective model figures. They also can choose child-rearing techniques conducive (or not conducive) to the development of moral reasoning. Social reinforcement can be used quite effectively. Parents who reinforce their children for high moral reasoning tend to have children who score highest on moral-reasoning scales (Holstein, 1969). Hoffman and Salzstein (1967) showed that children who scored highest on scales of moral reasoning tended to have parents who also scored highest. Parents who tended not to capitalize on their own power and authority in child rearing, but who, instead, focused on the consequences of their children's actions on others, tended to have the children most advanced in moral reasoning.

The Family, Sex-Role Identification, and Sex-Typing

Sex-role identification refers to the degree to which children regard themselves as male or female. *Sex-typing* refers to the selection of behavior that is considered socially acceptable for a given sex.

Identification with the same-sexed parent is learned through modeling and reinforcement.

Sex-role identification develops first through early identification with the prime caretaker. As children get older, identification with the same-sexed parent is learned through modeling and through reinforcement.

Preschool children learn sex-typed behaviors through a variety of cues, such as dress, body changes, and the behaviors of adults around them. We learned earlier (in Chapters 8 and 9) that, although social attitudes toward sex-typing are changing, the ways that sex-typed behaviors are learned still tends to differ for the two sexes in our society. American parents generally teach girls through positive reinforcement and boys through negative reinforcement. Still, by the time they reach school age, boys and girls are remarkably similar in their ability to identify socially accepted sex-typed behaviors (Maccoby, 1974). Williams et al. (1975) showed picture stories to young boys and girls from kindergarten through second grade, asking them to identify the picture characters in terms of known adult sex-typed stereotypes. As both boys and girls increased in age and grade, they tended to give responses increasingly similar to adult sex stereotypes. For example, male characters in the picture stories increasingly were described as aggressive, strong, or adventurous. Female characters were described increasingly as gentle, emotional, or appreciative.

Boys develop sex-role preferences earlier and more consistently than do girls. On measures of sex-role preferences—for example, on the "IT Scale for Children," which asks children to select either male- or female-stereotyped toys—girls tend to fluctuate between male and female choices until about age ten, when a rapid shift to femininity occurs. School-age girls tend to fluctuate in their preferences more than do boys (Hetherington and Parke, 1975). This ambivalence has been attributed by many psychologists to elementary-school girls' increasing awareness of greater privilege and prestige associated with the male role in our society.

THE WORLD OUTSIDE

As children increase in age, they come into daily contact with more and more people and objects. Elementary school brings new relationships with peers and teachers and affects personal-social development in a variety of ways.

Peer Relationships

For the preschool child, adult caretakers serve as primary model figures. In the school years, adult models, particularly teachers, continue to affect socialization (Hartup, 1970). During the school years, peers also begin to play more important roles as models both for socially acceptable and socially unacceptable behavior in games and play (Hartup, 1970; Perry et al., 1975). Children whose behavior is reinforced in some way, as through teacher approval for good homework, or even teacher attention given to unacceptable behavior, are likely to be imitated by other children in the class. Children whose behavior is reinforced through peer approval at play are likely to be imitated by others as well. What makes some children models and others imitators? The answer requires an understanding of how children's friendship groups and popularity evolve at this age.

Children's friendship groups The importance of games and play to socialization was described earlier in this text. Social play begins early in the preschool years with solitary play that involves objects rather than people. As children get older, their social play progresses in stages until they reach, after age three, cooperative play. By this stage, they have learned to use their peers for help and, in return, to provide help for others. By the time they enter elementary school, children often are accustomed to cooperative play in groups consisting of several children who interact on regular bases and who have common goals or motives. We call these *friendship groups*. Friendship groups can have a major impact on the personal-social development of both members and non-members. They serve as extremely important sources of positive and

Friendship groups serve as extremely important sources of positive and negative reinforcement.

negative reinforcement. Such groups often provide the first "we-they" referents for children, allowing the "we's" to experience a sense of belonging and affiliation and frequently leaving the "they's" feeling lonely and alienated.

Carson McCullers (1963) in her novel, *The Member of the Wedding*, poetically underscored the importance of group membership for elementary-school children. The following quotation describes a twelve-year-old's feelings of nonmembership and alienation:

*The long hundred miles did not make her sadder and make her feel more far away than the knowing that they were them and both together and she was only her and parted from them, by herself. And as she sickened with this feeling a thought and explanation suddenly came to her, so that she knew and almost said aloud: They are the "we" of "me." Yesterday, and all the twelve years of her life, she had only been Frankie. She was an "I" person who had to walk around and do things by herself. All other people had a "we" to claim, all others except her. . . . All members of clubs have a "we" to belong to and talk about. The soldiers in the army can say "we," and even the criminals on chain-gangs. But the old Frankie had had no "we" to claim.**

* From Carson McCullers, *The Member of the Wedding*. Copyright © 1946 by Carson McCullers. Reprinted by permission of Houghton Mifflin Company.

Friendship groups can be formal as well as informal. In either case, they provide bases for the social affiliation extremely important to the developing child. School clubs, for example, can be organized by teachers according to student interests. Among elementary-school children, sex often is used as the basis for both formal and informal groups. Separate clubs for boys and girls usually engage in socially determined sex-typed activities—for example, the girls' "sewing club" and the boys' "model airplane club."

Elementary-school children tend to base their informal groupings on commonalities of background. Among urban poverty children, informal groups frequently form along ethnic or racial lines. These groups are used through the school years increasingly to fulfill affiliation needs; the distinction between the "we's" and the "they's" becomes more and more magnified.

Although members frequently vow undying fidelity, friendship groups are not perpetuated indefinitely. As children progress through school, their interests change and they frequently leave one group to join another with more attractive goals.

Friendship and popularity Popularity refers to approval and acceptance by the group; popular children tend to serve as model figures for their peers. Popular and unpopular children differ in their knowledge of how

How do children select their friends?

Children of different ages and grades in elementary school frequently list different reasons for selecting friends. In one study, teachers asked elementary-school students to think about their best friends of the same sex and to write essays about what they expected from these friends that was different from what they expected of other acquaintances. The choices made were similar whether the essays were written by boys or by girls. Requirements for friendship, however, tended to increase with the grade level of the children writing the essays. Children in the second grade, for example, tended to think of their best friends primarily as "help-givers who share common activities." Third, fourth, and

fifth graders added a number of additional requirements, as, for example, stimulation provided in play activities, social acceptability, and loyalty. Seventh and eighth graders thought of their best friends in all of these terms. In addition, they stressed similarity of interests and values, and the potential for some form of intimate relationship.

The authors of the study (Bigelow and La Gaipa, 1975) related their findings to what they called a transition from "egocentric to sociocentric and sociocentric to empathic" views of children. How do these findings relate to Piaget's description of the social development of children?

to make friends, in the amount of reinforcement they provide their peers, and in their ability to identify emotions in the facial expressions of others (Gottman et al., 1975). According to Goslin (1962), popular children are able to *socioempathize*—that is, they have learned to perceive correctly the feelings and attitudes of others in their social group, and therefore are able to respond in appropriate fashion. Unpopular children, on the other hand, have not learned how to interpret the communications of their peers, or, in turn, how to communicate with others. Generally, popular children are considered to be friendlier, more sociable, and more outgoing.

Friendship groups and conformity Elementary-school children tend to conform to the behaviors of their peers. When it is popular to wear red sweaters to school, everyone wears red sweaters. When it is popular to carry lunch bags to school instead of buying hot lunches, everyone wants to carry lunch bags and asks for them at home.

According to Piaget (1932), conformity and age are directly related. The relationship is curvilinear—that is, very young preschool children are relatively uninfluenced by peer behavior. Conformity to peer-group behavior begins with elementary school and increases steadily until age eleven or twelve, when it begins to decrease. According to Piaget, adolescents stop conforming when they learn to develop their individual

Conformity to the peer group may be expressed through dress as well as behavior.

modes of responding. At the same time, they develop the ability to accept the opinions of others, even when these opinions differ from those of the friendship group. They begin to use rules as devices for meeting individual, rather than group, ends and goals.

Piaget attributed conformity in young elementary-school children to egocentric thinking—i.e., thinking that does not distinguish between ones' self and others. According to Piaget, children in the early grades are unaware that they respond to group pressure, because they cannot yet separate their own opinions from other sources of information. They are able to assimilate the points of view of others, but attribute to these views their own mental images.

A number of researchers have provided data to support Piaget's position. In a classic study of conformity to group pressure performed more than twenty-five years ago, Berenda (1950) showed that children, when asked to estimate the length of a line presented to them, gave estimates similar to those already provided by other children in the class, even when doing so meant estimating incorrectly. Some statements typical of Berenda's subjects follow:

> *I know they were wrong, but it was like a jury—we were nine and I was the only one against eight. The majority wins. Besides, how could I prove I was right?*
>
> *I had a funny feeling inside. You know you are right and they are wrong and you agree with them. And you still feel you are right and you say nothing about it. Once I gave the answer they didn't give. I thought they would think I was wrong. I just gave their answers. If I had the test alone, I wouldn't give the answers I gave.**

Berenda's study showed that younger children (seven to ten years of age) conformed in this situation more than did older children (ten to thirteen years of age).

Tierney and Rubin (1975) showed that elementary-school children measuring high in egocentricity tend to conform to group pressures more than do children who are less egocentric.

Social psychologists have related conforming behavior in elementary-school children both to self-esteem and to achievement. Coopersmith, in his study of self-esteem cited earlier, showed that conformity is inversely related to self-esteem: the lower the self-esteem of Coopersmith's subjects, the greater the likelihood of their conforming to peer-group norms. Slow learners in school are more likely to conform to group pressures than are higher achievers (Sams, 1974).

The School

School-age children spend an average of six hours per day in school. The effects of school-controlled factors on personal-social behavior become more pronounced with age.

---

* From R. Berenda, *The Influence of the Group on the Judgments of Children* (New York: King's Crown Press, 1950).

The school and self-esteem Coopersmith's study, described earlier, related the development of self-esteem in young boys to the behaviors of their parents. School also plays a major role in determining the quality of a child's self-concept. According to Erikson, during the early school years children first learn to perform academic tasks and develop feelings of either industry or inferiority. Erikson suggests that assistance and reward for learning by parents and teachers of children at this age leads to industry; lack of help at learning may lead to inability to deal with the school environment and, finally, to feelings of inferiority. (See Chapter 2 for a more complete discussion of Erikson's theory.)

One's concept of ability—a child's attitudes toward and perceptions of academic and social skills—is determined by a number of factors very early in the school years. These include success or failure at school tasks, rewards or punishments meted out during the learning process, and expectations of success held by both children and their teachers.

One's concept of ability and self-esteem, once learned, are difficult to change. Once children develop strong beliefs about what their abilities are, they tend to reject all new information inconsistent with these beliefs. Still, many educational programs designed to change self-concepts and increase self-esteem are being tried, some of them successfully. In general, educational programs designed to ensure that children will be rewarded for tasks they accomplish are more successful than others. Earlier in this book, we discussed the ways that behavior-management programs can increase appropriate behaviors. These programs also have been found effective in increasing the self-esteem and the concept of ability of young children (Parker, 1974; Rice, 1975).

Success or failure at early school tasks helps to shape a child's developing self-concept.

By school age, children vary widely
in physical size and coordination.

Physical development, motor performance, and self-esteem. Children
each develop at their own rates, and there are wide individual differences
in maturation (see Chapters 2 and 6 for review). By the time children
reach school age, they vary widely in terms of physical size, strength,
and ability to coordinate various parts of the body.

Coopersmith's investigation of self-esteem in school-age boys interestingly did not find that self-esteem and general physical and motor
development were related. Researchers have shown, however, that the
learning of at least some motor skills is related to extroversion, a characteristic found more frequently in high–self-esteem children than in children of lower self-esteem. Hardy and Nias (1971) reported a high positive correlation between extroversion in elementary-school children and
ability to learn to swim. This correlation was significantly higher than
those found between swimming ability and height, weight, or lung capacity. It was hypothesized by the researchers that extroverted children are
easier to teach.

Discipline One of the most difficult problems with which teachers regularly have to deal is discipline. Discipline, both in school and at home,
is a peculiarly misunderstood topic. In Chapter 3, we discussed at some
length the ways that punishment works to affect behavior. According to
one approach, punitive behavior on the part of teacher or parent changes
child behavior by strengthening escape responses. Of course, when

reasoning and explanation are used together with negative reinforcement, learning is more rapid than under other conditions (Leizer and Rogers, 1974). As you will recall, examples were given in Chapter 3 of ways that Tommy's parents can teach him to come home for dinner on time. It was suggested that they carefully make clear to Tommy just what time he is expected home, as well as the consequences if he is late. This way Tommy can learn in advance what he can do to avoid unwanted consequences.

Most psychologists prefer to discipline children by means other than negative reinforcement. Research shows that when parents or teachers do not adequately teach children exactly how to avoid the negative reinforcer, or when they are inconsistent in its use, they often teach other unwanted behaviors instead. Punitive disciplinary techniques, in some cases, are far less effective in eliciting desired behaviors than are less punitive techniques.

Many other factors also account for the frequent failure of classroom discipline. Classroom punishment meted out harshly and inconsistently has led to varieties of unwanted behaviors in children. Still, punitive discipline is very much a part of today's schools. Teachers, attempting to make children behave in desirable ways, use punishments that range

Inconsistent or harsh discipline may cause fearful withdrawal.

Interview with Miss P, a second-grade teacher in an urban elementary school

The following interview, with names deleted, was conducted recently by a graduate student in education in a typical school in a major city on the East Coast. What would you advise in order to help Miss P solve the problems she has in dealing with students in her class?

Interviewer How long have you been teaching at X School?

Teacher Forty-two years. I am planning to retire in two more years.

Interviewer What grade do you teach?

Teacher I was a first-grade teacher for the first ten years. Since then, I've taught second grade. I have actually been in the same classroom now for thirty-two years! I have had several sets of parents and children sit in the same seats over the years as my students.

Interviewer You've been in the school system a long time. Can you describe major changes you've seen during that time?

Teacher Well, I could talk about changes in clothing. When I first started out, the children all wore their best to school. You'd never see little girls in dungarees then!

Interviewer What do you think of the change in clothing style?

Teacher Well, it seemed more . . . ah . . . polite—to dress girls in girls' clothing and boys in boys'. Polite in the sense that I think it was more respectful to me. You know, if parents felt they were sending their children somewhere important, they wouldn't dress them in dungarees. I suppose the change in clothing isn't really what's im-

from ridicule or sarcasm to paddling and incarceration. In overcrowded elementary-school classrooms, where the teacher's attention is divided among many students, discipline too frequently is inconsistently applied. For example, sometimes when the teacher sees Tommy is disruptive, he or she will respond quickly and harshly; at other times, when the teacher is busy, the same misbehavior will go unnoticed and unpunished. As a result, Tommy will not learn that his disruptive behavior is wrong. He will learn instead that sometimes it is fine to behave this way, while at other times it is not. He may or may not learn when he will "get away" with this behavior.

Teachers cannot always control all of the contingencies in using behavior management. For example, the teacher might want to extinguish misbehavior by ignoring it. At the same time, the other children may reinforce the same behavior by laughing. In many cases, particularly in large classes, discipline may be delayed well beyond the time period portant. It's the whole change in attitude toward the school and toward the teacher.

Interviewer What do you mean?

Teacher Children are not taught respect for education anymore. They're rude—they don't obey. Why, when I first started teaching, if I disciplined a child, and he went home and told his parents, his parents would "whup" him again for being disobedient. Nowadays, children don't care what the teacher thinks, because their parents don't care. And we aren't even allowed to use discipline.

Interviewer What do you mean, you're not allowed to use discipline?

Teacher Well, when I first came here, the principal (he retired—I think it was twenty-one years ago this year) gave me a gift of a big wooden paddle. It used to hang right on the wall over there, right in the front where all the children could see it while I was teaching. I remember, he introduced me on the first day to the students, and he said, "Miss P is your new teacher. She may not look much older than you," he said (I was just turned twenty-one when I took the job here... it was my first job), "but I've told her to use it hard on any one of you who gives her trouble."

Interviewer Did you use it often?

Teacher Actually, I didn't have to. All I'd have to do is point to it now and then. The children would get the idea. Only a few times I had to take it down and use it. Now it's all different. The children have no respect for authority. And we have no authority. It's a long time since we were allowed to paddle children. And now we need it so much more than we did before, because the parents aren't disciplining their children. No one is!

most optimal for learning. The teacher may, for example, wait for a free moment to take the misbehaving child to the principal's office for disciplining.

Unwanted behaviors associated with inconsistent and harsh discipline range from fearful withdrawal and low creativity to more direct behaviors representing resentment against school. These behaviors all are associated with the feelings of low self-esteem reported by boys in the Coopersmith study cited earlier.

In 1971, *The Nation's Schools* polled administrators in fifty states. Seventy-four percent of those who responded said that they used corporal punishment in their districts; well over half felt the practice was an "effective educational instrument in assuring discipline." As the incidence of misbehavior in elementary schools, particularly in urban areas, has increased over the past several years, so also has the request by teachers' groups for increased use of corporal punishment. Discipline codes and procedures have been established at teachers' requests in many communities. The results? As most psychologists would have predicted, the results have included an increasing incidence of socially undesirable student behavior. In addition, more and more teachers are voicing despair, noting that "school just isn't the way it used to be."

The school and sex-typing Even as children enter kindergarten or first grade, they exhibit clear-cut behavior patterns associated with prescribed sex roles. Sex-typed behavior developed in the preschool years is reinforced in middle childhood by school activities and teacher expectations and behaviors.

Elementary-school teachers long have been known to anticipate and to perceive girls as more obedient, cooperative, and "better socialized" than boys (Wickman, 1928). Many studies since then have demonstrated that boys make up the majority of what teachers feel are their major behavior problems (Tolor et al., 1967). Teachers tend to discipline boys more harshly and, at the same time, give more attention to boys than to girls. The result, according to many researchers, is increased aggressive, assertive, and independent behavior in male students.

Girls, of course, do not remain unscathed through this procedure. Bronfenbrenner (1961) pointed out that elementary-school girls demonstrate behavior that is more anxious, timid, dependent, and sensitive to rejection that is the behavior of boys. Levy (1972) suggests that much of this behavior may be associated with patronizing attitudes of teachers: over time, girls get the message that they are inferior.

What other messages regarding sex-typing do children receive from school? For one thing, both boys and girls learn quickly that different sexes serve very different roles in the authority structure of the school. According to recent statistics approximately 85 percent of all elementary-school teachers in the United States are women; approximately 79 percent of all elementary-school principals are men.

The school furthers sex-typing also through a variety of formal and informal sex-segregated activities. Separate physical-education programs for boys and girls are a common example of formal sex-segregated activity. Sex-segregated team sports have been under attack in recent years by the Federal Office of Civil Rights. Although Title IX of the 1972 Education Amendment Acts specifically contained a ban on sex bias in these activities, new programs are only slowly being implemented in the majority of schools.

Sex-typing messages also can be communicated via the textbooks used in elementary schools, an issue that has drawn the attention of the Office of Civil Rights. In a recent two-year study of American elementary-school readers that included 134 "typical" texts published by twelve different companies, both stories and pictures depicted girls as being weak, uncreative, and timid as compared to boys. Boys and "male-type" behaviors were portrayed as more interesting than girls and their behaviors; the ratio of boy-centered stories to girl-centered stories was five to two. "Important" men were discussed much more frequently than were "important" women; the ratio of male biographies to female biographies was six to one. All books tended to describe boys as creative and attributed leadership qualities to males. Girls tended to be followers. When girls were highly successful at a given skill, the skill usually was

Checking for sexism in the classroom: advice from the National Education Association

According to the National Education Association, the key to dealing with sexism in the classroom is teacher awareness. Start with yourself. Do you have different expectations for boys than for girls? Do you expect boys to get higher scores in arithmetic? Do you expect girls to be better behaved?

One way to increase your sensitivity to the ways that sex-typing is taught in the classroom is to check the books on your own bookshelves. Jacobs and Eaton (1972) provide the following checklist for evaluating sexism in textbooks.

	Male	*Female*
1 Number of stories where main character is:	____	____
2 Number of illustrations of:	____	____

3 Number of times children are shown:

a. in active play	____	____
b. using initiative	____	____
c. displaying independence	____	____
d. solving problems	____	____
e. earning money	____	____
f. receiving recognition	____	____
g. being inventive	____	____
h. involved in sports	____	____
i. fearful or helpless	____	____
j. receiving help	____	____

4 Number of times adults are shown:

a. in different occupations	____	____
b. playing with children	____	____
c. taking children on outings	____	____
d. teaching skills	____	____
e. giving tenderness	____	____
f. scolding children	____	____
g. biographically	____	____

5 In addition, ask yourself these questions: Are boys allowed to show their emotions? Are girls rewarded for intelligence rather than for beauty? Are there any derogatory comments directed at girls in general? Is mother shown working outside the home? If so, in what kind of job? Are there any stories about one-parent families Families without children? Are baby-sitters shown? Are minority and ethnic groups treated naturally?*

How do your books stack up? What do you plan to do about it?

Reprinted by permission from *Today's Education*, Journal of the National Education Association.

related to domestic activities. Boys were shown to be good workers; girls, good mothers.

With increasing activity by feminist organizations such as NOW, educators have become more cognizant of the need to create positive models for schoolgirls to identify with and emulate. Teachers' organizations increasingly are developing programs for girls designed to foster improved self-concepts and greater senses of self-worth.

The school and values As noted earlier, morality is not taught by lessons on how to be moral. Moral-reasoning ability, according to psychologists, develops gradually in stages, beginning with early imitation and modeling of parental behavior. In school, teachers can help children to continue moral reasoning through the same informal processes.

According to Kohlberg, one way that teachers can increase the abilities of students to reason about moral issues is to give them practice at solving moral problems. (See Chapters 2 and 9 for a review of both Kohlberg's theory and applications of his work.) Kohlberg and his colleagues have recommended providing students with educational experiences that reflect real-life moral issues and concern them directly, either individually or collectively, as members of a society. They have recommended also that moral reasoning be facilitated by presenting to children models who operate at higher levels of moral reasoning than do the learners.

Implications for elementary-school education seem obvious: If school experience is to increase the ability of the child to reach qualitatively higher levels of moral reasoning, teachers must provide classroom experiences in solving morally relevant problems. They should themselves provide appropriate model figures. (In socialist countries, this method of teaching moral reasoning already has been formally set into practice. Children begin group practice at solving moral dilemmas at early ages. Peer teachers are selected often on the basis of their abilities to share and to help others, behaviors considered to be of prime importance in "moral upbringing." [Bronfenbrenner, 1970].)

In the United States, American parents and educators are still questioning whether the goals of moral education fall properly within the purview of the school or of the family. The question of moral education and the proper role of the teacher in this education is debated regularly. However, whatever the eventual answer, teachers and peers will continue to function informally as important role models.

Desegregation, busing, values, and attitudes. The school often is the battleground for major social and moral issues in our society. One timely example is the desegregation and busing issue of the 1970s. The 1954 United States Supreme Court decision that separate but equal schools are by nature unequal launched the massive and sometimes agonizing attempt in this country to integrate races and social classes within our educational system. The goal is to create equal educational opportunity for all, and, at the same time, to teach American children how to live and interact with others in socially desirable ways. Very few Americans disagree with the intent of the efforts; psychologists and educators agree that social interaction in situations in which all children are able to interact without threat to themselves is beneficial for developing self-esteem as well as democratic attitudes. In recent years, however, educators and lay people alike have been forced to initiate a serious reappraisal of the situation (Coleman, 1975; Jackson, 1975). To many observers, the progress of integration has been agonizingly slow; to many, it simply hasn't worked out. One of the recent attempts to increase the speed of integration in this country is enforced busing of children into different, and sometimes distant, areas of major cities. Busing, in some cities, has been highly successful; in others, it has produced turmoil, school shutdowns, and sometimes violence from those opposed. The issue has been a major factor in several political campaigns. In the confusion and emotionalism of the moment, the facts too often have been obscured.

Cooperation: a new subject matter for elementary-school curricula

The *New York Times* recently reported the results of a New York City public-school project designed to teach cooperation through games (Vidal, 1976). According to the report, after a year of "literally playing games," fifth and sixth graders enrolled in P.S. 75 and P.S. 101 displayed significantly greater ability to cooperate, to communicate with others, and to resolve group conflicts.

The program leading to these behavior changes involved a forty-five-minute weekly game period in which all children learned to create new responses to old situations through creative skits and games, such as "Simon Says" and "Know Your Orange."

Skits involved moral dilemmas similar to those studied by Kohlberg. Classes were broken up into small groups, each group acting out its own solution to the dilemma posed. The measure here was two-fold: moral dilemmas can be worked out in verbal communication; more than one solution is possible in a moral dilemma.

Project games were designed to develop skills that could help to reduce the likelihood of classroom conflict and competition. In "Simon Says," for example, all competition was eliminated by allowing children who did things that Simon didn't say to remain in the game. Instead, group cooperation and the individual need to listen was stressed. In "Know Your Orange," class members sat in a circle. Each child was given an orange. Children were given five minutes to study their own oranges and later were asked to identify them from among a batch of oranges. The message in this game was simple: Oranges, like people, are not all alike.

Just what are the facts? First, let's examine the effects of integration on attitudes and academic achievement of American school children. Psychologists have demonstrated that racial integration can be highly beneficial to minority-group children. Both self-concepts and academic achievement of minority children are significantly higher in integrated than in segregated school programs (Mondale, 1972).

In a study of black and white students attending both integrated and segregated schools, it was found that the most influential factor affecting students' self-concepts was not ethnic or racial membership, but the ethnic and racial composition of the school. White students were more accurate than black students in rating themselves on their social and academic abilities. However, both white and black students in integrated schools rated themselves considerably higher than did white and black students in segregated schools (Busk et al., 1973).

The National Assessment for Educational Progress, an extensive, federally funded research project investigating school children in all parts of the United States, found that black children in integrated programs had clearly benefitted educationally; further, white children in the same programs showed no decrements in achievement (McFeatters, 1976).

For many critics of northern city integration programs, it is not integration per se but enforced busing that causes alarm. Busing itself is not at all new in education. In fact, 65 percent of American children ride to

In some cities, busing has been highly successful; in others, it has produced turmoil and sometimes violence.

Integrated school programs will become more successful educationally when teachers learn how to deal effectively with individual differences.

school on buses every day for reasons other than school integration (Green et al., 1972). Even outspoken critics of busing admit that the "best education for everyone requires *some* busing." Teachers' groups have pointed out that integration of schools without busing is virtually impossible (Fondy, 1971; Spence, 1972).

Public concern about busing cannot be understood without examining the composition of American cities. It has proven much more difficult to integrate northern schools than those in the south because of segregated housing patterns in the north. For purposes of integration, northern urban schoolchildren often must be bused to schools outside their home neighborhoods. Distance has caused concern, as well as fear that inadequate instruction will be provided in distant neighborhoods. School boards in northern cities have tried various solutions. For example, in one urban area black children were bused to predominantly white areas and white children to predominantly black areas, using state and local financial support for the program. Children were bused only to schools whose facilities and instruction were considered at least as good as those in the neighborhood schools they would have attended without busing. The results of this program were considerably more successful than in programs where parents feared a decrease in the quality of their children's education.

Psychologists have provided evidence, also, that integrated programs will become more successful educationally when teachers learn to deal more effectively with individual differences. Studies have shown, for example, that children from lower socioeconomic backgrounds are more responsive to approval and more affected by disapproval than are middle-class children (Rosenham, 1966). Lower-socioeconomic children also have been shown to be more highly motivated by material incentives than are middle-class children (Terrell et al., 1959). If teachers are to be successful at teaching children of many different backgrounds—which is, perhaps, the only way to prove to parents that integration can be effective—they will have to be aware of these and other factors related to individual differences.

| Mass Media and Personal-Social Behavior | The development of values is affected by more than what goes on in the family and in the classroom. The mass media, one powerful intrusion from the outside world, provides messages daily to schoolchildren. |

Television has been recognized for some time as a major source of information about crimes and violence. Although it is true that properly programmed TV can teach socialized behavior, television also can teach aggression and tolerance for aggression (Eron et al., 1970; Lefkowitz et al., 1973; Sprafkin et al., 1975; Thomas and Drabman, 1975). Psychologists have found that children who watch violent models on television screens are likely to commit aggressive acts similar to those of the TV models when placed in similar situations themselves (Bandura, Ross, and Ross, 1963). Children who already exhibit problem behavior tend to be more affected by TV violence than are children who initially do not exhibit problem behavior (Feshbach, 1970). School-age children scoring lower on tests of cognitive ability tend to be more affected than are children who get higher scores (Fouts and Liikanen, 1975).

What should be done about aggression on TV? Some parents and educators have advocated monitoring television programming for the "safety of our society." But the issue is not as simple as that. First, we really are not certain how much monitoring is done at home. Parents have been shown to be very unreliable sources for this information (Rossiter and Robertson, 1975). Second, even though many people think that it is possible for TV to increase aggression, it has been extremely difficult to ascertain exactly what effects different TV programs have in real-life situations. In most programming, many different variables interact and affect the viewer simultaneously; the factors relevant to child behavior may, therefore, be extremely difficult to pinpoint. It was for many of these reasons that, in 1977, in the first court case in which a defendant pleaded innocent to a serious crime (murder) on the grounds that he had become "addicted" to television violence, the jury found him guilty. Finally, even if we could determine exactly the effect of each television program on behavior, we would still need to make some major decisions regarding who should be given authority to monitor the mass media. In a democratic society such as ours, such a decision poses some important moral questions.

As children increase in age, they increase also in their abilities to explore their environments, to interact with one another, and to affect and to be affected by others. Attitudes, values, and behaviors toward others change gradually during the school years. School children tend to develop attitudes and values similar to those of people they encounter in their play and other activities. Young schoolchildren gradually develop ability to play by rules. Piaget called the early school years the "stage of incipient cooperation." At the same time that children learn to cooperate in play, they learn to make moral judgments that include disapproval of intent to deceive. The first true self-concepts develop at this time, when children begin to express interest in who they are and what they can do.

The families of school-age children continue to play major roles in their socialization and in the development of their interests, attitudes, values, and behaviors. Studies show that parents, caretakers, and siblings continue to play important roles both as model figures and as sources of reinforcement. Child-rearing methods and parental behaviors are related directly to feelings of self-esteem in children and to their ability to solve problems related to moral issues. Sex-typing is learned usually through identification with the same-sexed parent. Modeling, of course, plays an important role in all of these learnings.

Changing family interactions associated with changing trends in American living patterns have affected child behavior in varieties of ways. Divorce, increasing numbers of working mothers, and a general decrease in attention given to children by their parents all have affected child development in the United States.

With increasing age, children more and more are affected by the world outside the family. Peer relationships become more important during the school years, with friendship groups becoming major sources of gratification. Elementary-school children tend to conform to the behaviors of peers in their friendship groups; popular children tend to serve as model figures.

School-age children spend an average of six hours per day in school. The effects of school-controlled factors on personal-social behavior be-

SUMMARY

come more pronounced with age and time spent in school. Interactions with peers and with teachers during the school day become increasingly important, affecting feelings of self-worth and self-ability. Physical development and motor performance, which vary greatly from child to child, similarly contribute to a child's self-esteem. The manner in which teachers elect to discipline children also is important to feelings of self-worth and to school performance.

During the school years, children are affected increasingly not only by attitudes and values taught at home, but by the attitudes and values of the society in which they live. Sex-typed behavior, for example, is reinforced during middle childhood by culturally defined school activities and teacher expectations. Unfortunately, in the past, this often has led to lowered expectations and decreased feelings of self-worth, particularly among female schoolchildren. However, changes in American attitudes in recent years toward the roles of both males and females in our society are gradually causing educators to recognize the need to provide more positive models for schoolgirls to identify with and emulate. School programs are being developed to foster improved self-concepts for female students.

Other changes in social values also have affected school programs. Since the 1954 Supreme Court decision calling for integration of all American public schools, efforts have been made to bring together in the same classroom children of different racial and ethnic backgrounds. In recent years, the program to integrate U.S. schools has included busing children to schools in neighborhoods other than their own. The results of busing and integration on the attitudes and achievement of children have depended on a variety of factors, including the school programs themselves, methods used to integrate schools, and teachers' and parents' attitudes toward the issues.

The behavior of children is affected by what they watch on television as well as by what is communicated through the other mass media. Psychologists have expressed the concern that TV viewing may encourage violent and aggressive behavior among American schoolchildren. In response, many parents and educators advocate some monitoring of programming. Such monitoring, of course, raises broader ethical questions—for example, what exactly should be monitored and who should have authority to exercise this judgment?

QUESTIONS FOR THOUGHT AND REVIEW

1 Consider the changes in family living styles that have taken place in the United States during the past decade. Which do you think are of greatest importance to the school-age child? What changes would you like to see Americans make in order to help produce a society of people with higher self-esteem? (For review, see pp. 344–358.)

2 American feminists in recent years have called for school programs in which behaviors would not be presented to children as exclusively "masculine" or "feminine"—in other words, they seek an end to the teaching of sex-typed behaviors. How do you think this unisex-typing might affect family patterning and future child rearing? (For review, see pp. 358–359 and 370–372. You might also refer back to Chapters 7 and 8.)

3 We discussed in this chapter some of the ways that children develop in their abilities to solve moral dilemmas. It has been said that one way to increase moral development is to provide appropriate model figures. What types of model figures have been provided in this country for children? Consider, in your answer, figures within families, schools, communities, and the nation as a whole. (For review, see pp. 353–354, 358, and 372–373).

4 Integration and forced busing have caused one of the major educational controversies of our generation. How would you suggest that our public schools provide equal educational opportunity for all, and, at the same time, increase the abilities of our young people to understand, interact, and communicate with one another? (For review, see pp. 372–376.)

FOR FURTHER READING

Bronfenbrenner, U. *Two Worlds of Childhood: U.S. and U.S.S.R.* New York: Basic Books, 1970. Bronfenbrenner's easy-to-read text has been suggested elsewhere for further reading. The student interested in the effects of American family life on the social and personality development of American youngsters would profit considerably by a review of Part II.

Coopersmith, S. *Antecedents of Self-Esteem.* San Francisco, Cal.: Freeman, 1967. Coopersmith's longitudinal study of youth in America and his findings concerning the relationship between school and familial variables and self-esteem are particularly valuable to parents or prospective parents.

Felker, D. *Building Positive Self-Concepts.* Minneapolis: Burgess, 1974. This is a very practical how-to-do-it book for parents and teachers. It deals primarily with the self-esteem of young children, but also considers behaviors associated with esteem.

Mussen, P., ed. *Carmichael's Manual of Child Psychology.* 3d ed. New York: Wiley, 1970. Carmichael's manual contains a series of research articles of use to the advanced student of personality and social development. Articles by Hoffman dealing with moral development and by Hartup dealing with peer interactions are particularly relevant.

Robertiello, R. *Hold Them Very Close, Then Let Them Go.* New York: Dial Press, 1976. This short primer for parents is written by a psychiatrist who views discipline as a very important form of parental love. Many of Robertiello's suggestions match closely the findings cited by Coopersmith.

REFERENCES

Bachman, J. *Youth in Transition.* Ann Arbor: Braun-Brumfield, 1970.

Bandura, A., D. Ross, and S. Ross. Imitation of film-mediated aggressive models. *Journal of Abnormal and Social Psychology* 66 (1963): 3–11.

Berenda, R. *The Influence of the Group on the Judgments of Children.* New York: King's Crown Press, 1950.

Berndt, T., and E. Berndt. Children's use of motives and intentionality in person perception and moral judgment. *Child Development* 46 (1975): 904–912.

Bigelow, B., and J. LaGaipa. Children's written descriptions of friendship: a multidimensional analysis. *Developmental Psychology* 11, no. 6 (1975): 857–858.

Bronfenbrenner, U. The changing American child—a speculative analysis. *Journal of Social Issues* 17 (1961): 6–18.

Bronfenbrenner, U. *Two Worlds of Childhood.* New York: Russell Sage Foundation, 1970.

Bronfenbrenner, U. Somebody—let it, please God, be somebody. *Time,* April 27, 1970.

Busk, P., R. Ford, and J. Schulman. Effects of schools' racial composition on the self-concept of black and white students. *The Journal of Educational Research* 67, no. 2 (1973): 60–63.

Coleman, J. Recent trends in school integration. *Educational Researcher* 4, no. 7 (1975): 3–12.

Condry, J., and M. Simon. An experimental study of adult vs. peer orientation. Unpublished manuscript, Cornell University, 1968.

Coopersmith, S. *The Antecedents of Self-Esteem.* San Francisco: Freeman, 1967.

Devereux, E. Authority and moral development among German and American children: A cross-national pilot experiment. *Journal of Comparative Family Studies* 3 (1972): 99–124.

Dorros, S. What you can do now. *Today's Education* 62 (1973): 41–42.

Eron, L., L. Huesmann, M. Lefkowitz, and L. Walder. Does television violence cause aggression? *American Psychologist* 27 (1972): 253–263.

Eron, L., L. Huesmann, M. Lefkowitz, and L. Walder. How learning conditions in early childhood—including mass media—relate to aggression in late adolescence. *American Journal of Orthopsychiatry* 44 no. 3 (April 1974).

Feshbach, S. Aggression. In P. Mussen, ed., *Carmichael's Manual of Child Psychology.* 3d ed. New York: Wiley, 1970.

Flavell, J. *The Developmental Psychology of Jean Piaget.* New York: Van Nostrand Reinhold, 1963.

Fondy, A. Testimony in behalf of Pittsburgh Federation of Teachers. In *Hearing on Busing for Racial Integration.* Basic Education Committee of the Pennsylvania State House of Representatives, November 11, 1971.

Fouts, G., and P. Liikanen. The effects of age and developmental level on imitation in children. *Child Development* 46 (1975): 555–558.

Garbarino, J. A note on the effects of television viewing. In U. Bronfenbrenner, ed., *Influences on Human Development*. Hinsdale, Ill.: Dryden Press, 1972, pp. 499–502.

Goslin, P. Accuracy of self-perception and social acceptance. *Sociometry* 25 (1962): 283–296.

Gottman, J., J. Gonso, and B. Rasmussen. Social interaction, social competence, and friendship in children. *Child Development* 46 (1975): 709–718.

Green, R., E. Smith, and J. Schweitzer. Busing and multiracial classroom. *Phi Delta Kappan* 53 (1972): 543–547.

Guilford, J. Maturation of values in young children. *The Journal of Genetic Psychology* 124 (1974): 241–248.

Guyatt, D. *The One-Parent Family in Canada*. Ottowa: Vanier Institute, 1971.

Hall, R., S. Axelrod, M. Foundopoulos, J. Shellman, R. Campbell, and S. Cranston. *Educational Technology Magazine* 10 (1971): 24–26.

Hardy, C., and D. Nias. An investigation of physical and personality factors involved in learning to swim. *Personality* 2, no. 1 (1971).

Hartshorne, H., M. May, et al. Testing the knowledge of right and wrong. *Religious Education Monographs* 1 (1927): 72.

Hartup, W. Peer interaction and social organization. In P. Mussen, ed., *Carmichael's Manual of Child Psychology*. 3d ed. New York: Wiley, 1970.

Herzog, E., and C. Sudia. Children in fatherless families. In B. Caldwell and H. Ricciuti, eds., *Review of Child Development Research*. Chicago: The University of Chicago Press, 1973.

Hetherington, E., and R. Parke. *Child Psychology: A Contemporary Viewpoint*. New York: McGraw-Hill, 1975.

Hoffman, M., and H. Saltzstein. Parent discipline and the child's moral development. *Journal of Personality and Social Psychology* 5, no. 1 (1967): 45–57.

Hoffman, M. Moral development. In P. Mussen, ed., *Carmichael's Manual of Child Psychology*. 3d ed. New York: Wiley, 1970.

Holstein, C. The relation of children's moral judgment level to that of their parents and to communication level in the family. Paper presented at the Biennial Meeting of the Society for Research in Child Development, Santa Monica, Cal., March 28, 1969.

Jackson, G. Reanalysis of Coleman's "Recent trends in school integration." *Educational Researcher*, November 1975, pp. 21–25.

Jacobs, C., and C. Eaton. Sexism in the elementary school. *Today's Education* 61 (1972): 20–22.

Kelly, J., and J. Wallerstein. The effects of parental divorce: experiences of the child in early latency. *American Journal of Orthopsychiatry* 46, no. 1 (January 1976).

Kenniston, K. In Abdicating American parents. *Newsweek*, September 22, 1975, p. 55.

Kirchner, E., and S. Vondracek. Perceived sources of esteem in early childhood. *The Journal of Genetic Psychology* 126 (1975): 169–176.

Lefkowitz, M., L. Eron, L. Walder, and L. Huesmann. Preference for televised contact sports as related to sex differences in aggression. *Developmental Psychology* 9, no. 3 (1973): 417–420.

Leizer, J., and R. Rogers. Effects of method of discipline, timing of punishment, and timing of test on resistance to extinction. *Child Development* 45 (1974): 790–793.

Levy, B. Do teachers sell girls short? *Today's Education* 61 (1972): 27–29.

McCullers, C. *The Member of the Wedding*. Philadelphia: New Directions, 1963.

Maccoby, E. Sex differences revisited: myth and reality. Paper delivered at the annual meeting of the American Education Research Association, Chicago, 1974.

McFeatters, A. School mix aids blacks, study says. *Pittsburgh Press*, 17 March 1976.

Miller, T. Effects of maternal age, education, and employment status on the self-esteem of the child. *The Journal of Social Psychology* 95 (1975): 141–142.

Mondale, W. Busing in perspective. *The New Republic*, March 4, 1972, p. 17.

Parker, H. Contingency management and concomitant changes in elementary school students' self-concepts. *Psychology in the Schools* 11 (1974): 70–80.

Perry, D., K. Bussey, and L. Perry. Factors influencing the imitation of resistance to deviation. *Developmental Psychology* 11 (1975): 724–731.

Piaget, J. *The Moral Judgment of the Child*. New York: Macmillan, 1932.

Rice, D. Educa-therapy: a new approach to delinquent behavior. *Journal of Learning Disabilities* 3 (1970): 18–25.

Robins, L. *Deviant Children Growing Up*. Baltimore: Williams and Wilkins, 1966.

Robinson, H., N. Robinson, M. Wolins, U. Bronfenbrenner, and J. Richmond. Early child care in the USA. *Early Child Development and Care* 2, 1973 (monograph issue).

Rosenham, D. Effects of social class and race on responsiveness to approval and disapproval. *Journal of Personality and Social Psychology* 4 (1966): 253–259.

Rossiter, J., and T. Robertson. Children's television viewing: an examination of parent-child consensus. *Sociometry* 38, no. 2 (1975): 308–326.

Sams, A. Conformity and peer groups in remedial nine-year-old children. *The Journal of Genetic Psychology* 124 (1974): 145–150.

Shouval, R., K. Venaki, U. Bronfenbrenner, E. Devereux, and E. Kiely. Anomalous reactions to social pressure of Israeli and Soviet children raised in family vs. collective settings. *Journal of Personality and Social Psychology* 32, no. 3 (1975): 477–489.

Spence, R. Best education for all children includes busing. *Phi Delta Kappan* 53 (1972).

Sprafkin, J., R. Liebert, and R. Poulos. Effects of a prosocial televised example on children's helping. *Journal of Experimental Child Psychology* 20 (1975): 119–126.

Terrell, G., K. Durkin, and M. Weisley. Social class and the nature of the incentive of in discrimination learning. *Journal of Abnormal and Social Psychology* 59 (1959): 270–272.

Thomas, M., and R. Drabman. Toleration of real life aggression as a function of exposure to televised violence and age of subject. *Merrill-Palmer Quarterly* 21, no. 3 (1975): 227–232.

Tierney, M., and K. Rubin. Egocentrism and conformity in childhood. *The Journal of Genetic Psychology* 126 (1975): 209–215.

Tolor, A., W. Scarpetti, and P. Lane. Teachers' attitudes toward children's behavior revisted. *Journal of Educational Psychology* 58 (1967): 175–180.

Vidal, D. Quaker project gives instructions by games. *New York Times*, 23 May 1976.

Wickman, E. *Children's Behavior and Teachers' Attitudes*. New York: Commonwealth Fund, 1928.

Williams, J., S. Bennett, and D. Best. Awareness and expression of sex-stereotypes in young children. *Developmental Psychology* 11, no. 5 (1975): 635–642.

Woods, M. The unsupervised child of the working mother. *Developmental Psychology* 6 (1972): 14–25.

Yarrow, M. The measurement of children's attitudes and values. In P. Mussen, ed., *Handbook of Research Methods in Child Psychology*. New York: Wiley, 1970.

12

The Cognitive Processes and School Learning

Learning objectives

After completing this chapter, you should be able to:

1
describe the stages of cognitive development of middle childhood; define and use the following terms in relation to these stages: classification; concrete operations; conservation; formal operations; inclusion; matching; seriation;

2
describe the cognitive styles children use in school learning; suggest ways to plan learning experiences so as to meet the needs of children with different cognitive styles;

3
explain how achievement motivation develops and why some children are more highly motivated to achieve than are others;

4
explain how IQ tests are used in schools today and discuss problems inherent in IQ testing.

© hapter 11 dealt with the personal and social concerns of school-age children: learning to get along with other children, learning to play and to satisfy needs in socially acceptable ways, and developing attitudes and values appropriate for their particular social milieus. All are tasks of major concern in middle childhood. Because children spend large periods of time each day in school, thinking and problem solving in school-related tasks also play increasingly important roles in development during middle childhood. Major developmental tasks of this period include expansion of knowledge and acquisition of academic skills, reasoning, and judgment—all tasks related to school learning. Associated with these tasks are others—for example, learning to make perceptual discriminations (a task associated with learning to read), development of manual dexterity (a task associated with learning to write), and so forth.

Chapter 12 deals with the cognitive processes and skills necessary for school learning. Since virtually all nonprimitive societies today provide some form of formal schooling for children, the skills discussed here are important for children the world over. The ways in which these skills are learned, as well as factors that affect skill learning for individual children, are the concerns of this chapter.

B y the end of the preschool years, children have developed the ability to solve increasingly complex problems. They still lack, however, what Piaget called "true reasoning"—that is, they are unable to think logically and objectively.

When children reach middle childhood, at about age seven, most begin to be able to perform mental operations using what Piaget called "true reasoning," the defining characteristic of the *operational stage of cognitive development*. When traditional teaching techniques are used with these children, teachers find that it is necessary to present concrete examples of all new concepts to the children, in order for them to grasp fully the notions being taught. A child might, for example, be able to count two blocks set before him or her, without being able to solve the problem $1 + 1 = ?$. In Piagetian terms, these children are operating at the *concrete operations stage*. Later, children develop thinking patterns that involve abstract concepts without the need for concrete examples. Piaget called this the *abstract* or *formal operations stage*.

Piaget's Stages of Cognitive Development: Middle Childhood

The concrete operations stage According to Piaget, the thinking of children, in the first several years of elementary school, is characterized by the development of reasoning and logic with respect only to the concrete

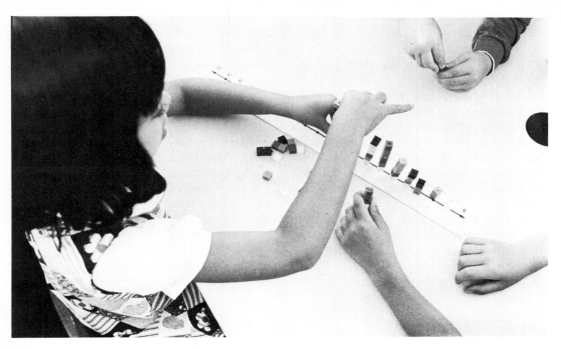

Children at the concrete operations stage use objects to learn new concepts.

objects around them. First-grade teachers in the United States have found that an effective way to have children learn the concept "2 + 2 = 4" is to present to the class a number line or a series of objects, like the blocks discussed earlier, that the children can count. Children learning to read also learn rapidly if learning materials are presented in concrete form. The highly successful Montessori method of teaching reading utilizes concrete stimuli matched to the cognitive level of the students. As noted in Chapter 10, Montessori used brightly colored alphabet figures cut out of sandpaper. Children learning the alphabet were encouraged to pick up each of the letters and handle them, as they learned their names and sounds (Montessori, 1914). When young children, at what Piaget called the concrete operations stage of cognitive development, are presented with concepts that adults deal with in abstract terms —for example, the concept of "God"—they tend to recreate the concept at a concrete level. First and second graders often talk to God as if He were another live human being, subject to all the feelings and emotions they themselves experience. Following is a very lovely and short example of the concrete thinking characteristic of this age level, in a letter written to God (Marshall and Hample, 1966):

Dear God:
We are going on vacation for two weeks Friday so we won't be in
church. I hope you will be there when we get back. When do you take
your vacation? Goodbye.

Donnie

Children at the concrete operations stage learn gradually to develop concepts on the basis of many different dimensions simultaneously. During the elementary-school years, they learn, over time, the concept of *conservation*—that is, that matter remains constant, regardless of how it changes form. Now they begin to understand, for example, that a ball of clay smashed flat on the table takes up the same amount of space in the universe as when it was round. They can also see that a short, fat container can hold the same amount of liquid as a tall, thin container, and also that two ten kilogram weights together are as heavy as one twenty kilogram weight. However, to understand this, according to Piaget, young children still need to touch or see the object in front of them; they are unable to understand without being able to use their senses to explore the objects before them.

Children at this stage learn also to differentiate between parts and wholes, greater and lesser. Schoolchildren will not accept a cookie broken into two parts as two cookies, as we learned earlier that preschoolers will do. By the time they reach school age, children know that a cookie broken in half consists of only two parts of the same cookie.

Other conceptual abilities are mastered gradually by the child, often before he or she has mastered the concept of conservation. *Seriation* involves the ability to order a series of objects along some dimension. Young children at the concrete operations stage can learn to pile blocks according to size, the largest block on the bottom and the smallest block on top with gradually decreasing blocks in between. Later, when children reach the formal operations stage, they are able to understand seriation abstractly, as in algebra. *Classification* involves the ability to sort objects according to some quality. Younger children may learn to classify according to such concrete attributes as color or size. Later, they will classify according to more abstract attributes, such as value. *Class inclusion* involves the ability to recognize that some classes of objects are subsets of other more inclusive classes of objects, and that an object may belong both to the subset and to the more inclusive classes as well. Thus dogs are a subset of the class of animals. Puppies belong to the subset dogs as well as the more inclusive animal class.

The formal operations stage From about age eleven on, children begin to be able to evaluate the world around them without relying on information gathered from concrete objects. According to Piaget, they now are ready to begin learning abstractly. Children at the stage of formal operations gradually develop the capacity to reason through use of hypotheses. When given information, they can start making logical deductions without first turning to concrete examples. According to Piaget, it is only at this stage that children are ready to solve problems in subjects such as algebra or calculus.

In the middle-school years, from ages eleven to thirteen, teachers in the United States usually utilize this newly developing capability to introduce a variety of abstract concepts into the curriculum. Now, to teach algebraic concepts, teachers present equations on the blackboard. Children are able to understand why, in order for the equation to retain its meaning, cancelling figures on one side of the equation requires cancelling figures on the other. Number lines or blocks are no longer needed. Teachers in middle schools (grades six, seven, and eight) begin to present new types of problems in other classes as well. Theme writing can begin to involve abstract concepts. For example, students writing about war might discuss the ethics involved rather than describing what they think wars are like.

Piagetian principles and concept learning According to Piaget and his followers, children pass through the stages of cognitive development in a specified order. In order to reach the concrete operational stages of middle childhood, they first pass through the preoperational stages of the earlier years. Similarly, in order to reach the formal operations stage characteristic of the later school years, they first pass through the concrete operations stage of the earlier school years (Piaget, 1952; Piaget and Inhelder, 1964).

At any given stage level, according to Piaget, children tend to learn concepts in specific order (Dimitrovsky and Almy, 1975). As just one example, they generally master the concept of conservation of quantity before they learn conservation of weight. Studies have shown a regular increase in ability to perceive part-whole differences; to understand conservation of mass, weight, and volume; to understand the additive composition of classes; and to understand the concepts "right" and "left" (Elkind, 1961a, 1961b, 1961c; Elkind et al., 1964).

Psychologists believe that the order in which concepts are learned can be affected by experience: more commonly experienced objects and concepts are assimilated into the child's cognitive structure before less commonly experienced objects and concepts. Indeed, research by Soviet psychologists, particularly in the past few years, has demonstrated that educational methods also play major roles in determining which specific concepts will be understood by a child at any given age (Markova, 1974; Salmina and Sohina, 1975). Soviet psychologists base their research on the belief that environment is critical to learning.

Matching learning materials and cognitive structures. Assimilation and accommodation processes require stimuli that are "matched in complexity to the child's cognitive structure" (see Chapter 2 for review). Piaget was skeptical of attempts to teach children advanced and complex concepts at too early an age. He felt that, in most cases, such attempts did not provide stimuli suitably matched to cognitive structure; thus, they were not likely to succeed. Researchers have shown that, as Piaget suggested, stimuli that are not matched to the cognitive structure of the child have little or no effect on cognition. However, they have also provided evidence that with careful and proper matching, children can progress more rapidly to the next developmental stage. Suchman (1960),

An exercise testing Piagetian-type tasks

When Piaget conducted his research, he often used tasks that could easily be performed at the kitchen table. The following Piagetian-type tasks were developed by an educational psychologist at the University of Pittsburgh to be used with young American children (Vasudev, 1976). To try out these tasks, find two children between the ages of five and ten. Use for your child subjects children whose ages are as far apart as possible. Ask them, one at a time, to perform the tasks described below. Write down their responses to your questions. When you are finished with both children, answer the questions that follow the tasks.

Task 1: Conservation of Mass

Step 1 Take two balls composed of equal amounts of clay or dough. Show them to the child and ask, "Are they both the same?" (If the child does not think that they are the same, allow opportunity for manipulation of the balls sufficient to demonstrate that this is the case.)

Step 2 Roll out one of the balls, in view of the child, into a "hot dog." Ask the child, "Is there the same amount of clay in the ball as in the hot dog?"

Step 3 Ask the child to explain his or her answer.

Task 2: Conservation of Continuous Quantity

Step 1 Take two glasses and fill them with the same amounts of water. Ask the child, "Is there the same amount of water in both glasses?" (If the child does not think that they are the same, demonstrate that this is the case.)

Step 2 In front of the child, pour the contents of one glass into a glass that obviously is taller and slimmer. Make sure the level of water is high in the tall glass. Ask the child, "Do the tall glass and the shorter glass have the same amount of water?"

Step 3 Ask the child to explain his or her answer.

Questions

1 Did the children respond differently to the questions you asked them? If yes, describe these differences fully.

2 Look back to descriptions of Piaget's stages of cognitive development described in this chapter and also in Chapters 2, 6, 7, 9, 10, and 11. According to these descriptions, at what level of development is each of these children responding? What evidence can you give to support your answer?

Stimuli, to be effective, must be matched to the child's cognitive structure.

for example, permitted a group of young children to observe, question, and discuss concrete examples of physical-science problems shown in movie shorts. Participating children who were presented these problems in concrete fashion understandable to them at their stage of development quickly became more adept at questioning and at formulating relationships between objects, abstract systems, and events. Compared to children who had not participated in the project, these children progressed to the formal operations stage much more rapidly.

COGNITIVE STYLES: AN EXAMINATION OF INDIVIDUAL DIFFERENCES

Piaget was interested in describing changes in children's thinking as they increase in age. Many researchers are interested also in explaining why children of the same age, cognitive stage, and intellectual ability often approach day-to-day problems in quite different ways.

Individual differences in the ways children organize what they learn, categorize concepts, and employ strategies to deal with problem solving are called *cognitive styles*. Because cognitive styles are indicative of different learning approaches, they sometimes are referred to as *learning styles*. Researchers have measured differences between children in learning approaches, personality, and motivations (DeCecco and Crawford, 1974).

Riessman categorized children's learning approaches into three basic groupings: *visual*—in which learning is accomplished most easily through reading; *aural*—in which learning is accomplished most easily through listening; and *physical*—in which learning is accomplished most effectively through touching, feeling, manipulating, and doing. Reissman's research on cognitive or learning styles was described in Chapter 3.) Nations (1967), using a different analytic method to describe cognitive styles, came up with two categories: the *response mode*—the manner in which children learn most effectively (e.g., alone or in a group); and the *thinking mode*—the way in which children approach each individual problem (e.g., by gathering details first for later organization, or by looking for the overall picture first and then supporting it with details).

Many factors that are related to personality development and motivation are related also to cognitive style and problem solving. For example, the *attention span* of children is related directly to the ways in which they approach problem solving (Shumsky, 1968). Some children need con-

Factors Related to Cognitive Style

Some children learn best visually—that is, through reading; others learn best physically—through touching, manipulating, and doing.

Some children take longer than others to solve the same problem, even though they are equally capable of coming up with the correct answer.

tinual monitoring in order to continue attending to a long problem, while others continue to work at a problem until it is solved.

Some children also have a greater *capacity for independent work* than do other children. Such children are able to work independently at solving problems without encouragement from others, while others need more praise and encouragement to keep from getting discouraged, particularly if a task is difficult.

Children also differ in *learning rate;* some take longer than others to solve the same problem, even though they are equally capable of coming up with the correct answer. Messick (1970) described individual differences in children's memories. Some children who have not had practice in differentiating between present and past, for example, tend to confuse time in describing what is taking place. Others the same age have difficulty seeing similarities between what they experienced last week and what is happening today.

One factor particularly interesting to psychologists because of its relationship to learning is *field dependence or independence.* Field dependence and independence are two different approaches to the perceptual organization of information. Field-independent children make fine discriminations in what they see before them and isolate items of importance from the surrounding material. We say that these children can discriminate figures from ground or background. Field-dependent children, on the other hand, often are overwhelmed if the materials presented to them appear in a complex context, for they have difficulty distinguishing figures from ground. Such children often are called "unanalytical." Field-dependent children have more difficulty solving the types of problems usually presented in the classroom than do field-dependent children (Messick, 1970).

Another variable important to psychologists because of its role in learning is *impulsivity-reflectivity*. Reflective children tend to take time in solving problems; they think over all possible alternatives before arriving at an answer. Reflective children may, because of this approach, make fewer errors en route than impulsive children. At the same time, they often take longer to solve problems than do impulsive children. They tend to persist for relatively long periods of time at different tasks and hold high standards for intellectual performance. Impulsive children, on the other hand, apparently have greater desire for quick success. They tend to solve problems quickly. They sometimes, however, test hypotheses too quickly and, as a consequence, come up with wrong answers.

In the classroom, teachers tend to rate impulsive children as "less attentive" and more often "hyperactive" than reflective children (Ault et al., 1972). They also rate impulsive children as less "task oriented" and "less considerate." Teachers tend to rate school-age boys as more impulsive and more distractible than girls, thus possibly initiating a self-fulfilling prophecy (Kagan et al., 1970; McKinney, 1975).

Psychologists are agreed that cognitive styles are shaped by early life experiences. Swan and Stavros (1973), in a provocative study of the relationship between children's cognitive styles and the child-rearing methods used by their parents, showed that parents who are helpful and encouraging and provide a great deal of pleasant and mutually rewarding verbal interaction during the preschool years tend to have children who enter school with the cognitive styles most conducive to academic success.

We learned earlier that children who are trained gradually to delay reinforcement attend to tasks at hand for longer periods of time without outside encouragement than do children without such training. Many of the differences in cognitive styles of children similarly can be explained in terms of early experience and learning theory. Kagan et al. (1970) suggests that the fact that boys in our society generally are more impulsive than girls can be explained by different early experiences.

Cognitive Styles and Child-Rearing Methods

Psychologists agree that cognitive styles are shaped by early life experiences.

Cognitive Styles and School Learning

What cognitive styles are most conducive to intellectual performance? According to Swan and Stavros (1973), problem-solving methods that allow children to listen carefully before making use of information presented to them, to try new approaches to problems when old ones do not work, and to take risks lead to greater intellectual performance and classroom success. Problem-solving methods that keep children from interacting successfully in group-learning situations or that lead to uncontrolled behavior, distractibility, or apprehension all lead to diminished academic success.

An exercise in instructional architecture: planning for different cognitive styles

Adults leading children's groups and responsible for providing instruction have many options in planning for different cognitive styles. For example, chairs in most classrooms or camp dining halls are not attached to the floor. Teachers or counselors can arrange them in any way that seems appropriate for the group, the individual children, and the instruction planned.

Teachers and group leaders might use other furnishings in different ways as well, so as to help each child learn in the way best suited to his or her individual needs. Bookcases may function as room dividers, in order to create separate quiet places for children who like to work alone or silently. Researchers have pointed out that young children like to have a "homey" atmosphere in which to learn. Accordingly, children can be allowed to bring in old, unwanted scatter rugs from home. A few, soft easy chairs can change the atmosphere considerably.

What about children who like to work in groups? Instructional architecture that meets the needs of these children will provide space where groups can work together on problems.

Some children learn more effectively aurally than they do visually. Equipment is available to-day to help these children, even in classrooms where other children require silence in order to read. Simple tape recorders have been found highly effective in teaching these children. If more money is available, teaching machines with auditory output are useful.

How should learning space be arranged to accommodate all of these innovations? Teachers and group leaders can become excellent instructional architects without too much practice. Following is a drawing of a typical traditional classroom, together with traditional classroom furniture. How would *you* arrange it to best plan for different cognitive styles? Use furniture similar to that provided in the drawing.

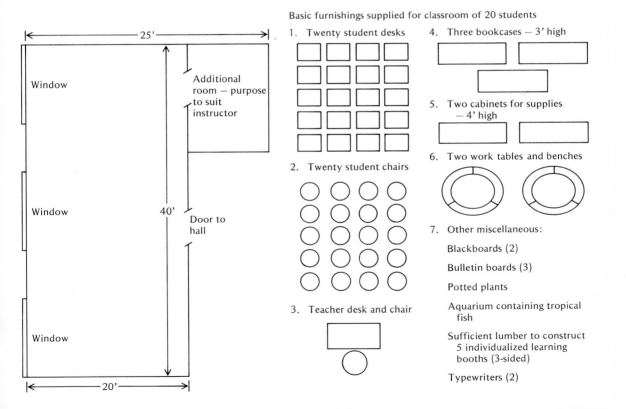

Planning for different cognitive styles Researchers agree that cognitive styles learned early in life are not subject later to very much change. Many psychologists suggest, therefore, that the best way to deal with cognitive styles is to accept them and to provide learning experiences most appropriate to the style of each child. For parents teaching their children at home, this means matching the lesson to the behavior of the child. For teachers with twenty to thirty children in a classroom, providing learning experiences appropriate to individual cognitive styles often is much more difficult.

Many psychologists and educators have argued that, in order for classroom teaching to be effective, class size should be greatly reduced, so that teachers will have sufficient time to deal individually with students. Results of studies relating class size to academic success have not been generalizable, however. For example, in some classes and with some subject matters, decreased class size clearly enhanced learning, while in other classes and with the same or different subject matters, it made no difference (Templeton, 1972). If class size affects learning, apparently its effects can be tempered by the instructional capabilities of the teachers.

In different studies, researchers studied the relationship between class size and instructional quality (ability of the teacher to individualize instruction, to provide individual attention, to be creative, and to conduct small-group programs). In these studies, smaller class size was related to increased quality of instruction. In other studies, a smaller class size was shown to be of particular benefit to slower students and younger students (Olson, 1971; Templeton, 1972).

THINKING AND SCHOOL LEARNING

During the school years, children first become seriously concerned with performance at academic tasks. Erikson described these years as ones in which children develop feelings of either industry or inferiority. According to Erikson, successful learning leads to industry; failure leads to feelings of inferiority. (See Chapter 2 for a review of Erikson's psychosocial theory.) All children are not equally motivated to be academically successful, however. It is children who are more motivated to achieve both in school and in other aspects of their lives who have the greatest success at school learning.

Achievement Motivation

What is meant by *achievement motivation*? Psychologists note that lower animals seem to "need" to explore their environments. Some suggest, that in human beings, a related need is to master the environment. Such mastery leads to feelings of competence (White, 1959). Motivation theorists tell us that some children strive more than others to obtain this mastery and to gain feelings of competence both in problem solving and in interactions with others. Such children are said to have a high need to achieve or high achievement motivation.

In any given classroom, some children will have a high need
to achieve, others will not.

High achievement-motivated children are more likely than are other
children to be challenged by the personal effort required in solving
problems. They also are more likely to persevere longer at learning tasks.
Children who have a high need to achieve usually are not gamblers:
they are more likely to use logic in solving problems than to take wild
chances without thinking. In selecting goals, they tend to select ones
that have intermediate possibilities of success—that is, goals they can
accomplish, but that still present learning challenges. Students lower in
achievement motivation tend to be more erratic: they more frequently
select either unrealistically high or unrealistically low goals (Mouly,
1970).

Children with high levels of motivation have high *levels of aspiration*
as well. That is, their expectations of themselves and predictions of future goals (such as grades desired or expected in school) usually are
higher than those of children with lower motivation to achieve.

Why are some children motivated to achieve while others are not?
Psychologists reply that children with high needs to achieve have developed a clear understanding of the specific goals to be obtained through
achieving. Through early successes, they have been able to observe self-

improvement firsthand. In addition, their social environments are highly supportive of their efforts (McClelland, 1965).

Level of aspiration is known to be affected by previous success or failure. In a classic study, Child and Whiting (1949) long ago showed that children who performed successfully raised their goals and increased their self-confidence. Children who failed at the same tasks tended to lower their levels of aspiration. However, the effects of failure seemed to be more variable than those of success: children either gave up or, in some cases, unrealistically raised their reported expectancies, almost as if the hope of success alone would bring success.

The period between six and ten years of age—approximately the first four years of school—appears to be a critical time in the development of children's achievement motivation. This is the period most predictive of adult motivation. Children, as they begin school, start to sever their parental ties and become more independent. At the same time, they are conceptually ready to develop skills that will allow them greater independence in later problem-solving situations. Children who easily develop these skills during this time achieve a high degree of self-confidence. It is this self-confidence, according to psychologists, that leads eventually to achievement motivation in adulthood (Sontag and Kagan, 1967).

Child-rearing methods, social-class differences, and achievement motivation Parents who give their children early training at being self-reliant tend to have children with higher achievement motivation than do parents who are highly restrictive and punitive in their child rearing. McClelland (1971) performed an experiment involving young, school-age boys who were blindfolded and then asked to stack irregular blocks with their left hands. McClelland found that boys whose mothers estimated in advance that they would do well and then encouraged them persevered at the task much longer than did boys whose parents were more prone to order the boys to perform the task properly and to try harder when they failed. The more successful boys also were found to be more highly motivated to achieve.

Psychologists have for some time related high need for achievement also to methods of discipline. McClelland et al. (1953) showed that mothers of children with high need to achieve often use guilt-inducing methods of discipline (as, for example, suggesting that bad behavior makes their parents unhappy) to make their children maintain achievement standards. This is not true of mothers of children with low needs to achieve.

Socioeconomic background also appears to be linked to variations in the achievement motivation of children. In one study of middle-class and poor seven-year-olds, it was found that being told they were right (that they had mastered the problem) served as greater reinforcement for middle-class boys than being given praise. The reverse was true for low SES boys (Zigler and Kanzer, 1962). A later study showed that parents higher on the socioeconomic scale have higher educational and occupational aspirations for their children than do parents in lower socioeconomic brackets. Presumably, their aspirations and corresponding encouragement affect their children's aspirations (Brook et al., 1974).

Sex and achievement motivation Girls tend to outperform boys academically during the first four years of elementary school. In addition, as we learned earlier, the social behavior of girls is generally regarded by teachers as being more acceptable than is the behavior of boys. Later, however, although girls continue to misbehave less in school, their academic achievement falls relative to that of boys. How can this be explained? Although there may actually be multiple causes for this male-female difference, psychologists have noted that, in the higher grades of elementary school and later in high school, the motivation of girls to master their school learning has tended in past years to decrease considerably. According to Kagan (1964), this decrease in achievement has corresponded to an increase in fear of success and of competitiveness. Although this fear may also occur in males, Kagan and other psychologists have noted that it is most frequent in females. In order to obtain the best grades in school, girls generally feel they must "defeat" their peers —a happening clearly incompatible with the sex-typed female characteristics of nonaggression and compliance.

Actually, as we have learned, vocational and occupational sex stereotyping in our society appears much earlier than elementary school. Child rearing for girls in our society differs greatly from that of boys. Mothers tend to be less accepting of assertiveness in daughters; accordingly, emphasis tends to be placed at very early ages on the development of social skills rather than of assertive behaviors. Girls are taught early that social approval is important for them and that mastery is important for boys (Harter, 1975). McClelland (1958) pointed out that training in independence and mastery is necessary to high achievement motivation; girls in our society are taught to be dependent, boys to be independent. Furthermore, boys are taught directly that achievement is important; girls are not. Masculine identification has long been known to be related consistently to high IQ, creativity, and superior problem-solving ability (Maccoby, 1966; Milton, 1957). For girls, identification is not related in similar fashion to intellectual and academic tasks.

What about educational and occupational aspirations? Parents' aspirations for their offspring differ according to the sex of their children (Brook et al., 1974). Vocational roles more often associated with men are also generally associated with aggressiveness, competition, and, worse, with social failure. The message is quite clear. A study of female television characters showed that female job holders in male-dominated

Today, society is becoming more willing to recognize achievement as appropriate for females.

fields were portrayed usually as unmarried or unsuccessful in their marriages (Manes and Melnyck, 1974). The range of different occupations to which girls aspire is considerably narrower than that of boys (Hewitt, 1974), presumably because girls have observed fewer successful women in a narrower range of outside activities. In addition, as they get older, girls increasingly fear social rejection of high achievement at intellectual tasks. Sadly, the higher the motivation to achieve, the higher the simultaneous fear of success (Horner, 1972).

Today, of course, society is more willing to recognize achievement as appropriate for females as well as males. Social pressure against achievement for women gradually is decreasing (Frieze, 1974). Female children more and more often are able to observe mothers who combine successful professional careers with happy, well-adjusted personal lives. Studies have shown in recent years that children of successful professional mothers have higher academic and vocational aspirations than do children either of nonworking mothers or dissatisfied working mothers (Etaugh, 1974). In one study of the motivation to avoid success in female children between grades five and eleven, it was found that only 4 percent of the girls studied were highly motivated to avoid academic success (Romer, 1975). Hopefully, this data suggests a relatively permanent trend associated with changing times and family styles.

Achievement motivation training We have, thus far, associated achievement motivation with a variety of factors related to upbringing. Can teachers and other adults with whom children interact during the school years affect achievement motivation? McClelland (1972) says, "Yes!" McClelland and his colleagues used achievement-motivation training with students and businessmen, and reported considerable changes in behavior oriented toward mastery. The steps McClelland suggests are: (1) teach children that they can and will succeed at the task before them; (2) give them clear ideas as to specific behaviors necessary to meet the desired goals; and (3) explain the relevance of the tasks both to everyday problems and to feelings about themselves and their peers.

Even when children are highly motivated to learn in school, success or failure is moderated by their ability in one crucial skill taught early in their school careers: reading. In recent years, educators have become more and more concerned with the seeming inability of American schoolchildren to learn to read. Often, they leave the elementary grades lacking this tool so crucial to the mastery of other skills.

Reading

Reading as a perceptual skill What process occurs in the thinking of children when they learn to read? Eleanor Gibson, a psychologist concerned with perceptual learning, suggests that, for one thing, reading requires the prior learning of a series of perceptual skills. Perceptual learning involves ability to extract meaningful and relevant information from one's environment as a result of practice and experience. According to Gibson, it is an active process (Gibson, 1965, 1969). Infants already have developed a great deal of perceptual ability when they learn to distinguish faces and to respond in certain ways to their mothers. Reading ability, according to Gibson, requires more complex discriminations. She suggests that, in learning to read, children first learn perceptually to differentiate among the many letters of the alphabet. Later, they learn to identify specific aspects of the printed word critical to meaning. It is important to realize that reading without meaning is a useless learning tool. In fact, most psychologists and educators suggest that "reading," by definition, must involve comprehension.

To answer the question, "What does a skilled reader do that an unskilled reader does not?" Gibson analyzed the process of learning to read. She derived from her analysis a hierarchy of four basic steps that must be learned in a prescribed order. More advanced steps require previous mastery of earlier steps. Gibson's hierarchy follows:

1 *Learning to speak.* This is the first prerequisite to learning to read. Without use of language, it is impossible for reading to acquire meaning.

2 *Learning to discriminate printed letters.* This step requires the ability to perceive differences in shapes of the individual letters. Gibson (1965) noted that very young children can be taught to point to a

Starting to read

My father's hands were a miracle of perfection. He could build a house single-handed. He could give you a haircut and butcher a cow. He could fix shoes and make tools and dies. He could farm and irrigate and build the prettiest doll houses in the world. He could make chairs, tables, cabinets; and even as I write this, I am staring at a pipe rack he made for me of hardwood set in a marble base. But it was not his genius as a craftsman which he passed on to me; it was his infatuation with reading.

My father immigrated from Russia in 1901 and through his manual skill became an assistant to the chief tool and die maker at the American Car and Foundry Company in Chicago. Ten years later, he became the chief tool and die maker himself. He was a man of activity, using his physical being all day long. But at night, after supper, he would retire to his favorite chair and open a book and smoke his pipe. Often, in the morning, he would arise from bed an hour earlier than necessary to finish reading what he had started the night before, so he could go to work "satisfied." It was a solitary addiction. He could not even discuss his reading with his near neighbors. Cohen, who lived on one side of us, couldn't put two words of English together. Rosenberg, our neighbor on the opposite side, couldn't care less. His only interests were pinochle and drinking tea (with lemon).

When I was a child, he often allowed me to go with him in the evening to the new public library that had just been opened on Homan Avenue, a distance of nearly three miles. The streets of Chicago's West Side were poorly lighted in those days, but it was possible to walk them without fear. My father would check out five books and depart with the books in one hand and my small hand in the other. Usually we walked in total silence until we got to Kobrick's grocery and delicatessen. As we approached the lighted window with its display of candies, bagels and honey cakes, and the salamis hang-

ing from the ceiling, my heart would almost stop. Would father, this night, decide to buy some pipe tobacco, then, looking down from his towering height, ask if I would like a sucker or a bag of polly seeds?

In time, we became co-conspirators in the love of reading. Books might not make me a better wage earner, he said, but they could prevent boredom. The experience of reading a good book was like getting unstuck and reaching out toward something entirely new, even though you still wore the same tie and shirt and met the same people.

But the great beauty of the thing, he said, was that when you are reading, you are never alone. For my father, to be *aleyn* (the Yiddish for loneliness) was one of the tragic elements in man's experience.

His favorite writer was Tolstoy. "When you read Dostoevsky," he would say, "you descend into a coal mine without a ladder for climbing out. When you read Tolstoy, it's like the sun after living in an icebox."

Anatole France's *Penguin Island* and the criticisms of Walter Pater were favorites of his. He liked Scott and Dickens. No one understood Dickens until he had read *Our Mutual Friend*, he said. It would be a grave mistake to die without having read that book. You may be sure I read Dickens until I couldn't see straight.

I became a teen-ager imbued with the desire to read everything, to know everything, to be everything. With the advent of the depression, the fulfilment of these modest ambitions required considerable ingenuity. The entire atmosphere of our household was altered. First, my sister and her husband and two children moved in. Her husband had lost his job after eighteen years as a pants cutter at Hart, Schaffner and Marx. Then, my brother who was a salesman for the wholesale division of Marshall Field lost his job, so he and his wife and three children joined our crowded household. Now the only place to read was either in the bathroom or the public library.

Even during these difficult and sometimes tragic years, there were evenings filled with affection and fun. Everyone crowded into the big kitchen and then, between tea and sweet cakes and perhaps a drop or two, or even three, of sweet home-made wine, they would talk and tell deprecatory tales of human stupidity and laugh and cry at the same time. The warmth and marvel of those days have never left me.

I was seldom without a book. I read walking along the street; I read standing up, sitting down, I read and read and read. Before the depression and the great influx of family members, the very best time to read was on Saturday mornings. Normally my mother baked on Friday, and she had a genius for failing to remember that something was in the oven. So if I was lucky, there would be plenty of cookies or cake or strudel left, slightly burned, that nobody else would touch. But I loved it. Then, too, the house was strangely still on Saturday mornings. No one was home and I could turn up the volume of the phonograph as loudly as I wished and sit and listen and read and eat cake. It was wonderful.

When reading became out of the question at home, I simply went to one of the two public libraries within walking distance. I liked best the one identified as the Douglas Park branch. It was newer, the seats more comfortable, the selection of books better.

While my remarkable father was responsible for my early love of books, Jesse Feldman, my teacher in senior-high-school literature, served to transform that love into an enduring and ever more passionate affair. His enthusiasm supported my own, and at the same time held the key to the wealth of possibilities that literature offers.

Through Jesse I learned the difference between a good book and a bad book. A good book is, very simply, a revealing book. A bad book is bad because it is dull. Its author is obviously

lying, not necessarily by purveying misinformation, but because he lards his work with any information that falls to hand—a sort of narrative treatment of the encyclopedia. A good book stirs your soul. You find yourself lost, not in a world of fantasy, but in a world where everything is understood.

Nobody can get along without an interior life. The soul must be fed, or something ugly and antihuman fills the void. Spiritual nourishment is not a frill, apart from everyday necessity. The everyday and the ultimate expression of man do not exist apart. Synge remarked: "When men lose their poetic feeling for ordinary life and cannot write poetry of ordinary things, their exalted poetry is likely to lose its strength of exaltation, in the way men cease to build beautiful churches when they have lost happiness in building shops."

So many years have passed since my father started me in reading as a way of life—marking a passage in a letter from Melville to Hawthorne, his workman's hands caressing the page: "My development," Melville wrote, "has been all within a few years past. Until I was twenty-five I had no development at all. From my twenty-fifth year I date my life. Three weeks have scarcely passed, at any time between then and now, that I have not unfolded within myself." How proud I was to have got an earlier start!

I think of those days when my hair was long and I wore the only pair of pants I had until they were in shreds. I used to sit in the classroom with my overcoat on so that the patches on my behind would not show, or stay in the library until closing time was called. Then I'd go out into the solitary night, walking thoughtfully home. I didn't want money or success or recognition. I didn't want a single thing from anybody. I wanted only to be alone, to read; to think; to unfold.

patch of color that matches the printed name of that color; this process alone, however, does not lead to reading of other words. She concluded that the process, called "reading letter patterns," is not true reading.

3 *Learning to decode letters to sound.* This step is particularly difficult in learning to read English, because, unlike phonetic alphabets, our alphabet does not have a one-to-one spelling-sound correspondence.

4 *Learning to perceive higher-order units and to make rapid visual discriminations between different words.* This final step is, according to Gibson, the step which discriminates good readers from poor readers (Gibson, 1968).

The importance of timing Readiness to learn was defined earlier as those behaviors of which children become capable because certain kinds of learning experiences previously were provided. Developmental psychologists theorize that there are *critical* or *sensitive periods* during which learning new skills first becomes possible. They further theorize that there are more favorable and less favorable periods in the lifespan for learning different skills. The effectiveness of teaching any skill, according to these psychologists, depends on proper timing of learning experiences.

Readiness and critical period both have been used as bases for arguing that instruction should wait until children are ready to learn. It has generally been assumed that the critical or sensitive period during which children first become capable of learning to read occurs during the sixth year. This assumption has been negated by the work of a number of educators, who, like Montessori, have shown that it is possible for children well under the age of six to learn to read if appropriate instruction is given. Of course, not everyone believes that preschool children should be taught to read. Many psychologists and educators contend that, even though it is possible for young children to learn, the time spent learning could well be used more effectively to master skills associated with socialization. Still others stress the importance of waiting until children are more capable of understanding the concepts presented in the reading books. Further, no psychologists or educators have indicated that *all* children are capable of learning to read at any given age; individual differences in the rate of cognitive development, as well as in learning experiences, make for individual differences in the age at which learning comes most easily. Clearly, we cannot suggest a specific age at which all, or even most, children ought to be able to read without knowing specific information about their past learning. From the work of Gibson, it is clear that children whose earlier language stimulation and perceptual-discrimination training were not adequate will not be able to learn to read as easily as children whose past experiences were enriched.

Teaching reading Intervention programs designed to provide enriched experiences for children who have not learned the early tasks of Gib-

The second step in learning to read involves perceiving
differences in the shapes of letters.

son's hierarchy were described earlier in this text. Included in Chapter 10 was a description of the Bereiter-Engelmann Program, which utilizes a deficit model of learning. Also discussed was Project Upgrade, a program that makes use of a difference model. Both programs provide language and perceptual learning tasks; both are successful at increasing reading skills at early ages.

Another interesting experimental reading program was tried out in this country a few years ago. Earlier, we noted that many children have difficulty learning to decode letters to sounds because there is no one-to-one spelling-sound correspondence in our language. Consequently, some educators took the radical approach of temporarily abandoning the English alphabet. They used instead a phonic alphabet (a special alphabet featuring a one-to-one correspondence between letters and sounds) called the *initial teaching alphabet* or I.T.A. (Pitman and St. John, 1968). Children using I.T.A. learned to read rapidly. Many, however, had some difficulty later in using the English alphabet (Warburton and Southgate, 1969).

Learning to decode letters to sound presents special problems for minority-group students who speak languages or dialects different from those of white, middle-class students. Communication difficulties between students and teachers or between students and their textbooks often occur because of discrepancies in speech patterns or environmental differences. Varieties of compensatory education programs have been designed for these children. In some cases, as in Project Upgrade, children are given materials prepared in their own dialects before they are presented with Standard English reading material. In other cases, the entire school curriculum is offered bilingually. Currently in the United States, bilingual education is being used primarily with Spanish-speaking children.

Creativity

Creativity, the ability to solve new and different problems in new and innovative ways, was discussed in Chapter 10. The creative preschooler is flexible, open to suggestions for revision in problem solving, unafraid to try out new courses of action, and willing to "play" with ideas. Chapter 10 suggested that parents and caretakers can increase preschool creativity by arranging unstructured and spontaneous play activities.

Creativity seems generally to decrease as children get older. Psychologists believe that age and culture together account for this decline. Maslow (1959) suggested that the potential for creativity is common to all babies at birth. However, as children get older, this potential decreases with enculturation.

Creative output tends to occur in spurts. During the first three years of school, most children increase their creativity. Some psychologists suggest that this might be because teachers in the primary grades tend to allow more freedom of expression. After grade three, however, a sharp drop in creativity occurs, followed by a gradual decrease during the remaining elementary and middle-school years (Bernard, 1973).

Is declining creativity related in some way to our educational system? Marx and Tombaugh (1967) suggest three possible links. First, teachers frequently discourage creativity because it disrupts lesson plans. Second, school tests tend to measure rote learning rather than new or innovative types of responding. Third, social stereotypes fostered by our society, such as rigid, sex-typed vocational expectations, frequently lead to stereotyped and noncreative student responses. Peers, teachers, and family all contribute in various ways to this stifling of creativity. "Curiosity killed the cat!" may be told to too many schoolchildren too often.

Can we make corrections? Can we teach children to think and behave creatively? Guilford and Torrance, two psychologists who have studied child creativity extensively, have suggested that we can. Guilford (1950, 1962) has suggested teaching in ways that allow for greater divergence of answers. The discovery method of teaching, in which teachers provide examples in order to let children "discover" the solutions is one way to do this. Torrance (1972) suggests that allowing children to work in small groups and to learn by themselves to make decisions might be another effective approach.

A discussion of the thinking processes and school learning of American children cannot be complete without a discussion of tests and grading. We pointed out earlier that some children are motivated to achieve in school in order to develop feelings of competence; others are motivated to achieve in order to receive praise and social reinforcement. One method used in schools to provide social reinforcement is grading. It is assumed by many teachers and parents that students are positively reinforced with good grades and negatively reinforced with bad grades.

Unfortunately, it's not that simple. Educators and psychologists have been increasingly concerned over the sometimes severe anxiety grading pressures create. A doctor in a midwestern state created quite a stir when he reported what appeared to be an alarmingly large number of first-through fourth-grade children with stomach ulcers. In discussing the report, educators suggested that these children were the victims of a "competitive, unreasonable, and demanding life . . ." (Georgiady and Romano, 1971). They suggested that, in spite of all we know about the shortcomings and inconsistencies of most grading systems, report-card grades are accepted too frequently as the "indisputable measure of success or lack of it."

What effect does emphasis on grades have on achievement motivation and on creativity? We already have learned that success tends to increase level of aspiration: children who are positively reinforced by high grades will strive harder for even better grades on the next report card. Children, on the other hand, who receive low grades are likely to have more

Grading

variable types of responses. As we stated earlier, giving up and unrealistic striving both can follow failure. What about creativity? If children are, indeed, reinforced by high grades, they will learn to make the kinds of responses required for those grades. Too often, according to the critics of testing, these responses require primarily rote learning rather than new or innovative responding. Pressures from family regarding grades also have been shown to be one of the causes of cheating on tests, a problem we will discuss in Chapter 14.

THINKING,
INTELLIGENCE,
AND THE IQ

Thus far in this chapter, we have discussed the ways that children change in their abilities to think and to solve problems as they get older. We have also discussed the ways in which a child's environment can affect these abilities. Many American psychologists look at cognitive ability from a different perspective. Rather than charting the progress of children over time, they are interested in comparing the abilities of many different children of the same age. The instruments they have developed to make these age-group comparisons are intelligence or IQ tests.

Earlier chapters reviewed a number of tests designed to measure the intelligence of infants and young children. As pointed out in Chapter 10 (p. 330), as this text was going to press, a United States district court trial in San Francisco was grappling with the question of whether, because of this cultural bias, IQ tests should be banned from our public schools. Why is the outcome of this trial important to education? Let's look more closely at how IQ testing relates to the thinking of school-age children.

IQ Testing: A
Description

We learned earlier that there are many definitions of intelligence, ranging from "ability to adjust to the environment" to "ability to perform school-learning tasks." IQ tests used today for schoolchildren make use primarily of problem-solving tasks similar to those presented in classroom situations. One reason is that most tests have been modeled after the Stanford-Binet Intelligence Scale. The first Binet Scale of Intelligence was designed by Alfred Binet in 1905 for the purpose of identifying slow learners in the Paris schools and detecting individual differences between them in degrees of retardation. In order to select items for his scale, Binet observed children in classrooms to see what they did. He decided that to learn successfully in school, children have to learn to use language, to memorize, to comprehend the problems being discussed, to make reasonable judgments, and to solve certain types of problems.

He then developed a scale to measure all of these abilities. Binet's early scale was revised for use in this country and has become the Stanford-Binet Scale of Intelligence (Terman and Merrill, 1937, 1960).

The developers of the Binet and Stanford-Binet Scales assume a *general-factor theory of intelligence.* That is, they accept the approach of early theorists like Spearman (1904) who suggested that intelligence is a general factor that increases a person's capability to do anything. For developers of the Stanford-Binet Scale, this means a single intelligence quotient that reflects a composite of responses to many different types of problems. Since school learning requires language, a large number of questions on the Stanford-Binet measure verbal ability.

Some psychologists believe the general-factor theory of intelligence is too simple. They take note of researchers like Thurstone (1938) who hypothesized that intelligence is composed of many different nonoverlapping abilities. One intelligence test that measures two abilities, verbal and performance, separately is the Wechsler Intelligence Scale for Children (WISC). The WISC separates questions that require verbal ability from questions that deal with symbols, pictures, blocks, and jigsaw puzzles and that require nonverbal or performance ability (Wechsler, 1949). The WISC can be used to obtain a general IQ score from a composite of the child's answers. It also can be used to obtain two separate verbal and performance IQ scores developed from answers on the verbal and performance parts of the test.

Both the Stanford-Binet Scale and the Wechsler Scale are known as individual tests of intelligence. They are administered on individual bases to children by a trained tester who asks the children questions, writes down their responses, and then computes an IQ score from the number of correct answers. Children administered individual tests of intelligence do not have to be able to read.

Intelligence tests have been designed to be administered by teachers in group situations as well. Public schools use these tests in order to determine as inexpensively and as rapidly as possible the IQs of groups of children. Two tests administered frequently by public schools in the United States are the Lorge-Thorndike Intelligence Test and the California Test of Mental Maturity (Gibson, 1972). Most of us who have been educated in the public schools can remember group IQ-test administration: questions are provided in test booklets; children are required to read each question and then answer by filling in the appropriate box on a computer-scored answer sheet. Clearly, more rapid readers have a decided advantage over slower readers.

Most group tests of intelligence have been designed to measure the same abilities as those measured by individual tests. However, different types of intelligence tests, as well as different tests, each ask different questions. Some tests have been designed to measure special abilities. The Arthur Point Scale, for example, is a performance test that measures

How stable is the IQ over time?

Psychologists tell us that the IQ, on even the best of tests, is not very *reliable*—that is, children who take the same test repeatedly are not likely to get the same score each time. Scores can rise or fall, dependent sometimes on the experiences of the children being tested and sometimes on natural fluctuations inherent in the tests themselves. IQ scores have been known, in some cases, to vary as much as thirty points in a single year, even when the same test was used. Consider the following sample case histories of fluctuating IQ scores. What does this tell you about the meaning of the IQ?

Robert P: a child with a gradually lowering IQ. Robert is an only child, born when his mother was forty-five, his father forty-two. The IQ of Robert's mother was estimated at somewhere between 70 and 75. She completed eighth grade, then dropped out of school. Robert's father is a skilled mechanic who completed the tenth grade of public school. His IQ is not known.

Robert initially was tested in the second grade. His Stanford-Binet IQ score was 115,

above average. In the fourth grade, Robert was examined by the school nurse; it was suggested that he see a doctor to help him solve an obesity problem. Medical advice was not followed. Robert's mother overindulged him. Her one desire was to feed him and keep him young, and she complained continually that Robert never gave her enough attention. She spent little time, however, helping Robert with his schoolwork or taking an interest in his intellectual activities. Robert's Stanford-Binet score in the sixth grade was 105. Medical advice concerning Robert's obesity problem finally was followed by Robert's family when he was fourteen years old, although little interest was shown in his schoolwork. His weight was normal when he was seventeen. Robert's IQ at seventeen was 85.

Philip J: a child with a gradually increasing IQ. Philip is a small, thin child with a history of ear infections, chronic bronchitis, headaches, and stomach pain. He has been hospitalized at least six times before entering first grade, three times because of serious illness and three times because of serious accidents. His mother and

ability to solve problems dealing with mazes, geometric puzzles, cubes, picture completions, and stencil designs. It is useful for measuring the abilities of children not fluent in language. The Terman-McNemar Test of Mental Ability asks questions dealing with information, synonyms, logical selection of words, word classification, analogies, and word opposites (Gibson, 1972). Clearly, children taking this test need to be fluent in the English language in order to receive high scores.

What Do IQ Scores Mean?

So far, we have discussed what IQ tests were designed to measure. What actually does a score obtained on a given test mean? IQ scores can range from mentally defective (usually considered to be IQs of 69 or under) to very superior (IQs of 131 and above). The classifications used most commonly for all standard intelligence tests are shown in Table 12.1.

The size of a child's IQ score depends on more than just the number of correct answers. It depends also on how these answers compare with father were divorced when he was five years old. He lived for some time with one aunt, later with his grandmother. His Stanford-Binet IQ at the time he entered first grade was 77. His learning ability, as measured by school grades, seemed at the time to indicate that this low IQ reflected low ability to learn. Philip's grandmother, with whom he was living at the time, was asked by school authorities if she wanted Philip to be placed in a class for low-ability children. She decided against this plan of action, even though she admitted that Philip's low grades warranted it. Philip's tested ability began to increase after age seven. At age eleven, his Stanford-Binet IQ was 104, average for students in the class. From that time on, according to the school psychologist, Philip has maintained average intellectual interests and achievements and has made good social adjustment.

Sarah J: a child with fluctuating IQ scores. Sarah presents a history characterized by intermittent but severe eczema and asthma throughout elementary school. At age nine, she had serious visual problems, which eventually were alleviated by glasses. At age ten, doctors were able to bring her asthma under control through medication. In addition to her health problems, Sarah had a number of social problems. Particularly during the last years of elementary school, when other girls were first becoming interested in boys, Sarah was concerned more with a disfiguring weight gain and eczema. She was, however, extremely interested in school and school learning and seemed to get a great deal of her social reinforcement from her teachers. Sarah's parents both were high-school graduates.

Sarah's IQ scores, as measured by the Stanford-Binet Scale during elementary school, varied from 110 to 165. Her lowest score was obtained at age eight, prior to the time that she began to wear glasses. Her highest score was obtained at age ten, when she was under medication for her asthma. Sarah's IQ score contined to fluctuate during the rest of her elementary-school years. Even though she was greatly interested in school learning in the eighth grade, her IQ score began to drop at this time when new social strains began to develop.

TABLE 12.1 Commonly accepted intelligence classifications

CLASSIFICATION	IQ
Mentally defective	69 and below
Borderline defective	70–79
Low average	80–89
Average	90–110
High average	111–120
Superior	121–130
Very superior	131 and over

those of the *standardization population,* a sample population of children who have taken the same test. If Johnny receives more correct answers than most children of his age in the sample population, he will receive a higher-than-average IQ score; if his correct answers are fewer than

IQ tests standardized on middle-class children are unfair to children from minority or poverty backgrounds.

those of children of his age in the sample population, he will receive a lower-than-average score. From this information, we can see that the sample population or the standardization population, as it is called, is very important to IQ determination. As we know, learning experiences play a major role in determining ability to speak and to perform problem-solving tasks. Thus, for the IQ score of any child to be a meaningful indicator of ability, it is necessary that the children in the standardization sample have learning experiences similar to that child.

Designers of intelligence tests do their best to get standardization samples truly representative of the populations for whom the tests are designed. However, test standardization is a time-consuming and expensive task. It has proven less costly for testers to select standardization samples from urban areas, so that many children can be tested at a time. It often is simpler for testers to get permission from middle-class parents to test their children than to get the permission of parents of lower-income backgrounds. Most urban, middle-class children are both white and Protestant; most standardization samples are composed primarily of white, urban, middle-class, Protestant children.

Sociocultural Differences, Teacher Expectancy, and IQ Tests

Earlier, we discussed the cultural bias inherent in IQ tests used today in the United States (see Chapter 4 for review). Because most standardization samples are biased in favor of middle-class children, most IQ tests give invalid estimates of the abilities of children of other-than-middle-class background. In addition, tests that make use of verbal skills taught in middle-class homes also are biased against children who have not been taught Standard English at home. Attempts have been made to develop "culture-free" tests (tests free of cultural bias), as well as "culture-fair" tests (tests fair to a particular society or group). For example, the Culture-Fair Intelligence Tests require no language skill. The Raven Progressive Matrices test uses abstract drawings instead of language to test general intellectual ability. Neither of these tests, however, is totally free of cultural influence (Cronbach, 1970). It is the lack of ability of researchers to develop such tests that led, presumably, to the test case in San Francisco discussed on pp. 330 and 410.

Using teachers' judgments to estimate intellectual ability

The school systems have long been aware of problems related to IQ testing. The New York City School System and the Educational Testing Service, in the late 1960s, embarked jointly on a project designed to assess the intellectual abilities of schoolchildren. The project grew out of the conviction that teachers' judgments would be more reliable than group IQ tests in gauging ability, especially if certain guidelines were established and if the judgments were supplemented by achievement testing.

To develop the guidelines, the project directors used specific descriptions of behavioral clues to intellect drawn from the research observations of Piaget, Guilford, Bruner, and other psychologists. Then, teachers were asked to supplement these clues by describing the behavioral signs of intellect they saw in their own classrooms. Some sample teacher responses reported by Clark (1967, p. 50) follow:

Teacher A: Juan seldom speaks in class, apparently doesn't know much English, and will fall out of the bottom of the readiness tests, BUT . . . he can take the right bus to get him across town with the laundry, work all the right buttons in the laundromat, and go home again on the bus in rush hour. No matter

what the IQ tests show, Juan is a bright six-year-old in my book!

Teacher B: Grace can't or won't do much in language or arithmetic, but in art she reveals perceptions and understandings that would be a credit to a child twice her age.

Teacher C: If children at this age can communicate well—with each other and with me—I suspect they are pretty bright. Not all the bright ones can communicate, of course, but all the good communicators seem to me better than average in mental alertness.*

The combined researchers' list and New York City teacher list was printed in a booklet, *Let's Look at First Graders: An Observational Guide for Teachers*. Its authors suggest that the manual represents a "giant step in education" and that, if it is used by the teacher to direct attention to the "actualities of behavior" rather than to some vague notion about capability, it will serve a very important function.

Is actuality of present behavior rather than future ability or capability your idea of intelligence?

* From D. Clark, *The Psychology of Education* (New York: The Free Press, © 1967). Reprinted by permission.

Evidence suggests that attitude toward self is affected not only by performance, but also by children's expectations of how they will perform. Studies have shown that children's academic progress is related directly to their attitudes toward their own perceived abilities as measured by, among other things, IQ. Children with expectations of failure have long been known to lower their levels of aspiration and to fail more frequently than do children with expectations of success (Child and Whiting, 1949). Psychologists suggest also that children whose teachers expect them to do poorly may perform less well on future tasks; they refer to this as *teacher-expectancy effects* or the *self-fulfilling prophecy*. (See, for example, studies by Barbar et al., 1969; Claiborn, 1969; Fleming and Antonnen, 1971; José and Cody, 1971; and Rosenthal and Jacobsen, 1968). If the self-fulfilling prophecy is real, then low IQ scores obtained by children whose backgrounds differ considerably from those children for whom the test was designed will be adversely affected in their school learning. In some major cities the law has responded, as the current test case of IQ testing in the public schools shows.

Most psychologists agree that IQ tests are unfair to children of minority and poverty backgrounds and also that the self-fulfilling prophecy presents a very real danger. Some psychologists point out, however, the hazards of oversimplifying a necessarily complicated problem and acting with too much haste. Intelligence tests can be used to diagnose learning problems and removing these tests or modifying them does not always resolve the critical problem. Cronbach, for example, suggests that "the critical problem is not one of modifying tests, but of inventing educational procedures suitable for children who are prepared neither intellectually nor motivationally for the traditional school" (Cronbach, 1970, p. 306). Certainly, studies have shown that changes in achievement as well as in ability to learn and problem solve are related more to adaptive instructional environments than they are to changes in IQ scores. We discuss this problem further in Chapter 13.

SUMMARY

According to Piaget, the abilities to think and to solve problems increase in two major stages during middle childhood. During the school years, children progress gradually from a concrete operations stage, in which they are able to solve problems in a logical manner, providing that concrete examples are set before them, to a formal operations stage, in which they are able to evaluate the world around them in abstract terms.

Children at the concrete operations stage learn gradually to develop concepts on the basis of many different dimensions simultaneously. During the elementary-school years, they learn the concepts involved in seriation, classification, class inclusion, and conservation. Children at the stage of formal operations gradually develop, additionally, the capacity to reason through use of hypotheses and use this reasoning ability to deal with more abstract concepts taught during the middle-school and high-school years. Children tend to learn concepts in a specific order, although psychologists and educators have shown that the order in which concepts are learned can be affected by experiences.

Although children pass in similar fashion through more and more complex stages of cognitive development, children of the same age and stage often approach problem solving in quite different ways. A number of different approaches or cognitive styles have been described by psychologists. For example, some children seem to learn most effectively through reading; some through listening; and others through touching, feeling, and manipulating objects in front of them. Some children learn most effectively by themselves; others, in groups. Children tend to organize and respond to material presented to them in different ways. Many factors are related to learning styles, including attention span, capacity for independent work, and learning rate. The fact that so many different learning styles, as well as so many factors affecting these styles, exist makes it important that teachers individualize instructional methods.

Children who are highly motivated to master their environments and to gain competence are said to have high achievement motivation. Such children are more likely to be challenged by personal effort at problem solving and to persevere longer at tasks, two characteristics associated with success at school learning. Research indicates that children who are high in achievement motivation aspire to higher levels of achievement following success at problem solving. Failure leads to more variation in level of aspiration. During the school years, girls gradually tend to decrease their achievement motivation and to increase their fear of success. Psychologists attribute this trend in behavior to social stereotyping of the female sex role in our society. Social stereotyping may also decrease the creativity of children as they get older.

Even when children are highly motivated to achieve in school, success or failure is moderated by their ability to read. According to Eleanor Gibson, reading requires the prior learning of a series of perceptual skills involving ability to extract meaningful and relevant information from the environment. This requires, according to Gibson, first learning to speak, then learning to discriminate printed letters, learning to decode letters to sound, and, finally, learning to perceive higher-order words and make rapid visual discriminations between different words. Reading, by definition, involves comprehension. Children lacking in adequate language and perceptual discrimination learning will not be able to learn to read as easily as children whose past experiences were enriched, regardless of timing or teaching method used. Current teaching methods have had variable success.

Creativity, the ability to solve new and different problems in new and innovative ways, seems generally to decrease as children get older. Psychologists believe that age and culture together account for this decline. Our educational system often contributes to the stifling of creativity, both through teachers who do not want to disrupt rigid lesson plans and through grading systems that reinforce rote learning.

Children change in their abilities to think and problem solve as they increase in age. They also are characterized by differences individual to each child. Intelligence testing is an attempt to measure these individual differences. IQ testing is fraught with dangers, however, if used inappropriately. Tests are invalid for measuring IQs of children whose backgrounds do not match those of the standardization sample of the test. Most IQ tests are verbally saturated, making them meaningless for children who are not fluent in the language or who have language difficulties. Psychologists suggest that children whose teachers expect them to do poorly on the basis of their IQ scores may perform less well on future tasks; they refer to this as the self-fulfilling prophecy. If the self-fulfilling prophecy is real, then low IQ scores obtained by children whose backgrounds differ considerably from those children for whom the test was designed will be adversely affected in their school learning.

QUESTIONS FOR THOUGHT AND REVIEW

1 Piaget stressed the importance of matching learning materials to the cognitive structure of the child. Reread the descriptions of Piaget's concrete operations stage and Piaget's formal operations stage. Assume that you would like to teach a lesson on the law of supply and demand to a group of second graders and a group of eighth graders. How would you go about designing the lessons for these two groups? What would be different about them? What would be the same? Be specific. (For review, see pages 387–392.)

2 Review the description of instructional architecture on page 396. After you have completed the exercise and designed the classroom space, answer the following question: Do you think that educators, parents, psychologists, or architects have the greatest knowledge concerning how to design classroom space for different cognitive styles? Explain your answer.

3 What trends do you expect to see in achievement motivation of elementary-school girls over the next decade? Why? (For review, see pages 398–403.)

4 Chapter 10 described many problems related to the use of IQ tests in the public schools. Suggest an alternative means of measuring individual differences in ability. Discuss its pros and cons. (For review, see pages 410–416.)

Becker, W. *Parents Are Teachers: A Child Management Program.* Champaign, Ill.: Research Press, 1976. Becker's manual provides practical information for the parent who wants to turn the home into an environment supportive of educational and social growth.

Crandall, V., and E. Battle. The antecedent and adult correlates of academic and intellectual achievement effort. In J. Hill, ed., *Minnesota Symposia on Child Psychology.* Vol. 4. Minneapolis: University of Minnesota Press, 1970, pp. 36–93. This article deals in interesting fashion with those environmental variables related to performance on intellectual tasks, rather than to IQ.

Hess, R., and V. Shipman. Cognitive elements in maternal behavior. In J. Hill, ed., *Minnesota Symposia on Child Psychology.* Vol. 1. Minneapolis: University of Minnesota Press, 1970, pp. 57–81. Another study for advanced students, this report illustrates some of the ways that cultural and social environments influence the thinking patterns of children.

Kipnis, D. Inner direction, other direction, and achievement motivation. *Human Development* 17 (1974): 321–343. Kipness relates the concept of achievement motivation to Reissman's theory of inner and other direction, and uses this relationship to explain sex differences in motivation.

Ault, R., D. Crawford, and W. Jeffrey. Visual scanning strategies of reflective, impulsive, post-accurate, and slow-inaccurate children in the Matching Familiar Figures Test. *Child Development* 43 (1972): 1412–1417.

Barbar, T., D. Calverley, A. Forgione, J. McPeake, J. Chavas, and B. Bowen. Five attempts to replicate the experimenter bias effect. *Journal of Consulting and Clinical Psychology* 33 (1969): 1–6.

Bernard, H. *Child Development and Learning.* Boston: Allyn and Bacon, 1973.

Brent, S. Starting to read. *University of Chicago Magazine,* Winter 1975.

Brook, J., M. Whiteman, E. Piesach, and M. Deutsch. Aspiration levels of and for children: Age, sex, race, and socioeconomic correlates. *Journal of Genetic Psychology* 124 (1974): 3–16.

Child, I., and J. Whiting. Determinants of level of aspiration. *Journal of Abnormal and Social Psychology* 44 (1949): 303–314.

Claiborn, W. Expectancy effects in the classroom. *Journal of Educational Psychology* 60 (1969): 377–383.

Clark, D. *The Psychology of Education.* New York: The Free Press, 1967.

Cronbach, L. *Essentials of Psychological Testing.* 3d ed. New York: Harper & Row, 1970.

DeCecco, J., and W. Crawford. *The Psychology of Learning and Instruction: Educational Psychology.* 2d ed. Englewood Cliffs, N.J.: Prentice-Hall, 1974.

Dimitrovsky, L., and M. Almy. Linkages among concrete operations. *Genetic Psychology Monographs* 92 (1975): 213–229.

Elkind, D. Children's discovery of the conservation of mass, weight, and volume. Piaget replication study II. *Journal of Genetic Psychology* 98 (1961a): 219–227.

Elkind, D. The development of the additive composition of classes in the child. Piaget replication study III. *Journal of Genetic Psychology* 99 (1961b): 51–57.

Elkind, D. The child's conception of right and left. Piagetian replication study V. *Journal of Genetic Psychology* 99 (1961c): 269–276.

Elkind, D. Piaget and Montessori. *Harvard Educational Review* 38 (1968): 335–545.

Etaugh, C. Effects of maternal employment on children: a review of recent research. *Merrill-Palmer Quarterly* 20 (1974): 71–98.

Fleming, E., and R. Antonnen. Teacher expectancy or My Fair Lady. *American Educational Research Journal* 8 (1971): 241–252.

Frieze, I. Women's expectations for and causal attributions of success and failure. In M. Mednick, S. Tangri, and L. Hoffman. *Women and Achievement: Social Psychological Perspectives.* New York: Holt, Rinehart and Winston, 1974.

Georgiady, N., and L. Romano. Ulcerville, USA. *Educational Leadership* 29, no. 3 (December 1971): 269–272.

Gibson, E. Learning to read. *Science* 148 (1965): 1066–1072.

Gibson, E. Perceptual learning in educational situations. In R. Gagne and W. Gephart, eds., *Learning Research and School Subjects.* Itasca, Ill.: Peacock, 1968.

Gibson, E. *Principles of Perceptual Learning and Development.* New York: Appleton-Century-Crofts, 1969.

Gibson, J. *Educational Psychology.* 2d ed. New York: Appleton-Century-Crofts, 1972.

Guilford, J. Creativity. *American Psychologist* 9 (1950): 444–454.

Guilford, J. Factors that aid and hinder creativity. *Teachers' College Record* 63 (1962): 380–392.

Harris, T. To know why men do what they must: a conversation with David McClelland. *Psychology Today,* January 1971, pp. 35–39.

Harter, S. Developmental differences in the manifestation of mastery motivation on problem-solving tasks. *Child Development* 46 (1975): 370–378.

Hewitt, L. Age and sex differences in the vocational aspirations of elementary school children. *Journal of Social Psychology* 97 (1975): 173–177.

Horner, M. Toward an understanding of achievement related conflicts in women. *Journal of Social Issues* 28 (1972): 157–176.

José, J., and J. Cody. Teacher-pupil interaction as it relates to attempted changes in teacher expectancy of academic ability and achievement. *American Educational Research Journal* 8 (1971): 39–49.

Kagan, J. Acquisition and significance of sex typing and sex role identity. In M. Hoffman and L. Hoffman, *Review of Child Development Research*. Vol. 1. New York: Russell Sage Foundation, 1964.

Kagan, J., H. Moss, and I. Sigel. Psychological significance of styles of conceptualization. In Society for Research in Child Development, *Cognitive Development in Children*. Chicago: University of Chicago Press, 1970, pp. 203–242.

McClelland, D., J. Atkinson, R. Clark, and E. Lowell. *The Achievement Motive*. New York: Appleton-Century-Crofts, 1953.

McClelland, D. The importance of early learning in the formation of motives. In J. Atkinson, ed., *Motives in Fantasy, Action, and Society*. Princeton: Van Nostrand, 1958.

McClelland, D. Toward a theory of motive acquisition. *American Psychologist* 20 (1965): 321–333.

McClelland, D. What is the effect of achievement motivation training in the schools? *Teachers' College Record* 74 (1972): 129–145.

McKinney, J. Teacher perceptions of the classroom behavior of reflective and impulsive children. *Psychology in the Schools* 12 (1975): 348–352.

Maccoby, E. Sex differences in intellectual functioning. In E. Maccoby, ed., *The Development of Sex Differences*. Stanford: Stanford University Press, 1966.

Manes, A., and K. Melnyck. Televised models of female achievement. *Journal of Applied Social Psychology* 4 (1974): 365–373.

Markova, A. *Psihologia Chsvoenia Yazika kak Sredstva Obsheniya*. Moscow: Pedagogika, 1974.

Marshall, E., and S. Hample, eds. *Children's Letters to God*. New York: Simon and Schuster, 1966.

Marx, M., and T. Tombaugh. *Motivation*. San Francisco: Chandler, 1967.

Maslow, A. Creativity in self-actualizing people. In H. Anderson, ed., *Creativity and Its Cultivation*. New York: Harper & Row, 1959.

Messick, S. The criterion problem in the evaluation of instruction. In M. Wittrock and D. Wiley, eds., *The Evaluation of Instruction: Issues and Problems*. New York: Holt, Rinehart and Winston, 1970.

Milton, G. The effects of sex-role identity upon problem-solving skills. *Journal of Abnormal and Social Psychology* 55 (1957): 208–212.

Montessori, M. *Dr. Montessori's Own Handbook*. New York: Schocken, 1914.

Mouly, G. *Psychology for Effective Teaching*. 3d ed. New York: Holt, Rinehart and Winston, 1970.

Nations, J. Caring for individual differences in reading through nongrading. Lecture at the Seattle Public Schools, May 13, 1967.

Olson, M. Ways to achieve quality in school classrooms. *Phi Delta Kappan* 53 (1971): 63–65.

Piaget, J. *The Child's Conception of Number*. New York: Humanities Press, 1952.

Piaget, J., and B. Inhelder. *The Early Growth of Logic in the Child*. New York: Harper & Row, 1964.

Pitman, J., and J. St. John. *Alphabets and Reading*. New York: Pitman, 1969.

Romer, N. The motive to avoid success and its effects on performance in school-age males and females. *Developmental Psychology* 2, no. 6 (1975): 689–699.

Rosenthal, R., and L. Jacobsen. Teachers' expectancies: determinants of pupils' IQ gains. *Psychological Reports* 19 (1966): 115–118.

Salmina, H., and V. Sohina. *Obuchenie Matematike v Nachalnov Shkole*. Moscow: Pedagogika, 1975.

Shumsky, A. *In Search of Teaching Style*. New York: Appleton-Century-Crofts, 1968.

Sontag, L., and J. Kagan. The emergence of intellectual achievement motives. *American Journal of Orthopsychiatry* 37 (1967): 8–21.

Spearman, C. General intelligence objectively determined and measured. *American Journal of Psychology* 15 (1904): 201–293.

Suchman, J. Inquiry training and science education. In H. Ruchlis, ed., *Laboratories in the Classroom*. New York: Science Materials Center, 1960.

Swan, R., and H. Stavros. Child-rearing practices associated with the development of cognitive skills of children in low socio-economic areas. *Early Child Development and Care* 2 (1973): 23–38.

Templeton, I. Class Size. *Educational Management Review Series* 8 (1972): 1–7.

Terman, L., and M. Merrill. *Measuring Intelligence*. Boston: Houghton Mifflin, 1937.

Terman, L., and M. Merrill. *Stanford-Binet Intelligence Scale (Manual for 3rd Revision, Form L-M)*. Boston: Houghton Mifflin, 1960.

Thurstone, L. Primary mental abilities. *Psychometric Monographs*, 1938.

Torrance, E. Can we teach children to think creatively? *Journal of Creative Behavior* 6 (1972): 114–143.

Vasudev, J. An exercise testing a Piagetian-type task. Unpublished manuscript, University of Pittsburgh, 1976.

Warburton, F., and V. Southgate. *I.T.A.: An Independent Evaluation*. London: Murray and Chambers, 1969.

Wechsler, D. *Wechsler Intelligence Scale for Children Manual*. New York: Psychological Corp., 1949.

White, R. Motivation reconsidered. *Psychological Review* 66 (1959): 297–333.

Zigler, E., and P. Kanzer. The effectiveness of two classes of verbal reinforcers on the performance of middle-class and lower-class children. *Journal of Personality* 30 (1962): 157–163.

13

Children Who Need Special Help

Learning objectives

After completing this chapter, you should be able to:

1
identify adjustment problems particular to handicapped children;

2
describe the problem behaviors most common to American children and suggest ways to help children reduce these unwanted behaviors;

3
explain some of the reasons that socially disadvantaged children have difficulty in school and suggest intervention programs to reduce the difficulty;

4
compare and contrast special education with mainstreamed programs as regards their effectiveness in helping children with special needs;

5
discuss professional services available in the community to help children with special needs and the families of these children.

We have discussed in earlier chapters how most children learn to think and solve problems, how they learn to interact socially with others as they get older, and how they adapt to the world around them. We have noted that all children do not have equal ability or opportunity to learn. Some children, for example, have difficulty making the adjustments necessary for "normal living."

Difficulties can occur for a variety of reasons. Some children are born with noticeable physical deformities. Others, because they are born mentally retarded or because of nutritional inadequacies or lack of environmental stimulation early in life, later have difficulty learning and quickly fall behind others their age.

Children sometimes develop behavior patterns that set them apart from other children and make it more difficult for them to acquire expected social learnings. Such children may become extremely shy and withdrawn, shrinking from attention. Or, they might become excessively aggressive and destructive.

Some social-emotional problems—for example, autism—make their appearance long before children are ready to enter school. Parents usually are the first to notice that their children are not learning to speak as other children are or that they are acting in bizarre ways, repetitively banging their heads against the wall and so forth. Some children with average or above-average intelligence suddenly may have difficulty in school; they may not be able to learn to read, may write backwards long after other children have learned to write properly, or may produce mirror images of printed letters.

Sometimes children who are not handicapped in the ways described above still have difficulty learning in school. Highly intelligent children may have difficulty in school because their past learning experiences have not prepared them for the middle-class–oriented public schools in this country. We call these children "socially disadvantaged." Socially disadvantaged children, as well as handicapped children, often require special help in order to develop their abilities and to adjust satisfactorily to the world around them.

Handicapped children, according to federal government classification, include "mentally retarded, hard-of-hearing, deaf, speech impaired, visually handicapped, seriously emotionally disturbed, crippled, or other health-impaired children who by reason thereof require special education and related services" (LaVor and Harvey, 1976).

Children with sensory, speech, or other physical handicaps Infants and young children explore the world through their visual and auditory senses. When either of these senses is impaired, it may be difficult for children to learn. With special training, some of these children can be

A teacher helps a deaf student learn to pronounce
words by watching lip movements in a mirror. (UPI)

taught to compensate. One extraordinary example of compensation with
special training was described in Chapter 10: the teaching of a blind,
deaf child, Helen Keller, to communicate with the outside world and
to develop socialized responses.

Children who have sensory handicaps usually do not have such extreme loss as Helen Keller. Some simply have poor eyesight or have
difficulty hearing. Such children often exhibit behavioral symptoms, such
as inattention or failure to respond to normal visual or auditory cues,
that signal their difficulties. One mother reported, for example, that her
young son had developed problem behavior: he never came when she
called him. This mother thought her son was just disobedient, until
one day she realized he was reading her lips! Teachers frequently report
that children who "act out" in the classroom frequently do so because
of frustration associated with never knowing what is happening. Frequently these children later are found to have sensory handicaps.

Children with slight visual or auditory impairments often can be
helped by such simple aids as glasses or hearing aids. Others, however,

are sufficiently handicapped that they are unable to learn through normal channels of communication. These children require additional special assistance.

Some children, even though they can see and hear as well as others, still develop problems in speaking. Speech problems are not always strictly physically caused. They may arise from simply learning wrong ways to speak when young, from mental retardation, from a severe emotional disturbance, or from neurological impairment. Of course, the child who has trouble hearing also will have trouble speaking. Children with speech handicaps have a special burden when they enter school: other children, when they can't understand them, tend to ridicule and make fun of them.

Children who are considered physically handicapped may have any one of a number of afflictions. Children crippled by accident or by a disease such as cerebral palsy, muscular dystrophy, paraplegia, scoliosis, or arthritis fall into this category. Other handicaps, such as neurological impairments caused by epilepsy, also are included in this category.

Many children with one physical handicap also are handicapped in other ways; we call these multiple-handicapped children. Such children,

"My goal in life"

The following essay was written for a ninth-grade English class by a fifteen-year-old girl who was paralyzed from the waist down as the result of an automobile accident. It portrays poignantly the multiple effects that disability can have on psychological and social functioning.

My goal in life is to become a good teacher. Since I probably will never be able to be married and have children of my own, I would like to teach students like me who have problems. Not many people realize the kinds of problems that crippled students face. There are many things that other students take for granted that are difficult for us. Even getting up the ramp to get to class is harder for me than for other students at South High.

If I am able to become a teacher, I would arrange ways to make special activities fun for crippled students. So many regular activities are closed to them now. I wouldn't punish students for missing work when they have to be out sick a lot. Most of all, I would help them to get along with other kids in the school, and teach other kids that handicapped students have feelings just like they do.

I don't know if I will ever be able to become a teacher because education is especially expensive for students who need special medical attention. And because I must be out of school a lot when I am not feeling well, sometimes my grades are bad. But I am going to try to learn enough to go to college to become a teacher. That's the only way that I will be able to do something important.

Pamela Roberts, English I
Miss Philips—6th period

because of their deformities as well as the difficulties they face in communicating and socializing with other children, often have social-emotional adjustment problems. Again, ridicule by peers complicates the problem (Karagianis and Merricks, 1973).

How can children with sensory and physical handicaps be helped? Parents of such children need to realize first that the teaching of self-care skills related to simple tasks such as eating or dressing is critical. Children, particularly when they reach school age, need to be able to care for themselves to the best of their abilities and to learn the "social graces" necessary for social approval. The multiple-handicapped child particularly needs to learn safety skills, directions necessary for orientation in the environment, and mobility skills.

When loss occurs in one specific sensory area, as is true of blind or deaf children, help often comes through increasing skill in another area. Blind children, for example, can be helped through teaching listening skills. Parents can do this most effectively early in the blind child's life by selectively reinforcing listening behavior. Word games played with young children reinforce careful listening. The listening skills of older blind children can be increased through practice with taped or recorded material (Brothers, 1972).

Sometimes, if impairment is not severe, special equipment can facilitate learning. Partially sighted children, for example, have been helped through a closed-circuit TV system called Randsight. Randsight works like a giant magnifying glass, producing a bright, high-contrast image of whatever the camera focuses on. In the classroom, it can focus on the teacher or the blackboard. The device can be used at home as well to focus on books or papers (Closed-circuit sight, 1975).

Mentally retarded children It has been estimated that 126,000 Americans who will be labeled as mentally retarded sometime during their lives are born annually (Karagianis and Merricks, 1973).

What is mental retardation? Retardation is a relative classification of ability to adjust to the environment and is made on the basis of average rate of developmental progress. Specific classifications vary according to agencies providing special services. However, children who are unable to learn sufficiently to meet the standards of personal independence and social responsibility expected of their age and cultural group generally are placed in this category. Such children are said to have "impaired adaptive behavior" and require special training or education (Florida State Department of Education, 1974).

Causes of mental retardation vary considerably. We discussed early in the text some of the genetic factors that cause retardation. Mongolism, for example, is caused by a chromosomal defect. But, as we learned, genetic causes are minor in comparison to other critical factors, such as certain maternal diseases or malnutrition during the fetal period or brain injuries due to birth trauma, infections, disease, or metabolic disorders.

Degree of retardation usually is described in terms of the help necessary for these children to adapt. The *profoundly retarded* are children who require lifelong care. They are characterized often by considerable central nervous system impairment and gross physical abnormalities. Frequently, they are blind and/or deaf. They tend to exhibit patterns of repetitive behavior, such as head-banging or rocking movements. Such children are incapable of learning even the most basic self-care skills and often are bedfast. Most profoundly mentally retarded are institutionalized, so that the extensive medical and nursing services they require can be provided. Families that choose to keep the profoundly retarded child at home must drastically alter normal family routine to accommodate the extremely time-consuming day-to-day care needs of the retarded child.

Severely retarded children also are totally dependent during their lifetimes, although these children, with intensive and prolonged training, can learn many of the basic self-care skills, such as toileting and dressing. Severely retarded children often are multiple-handicapped. Some, because of organic brain damage, are difficult to control. Because of the intensive training necessary for these children, they often are cared for in institutional settings, although they may be adequately cared for at home.

Trainable children are children capable of learning self-help skills such as toileting, feeding, and bathing. These children usually are considered moderately retarded in comparison to other children. They tend to have fewer additional handicaps when compared to the profoundly or seriously retarded. Their motor abilities tend to approach normalcy. Trainable children can score between 25 and 50 IQ points on a Wechsler or Stanford-Binet IQ test. With special help, they can live within family settings and often adjust quite acceptably to community living.

Educable mentally retarded children are more capable of learning than children falling in any of the other categories listed. The educable mentally retarded can score between 51 and 75 on a Wechsler or Stanford-Binet Scale of Intelligence. They are slower than most children in developmental progress. However, both their physical appearances and their motor development are close to normal. The poor learning ability of these children usually is first noted together with their inability to learn at the same rate as others in school. Educable children can be given much more freedom than can children with lower levels of ability. They often can be taught skills sufficient for satisfactory adjustment to the outside world. They can learn to care for themselves in their own living quarters and can hold simple jobs. Since the educable mentally retarded tend to have some difficulty managing their own affairs, they still may have special problems and require help interacting with other people.

What is the best way to help retarded children develop to their fullest potential? The answer to this question clearly is affected by a number of factors, including the child's degree of retardation. Profoundly and severely retarded children may require daily help that institutional living seems most able to provide. Even in the case of trainable or educable retarded children who are able to live at home, it is important to realize that the amount of help a family can provide is dependent on a variety of factors. These include both the emotional stability of family members and community tolerance of the handicapped child.

The discussion of placement and/or special training often is fraught with indecision and guilt. The presence of a retarded child at home can cause tension and adjustment problems for all family members. The National Association of Parents and Friends of Mentally Retarded Children was established in 1960 to help families raise their retarded children; to encourage new community attitudes of acceptance; and to exert pressure on legislative, educational, and medical services to assist in these areas.

The goal, of course, for the retarded child is the development of skills sufficient to live as independently as possible. Many retarded children who have been helped to learn self-care and vocational skills have been able to move to relatively independent living environments, together with peers, as they have gotten older. With sufficient help, educable mentally retarded have been able to support themselves financially and, in some cases, to marry and raise their own families.

Research on retardation has taken two major directions. Broad programs were begun in the 1960s in the United States and in several other nations, notably the USSR, England, and Sweden, both to reduce the causes of retardation and to provide help in adaptation when it occurs. One of the largest and best-known research centers in the United States is the George Peabody College for Teachers in Nashville, Tennessee. Research during the past two decades has been stimulated greatly also by the influence of the Joseph P. Kennedy Foundation and by efforts initiated by President John F. Kennedy.

Learning-disabled children Some 10 to 14 percent of children, many with average or above-average IQ scores, suddenly encounter learning difficulties when they enter school. Psychologists and educators report many different types of learning problems that become apparent when children first begin to learn to read and write. Golick (1971) listed poor awareness of body, poor ability to combine vision and movement, low visual efficiency, poor listening ability, poor grasp of sequence and rhythm, and difficulty in taking information from several sensory channels at the same time as some of the problems that plague these children. Other symptoms include intersensory confusion and confusion in orientation in time and space. Learning-disabled children frequently confuse

Some 10 to 14 percent of children in the United States
encounter learning difficulties when they enter school.

concepts such as yesterday and tomorrow, left and right, up and down,
and so on. Many of these children also exhibit poor memory and motor
coordination, as well as disruptive behavior (Bradbury, 1972). Some children have problems understanding written and spoken language. Because all of these problems result in learning difficulties, in the past,
many of these children have been incorrectly identified as retarded. Of
course, for some learning-disabled children, psychological and physiological tests do indicate a minimal amount of brain damage. For others,
however, there seems to be neither mental retardation nor any indication of cause.

Dyslexia. The most common category of learning disabilities is called
dyslexia, a term derived from the Greek roots "dys" meaning "difficulty"
and "lexia," "pertaining to words." Dyslexic children exhibit a range
of symptoms. They may have difficulty in developing spatial relationships, often confusing left and right or up and down. They may make
letter reversals in reading and in writing, confusing letters like "p" and
"b" and numbers like "6" and "9". Dyslexic children may reverse or
rearrange letters in a group, thus mistaking "spilt" for "split," "god"

for "dog," or "not" for "ton." Further, they might not be able to discriminate geometric shapes and designs. Dyslexic children can be found at all IQ levels. Sometimes dyslexic children have sufficiently high mental ability that their difficulties are not very noticeable in the classroom; at other times, regular teaching methods seem sorely inadequate.

Ever since dyslexia was identified late in the nineteenth century as a disorder by German and British ophthalmologists, it has been studied and debated. What causes dyslexia? Researchers still are not certain. Many feel that there are a variety of different causes related to similar symptoms. These researchers feel that the label "dyslexia" tells little about the etiology of the disorder and thus is misleading.

What can be done for learning-disabled children? Some experts suggest that the first step should be to forget the classification "learning disability" altogether. They point out that use of this label might actually cause some children to have more difficulty learning. Learning disability, or LD, as the public has come to know it, often is misunderstood as a dreaded disorder for which there is no known cause or cure. The label, many psychologists fear, may cause the frightened child and/or parents simply to "give up" (Silberman, 1976).

Experts are agreed that there is no panacea: each child must be considered individually. Behavioral assessment of individual performance and individual help with each problem is recommended. Small-group learning for children with learning disabilities seems to work most effectively. Teachers and parents who are patient in evaluating and planning instruction have the best results. The most effective teachers "like" children, take small steps, and provide a great deal of reinforcement (Haring, 1970; Woestehoff, 1970).

Two examples of special programs that have reported good results with learning-disabled children are those that have been operated by The McGlannen School in Miami and the Delacato School in Philadelphia. The McGlannen School is a small, research language-arts center. Its program has made use of an ungraded curriculum with individualized instruction to teach children who seem to be having difficulty receiving clear messages via their sensory channels.

The more controversial Delacato program is based on Delacato's (1959) assumption that the learning-disabled child's problem lies in incomplete neurophysical development, caused by inadequate muscle development. Using the Dohman-Delacato Developmental Profile, Delacato has selected those children who are retarded in what he calls "neurological age." His program gives them practice developing their muscles and their brain functioning through special exercises. The Delecato method also uses individualized instruction designed to meet the needs of each student. Critics point out that there is a lack of research supporting the program. Some suggest that if the method does work for some children, it may be because of the individual attention rather than the specific exercises prescribed by Delacato.

Children who exhibit problem behaviors Some children have learning problems that cannot be explained by the intellectual, sensory, or other factors we have discussed. These children have trouble building relationships, because their behaviors consistently antagonize others or are inappropriate for given situations. They are referred to as emotionally disturbed children or children with problem behaviors.

Just what causes problem behavior? According to many psychologists, problem behavior occurs when children have difficulty learning to adjust satisfactorily to others and, as a result, use to excess the defense mechanisms discussed in Chapter 11. The behavior that results deviates considerably from acceptable behavior. It is said to be maladaptive; that is, it is ineffective in reaching the child's desired goal of satisfactory interactions with others (Sarason, 1972).

Many handicapped children, because they feel different from others and because others feel they are different, have difficulty adjusting to people and often exhibit problem behavior. Other children, who are average in all other respects, still persistently exhibit behavior that interferes with their attaining desired goals. In many cases, these children can be helped by understanding adults. Home and school environments that provide stable and consistent caretaking help reduce problem behavior. In some cases, however, this is not enough: more help is needed. According to the National Institute of Mental Health, some 10 to 12 percent of elementary-school–age children exhibit problem behaviors that require some form of professional therapy (Rogeness et al., 1974).

Hyperactive children find it difficult to sit still long enough to learn.

Hyperactivity. Some children classified as learning disabled actually are hyperactive. These children often have difficulty simply because they can't sit still long enough to learn. They tend generally to be impulsive and aggressive, and may often have temper tantrums. Antisocial be-

Seeking help in reducing problem behavior

Many people write to the Department of Health, Education and Welfare to ask for help in handling problem behavior—either their own or that of their children. Often they ask the same questions. Some of the most commonly asked questions addressed to the Public Health Service, and their answers, follow:

Q If I do seek help, where would I go?

A You could start by contacting your local community mental-health center. More than 500 of these centers in different parts of the country have been funded by the federal government and are being operated by state and local groups and agencies.

Q I don't have any hospitalization coverage—where would I get the money to pay for all this?

A The cost of any of the services should depend on what you can afford to pay. So, if you have no money, or very little, services are provided free at these centers.

Q Wouldn't it be better just to tough it out? I don't like to bother other people with my problems—and things could blow over if I just hang on.

A That's like having a toothache and not going to the dentist. The price you pay is exactly the same—you keep on hurting.

Q Suppose I decide to go ahead and visit one of these centers . . . what goes on in one of those places? What's their treatment all about?

A A specially trained staff member will talk with you about the things that are worrying you.

Q Talk? I can talk to anyone for free. Why pay a doctor?

A You're quite right. If you have a wise and understanding friend who is willing to listen to your problems, you may not need professional help at all. But often that's not enough. You may need a professionally trained person to help you dig out what's really bothering you and you may need some medication.

Q How can just talking make problems disappear?

A Well, when you're talking to someone who has helped many others with problems similar to yours, that person is able to see the patterns in your life that have led to your unhappiness. In therapy, the job is to help you recognize those patterns—and you may then try to change them.

Q Does therapy for mental and emotional problems always work?

A Sometimes it does and sometimes it doesn't. It depends on you and the therapist. You may not "click" with a particular person, and someone else—or some other method—may be more suitable for you. You can ask your therapist for a referral to another mental-health professional or, if you prefer, you can call one of the associations listed in this booklet for the names of other therapists.*

* Reprinted from *A Consumer's Guide to Mental Health Services*, DHEW Publication No. (ADM) 75-214, 1975 HEW Public Health Service (Alcohol, Drug Abuse, and Mental Health Administration, Rockville, Md. 20852).

haviors such as lying, stealing, or cruelty to animals are not uncommon among these children (Stewart, 1970).

Hyperactive children often have histories of restlessness, tantrums, and inability to relax. When very young, they are considered "difficult" children; in school, they often are considered "impossible." Faced with angry teachers, they become increasingly aggressive and often hostile.

The causes of hyperactivity still are largely unclear. Some researchers suggest that hyperactive behavior may result from homeostatic mechanisms that allow some children to acquire additional needed sensory stimulation through more active behavior (Zentall, 1975).

What can be done for the hyperactive child? One controversial method use has been drug therapy. Amphetamines, such as ritalin and dexedrine, used with other people as stimulants, have been found frequently to reduce hyperactivity (Bradbury, 1972). There has been much controversy concerning the use of drugs with hyperactive children, however. Concerns have been voiced over the safety of the children—some fear negative side effects, such as further behavioral abnormality or addiction. Further, the qualifications of those administering the drugs in school have been challenged. Many psychologists as well as medical experts agree that there is "no doubt" but that drugs have been misused (Cole, 1975; Stewart, 1975; Weithorn and Ross, 1976).

Interestingly, investigations have shown that hyperactivity can be reduced considerably by eliminating food additives, artificial flavors, and artificial colors (Feingold 1975a, 1975b). Pursuant to these findings, the state of California has revised public-school menus, so as to reduce food additives. Feingold (1975b) and others have urged that all food packages should bear labels stating the presence of food additives.

Another method of treatment involves training hyperactive children in improved self-control. Simpson and Nelson (1974), for example, used breathing techniques and other body controls to help hyperactive children control various motor behaviors and maintain concentration. The research findings suggest that such training can, indeed, help hyperactive children develop better self-discipline.

Excessive anxiety. Children characterized by short attention spans, high levels of distractibility that are not age-appropriate, and hyperactivity associated with persistent feelings of anomie or personal disorientation are said to be excessively anxious. Unlike the behavior of hyperactive children, the behavior of excessively anxious children seems to be due primarily to difficulties in the environment. Children may exhibit "anxiety attacks" or "panic reactions" in certain frightening situations. In other more serious cases, the anxiety is chronic with unclear causes.

Drugs reportedly have been administered mistakenly to excessively anxious children. The results in many cases have been poor. In many cases, when the cause of anxiety can be discovered and "talked out" through interpretive therapy, these children are greatly helped (Doyle and Freedman, 1974). Behavior management, described in Chapter 3, has been shown also to produce excellent results when the specific situation causing the anxiety can be identified (Cooper, 1973).

Excessive withdrawing. Opposite to the hyperactive child is the extremely shy, withdrawn child. Withdrawn children tend to spend large amounts of time daydreaming and fantasizing, instead of interacting with those around them. Zimbardo et al. (1975) reported, in a survey of high-school and college students, that 40 percent of those interviewed reported that extreme shyness has accompanied and affected their interpersonal reactions throughout their growing-up periods. One interviewee reported that he could remember as far back as four years of age exhibiting behaviors specifically designed to hide from interactions with others. He would look the other way when seeing people he knew, in hopes they wouldn't notice him. He never raised his hand to answer teachers' questions in class. These behaviors were accompanied by blushing, excessive perspiring, and having "butterflies in the stomach" whenever he was forced into social interactions.

Excessively withdrawn children appear to be fearful, secretive, and apathetic. Frequently, they dislike interacting with others so much that

"Talking out" problems

The following paper was written by an eleven-year-old boy after he was sent to visit the school psychologist. His behavior in class, according to his teacher, was withdrawn. He refused to participate in regular classroom activities. The psychologist, after trying to get the boy to "talk out" his problems, asked him if he wanted instead to "talk them out" on paper. The results appear below.

Consider the problems expressed by this student. What do you think the psychologist can do to help? What can the child's teacher do? His parents?

1. I like to work by myself.
2. I don't like the kids in my class.
3. I wish people wouldn't always ask about my mother.
4. My father is too strict.
5. People call me names.
6. I'm always getting into fights.
7. I have bad dreams at night.

Opposite to the hyperactive child is the extremely shy and withdrawn child.

it becomes painful for them to go to school. In this case, hypochondriacal symptoms are not at all uncommon, with children complaining of headaches, stomachaches, and other ills that appear just as they are ready to depart for school. Sometimes the hypochondriacal (or sometimes real) physical symptoms keep the withdrawn child at home and away from school altogether. This is called school phobia.

Asthmatic coughing, high blood pressure, skin disorders, and gastrointestinal disturbances, all are physical ailments that, in many cases, may be psychosomatic—that is, associated with tension and extreme emotion rather than with physical causes only. Children with severe school phobia, when required to attend school, may simply refuse to go. If physically forced to go to school, they may spend most of the time either mute or crying. Sadness and deep depression are not uncommon (Freedman and Doyle, 1974).

What can be done to help the withdrawn child? One of the first concerns of psychologists is simply to alert people to the problem. Wickman (1928) studying the incidence of behavior problems in children noted long ago that shy, withdrawn children too frequently are not noticed by anyone, including their families and teachers. Unless they interfere in what is going on around them (as in "acting out" in school), they often are not even considered behavior problems. Once selected for attention, the withdrawn child has great hopes of being helped. Behavior management, in which reinforcement is given consistently for interaction, has been one of the more successful methods used (Phillips, 1972). Group-centered therapy approaches, based on the theory that in a group individuals can receive acceptance and encouragement from many members, have been effective in many cases in allowing withdrawn individuals to work out their problems within an interpersonal context (Harper, 1974). In using group-centered approaches, it is important to note that a skilled therapist must always be present in the group, so as to clarify matters or intervene when necessary.

Unsocialized aggression. Children characterized as unsocialized and aggressive behaviors are quickly spotted by teachers and families alike. These children are hostile, disobedient, and destructive. Like hyperactive children, they may have frequent temper tantrums. They tend also to be both verbally and physically abusive toward others. Assaults on people or property are not uncommon. Unsocialized, aggressive children tend frequently to lie, steal, and vandalize. They regularly get into fights with other children. Teachers are particularly aware and highly critical of

Hostile children are often unhappy and easily frustrated.

aggressive children and tend to consider this behavior as much more serious than withdrawn behavior. Unfortunately, teachers and parents often respond to the aggressive child with aggression of their own. As pointed out in earlier chapters, this return aggression frequently increases rather than reduces the unwanted behavior.

Psychologists offer many explanations for children's aggressive behavior. Children may first learn aggression by modeling the behavior of punitive caretakers. Hostile aggressive behavior has long been associated with extreme frustration (Miller and Dollard, 1941; Miller, 1948). Not surprisingly, children who tend to exhibit unsocialized aggression in their interactions with others tend also to be unhappy children who are frequently and easily frustrated. One method of helping these children is to carefully and systematically provide nonfrustrating environments in which positive reinforcement can be meted out immediately following appropriate behavior. This involves, in therapeutic learning situations, placing children in small groups where a great deal of atten-

Problem behaviors of American children

What are the most common problem behaviors of children? The following behaviors were described originally over thirty years ago by Long (1941), in a study of children from the ages of three to fourteen. Teachers and parents today still report the same behaviors, as well as some others. Looking at this list of behaviors described by parents, why do you think that each has been listed as a problem behavior? Why do you think that these behaviors occur? What do they tell you about our society?

Age	Behavior Problem
3–5 years	Disobedience Temper tantrums Thumb sucking Bedwetting
7–10 years	Disobedience Fears of all sorts
11–14 years	Disobedience Overconscientious in school and tension associated with this overconscientiousness

tion can be given (Culbertson, 1974). Group-centered therapies, of the type discussed earlier for withdrawn children, can be useful with aggressive children as well. Therapists and others dealing with these children must be extremely careful, however, not to respond to aggression with aggression and thus, unwittingly, provide models for imitation.

More severe behavior disorders. Thus far, we have been discussing children who exhibit behaviors that are problems to them and to those around them. Most of these children are able to function in society, although they may do so with some difficulty. Other children, as, for example, severely autistic children, exhibit behaviors so bizarre that they need to be cared for away from other children.

Autism is first exhibited at extremely early ages: mothers of autistic children often report that their babies appeared unresponsive even in the first year of life, while being fed and held. Babies later diagnosed as autistic frequently have histories of crying day and night in infancy. Later, as they get older, they exhibit what psychologists suggest is extreme withdrawal: they exhibit repetitive behaviors such as head knocking, do not speak, and appear totally disinterested in the world around them. Autistic children are failures at socialization. They can't communicate, nor do they appear to be interested in communicating. Some psychologists suggest that this behavior is a defense mechanism that allows these children to shut themselves off from the rest of the world. Thus far, however, little is known of the true etiology of autism. For this reason, therapy related to this disorder has been less successful than for some of the other problem behaviors discussed. One of the most successful methods of providing help for autistic children has been through extensive use of behavior-management techniques. Behavior management has been used both in institutions and in public-school programs designed for autistic children (Sage, 1975). It is clear, however, that, until the true etiology of autism is discovered, no completely effective therapy program can be developed.

Another serious behavior disorder noted in childhood is *childhood schizophrenia*. Childhood schizophrenics may exhibit a wide variety of symptoms. To the outside world, they communicate very mixed messages. Child schizophrenia is characterized by extremes of activity, sudden mood changes, and verbal disturbances. The approximately one million children in the United States diagnosed as schizophrenic have great difficulty adjusting. Unlike autistic children, who tend to exhibit repetitive behaviors, these children exhibit a wide variety of changing behaviors.

Childhood schizophrenia is, as yet, not well understood by psychologists and psychiatrists. For this reason, there is considerable debate in the profession concerning the most effective therapy. Therapy of many different sorts has been used with these children, with varying degrees

of success. When severe, many psychologists believe that childhood schizophrenia is treated most effectively by removing the child from the family and providing full-time therapy.

Socially Disadvantaged Children

The bottom 15–20 percent of our population in terms of income and educational level has been labeled by sociologists the "lower-lower social class" (Havighurst and Neugarten, 1967). This population is characterized by absence of steady employment, low level of education and technical skills, dependence on assistance programs, and isolation from other segments of the population. It is not characterized by any single race or minority group, but includes approximately 20 million whites, eight million blacks, 700,000 Puerto Ricans, two million other Spanish Americans, and 500,000 American Indians. The children of this population, according to psychologists and sociologists, have one major factor in common: they grow up in a "culture of poverty." Most such children are destined to live at or near subsistence levels most of their lives. Regardless of potential ability, they tend to fail and then drop out of school. As a consequence, they are limited later to unskilled jobs. It is these children who are the *socially disadvantageed* (Havighurst, 1969; Lewis, 1966).

Problems of socially disadvantaged children As we learned in earlier chapters, the children of poverty are plagued with problems even before birth.

Health. Chapters 5 and 6 dealt extensively with the effects of poor malnutrition and disease on prenatal and early development. The children of the poor are characterized by continuing malnutrition. Seventy-five percent of poor children seen in free clinics in the 1960's suffered from malnutritional deficiency anemia (Citizens' Board of Inquiry, 1968). Today, in many areas, the situation has worsened. Diseases and environmental poisoning, such as lead poisoning, are frequent among the poor. Medical researchers have recently noted that lead poisoning, caused by eating peeling paint in old houses, is quantitative in its effects and can be shown to have decreased the health and abilities of poor children within both the normal and abnormal range.

Behavior, values, and attitudes. Psychologists, psychiatrists, and educators tell us that socially disadvantaged children exhibit considerably more problem behavior both in and out of school than do children coming from wealthier homes. Many suggest that these problem behaviors are caused by the early learning of values and behaviors that later turn out to be "out of place" in middle-class schools (Evans, 1975; Karnes et al., 1971; Langner et al., 1974). The result often includes defense responses equally inappropriate to the school setting in which children spend the major portion of each day. Children who have learned, for example, that it is acceptable to come and go from their homes at times that vary according to what is happening that day, suddenly find that it is inappropriate to be even two minutes late to school in the morning. Children of some minority groups who have learned to speak one language or dialect in the home, suddenly find that this speech is considered inappropriate in the new school setting. The psychological cost often is high and may include feelings of low self-esteem, powerlessness, and worthlessness, signalled by low motivation, inappropriate social behavior, and lowered intellectual functioning.

Psychologists suggest that the psychological cost is particularly high for poor black children living in our predominantly white country. Some have suggested that lower self-esteem is one of the most significant of these costs (Rosenham, 1969). Others suggest that today the problem for black children is more complex and involves primarily cultural patterns that differ considerably from the white majority (Taylor, 1976).

Providing help for the socially disadvantaged child Many solutions to the problems of socially disadvantaged children have been posed. Some suggested earlier in this text include better and more extensive day-care programs and early intervention (see Chapters 7 and 10 for review). In addition to the governmental and private experimental programs designed to teach appropriate learning habits and thereby increase young children's abilities to learn, varieties of individual neighborhood programs have been operating through community centers throughout the United States with varying degrees of success (Jason et al., 1973). Summer programs have been less effective than full-time, year-round pro-

Teachers can help

Research has shown that individualized, intensive, and integrated remediation programs are particularly helpful to socially disadvantaged children having trouble learning in school (Feshbach and Adelman, 1974). What do individualized programs do? Marshall (1974) suggests that the following probably are most important to disadvantaged kids:

1 reducing emphasis on competition and test scores;
2 spending more time developing quality of the lives of children in the "here and now" rather than in some vague future time;
3 realizing that IQ scores are not unchangeable;
4 providing help and understanding to children who otherwise would begin to cut class and, later, drop out;
5 doing away with elitist ability tracking and realizing that every child has the potential for success.

Can you design a program that would take all of these into consideration?

grams (Austin et al., 1972). Once children reach the school years, psychologists have learned, it is more difficult to help.

Within the public schools. Psychologists have suggested that public schools in the United States are particularly adept at "programming kids for failure" (Havighurst, 1970; Richmond, 1970). What do they mean? For one thing, they mean that teachers often do not take into consideration the past learning experiences of children. They tend often to select reinforcements that have been proven effective among middle-class children; then, if poor children do not respond to these reinforcers, teachers assume they are "incapable of learning." According to critics, the main problem in schools today often is misunderstanding. Havighurst (1970) reported the case of a substitute teacher entering a classroom of second graders who, according to school records, could not count. The substitute teacher tried an interesting experiment. It was Valentine's Day, and she came prepared with boxes of candy hearts. She suggested to the children that they each could have as many candy hearts as they could count. One child, who was reported in the school records to be unable to count above three, counted to fourteen and received an equal number of candies!

Helping hand for Black English

One factor that sets many socially disadvantaged children apart from other children is the language they speak at home. This is particularly true of children who are both socially disadvantaged and members of minority groups. In recent years, many educators have experimented with teaching these children in whatever language they speak at home. One exception to this approach is that taken by the U.S. Labor Department in its pilot program to teach Standard English to children speaking Gullah, a dialect that has been called by some "pure Black English." Gullah is spoken in isolated areas along the South Carolina coast. Children speaking Gullah reportedly have trouble understanding most other Americans (McNeese, 1976).

Gullah, a language that dates back to the period of slavery in the United States, combines English with elements of several African languages. One of its more noticeable traits is a shortening of English words which eliminates both plurals and past tenses.

According to John Gadson, Director of the Sea Island Language Project at Beaufort, South Carolina, Gullah is a legitimate language that should and can be spoken without criticism. However, a more standard English is necessary for the world of work. Gadson feels that children, as part of their preparation for functioning in the outside world, should learn Standard English for this purpose.

The Labor Department program seeks to show that overdependence on Gullah will prevent Gullah-speaking young people from holding jobs for which they otherwise would be qualified. Some educators take this view one step further: they suggest that, since speaking and thinking on most jobs will be done in Standard English, minority children should learn English first, rather than be reinforced in a language that will become increasingly difficult for them to use in the outside world (Vail, 1970).

What approach do *you* think would be most effective?

Black children who speak Black English may suffer severe communication problems in schools where only Standard English is used.

Language, for many socially disadvantaged children, is a major problem in school. A dialect different from Standard English or, sometimes, an entirely different language may be spoken in the child's home. This is particularly true for many black children in America who speak Black English at home and for Puerto Rican children who speak Spanish. Communication becomes a major problem. One approach to helping the socially disadvantaged child who speaks a language different from "school language" is bilingual education, in which instruction is given in the home language until Standard English is learned. Project Upgrade, a successful intervention program discussed in Chapter 10, used this method. The Bilingual Education Act, passed in the United States in 1968, calls for the teaching of subject matters in both English and native language for children unfamiliar with Standard English.

In other social settings. Socially disadvantaged children have a great deal of difficulty in other social settings as well. Children who have difficulty learning to read may be unable to decipher street signs and may not be able to find their way to the office of a social worker or to a clinic

in time to make an appointment. They may be more fearful than other children of authority figures such as police, with whom they may associate unpleasantness rather than help. Fear of authority figures may generalize to others, particularly those in uniform, such as doctors and nurses. The lower self-esteem of socially disadvantaged children may lead them to respond to criticism of this behavior in nonsocialized or aggressive ways. According to psychologists, what these children need in all situations is a great deal of individualized help, attention, and, particularly, understanding.

SPECIAL SERVICES FOR SPECIAL CHILDREN

We have talked so far in this chapter about the unique needs of handicapped and disadvantaged children, and procedures that have been most useful in helping these children develop their capabilities. Caring for special children has long been one of the functions of our government. When children are capable of being educated in our public-school systems, special programs have been developed for them. When other help is required, governmental and community agencies have provided services to assist parents in obtaining needed aid.

In the Schools

Special education Public-school education for children with special needs has for years provided special programs and classes. Special education is designed to separate out from regular classes children who learn more slowly than do others in their age group or children who need special help in controlling themselves. The objective is to provide extra attention and individualized instruction by specially trained teachers. Teachers in special-education programs often hold master's degrees in special-education methods.

In the United States, children who are mentally retarded, learning disabled, or who exhibit problem behaviors traditionally have been placed in special-education classes. Critics of special education point out that a disproportionate number of socially disadvantaged children also have been placed in these classes.

In recent years, special education has been on the firing line. Critics have pointed out that, in many instances, children who are having problems in regular classrooms are placed together, regardless of the individual causes of the problems. Thus, many special-education classes actually are more heterogeneous in terms of ability to learn than are regular classes. It is said that many special-education teachers are burdened by lack of resources and have difficulty, therefore, effectively individualizing instruction. Critics point out, also, that the social stigma often attached to special-education classes can have a detrimental effect on both teachers' and students' attitudes, as well as on students' abilities to learn. Studies have shown that special-education students labeled "retarded" or "disturbed" are given "negative halos" by their teachers. That is, their teachers tend to expect poor learning and, as a result of the expectation, often receive poor performance (Jones, 1972). One study showed that student teachers, when shown photos of average children in regular classrooms and told that these were emotionally disturbed children, then viewed them as emotionally disturbed. The teachers actually reported that they "could see" in the photos the "disturbed behavior" being exhibited. The authors of the study (Foster et al., 1975) entitled it, "I Wouldn't Have Seen It If I Hadn't Believed It."

Mainstreaming. Because of these and other concerns, parents of children with special needs increasingly have requested that their children, whenever possible, be allowed to remain in regular classes. Parents claim that their children have the same right as other children to regular classes, as long as their education does not interfere with the rights of others. Courts in state after state have agreed and have mandated integration of special students into the mainstream of public-school life (Pedrini and Pedrini, 1973; Stearns and Swenson, 1973).

Mainstreaming is the term coined to describe public education that permits average children, physically and mentally disabled children, and children with problem behaviors to be taught together by one teacher. Experimental studies in the United States have shown that, if done well, teaching can be very effective in mainstreamed classes, both for children with special needs and for average children (Haring and Krug, 1975).

Mainstreaming already has been effective in British classrooms (Anderson, 1973; Central Advisory Council for Education, 1967).

Mainstreaming clearly is not a panacea for all the problems of special education. Children with severe behavior problems, for example, may be too disruptive to be allowed to attend special classes. It has been shown that many highly aggressive children enrolled in mainstreamed programs still need to attend special classes at least part of the time to receive help with their behavior problems (Karagianis and Merricks, 1973). Special psychological, counseling, and instructional services are required for teachers who usually have not been prepared to deal with the many problems of children from special classes. In some cases, help is required also from physicians, physical and occupational therapists, and social workers working within the schools.

To be successful, mainstreamed programs must take into consideration the needs of both teachers and students. Teachers' concerns for their curricular planning and for the needs of their classes must be considered. Special preparation must be given teachers and students alike to deal with the new members of the class. Research has shown that telling classmates about problems of a student, if not done with extreme cau-

What is mainstreaming ?

The term "mainstreaming" has been used frequently and in different ways during the last few years. As a result, there is some confusion regarding what the term really means. While there may not be a definition that is universally agreed on, some basic themes can be looked to for an understanding of the intent of mainstreaming.

Mainstreaming is:

1 providing the most appropriate education for each child in the least restrictive setting.
2 looking at the educational needs of children instead of clinical or diagnostic labels such as mentally handicapped, learning disabled, physically handicapped, hearing impaired, or gifted.
3 looking for and creating alternatives that will help general educators serve children with learning or adjustment problems in the regular setting. Some approaches being used to help achieve this are consulting teachers, methods and materials specialists, itinerant teachers and resource room teachers.
4 uniting the skills of general education and special education so that all children may have equal educational opportunity.

Mainstreaming is not:

1 wholesale return of all exceptional children in special classes to regular classes.
2 permitting children with special needs to remain in regular classrooms without the support services they need.
3 ignoring the need of some children for a more specialized program than can be provided in the general education program.
4 less costly than serving children in special, self-contained classrooms.*

* This material is provided as a service from the Council for Exceptional Children, 1920 Association Drive, Reston, Virginia 22091. Reprinted from *Exceptional Children* 42 (1975): 174.

When parents understand the nature of their children's
problems, they often can help in providing therapy.

tion, can increase their negative responses. Clearly, attitudes of teachers,
parents, and students must be considered (Birch, 1974; Novak, 1975).

It is clear that teaching in both special-education and mainstreamed
classes will benefit from special services provided by professionals. Children who need special help do not always receive all they need through
the school systems alone, however. In most cases, both these children
and their parents must rely also on help from private, community, or
governmental agencies. What sorts of supportive services can be found
in the community?

In the Community

Psychological and psychiatric services These services are found in most
communities both privately and through clinics. Psychologists and psychiatrists provide important help in diagnosing learning and behavior
problems, and also in providing therapy when necessary. Psychologists

report that early diagnosis of problem behaviors such as hyperactivity leads to more effective therapy. When parents understand the nature of their children's problems, they also can provide therapy. In many cases, psychiatric and psychological services are most useful in simply helping parents to understand both their own anxieties and their children's problems.

Counseling services Counseling services are available privately, as well as through school, community, and governmental agencies. Rehabilitation counselors are helpful in providing vocational assistance. Often, the parents of children who need special help are in need of counseling services themselves, in order to learn how best to cope with the many problems they face each day. In recent years, family group counseling has become particularly popular. When should help be requested from a psychologist or psychiatrist and when from a counselor? There is a disagreement within the professions as to specific rules. Some researchers suggest that a good policy to follow is to make use of psychological or psychiatric help for involuntary referrals (as when the school principal sends an unsocialized, aggressive child for help) and that counseling be reserved for voluntary referrals (Nugent, 1973; Taylor and Hoedt, 1974).

Social workers Social workers usually are available through agencies in the community to help both the child and the family with school or other problems. The most important attribute of the social worker is his or her ability to function as a liaison between the family and other service agencies. The social worker also is trained to understand the needs of people of different backgrounds, an important asset in dealing with socially disadvantaged children and their families (Lurie, 1974).

Medical help Physicians of all sorts are available in many communities to deal with the problems of children. In the cases of the children described in this chapter, pediatricians, pediatric neurologists (who can diagnose central-nervous-system problems), ophthalmologists, audiologists, and other specialists are needed both for diagnosis and for therapy. In large cities, these professional people are available both privately and through clinics.

Therapists Another professional service frequently required by the child with special needs is therapy. Physical and occupational therapy is necessary to help physically handicapped children learn to use their bodies to the best advantage and to develop self-help skills. Speech correctionists and audiologists help children deal with speech and hearing handicaps. All of these therapists are available in clinics; in some cities, they are available to special-education students and handicapped students in mainstreamed classes through the school systems.

Some children have greater difficulty than do others making the adjustments necessary for "normal" living. Difficulties can occur for a variety of reasons. Some children are set apart from others in their behavior or learning ability because of physical, mental, or social-emotional handicaps, or because they are what we call "socially disadvantaged." Such children need special help if they are to adjust satisfactorily to the world in which they will live as adults.

Children with speech, sensory, or other physical handicaps often have problems in school interacting with other children. Physically handicapped children may have only one affliction, although many are multiple-handicapped. Such children, because of deformities as well as the difficulties they face in communicating and socializing with others, need special help in adjusting.

Mentally retarded children usually are classified by degree of retardation. Profoundly retarded children need lifelong care; severely retarded children also are totally dependent on their caretakers, but can learn some self-care skills with long and intensive training. Trainable children are more capable of learning all self-care skills. With special help, they can live within family settings and often adjust quite successfully to community living. Educable mentally retarded children are slower than most normal children in developmental progress, but, with help, their appearance, motor development, and cognitive abilities can be brought close to normal. Many educational programs have been designed for these children.

Many children with average or above average IQ scores suddenly encounter learning difficulties when they enter school. Psychologists and educators report many different types of learning problems that first become apparent when children begin learning to read and write. These children are called learning-disabled, and have, among their problems, poor body awareness, poor ability to combine vision and movement, low visual efficiency, poor listening ability, poor grasp of sequence and rhythm, and difficulty in taking information from several sensory channels simultaneously.

Learning-disabled children with particular problems in learning to read and write are called dyslexic. These children have particular problems in developing spatial relationships, often confuse left and right and up and down, and make common letter reversals in reading and writing. The causes of dyslexia are not known; many feel that there are a variety of causes related to similar symptoms. The many different programs developed to help these children have met with varying degrees of success.

Many children exhibit behavior that is socially unacceptable to those around them. Problem behavior can be exhibited for a variety of reasons —for example, as a defense mechanism to hide other problems. In some cases, problem behavior may be caused by physiological conditions. Hyperactivity, for example, may be related directly to the chemical contents of food additives and thus may be eliminated by removing these substances from the hyperactive child's diet. Children characterized by short attention spans, excessive distractibility, hyperactivity, anomie, and personal disorientation are said to be excessively anxious. The extremely withdrawn child is fearful, secretive, and apathetic and spends large amounts of time daydreaming and fantasizing, instead of interacting with those around him or her. The behavior of both excessively anxious and excessively withdrawn children seems to be directly related to difficulties in the environment. Help can frequently be provided through therapy. Autism and childhood schizophrenia are severe behavior disorders that cause children to exhibit behaviors so bizarre that they frequently must receive care away from other children.

Socially disadvantaged children are the children of the poor—children who have grown up in a "culture of poverty" at near subsistence or subsistence levels most of their lives. Problems of children of poverty include poor health, hunger, and, often, the learning of values and behaviors that are inappropriate to successful adjustment to the majority culture. Regardless of potential ability, without special help these children tend to fail to learn in school. Ultimately, they may drop out, limiting themselves later to semiskilled and unskilled employment possibilities.

What can be done to help children with special needs? School, local, state, and federal agencies are available to provide services. Within schools, children in this country have been placed in special-education classes with teachers specially trained to work with them. In recent years, schools have opened their regular classes to these children—providing what is called "mainstream education." Mainstreaming has proven effective, providing that other services are available as well. In addition to teachers specially prepared for the problems of children with special needs, psychologists, psychiatrists, counselors, social workers, physicians, and varieties of therapists are available in many communities to help children with special needs and their families.

QUESTIONS FOR THOUGHT AND REVIEW

1 Assume that you are a physically disabled child who needs to use a wheelchair to get to school. What day-to-day problems would you encounter in elementary school? How could the school best help you? What special services outside the school would be most useful? (For review, see pp. 425–428.)

2 Excessively withdrawn children often overlooked by the teacher because they do not interfere with regular classroom activities. What can the teacher do to help the withdrawn child to interact more successfully with others? Outline some class activities that might help. (For review, see pp. 433–434 and 436–437.)

3 Research has shown that hyperactivity may be related to the presence of food additives. Assuming that further research clearly shows that food additives are the cause of this behavior problem, recommend a program that would successfully reduce this problem for our children. How would you convince the public to follow this program?

4 Socially disadvantaged children tend frequently to be unsuccessful in their interactions with authority figures, such as policemen, teachers, doctors, and nurses. Why? Outline a program that would help disadvantaged children to interact more successfully and, at the same time, would teach authority figures ways to communicate more effectively with these children. (For review, see pp. 442–446.)

5 Which would you prefer for your child, a special-education class or a mainstreamed class? What specific special services would you like to have provided? Which do you think are the most important? Why? (For review, see pp. 446–450.)

Baker, B., A. Brightman, L. Heifetz, and D. Murphy. *Steps to Independence: A Skills Training Series for Children with Special Needs.* Champaign, Ill.: Research Press, Inc., 1976. This text provides how-to-do-it help for anyone working with parents of children with special needs. It deals primarily with early, intermediate, and advanced self-help skills, as well as behavior problems.

Dempsey, J. *Community Services for Retarded Children.* Baltimore, Md.: University Park Press, 1975. Dempsey's book is a major source of information related to service systems in detection, diagnosis, and treatment of the mentally retarded.

Kaufman, B. *Son Rise.* New York: Harper & Row, 1976. This is a personal story of an autistic child, written by the child's father. It describes not only the behavior of the child during his first two and one-half years, but also the intensely emotional reactions of parents, siblings, and family members. Kaufman relates the family's efforts, assisted by doctor care, to help.

Karagianis, L., and D. Merricks, eds. *Where the Action Is: Teaching Exceptional Children.* St. John, Newfoundland: Memorial University, 1973, ERIC Document Reproduction Service No. Ed 084 764. This is a collection of readings dealing with a variety of special needs. Identification of children with special needs and suggestions for treatment are discussed.

Sarason, I. *Abnormal Psychology: The Problem of Maladaptive Behavior*. New York: Appleton-Century-Crofts, 1972. This textbook is useful reading for students with some background in psychology. Social-emotional problems and their etiologies are described in some detail.

Schiefelbusch, R., ed. *Language of the Mentally Retarded*. Baltimore, Md.: University Park Press, 1972. Theoretical and practical aspects of language development of children in general, and of retarded children in particular, are examined in this collection of articles.

REFERENCES

Anderson, E. *The Disabled School Child*. London: Methuen, 1973.

Austin, J., B. Rogers, and H. Walbesser. The effectiveness of summer compensatory education: a review of the research. *Review of Educational Research* 42 (1972): 171–181.

Birch, J. *Mainstreaming: Educable Mentally Retarded Children in Regular Classrooms*. Reston, Va.: Council for Exceptional Children, 1974.

Bradbury, W. An agony of learning. *Life*, October 6, 1972, pp. 57–58.

Brothers, R. Is listening the answer? Paper presented at the Biennial Conference of the Association for the Education of the Visually Handicapped. Miami Beach, Florida, June 1972.

Central Advisory Council for Education. *Children and Their Primary Schools*. Vols. 1 and 2. London: Her Majesty's Stationery Office, 1967.

Citizens' Board of Inquiry into Hunger and Malnutrition in the U.S. *Hunger USA* (A report). Boston: Beacon, 1968.

Closed-circuit sight. *Human Behavior*, February 1975, p. 30.

Cole, S. Hyperkinetic children: The use of stimulant drugs evaluated. *American Journal of Orthopsychiatry* 45, no. 1 (January 1975): 28–35.

Cooper, J. Application of the consultant role to parent-teacher management of school avoidance behavior. *Psychology in the Schools* 10 (1973): 259–262.

Culbertson, F. An effective, low-cost approach to the treatment of descriptive school children. *Psychology in the Schools* 11 (1974): 183–187.

Delacato, C. *The Treatment and Prevention of Reading Problems*. Springfield, Ill.: Charles C Thomas, 1959.

Dollard, J., N. Miller, L. Doob, O. Mowrer, and R. Sears. *Frustration and Aggression*. New Haven: Yale University Press, 1939.

Doyle, G., and R. Freedman. Anxiety in children: some observations for the school psychologist. *Psychology in the Schools* 11 (1974): 161–164.

Evans, W. The behavior problem checklist: data from an inner city population. *Psychology in the Schools* 12 (1975): 300–303.

Feingold, B. *Why Your Child is Hyperactive.* New York: Random House, 1975a.

Feingold, B. Hyperkinesis and learning disabilities linked to artificial food flavors and colors. *American Journal of Nursing 75*, no. 5 (May 1975): 797–803.

Feshbach, S., and H. Adelman. Remediation of learning problems among the disadvantaged. *Journal of Educational Psychology 66*, no. 1 (1974): 16–28.

Florida State Department of Education, Division of Elementary and Secondary Education. *District Procedures for Providing Special Education for Exceptional Students: 1974 Guidelines.* Vol. 2. (ERIC Document Reproduction Service No. ED 087 164).

Foster, G., J. Ysseldyke, and J. Reese. "I wouldn't have seen it if I hadn't believed it." *Exceptional Children 41* (1975): 469–473.

Freedman, R., and G. Doyle. Depression in children. *Psychology in the Schools 11* (1974): 19–23.

Gibson, J. *Psychology for the Classroom.* Englewood Cliffs, N.J.: Prentice-Hall, 1976.

Golick, M. *A Parent's Guide to Learning Problems.* Montreal: Quebec Association for Children with Learning Disabilities, 1970.

Haring, N. The new curriculum design in special education. In R. Burns and A. Brooks, eds., *Curriculum Design in a Changing Society.* Englewood Cliffs, N.J.: Educational Technology Publications, 1970, pp. 159–184.

Haring, N., and D. Krug. Placement in regular programs: procedures and results. *Exceptional Children 41* (1975): 413–417.

Harper, R. *Psychoanalysis and Psychotherapy.* New York: Jason Aronson, 1974.

Havighurst, R., and B. Neugarten. *Society and Education.* 3d ed. Boston: Allyn and Bacon, 1967, p. 19.

Havighurst, R. Minority subcultures and the law of effect. *American Psychologist 25* (1970): 313–322.

Jason, L., S. Clarfield, and E. Cowen. Preventive intervention with young disadvantaged children. *American Journal of Community Psychology 1*, no. 1 (1973): 50–61.

Jones, R. Labels and stigma in special education. *Exceptional Children 38* (1972): 553–564.

Jones, N., J. Loney, F. Weissenburger, and D. Fleischmann. The hyperkinetic child: what do teachers know? *Psychology in the Schools 12* (1975): 388–392.

Karagianis, L., and D. Merricks, eds. *Where the Action is: Teaching Exceptional Children.* St. John, Newfoundland: Memorial University, 1973 (ERIC Document Reproduction Service No. ED 984 764).

Karnes, M., R. Zehrbach, and G. Jones. *The Culturally Disadvantaged Student and Guidance.* Boston: Houghton Mifflin, 1971.

Langner, T., J. Gersten, E. Greene, J. Eisenberg, H. Herson, and E. McCarthy. Treatment of psychological disorders among urban children. *Journal of Consulting and Clinical Psychology* 42, no. 2 (1974): 170–179.

LaVor, M., and J. Harvey. Headstart, economic opportunity, community partnership act of 1974. *Exceptional Children* 42 (1976): 127–230.

Lewis, O. The culture of poverty. *Scientific American*, October 1966, pp. 19–25.

Long, A. Parents' reports of undesirable behavior in children. *Child Development* 12 (1941): 43–62.

Lurie, O. Parents' attitudes toward children's problems and toward use of mental health services. *American Journal of Orthopsychiatry* 44, no. 1 (January 1974): 109–119.

McNeese, F. Helping hand for "Black English." *Pittsburgh Press*, 3 October 1976.

Marshall, K. Who's afraid of Christopher Jencks? Only those with blindfolds still in place. *Learning Magazine* 11, no. 5 (January 1974).

Miller, N., and D. Dollard. *Social Learning and Imitation*. New Haven: Yale University Press, 1941.

Miller, N. Studies of fear as an acquired drive. I. fear as motivation and fear-reduction as reinforcement in the learning of new responses. *Journal of Experimental Psychology* 38 (1948): 89–101.

Novak, D. Children's responses to imaginary peers labelled as emotionally disturbed. *Psychology in the Schools* 12 (1975): 103–106.

Nugent, F. School counselors, psychologists, and social workers: a distinction. *Psychology in the Schools* 10 (1973): 327–333.

Pedrini, B., and D. Pedrini. *Special Education*. ERIC Document Reproduction Service No. ED 085 927, 1973.

Phillips, D. We have a successful tool here—let's use it. In J. Jordon and L. Robbins, eds., *Let's Try Doing Something Else. Behavioral Principles and the Exceptional Child*. Arlington, Va.: The Council for Exceptional Children, 1972.

Richmond, J. Disadvantaged children: what have they compelled us to learn? *Yale Journal of Biology and Medicine* 43 (1970): 127–144.

Rogeness, G., R. Bednar, and H. Diesenhaus. The social system and children's behavior problems. *American Journal of Orthopsychiatry* 44, no. 4 (July 1974): 497–502.

Rosenham, D. The kindnesses of children. *Young Children* 25 (1969).

Sage, W. Classrooms for the autistic child. *Human Behavior*, March 1975.

Sarason, I. *Abnormal Psychology: The Problem of Maladaptive Behavior*. New York: Appleton-Century-Crofts, 1972.

Silberman, A. If they say your child can't learn. *McCalls*, January 1976.

Simpson, D., and A. Nelson. Attention training through breathing control to modify hyperactivity. *Journal of Learning Disabilities* 7 (1974): 274–283.

Stearns, K., and S. Swensen. The resource teacher: an alternative to special class placement. *Viewpoints* 49 (1973): 11.

Stewart, M. Hyperactive children. *Scientific American,* April 1970, pp. 94–99.

Taylor, R. Psychosocial development among black children and youth: a reexamination. *American Journal of Orthopsychiatry* 46, no. 1 (January 1976).

Taylor, W., and K. Hoedt. Classroom-related problems: counsel parents, teachers, or children? *Journal of Counseling Psychology* 21, no. 1 (1974): 3–8.

Vail, E. What will it be? reading or machismo and soul? *Clearing House* 45 (October 1970): 92–96.

Weithorn, C., and R. Ross. Stimulant drugs for hyperactivity: some additional disturbing questions. *American Journal of Orthopsychiatry* 46, no. 1 (January 1976): 168–172.

Wickman, E. *Children's Behavior and Teachers' Attitudes.* New York: Commonwealth Fund, 1928.

Woestehoff, E. Students with reading disabilities and guidance. *Guidance Monograph Series.* Boston: Houghton Mifflin, 1970.

Zentall, S. Optimal stimulation as theoretical basis of hyperactivity. *American Journal of Orthopsychiatry* 45, no. 4 (July 1975): 549–560.

Zimbardo, P., P. Pilkonis, and R. Norwood. The social disease called shyness. *Psychology Today,* May 1975, pp. 69–72.

PART 5

The End of Childhood

14

The Adolescent Period: From Middle School through High School

Learning objectives

After completing this chapter, you should be able to:

1
describe the physical changes and psychological changes experienced by adolescents in our society;

2
describe the problems associated with adolescence in the United States;

3
explain how familial and cultural variables can affect adolescent behavior;

4
evaluate some of the intervention strategies being used to help adolescents solve their problems.

T he stage we call adolescence marks the end of childhood. In our society, it is a period of dramatic change, which can significantly affect both the adolescent and his or her family.

Adolescence has been defined as the period from pubescence (the stage at which body growth suddenly increases rapidly) to full physical, social, and emotional maturity. In our society, it is marked by both physical and psychological changes.

Physical changes The beginning of pubescence is signalled by a sudden spurt in growth, which occurs about two years prior to *puberty* or sexual maturity. For girls, this spurt occurs between nine and twelve years of age; for boys, between ten and fifteen years of age. Growth rate for boys during this period often is enormous; indeed, an eight-inch height increase is not uncommon. Parents report that clothing is outgrown before they turn around! Only later, when puberty (measured in girls usually by menstruation and in boys by appearance of sperm) is reached, does growth rate slow.

In addition to changes in physical size, pubescence is marked by a number of other changes. For example, there is considerable change in the shape of the body, rapid development of the sexual organs, and development of hormonal secretion in relation to sex-organ development.

The end of childhood is marked by a sudden, absorbing interest in one's personal appearance.

The pituitary gland encourages development of growth and, at the same time, secretion of the sex hormones testosterone and estrogen.

Secondary sex characteristics make their appearance at this time. For girls, this means development of breasts and axillary hair, as well as changes in general body proportion. For boys, voices deepen and axillary and facial hair develop. Other changes occur for both boys and girls as sweat glands develop and step up their secretions. A sudden interest in deodorant appears.

Development of secondary sex characteristics has a major impact on the self-image of the adolescent. Boys and girls often spend hours before the mirror studying their appearances. Many keep diaries that attest to their new feelings of self-importance and to what psychoanalysts call their egocentricity. This egocentrism manifests itself as well in excessive self-consciousness (Elkind, 1967).

Only later, after puberty, will production of sex hormones inhibit physical growth; after full maturity, growth and corresponding rate of change in other physical characteristics slows. So does the turbulence of the period.

Although physical changes that take place at the end of childhood have been consistent throughout history, slow, evolutionary changes have altered the rate of change somewhat. Boys and girls mature earlier today than they did two centuries ago. The age at which they reach puberty has decreased considerably in just the past four decades. Tanner (1971) reports, for example, that British girls begin to menstruate a full two years earlier than they did only forty years ago. Researchers attribute this decreased pubertal age to improved nutrition and decreased childhood illness.

Psychological changes In centuries past, as we learned at the beginning of this text, the stage of childhood was given no special attention by adults. Similarly, the period of adolescence as a significant stage of life was given no special recognition. It was not until the early 1940s in this country, in fact, that adolescents began to consider themselves—and to be considered by others—as a special group, characterized by specific patterns of interests, attitudes, and behaviors. During World War II, when many fathers were away at war and mothers first began to be employed on regular bases outside the home, adolescents began to band together in peer groups to pursue common activities and interests. The "peer culture" and independent establishment of values that resulted caused observers finally to see adolescence as an important life stage (Lowe, 1972).

Adolescence in our society has been called a period of "storm and stress," a stage of "being partway." It is a period frequently dismissed by adults as a stage of life remembered as "unhappy" (Gibson, 1972). The late Judy Garland once described female adolescence poetically as

Adolescence is a period of looking for people and ideas in which to have faith.

"just an in-between—too old for toys, too young for boys." Adolescents today, unlike those of Judy Garland's era, no longer feel themselves too young for many adult activities. And, unlike earlier adolescents, many have had firsthand opportunity to discover that freedom alone is not what they're looking for.

Identity and self-actualization. Adolescence is a period when individuals try to determine who they are and where they are going. Erik Erikson, a stage-dependent theorist, described the adolescent stage as one of crises and potential turning points. According to Erikson, adolescents are most interested in answering the question, "Who am I?" They must answer satisfactorily in order to develop to full emotional maturity. Since one of the important developmental tasks for this period involves finding an occupation, *role identity* becomes critical.

"Who am I" is a complex question. According to psychologists, to answer the question, adolescents must understand the physical changes that take place at the time, define their external environments, and define their roles within those environments. Adolescents are concerned also with making explicit their own personal positions in relation to the values and beliefs of society. The question, "Who am I?" coincides with the development of formal thought in Piagetian terms. Concurrent with this is the development of moral reasoning. When adolescents discover existing inconsistencies—for example, in values and beliefs regarding what is proper sexual or moral behavior—their overriding concern becomes clarification. Adolescence is a period of looking for people and ideas in which to have faith. Sometimes trustworthy people can be found in the adult community; sometimes, however, adolescents decide they can only be found in the adolescent peer group.

Many adolescents look to music as a means of emotional expression. Popular music often expresses many of their conflicts and desires, and popular musicians frequently become adolescent "folk heroes." Frank Sinatra and Elvis Presley were two of the first folk heroes to develop from the youth culture; the Beatles were more recent ones. To many adolescents, such figures represent consistent ideas and values not found in the adult culture. When parents disapprove, so much the better. When

A case study of a ninth-grader

I. Identification and sources of information
Name: Richard Harris, 7521 Bennett St., Chicago, Illinois

Race: White
Sex: Male
Age: 14 years, 2 months
School: Hudson High School
Grade: Nine

Sources of information:
1. Personal observation
2. Interview with student
3. Interview with mother
4. Interview with teacher

II. Family history
Richard is the oldest of four children, all males. His three younger siblings are in grades five, six, and eight at Harrington Elementary School. All are in good health and doing well academically. Mrs. Harris appears to be interested in her sons, is an active member of the PTA, and is well

known to the teachers both at Hudson High and at Harrington because of the time she has put in doing lunchroom duty and helping out in extracurricular activities.

Mrs. Harris is forty-five, a graduate of an exclusive "ivy league" college. She married shortly after graduating and has never been employed outside the home. Mr. Harris has a master's degree in business administration, and is employed in a local brokerage house. Economic status of the family is high.

III. Case history
Richard was a good student throughout his eight years at Harrington Elementary School. He got along well with his family and peers, seemed to make friends easily, and generally appeared to be a well-adjusted child. However, when he enrolled in the fall at Hudson High, his behavior seemed to change abruptly. Richard still obtains moderately good grades, although his first two report cards in the ninth grade contained some

parents ridicule the heroes ("How can you like a singer who can't sing?"), so much the better. Teenagers identify with their folk heroes—their "poor" voices, their unconventional appearances. After all, they themselves are just learning about their own strange voices and appearances.

At the same time that adolescents begin the process of clarifying their values, according to Erikson (1959), they try to separate themselves out from their environments and to consolidate their identities as human beings. Life for adolescents presents a variety of conflicting possibilities and choices. Deep down, they are not yet sure that they know who they are, what they want to be, how they appear to others, and whether they really are capable of providing correct answers to these extremely important questions. It is resolution of these questions that brings what Erikson referred to as "identity instead of identity confusion" and the beginning of adulthood. The resolution of these questions brings also what Maslow referred to as "self-actualization," the highest in his hierarchy of needs discussed in Chapter 3.

C's and a D—the first in his academic history. His parents were not as concerned about the grades on Richard's report as they were upset at the belligerent attitude Richard seemed to take about the grades. When his father suggested that he be punished, Richard became very angry, stormed out of the house, and stayed away from home through the dinner hour. When he finally returned home, he refused to talk with anyone in the house and locked the door of his room, so that he could not be disturbed.

The Harrisses decided to call in a psychologist when Richard's behavior had been hostile and aggressive for several months. He refused to eat with other members of the house, often staying out at a hamburger joint until after nine o'clock each evening. His teachers reported that he attended classes regularly and did not misbehave there, but that he seemed uninterested in anything going on around him.

In an interview with the psychologist, Richard reported that school was dull and uninteresting and, further, that his family was as dull as school. He said that he didn't want to grow up and be "dull like them." He said, also, that many of the students in his class had experimented with drugs, but that he had not as yet tried them. He didn't see any reason why he shouldn't experiment, however, since, whatever he did, he knew in advance that his parents "would say it was wrong."

IV. Present status; diagnosis and prognosis
For the present, at least, Richard is not in serious trouble. There is no reason that he should not be able to successfully complete the ninth grade if he tries. But, according to the psychologist preparing the case history, Richard may well be in serious difficulty if he does not learn how to communicate with his parents, and his parents with him. It is recommended that Mr. and Mrs. Harris and Richard come together for family therapy at the local guidance clinic. Since Mr. and Mrs. Harris have sufficient funds, they may decide, instead, to seek guidance from a private practitioner.

According to Erikson, adolescence is a crucial turning point, during which development must move in one direction or another. For adolescents to build positive identities, they must arrive at satisfactory role commitments. Whereas earlier their concerns revolved around immediate successes or failures, now these concerns are more far reaching, involving occupation and ideology. Positive identities lead to self-esteem, self-sufficiency, and stability in adulthood. When the identity crisis is not resolved, what Erikson calls *identity confusion* or *identity diffusion* occurs. Adolescents who are unable satisfactorily to answer the question "Who am I?" and "Where am I going?" can be expected, according to Erikson, to have deep problems adjusting to their environments and to life.

Role confusion can occur, Erikson suggests, when particular roles are sought, but are found impossible or difficult to attain. Since choice of occupation assumes major significance during this period, role confusion often is associated with occupation. Many adolescents observing a standard of living on TV that far surpasses anything available in their real worlds, plan in childhood to obtain that standard of living for themselves. Elementary-school children who are failing in school, for example, may report that they plan to be doctors or lawyers. But, by the time they reach the age at which they are ready to make the occupational decisions that will allow or not allow them to achieve this goal, they become painfully aware of the barriers that stand in their way. The result is *role confusion*—a desire not to accept a less-than-satisfactory role coupled with knowledge (real or imagined) that a satisfactory role will not be available to them. A variety of unwanted behaviors common to adolescents can result—for example, excessive daydreaming, role playing, and acting out of subconscious wishes (Erikson, 1963).

Sometimes role confusion occurs even when the real goal is attainable. In such instances, the adolescent simply can't decide what to do. Biff portrays this type of confusion clearly in his famous lines in *Death of a Salesman*: "I just can't take hold, Mom. I can't take hold on some kind of life" (Erikson, 1968, p. 131).

Sometimes role confusion is associated with social conditions. The socially disadvantaged children described in Chapter 13 are more likely to exhibit role confusion than are more advantaged youngsters. Pettigrew (1964) pointed out that social conditions that exist for most poor black teenagers can lead easily to role confusion or to negative identities. The following statement made by a black, teenage school dropout is typical of many such statements heard by counselors:

I don't care what happens to me, man. Nothing I do turns out anyway. I never made the grade, and I don't care. When I had to go to that school, I learned that it wan't worth a try. I couldn't do no better than last place. And then, when I got out, man, then it really was bad. All's I wanted was a job and some bread, man. But I couldn't do it; I ain't no good.

The question, "Who am I?" must be answered in order that later development not be hampered, according to Erikson. It is important to note, however, that resolution of these problems does not require previous resolution of all the problems and conflicts of previous stages. Where there is logical sequence to Erikson's stages, they are not hierarchical in the way cognitive stages are. "Who am I?" can be answered by an adolescent failure as well as by an adolescent success. The answers will be very different, however (Kohlberg and Gilligan, 1971).

Dealing with sexuality. Freud called the period from age eleven to eighteen the *genital stage*. In the early part of this stage, he said, there is a revival of infantile behaviors. Later, during the pubertal stage, there is an increase in the desire to obtain pleasure through adult sexual activities. Conflicts associated with changing from infantile to adult sexual activities are common.

The physical changes associated with adolescence are accompanied by the need for major psychological adjustments. For adolescents, the physical changes of greatest importance are those associated with sexuality. Acquiring sexual interests and developing more mature peer relation-

Adolescents, especially in our society, often find it difficult to sort out sexual values and handle their new feelings of sexuality.

ships that take into account these interests are described by Havighurst as developmental tasks for this period.

Adolescents in our society handle feelings of sexuality with some difficulty. They become increasingly aware, both through the mass media and through the activities of their peers, of just what their new feelings mean, and they are afraid that they won't be adequate. They learn that many of the moral rules regarding sexuality that they were taught as children do not apply to adult behavior and, further, that many of these rules have no logical basis. They begin seriously to question sexual as well as other basic values.

The first major sexual outlet for adolescents in our society is masturbation (Kagan, 1971; Mitchell, 1974). Adolescents who have learned as children that masturbation is evil or dangerous may still masturbate, but they will experience guilt, fear, and conflict. With sexual freedom increasing in our society, there is more and more opportunity for sexual experimentation. Adolescents who read in the mass media about the sexual experiments of their peers and of adults are being encouraged to experiment more and more themselves. The old taboos are fast disappearing. In 1974, some 59 percent of all males and 45 percent of all females between thirteen and nineteen reported that they already had had sexual intercourse (Vener and Stewart, 1974). Unfortunately, many adolescents involved in sexual experimentation have not had sex education. Experimentation for them often leads to such unhappy conclusions as venereal disease or an unwanted pregnancy. Three in every ten

Sex education: when should it begin?

Sex education should begin between the ages of twelve to fifteen, according to junior-high-school students surveyed by the Encyclopedia Britannica Corporation. Asked if sex education should be taught in the schools, the majority said, "Yes." Over 50 percent said sex education already was taught in their schools.

Encyclopedia Britannica asked the 1000 students polled which medium most influenced them in their sexual activities. Fifty-eight percent said television; 18.5 percent said books; 12 percent said radio; 5.5 percent said newspapers; 2.5 percent said magazines.

Respondents to the survey felt that marriage probably will still be here in the year 2000, that their parents still exercise strong influences on their lives, and that education is important in obtaining a good job (*Pittsburgh Press Parade*, February 29, 1976).

Many parents object strongly to sex education in the schools. Sometimes they forget that, before they were parents, they were lovers, a fact that some psychologists suggest can affect how they deal with their child's emerging sexuality (Gordon, 1974).

What do *you* think should be done about sex education? Does it belong in school or only in the home? Why?

teenage girls who engage in premarital intercourse become pregnant (Kantner and Zelnick, 1972).

Why are adolescents today so involved in sexual experimentation? Psychologists report that the goal usually is not sexual gratification (Josselyn, 1974). In fact, most adolescents frequently experience in their experimentation what they interpret as "sex failure." Sexual experimentation is not considered by most adolescents as promiscuity. Young people who feel increasingly alienated from an adult world of confusing and conflicting values often view sex as a way to experience closeness with others.

Puberty is interpreted by adolescents as a signal that childhood is over and what they consider to be regressive attitudes, beliefs, and behaviors must stop. Sometimes this stopping of infantile behaviors is difficult and poses more conflict for the adolescent. Kagan (1971) described a fifteen-year-old girl recalling her first menstrual period: she suggested that the real meaning to her was that she was finally too grown up to ride her bicycle. Puberty is interpreted also in terms of sex-typing. Adolescent boys feel the necessity to be more autonomous, active, and independent. Girls feel the need to be more socially sensitive and passive. These behaviors are consonant with culturally defined masculinity and femininity and strongly shape the behavior of this age group. Feelings, attitudes, motives, and wishes become sex-typed as never before (Kagan, 1964).

Achieving and making vocational choices. Childhood comes to an end with the establishment of a good relationship with the world of skills and to those who teach and share these skills (Erikson, 1959). During adolescence, tentative decisions are made concerning future life work. Indeed, courses that children select in school, as well as their academic performance during this period, clearly affect later career possibilities. Children from eleven to twelve years of age tend to select prospective occupations on the basis of current interests. By thirteen to fourteen, they begin to take their aptitudes into consideration. By fifeen to sixteen, they consider personal values and goals as well. Only after age seventeen do most adolescents begin to make realistic decisions regarding future occupations.

Even though many alienated adolescents and school dropouts deny it, school and school achievement become particularly important during adolescence. Gordon (1971) suggests that achievement is a symbolically validated performance that can be compared with a socially defined standard of excellence long before adolescents can prove themselves in the adult field of work. Achievement (or lack of it) forms major grounds for the development of self-esteem among adolescents. It also is an important determinant of popularity.

Exploring new interests and abilities and selecting an occupation are adolescent developmental tasks. Sex-typing plays an important role here.

Academic achievement becomes particularly important during the high school years.

During early adolescence, boys learn that they are expected to become serious students, to develop ways to take care of themselves and, later, to take care of their own families. Girls learn frequently that they are expected to be "feminine" and attract boys. It is not surprising, therefore, that during adolescence boys begin to do better in their schoolwork than do girls. Boys excel particularly in such "masculine" subjects as mathematics and science. Girls tend to excel at more "feminine" subjects, such as art. Interestingly, girls have excelled at math problems when these problems are placed in a socially accepted feminine context, such as problems involving recipes (Kagan, 1964). The advent of the women's movement in the United States is only just beginning to effect changes in this stereotypic behavior.

All adolescent males are, of course, not high achievers. Neither are all adolescent females low achievers. Major differences in orientation toward achievement seem to occur with differences in social-class background and mothers' occupations. High-achievement-oriented girls tend to come from lower-middle-class homes. These girls use achievement as a means of social mobility. Girls with professionally successful mothers also tend to be more highly achievement-motivated than are girls whose mothers do not have careers.

Today, more and more adult women are entering previously male-dominated professional fields. With women gradually throwing aside accepted sex-typed occupations, corresponding changes can be expected in the attitudes, behaviors, and choices of adolescent females.

Making moral decisions. Lawrence Kohlberg's theory of the development of moral reasoning was described first in Chapter 2. Kohlberg, it will be remembered, hypothesized six stages of moral reasoning defined by the ways individuals think about moral matters and by the bases on which they make choices when confronted with a moral dilemma. Kohlberg's first two stages, orientation to punishment and reward and hedonistic orientation with an instrumental view of human relations, were described in relationship to the development of young children. According to Kohlberg, most children respond at these levels. Kohlberg's third and fourth stages, good-boy orientation and orientation to authority, law, and duty, both are characterized by choices made in response to concern for group values. These stages constitute the "conventional" level at which most adults and some adolescents operate. At stages five and six, decisions are made on the basis of ethical principles, these stages are characteristic, according to Kohlberg, of perhaps only 20 to 25 percent of the adult population, with perhaps 5 to 10 percent arriving at the most advanced stage six.

Initially, when considering typical adolescent moral decisions, particularly those associated with rejecting inconsistent or hypocritical adult behaviors, observers often conclude that these young people are operating on the basis of principled stages of moral reasoning. Kohlberg and his colleagues suggest that this may well be true of some adolescents. They suggest, however, that observers be cautious in making such assumptions. Many adolescents make decisions based on considerably lower levels—for example, Kohlberg's stage 2 hedonistic orientation (Do your own thing!) or stage 3 good-boy orientation (Be nice and loving). While behavior may appear to be the same as stage five or six behavior, because these adolescents also reject societal values, the reasons for their behaviors may be considerably different (Kohlberg and Gilligan, 1971).

Increasing numbers of elementary, middle-school, and high-school children in the United States cheat on examinations and do not consider this behavior immoral. What causes cheating? Interestingly, most students who cheat do not do so to keep from failing, but do so in order to protect high grades (Fisbe, 1975).

As we discussed in Chapter 12, the grading systems used in our schools are anxiety producing for many students. Students particularly affected are those whose parents are not concerned that they receive high grades. Unfortunately, anxious students are often less able to obtain high grades than are students who are less anxious and pressured. Psychologists suggest that strong parental pressure for high grades is one factor that leads to student cheating (Pearlin et al., 1967). High parental aspiration for children coupled with limited resources can lead to the greatest pressure and the highest probability of cheating.

Many students whose parents do not pressure them to do well also cheat frequently on examinations. Some students report that they cheat because their friends cheat and their friends "would laugh at them" if they didn't. Clearly, cheating is such a common occurrence in today's schools that it is difficult to attend school and not regularly observe successful "cheater" models.

Successful cheating can be observed in every sphere of scholastic and professional endeavor in the United States. Cheating on college campuses has become a lucrative and well-organized national enterprise, grossing millions of dollars annually. Some outfits have coast-to-coast

Anything for a grade

The following classroom experience actually occurred at a major American University several years ago, and was described in several United States newspapers at the time:

In the fall quarter, Dr. James Smith (not his real name), Visiting Professor of Economics, strode into the principles of economics class and made the following surprise announcement: "You people have won. I'm going to sell grades. Grades will go to the highest bidder. If you people are so happy with the free-market process, why don't we just let the market system dictate who gets what?"

According to newspaper reports of the event, Dr. Smith then called in a colleague to "auction off the grades without prejudice." While a few students objected to the auction —some even complained to the Dean and Department Chairman—approximately 90 percent of the class participated. Professor Smith collected almost $2000, averaging $85 for an A in the course, $55 for a B, $35 for a C. Smith accepted IOUs from most of the students. One student, however, insisted on his accepting $80 in cash. Another student, observing the absence of several friends who *were cutting class, bought extra C's and D's, and tried to make a profit by advertising them for sale in the school newspaper.*

All students participating in the auction were dismayed later to find out that it was a hoax.*

Consider Dr. Smith's auction in relation to our discussion of cheating and grades. Then answer the following questions:

1 If you were given the same opportunity to buy your grade as the students in Dr. Smith's class, what would you do?
   a. Go along with the class and bid.
   b. Complain to the dean.
   c. Other (list) _____
   _____
   _____

2 Are you sure that you were truthful in your first response? _____

3 What do you think should be the purpose of grades in any program? _____
   _____
   _____

* From *Pittsburgh Press Parade*, March 19, 1975.

The peer group increasingly replaces the family as a source of support for the teenager.

networks of franchises established to sell already-prepared term papers and theses; others prepare research papers to order. Students can now pay for theses, term papers, dissertations, lecture notes, class outlines, and language translations. Cheating in the business and political worlds makes headlines daily (*Newsweek*, March 20, 1972).

Conforming to the peer group. Adolescence brings increasing freedom of behavior and, with it, the need to develop independence from the family and new, mature relationships with peers. What special role does the peer group play in adolescent lives? Why is conformity to the peer group suddenly so important?

Psychologists have proposed a number of explanations for the importance of the peer group. For one thing, the adolescent is increasingly alienated from the adult world. It has been suggested, for example, that this alienation has its roots in parental attempts to develop independence in their children, and that these attempts often are viewed by children as rejection. Other psychologists suggest that parental rejection, more simply, is just a matter of too little time: American parents are so busy with their own lives that they simply don't pay enough attention to their children. Fathers, who can be important model figures to their children, are more and more unavailable to their children because of increased time spent on the job. Adolescents thus grow up in households with little parental supervision and attention (Bettelheim, 1971; Bronfenbrenner, 1972).

Many theorists have related alienation from adults and dependence on the peer culture to permissive, inattentive child rearing. Others suggest that this is too simple an explanation—factors such as lack of continuity in our society, conflicting values, and lack of personal security all contribute to feelings of alienation (Thornburg, 1971). It is clear that concern for the meaning of life is important in the peer culture; group identification reduces loneliness and gives some meaning to existence.

Conformity, a hallmark of adolescent behavior, seems to have a curvilinear relationship to age. As children progress through elementary school, they become more and more conforming in their behavior to those around them. Floyd and South (1972) suggest this comes from both a "push" from parents and a "pull" from the peer group.

Sometime early in high school, this conforming behavior begins to decrease. In the later years of high school, students are more apt to make decisions because they agree with the idea involved, rather than because they think that's how their friends would respond.

The peer group also has been described by some as a solution for the lack of a "rites of passage" in our society to express the change in status from childhood to adulthood. It provides adolescents with the opportunity to disengage simultaneously from both childhood and adulthood. According to Keniston (1962), the peer culture which develops is not rebellious; adolescents tend, on the whole, to appreciate their parents. At the same time, they see the problems of their parents and do not wish to become carbon copies of them. According to this view, adolescent values are liberalized versions of their parents' values.

All psychologists do not agree with this view. Coleman (1961, 1970) believes that the adolescent subculture is distinct in appearance, speech, social values, and associational patterns. The heroes of adolescents, according to Coleman, are significantly different from those of their parents.

The politics of adolescence   Erikson (1970) suggests that a major portion of the stage of adolescence is devoted to ideological experimentation. During the 1960s, young adults turned their attention to politics. Political activism of American adolescents during this period ranged from militant demonstrating to "peace and love" movements. Just as previous peer cultures had developed their values more from family traditions than from rebellion, student activists based their political activity on family values. That is, although they tended generally to be more radical than their parents, at the same time, their parents tended to be more liberal in their political beliefs than were the average American parents of the time. Student activists seemed to be living out expressed, but unimplemented, parental values (Flacks, 1966; Keniston, 1967).

Many researchers have associated student activism in the 1960s with the child-rearing methods used by the activists' parents. A common belief has been that the sixties student activists came from homes in which permissive child-rearing methods were used. However, researchers have come to realize that student activism developed for many different reasons. Block et al. (1969) noted that some activists came from homes in which liberal political values were stressed and in which democratic methods of child rearing were used. These activists usually behaved in ways they believed their parents had taught them to behave. A second type of adolescent activist, however, came from a home in which child-rearing methods were, by turns, permissive and harsh. Such individuals became activists for a quite different reason: they used their activism to register their dissent from the adult culture. Finally, some adolescents in the 1960s and early 1970s tended to withdraw rather than become politically active. Many of these were culturally alienated adolescents who had learned not to expect reinforcement from the adult culture. Their response was to withdraw.

In selecting political stances, adolescents generally are more dogmatic than are their parents, whatever view they decide to take. Not until they get older are they able easily to see the other's point of view (Gallatin and Adelson, 1971).

According to many observers, the end of the Vietnam War marked the beginning of youth apathy regarding international political problems. By 1975, a survey of undergraduate students at the University of Pittsburgh suggested that ideological concerns had been replaced by

How did Watergate affect the views of teenagers?

The New Left died away with the passing of the sixties and was followed by a general apathy and disinterest in politics among teenagers. The 1970s were marked by a series of political scandals and the resignation of a president in disgrace. How did Watergate affect the views of the teenagers who observed it?

According to Rick Trow Associates, a Philadelphia-based company that staged patriotic assemblies in high-school auditoriums throughout the country in 1975, Watergate and related scandals seemed to revive interest in politics—in a new way. "Waving a flag in front of a high-school assembly five years ago would have brought more boos than yeas. Now it often brings a standing ovation," commented Trow. "Students seem to feel today that the system really works, and that those who behaved inappropriately are being removed from office. The mood is more 'I want to feel good, succeed professionally, get established, and enjoy the good life with the family'" (Swift, 1976).

Do you agree with Trow? Do you think that the lack of interest today in politics and political injustice is due to students feeling that they have a good life now and a good future to look forward to? Or can the behavior of today's students be explained in other ways?

concerns regarding the economy and unemployment. Students tended generally to be apathetic about political matters. They even had difficulty deciding which issues were important. When pressed, however, their voiced concerns dealt less with ideology than with themselves (*The Pitt News*, 8 September 1975).

Remnants of the 1960s linger in a variety of flourishing youth cultures, less related to politics than to withdrawal from a nonreinforcing adult culture. Alternate life styles, as we have suggested earlier, often are marked by greater sexual freedom and use of some of the products of the adult culture: alcohol and drugs.

Special problems of adolescence Problem behavior was defined in Chapter 13 as behavior that is not accepted by society. Problem behavior particular to adolescents has its roots in childhood.

Dropping out. School absenteeism and dropping out continue to be major problems in the United States. The reasons that adolescents give for leaving school are varied and are generally related to continued failure to learn. But dissatisfaction with achievement is generally part of a larger picture of discontent. Dropouts report that they feel "useless"; they often leave school in order to get relief from unbearable conditions, only to find that conditions away from school are equally unbearable.

Running away. Running away frequently is triggered by many of the same feelings that cause a student to drop out. But, in this case, the adolescent is running away not only from school, but from home as well. The results are more severe, because all adult help is rejected by the runaway.

Delinquency. Delinquency among adolescents, as among younger children, is increasing at an alarming rate. In urban high schools today, teaching has become a dangerous profession, because of the high incidence of serious crimes, including shootings, by teenagers and teenage gangs. According to security police, shootings occur for a variety of reasons, ranging from protection to extortion. There have been so many gun episodes in recent years in urban schools throughout the country that authorities in Chicago and other cities have permitted school guards to arm themselves.

There is no simple explanation for the increase in crimes involving adolescents. Delinquency, like alienation, has been related by many psychologists to child rearing. The delinquent is more likely than the nondelinquent to come from a home with restrictive policy making, loose policing, and lenient punishing. The parent of the delinquent is likely to be highly inconsistent in child rearing (Singer, 1974).

Drugs. Illegal drug use, of course, involves delinquent behavior. The drug user, however, may be withdrawn and not necessarily antisocial. Adolescents who become heavy users of drugs tend to have strong feelings of *anomie*—separation of themselves from the norms of society—and alienation. They report often a lack of authentic, meaningful relationships with others, including their peers. They tend to have confused senses of identity and frequently feel inferior or powerless. Often, they are fearful of independence (Coleman and Broen, 1972).

Drug use, like other forms of delinquency, is on the increase in the United States. Why? One explanation given by psychologists is that adolescent drug use, in the eyes of the users, may be seen as an extension of adult behavior rather than as a rebellion against adult values. We learned earlier that drug use certainly has precedent in our adult culture: three-quarters of all adults in this country drink alcohol; one-tenth are problem drinkers. Use of other drugs, from tranquilizers to pain killers, is higher than in most other countries.

Some drugs, such as marijuana, frequently are used by adolescents in groups for the purpose of increasing intimacy and intensifying awareness. For this reason, Goode (1969) classified marijuana as a "sociogenic drug"—a drug that stimulates social activity. There seems to be a strong preference among adolescents for marijuana over alcohol, although use of alcohol among high-school students is on the rise, perhaps because it is more readily available.

Clearly, drug use has some roots in alienation from the adult culture. Writers like Ken Kesey, Timothy Leary, and Allen Ginsburg have spread the message that many drugs are good and the Establishment is bad. The fact that many adults, although unclear as to the actual effects of marijuana, have supported harsh penalties for its use, has strengthened the beliefs of many adolescents that the adult culture is misdirected and unwilling to consider the issue more clear-sightedly.

In addition to use of marijuana and alcohol, use of hallucinogens and harder drugs is on the increase and now is considered a serious prob-

The new "junkie"

The new "junkie" is a middle-class junkie as well as a teenager. Following are some personal accounts of a few who have shaken the habit— at least for now.

Marilyn is a fifteen-year-old, attractive girl from an upper-middle-class neighborhood in Cleveland. Marilyn's father is a buyer at a department store in town. Her mother is employed as a legal secretary. Marilyn reports that she began using heroin at age thirteen.

I guess I started using drugs because I wanted to be like the other kids in class, and because I wanted to impress my boyfriend. All the older kids were using drugs, and we all wanted to see what it was like. First I messed around with pills and pot. Later, my boyfriend got ahold of some heroin at a party. I snorted a couple of times, skinned a lot, and, after that, I mained it. I stopped going to school. After awhile, my mother caught me stealing silverware from the house to sell it and my folks sent me to a special school for kids who are emotionally disturbed. But it was easier for me to get heroin there than out on the streets. All the other kids got it from their friends, and we shared. Looking back, I'm not sure I would have had any friends if I hadn't used drugs. Everybody was doing it, and I wanted to be like everyone else. My parents never spoke to me once about drugs before

I started. Not even after I started. I guess they tried to pretend they didn't know. I used to go and tell my mother what I did. I guess I kinda hoped she'd make me stop. But she didn't.

Phil, a sixteen-year-old, started on marijuana at thirteen, and went through LSD and amphetamines before getting into heroin at fifteen. Phil's father is a successful surgeon, but Phil never completed high school once he started his habit.

I started on smack exactly on the third anniversary of the first time I smoked pot. I was really scared. I'd never stuck a needle in my arm before, for one thing. It was a thrill thing with me. First, I started hitting up once a day. After awhile, I was hitting up two and three times a day. I stopped school. It's not the same high with heroin that it is with amphetamines. It's the first wild rush for the first minute, that's what it is. After that it's good, but it's never the same as that first minute. As soon as it starts wearing off, you get a sick kind of feeling wondering how you'll get more. I want to stay off because I saw such messes from it. One girlfriend of mine died from hepatitis. I used to main it with her—I never knew why I was so lucky I didn't get it. Another kid I know landed up in the hospital with a $100 a day habit. Everytime you stick that needle in, you're playing with your life.

Some teenagers use marijuana to increase intimacy and intensify social interactions.

lem in this country. The news media tell us that addiction among adolescents is more and more common. What is the adolescent addict like? More often, the addict is male rather than female. Unlike the delinquent high-school student carrying a gun, the addict is likely to be quiet, polite, easily influenced, and withdrawn in his behavior. He generally has few friends among his peers. Withdrawal and alienation from adult and peer society increases with drug addiction. The adolescent addict usually has obtained drugs from an acquaintance of his own age in school, rather than from an adult pusher. The fact that his parents and the law are more concerned with what often is a nonexistent adult pusher than with the real people in his narrowing world makes the addict feel even more alienated from adult society (Jalkanen, 1973).

Intervention strategies for the American adolescent appear at all levels of society. We will talk here about strategies for helping adolescents in school, as well as strategies used outside of school.

WHAT'S BEING DONE TO HELP? SOME INTERVENTION STRATEGIES

Open methods of teaching We talked in Chapters 11 and 12 about curricular methods used to motivate disinterested students. One approach that has sparked interest in elementary-school children is the open classroom. The open-classroom concept is based on the belief that children

Educational Strategies

learn best when they themselves help design their learning experiences and when they are permitted to pursue interests independently and at their own desired pace. The open classroom is not, however, a "free school": the learning environment is carefully structured to engage the students' attention with many options and alternatives. Much has been written about the advantages of open-classroom methods for young children when used carefully by well-trained teachers. Open-classroom methods have proved effective also for adolescents, who have a growing need to be independent and to learn how to make decisions. Variations of the open classroom have been implemented with some success at the high-school level, both in regular schools and in special programs for dropouts and potential dropouts. One example is the Parkway School, a remarkable alternative school operating in Philadelphia since 1967 under the auspices of the Philadelphia Board of Education. The Parkway School is a "school without walls"; it has no permanent building of its own. It uses the surrounding community—museums, hospitals, businesses, libraries, and colleges—to teach high-school students meaningful information about real life (Resnik, 1971).

Open methods have been used also at the college level. The Alternative Curriculum at the University of Pittsburgh is a special program for transition students—freshmen who are not certain what they want to do and who desire more freedom to experiment than is permitted in the traditional program. Students plan their own learning experiences and organize their study time themselves. They rely much less than do students in traditional programs on individual staff members, for they develop their own goals and are not required to conform to any teacher-defined goals (Townsend, 1974).

The middle schools In the past decade, many American cities have developed special middle-school programs for sixth-, seventh-, and eighth-grade students. Unlike the older junior-high-school concept, in which a special school was provided to bridge the gap between the sheltered elementary school and the larger, freer high school, the middle school does more than provide a miniature high-school program. The middle school was designed to meet the separate and special needs of the pubescent and early adolescent years. Advocates of the middle-school concept point out that all adolescents are not the same and that, in fact, the period we call "adolescence" can be broken into smaller substages, each characterized by certain degrees of physical, social, emotional, and cognitive development. Different sorts of problems arise in the early pubescent and later pubertal years of adolescence. Ideally, the middle school can provide special programs that cater particularly to the needs of less socially assured, often still regressive, early adolescents—or, as they are called, "transescents." The success of these programs, and, indeed, of the middle-school concept, is still to be determined. Success of each in-

Middle schools meet the special needs
of the early adolescent years.

dividual middle school, of course, is dependent on the particular programs established within it.

Skill training One of the main goals of adolescents is to develop vocational skills. Of great importance to this age group are vocational counselors who can not only teach the importance of skills, but can provide greatly needed information on the steps necessary for skill attainment. One method that has been used successfully with dropouts and potential dropouts is the work-study program, in which skill training is incorporated into work settings (Borow, 1973).

"Real-life" teaching As more and more personal freedoms are given young people in our society, more and more information is needed concerning ways to deal with that freedom. Sex education, including methods of birth control and information regarding venereal disease, is becoming vital as adolescents experiment more and more freely with sex. Controversy still exists today as to whether the proper place for sex education is in school or in the home. However, with the increase in young unmarried mothers, there is almost no dispute that sex education in some form is important (Libby, 1974). A number of public-school programs have also experimented with role-play courses in marriage. One high school, in Portland, Oregon, has even designed a course in which students role play divorce and then work out the consequences of their decision together (*Time*, December 2, 1974).

Medical Strategies

Obviously, all the problems of the adolescent cannot be resolved in the classroom. Dealing effectively with physical changes and psychological problems often requires help only available outside the school setting.

Special medical programs for adolescents Recognizing that adolescents not only have difficulty communicating their problems to others, but that they also have special problems related specifically to their age, many physicians have begun to specialize in adolescent medicine. Adolescent pediatricians frequently are used as sounding boards by their patients who want to talk about anything from acne to venereal disease, from weight control to birth control. Some large cities, such as New York, have set up special medical clinics catering to adolescents on an out-patient basis. Psychologists and psychiatrists are establishing special adolescent practices to deal exclusively with adolescent problems. Today, it is possible in many cities for adolescents to receive birth-control information and to be tested for venereal disease or pregnancy without their parents' knowledge through free clinics. Currently, legislation that would permit adolescents independently to decide to have an abortion is being debated in some states.

Drug-abuse programs What about the adolescent drug user? Most large cities today have drug-abuse centers that offer special programs for adolescents—places where young people can drop in and talk with counselors or other young people about their problem, crisis centers where adolescents can call for immediate help, and education centers where they can be helped. One method that has proved most effective uses therapy programs in which young people help each other. The helper-therapy principle works, according to its developer, because it provides support for both the drug abusers and the therapists (Jalkanen, 1973; Reisman, 1965).

SEVERAL APPROACHES TO EXPLAINING ADOLESCENCE

In earlier chapters, we discussed child behavior from several different theoretical viewpoints. Chapter 2, for example, described theories that explain child behavior by relating behavior to specific ages and stages. Chapter 3 described theories of learning that explain child behavior by focusing on children's interactions with their environments. In addition, we have adopted a cross-cultural perspective, comparing the experiences of children in our culture with those of children growing up in other cultures.

Adolescence, as well as childhood, can be described both as a stage of life and also as a product of a history of learning experiences. Adolescents in our society have problems different from those in other societies. How can different theorists help us to understand just what adolescence is all about?

Major themes of adolescence have been described by stage-dependent theorists, from the adolescent's continual search for identity as described by Erikson to the adolescent's transition to conventional morality in decision making as described by Kohlberg. Keniston (1970) lists the adolescent's major psychological problem themes as tension that develops between the self and society, refusal to accept the responsibility to socialize, and fear of growing up. The adolescent peer culture, Keniston suggests, relieves to some extent the problems of adolescence and satisfies the adolescent's need for closeness. Adolescents, according to Keniston, all are in strong need of attention from the adult culture. With attention and reinforcement, they will find themselves and progress to the next-stage: adulthood.

Stage-Dependent
Approaches

Learning Approaches

Adolescence has been characterized by withdrawal from the norms of the adult culture. According to learning theorists, whether this withdrawal occurs with unwanted antisocial behavior or whether it is manifested through acceptable peer cultures depends on the individual's history of learning experiences. We noted earlier in the chapter that extreme alienation and delinquent behavior during adolescence are associated with harsh and inconsistent parental attitudes. Parental and mass-media models can serve to teach unwanted behaviors to young children. Mothers who are highly punitive toward aggressive children tend, for example, to have the most aggressive children on the block. Children who spend a great deal of time watching TV models aggress toward one another are more apt to use those same modes of aggression later in real-life situations if frustrated. Psychologists have shown that aggressive behavior learned in this fashion is highly stable over time. The aggressive child is likely to become the aggressive adolescent (Eron et al., 1974). Similarly, the shy, unhappy child is likely to become the withdrawn, unhappy adolescent.

A Cultural View of Adolescence

Is the adolescent behavior that we see in our own children a necessary part of growing up in all societies, or is it a reflection of the particular learning experiences of children in our own culture? Cultural anthropologists such as Mead and Benedict have pointed out that adolescence is not a period of difficulty in all societies. In some, particularly those societies in which the rules of adulthood are clearly prescribed and in which there is not much freedom of choice for the adolescent, parents and children tend more easily to share the same values and make similar decisions (Benedict, 1938; Mead, 1949; Mead and Heyman, 1965). Bronfenbrenner (1967) reported that Soviet children similarly share the values of their parents during this period more readily than do American children.

What accounts for these differences? First, the behavior of adolescents growing up in societies in which their future roles are predetermined differs markedly from the behavior of adolescents who have a great deal of choice as to which roles they will take. Interestingly, as societies industrialize and provide more opportunity for different occupational roles, parent-child tensions during adolescence seem to increase. Levy (1949) reported that with greater urbanization, increased ability of young people to find employment outside the home, and less dependence of young people on their immediate families in modern China, adolescent Chinese began long ago to develop patterns of parent-child conflicts. More recently, studies of urban-area Australian adolescents also showed conflict patterns essentially similar to those of American children (Collins and Harper, 1974).

Another source of adolescent conflict, according to cultural anthropologists, is the absence in our society of a specific "rites of passage" or

During adolescence, individuals learn that social status comes only through work and self-sufficiency.

initiation experience in which adolescents are symbolically divested of childhood and invested with adulthood (Benedict, 1938; Eisenstadt, 1962; Knepler, 1969). Americans particularly seem to be very ambivalent about the social status of adolescents and are inconsistent in their behavior toward their children. On the one hand, parents might suggest to adolescents that they are old enough to take on some responsibility around the house—like cleaning up the kitchen, mowing the lawn, or emptying the dishwasher. At the same time, they might point out that adolescents are too young to borrow the family car or to stay at a party past midnight. Many studies show that, although American adolescents are given much more freedom in terms of opportunity to interact with their peer groups, they are treated in many ways as children longer than children in other societies (Kandel and Lesser, 1969).

Some theorists suggest that our society exhibits an extreme concern with rejecting dependence and promoting independence. They further suggest that it is this rejection of dependence that leads to adolescent frustration. During adolescence, individuals learn that social status comes only through work and self-sufficiency. Because they are not yet employed in the labor market, they cannot yet be taken seriously. Frustration associated with this inability to be taken seriously provides the major impetus for rejection of adult values (Lyell, 1973).

Finally, why is our society so compelled to reject dependence? Conger (1971) and others suggest that we need to look closely at changing family relationships, contemporary parental roles, and rapid social change, phenomena discussed at length in the early chapters of this text. We have come full circle; to understand the adolescent and, later, the adult, we must begin at the beginning. We must study the child from conception on, watching each step of the way as the child grows, develops, and interacts with the world. Only in this way can we begin to solve the many enigmas of human behavior.

SUMMARY

Adolescence is the period from pubescence, the stage at which body growth suddenly increases rapidly, to full physical and emotional maturity. In our society, it is regarded as a period of dramatic change which can significantly affect the adolescent and his or her family.

During adolescence, changes take place in physical size, shape of the body, and development of the sex organs and hormones. Development of secondary sex characteristics has a major impact on the self-image of the adolescent. Psychological changes also take place during this time. Adolescence in our society has been called a period of storm and stress when individuals try, often emotionally, to determine their own personal and role identities in relation to the rest of society. During this period, adolescents also begin the process of clarifying their values and moral beliefs in a society that presents, for most of them, a variety of conflicting possibilities and choices.

According to Erik Erikson, adolescence represents a crucial turning point during which development must move in one direction or another. Positive identities developed during this period lead to self-esteem, self-sufficiency, and stability in adulthood. When the identity crisis is not resolved, Erikson suggests that identity confusion or role confusion results.

Adolescents must learn to deal in some satisfactory way with their rapidly developing sexuality. Physical changes associated with sexuality assume major importance. Adolescents become increasingly aware, both through the mass media and through the activities of their peers, just what their new feelings of sexuality mean. They begin seriously to question sexual as well as other basic values. Many adolescents engage in sexual experimentation at this time.

During adolescence, tentative decisions are made concerning future life work. Achievement (or lack of it) in school forms has a significant effect on the development of self-esteem and career expectations.

The making of moral decisions becomes increasingly important during this time. Kohlberg hypothesizes that although some adolescents operate at what he calls the "principled stage of moral reasoning," many others make decisions based on considerably lower stages. In the United States today, increasing numbers of students cheat on examinations and do not consider their behavior immoral. Most students who cheat do so not to keep from failing, but rather to protect high grades. Society seems to foster cheating by providing successful models well advertised in the mass media. Lucrative and well-organized national enterprises sell term papers, theses, and lecture notes openly. Cheating in the business and political world makes daily headlines.

Adolescence brings increasing freedom of behavior and, with it, the need to develop independence from the family and new, mature relations with peers. The peer group is viewed by the adolescent as a source of solace and support in what often appears to be a hostile world. Sometimes, however, the particular peer group chosen may provide impetus for socially unwanted behavior. Given the adolescent tendency to conform to peer behavior, such peer groups may increase problems for the adolescent. Importance of the peer group increases in our society at the same time that parents tend to increase their own extrafamilial activities and devote less time to their children.

Society has long associated student political activism, as it existed in the United States in the 1960s, with the child-rearing methods used by activists' parents. A common belief has been that student activists come from permissive homes. Researchers have found, however, that student activism so common in the 1960s evolved for many reasons, including the belief of some activists that they were behaving in the only moral way possible and also the desire of other activists simply to dissent from an unacceptable adult culture. In the 1970s, ideological concerns seem to be replaced by concerns regarding the economy and potential unemployment.

Special problems associated with adolescence in the United States include dropping out of school, running away, delinquency, and drug use. Many of these unwanted behaviors are responses to a social environment that provides little security, inconsistencies in reinforcement, and, too often, little attention. To deal with problems of adolescence, many intervention strategies are being tried. These include educational strategies, such as open methods of teaching, new middle-school programs, skill-training programs, and real-life teaching; and medical strategies, including special pediatric and psychiatric programs for adolescents and drug-abuse programs.

Major themes of adolescence have been described by stage-dependent theorists such as Erikson, Kohlberg, and Keniston. These theorists are concerned with describing the period we call "adolescence." Adolescence also has been described by learning theorists primarily in terms of behaviors resulting from what, in our society, often are harsh, inconsistent, and disinterested parental attitudes. Cross-cultural studies have shown that societies that provide consistently warm methods of child-rearing or that provide clear-cut rules of behavior for adolescents to follow tend to have children who grow up without exhibiting disruptive behavior. It is quite clear that child care is an extremely important occupation at all stages of development.

QUESTIONS FOR THOUGHT AND REVIEW

1 Much material has been published lately describing the increased incidence of cheating in American high schools and in colleges. Students who cheat frequently report that they do so "because everyone does." Other students who don't cheat report that they behave honestly because they fear getting caught. At what level of moral development are these students operating? Can you make some suggestions on what might be done to help these students reach a higher level of moral development? (For review, see pp. 473–476 in this chapter, and p. 358 in Chapter 11.)

2 We talked in this chapter about continued apathy of students as regards the current political situation. Why do *you* think students are apathetic? Do you agree or disagree with Trow's statement about how Watergate has affected student patriotism? Explain. (For review, see pp. 476–478.)

3 What major social changes in family structure in the United States have contributed to the problems of adolescents in our society? Explain your answer. (For review, see pp. 484–488 in this chapter, and relevant sections in Chapters 8 and 11.)

4 Do you think the intervention programs described in this chapter will meet the needs of young people in our society? Or will more drastic methods of intervention be necessary? Why? Have you any suggestions for further intervention? (For review, see pp. 481–484.)

FOR FURTHER READING

Adolescence. Libra Publishers, Inc., P.O. Box 165, 391 Willets Rd., Roslyn Heights, New York, 11577. This quarterly journal is devoted entirely to issues dealing with adolescents. The journal attempts to represent all points of view on topics dealing with life between twelve and twenty.

Coleman, J. *The Psychopathology of Adolescence*. New York: Grune and Stratton, 1970. Coleman has studied extensively the problems of adolescence. This text represents a summary of his research and theory.

Coles, R., J. Brenner, and D. Meagher. *Drugs and Youth*. New York: Behavioral Publications, 1972. The three authors of this text—a physician, a psychiatrist, and a lawyer—discuss the drug problem from their own professional standpoints. The book is written for lay people concerned with taking proper courses of action when confronted with drug-related problems.

The early adolescent. *Daedalus* (Fall Issue, 1971). This entire issue of *Daedalus* is devoted to adolescence and adolescent problems. Social, cognitive, emotional, and physical development are discussed, as well as the major conflicts of the adolescent period. Major theorists have their say.

Erikson, E. *Identity, Youth, and Crisis.* New York: Norton, 1968. Erikson's book remains one of the most extensive analyses of adolescent conflict based on the stage-dependent approach to development. His discussion of identity should be read by anyone expecting to work with, and sensitively deal with, adolescents during their careers.

REFERENCES

Benedict, R. Continuities and discontinuities in cultural conditioning. *Psychiatry* 1 (1938): 161–167.

Bernard, H. *Adolescent Development.* Scranton: Intext Educational Publishers, 1971.

Bettelheim, B. The roots of radicalism. *Playboy Magazine*, March 1971.

Block, J., N. Haan, and M. Smith. Socialization correlates of student activism. *Journal of Social Issues* 25, no. 4 (1969): 143–177.

Borow, H. Career development in adolescence. In J. Adams, ed., *Understanding Adolescence.* Boston: Allyn and Bacon, 1973, pp. 421–452.

Bronfenbrenner, U. The roots of alienation. In U. Bronfenbrenner, ed., *Influences of Human Development.* Hinsdale, Ill.: The Dryden Press, 1972.

Coleman, J. Social climates in high school. In *Cooperative Research Monograph.* No. 4. Washington, D.C.: U.S. Office of Health, Education and Welfare, 1961, pp. 10–34.

Coleman, J. *The Adolescent Society.* New York: Free Press, 1971.

Coleman, J., and W. Broen, Jr. *Abnormal Psychology and Modern Life.* Glenview, Ill.: Scott, Foresman, 1972.

Collins, J., and J. Harper. Problems of adolescents in Sydney, Australia. *The Journal of Genetic Psychology* 125 (1974): 187–194.

Conger, J. A world they never knew: the family and social change. *Daedalus* 100 (1971): 1105–1138.

Eisenstadt, S. Archetypal patterns of youth. *Daedalus* 91 (1962): 28–46.

Elkind, D. Egocentrism in adolescence. *Child Development* 38 (1967): 1025–1034.

Erikson, E. Identity and the life cycle. *Psychological Issues* 1 (1959): 18–172. (Monograph)

Erikson, E. *Childhood and Society.* New York: Norton, 1963.

Erikson, E. *Identity, Youth and Crisis.* New York: Norton, 1968.

Erikson, E. Reflections on the dissent of contemporary youth. *Daedalus* 99 (1970): 154–176.

Eron, L., L. Huesmann, M. Lefkowitz, and L. Walder. How learning conditions in early childhood—including mass media—relate to aggression in late adolescence. *American Journal of Orthopsychaitry* 44, no. 3 (April 1974): 412–423.

Fisbe, E. Colleges are finding their honor systems short on honor. *New York Times,* 11 October 1975.

Flacks, R. The liberated generation: an exploration of the roots of student protest. *Journal of Social Issues* 23 (1966): 52–75.

Floyd, H., and D. South. Dilemma of youth: the choice of parents or peers as a frame of reference for behavior. *Journal of Marriage and the Family* 34 (November 1972): 627–634.

Gallatin, J., and J. Adelson. Legal guarantees of individual freedom: a cross-national study of the development of political thought. *Journal of Social Issues* 27, no. 2 (1971): 93–108.

Gibson, J. *Educational Psychology: A Programmed Text.* New York: Appleton-Century-Crofts, 1972.

Gibson, J. *Psychology for the Classroom.* Englewood Cliffs, N.J.: Prentice-Hall, 1976.

Goode, E. Marijuana and the politics of reality. *Journal of Health and Social Behavior* 10 (1969): 83–94.

Gordon, C. Social characteristics of early adolescence. *Daedalus* 100 (1971): 931–960.

Gordon, S. Why sex education belongs in the home. *PTA Magazine,* February 1974.

Jalkanen, A. Drug use and the adolescent. In F. Adams, ed., *Understanding Adolescence.* 2d ed. Boston: Allyn and Bacon, 1973.

Josselyn, I. Sexual identity crises in the life cycle. In G. Seward and R. Williamson, *Sex Roles in Changing Society.* New York: Random House, 1974.

Kagan, J. Acquisition and significance of sex-typing and sex-role identity. In M. Hoffman and L. Hoffman, *Review of Child Development Research.* Vol. 1. New York: Russell Sage Foundation, 1964.

Kagan, J. A conception of early adolescence. *Daedalus* 100 (1971): 997–1012.

Kandel, D., and G. Lesser. Parent-adolescent relationships and adolescent independence in the United States and Denmark. *Journal of Marriage and the Family* 31 (1969): 348–358.

Kantner, J., and M. Zelnick. Sexual experience of young unmarried women in the United States. *Family Planning Perspectives* 4 (October 1974): 9–18.

Keniston, K. Social change and youth in America. *Daedalus* 91 (1962): 145–171.

Keniston, K. The sources of student dissent. *The Journal of Social Issues* 23, no. 3 (1967): 108–137.

Keniston, K. Youth: a "new" stage of life. *The American Scholar* 39, no. 4 (Autumn 1970).

Knepler, A. Adolescence: an anthropological approach. In G. Winter and E. Nuss, eds., *The Young Adult: Identity and Awareness*. Glenview, Ill.: Scott, Foresman, 1969.

Kohlberg, L., and C. Gilligan. The adolescent as a philosopher: the discovery of the self in a post conventional world. *Daedalus* (Fall 1971): 12–16.

Levy, M. *The Family Revolution in Modern China*. Cambridge: Harvard University Press, 1949.

Libby, R. Adolescent sexual attitude and behavior. *Journal of Clinical Child Psychology* 3 (Fall–Winter 1974): 36–42.

Lowe, G. *The Growth of Personality: From Infancy to Old Age*. Middlesex, England: Penguin Books, 1972.

Lyell, R. Adolescent and adolescent self-esteem as related to cultural values. *Adolescence* 8, no. 29 (Spring 1973).

McCandless, B., and E. Evans. *Children and Youth: Psychosocial Development*. Hinsdale, Ill.: Dryden Press, 1973.

Mead, M. *Coming of Age in Samoa*. New York: New American Library of World Literature, 1949.

Mead, M., and K. Heyman. *Family*. New York: Ridge Press, 1965.

Mitchell, J. Moral dilemmas of early adolescence. *School Counselor* 22 (1974): 16–22.

Pearlin, L., M. Yarrow, and H. Scarr. Unintended effects of parental aspirations: the case of children's cheating. *American Journal of Sociology* 73 (1967): 73–83.

Pettigrew, T. *A Profile of the American Negro*. Princeton, N.J.: Van Nostrand, 1964.

Reisman, F. The "helper" therapy principle. *National Association of Social Workers Journal* (April 1965): 27–32.

Resnik, H. Parkway: a school without walls. In R. Gross and P. Osterman, eds., *High School*. New York: Simon and Schuster, 1971.

Singer, M. Delinquency and family disciplinary configurations. *Archives of General Psychiatry* 31 (December 1974): 795–798.

Sorenson, R. Adolescent sexuality: crucible for generation conflict. *Journal of Clinical Child Psychology* 3 (Fall–Winter 1974): 44–45.

Swift, P. Keeping up with youth: changing youth. *Parade*, 20 September 1976, p. 21.

Tanner, M. Sequence, tempo, and individual variation in the growth and development of boys and girls aged twelve to sixteen. *Daedalus* 100 (1971): 907–930.

Thornburg, H. Peers: Three distinct groups. *Adolescence* 6 (1971): 59–76.

Townsend, J. Learning strategies and tactics. Unpublished manuscript, University of Pittsburgh, 1974.

Vener, A., and C. Stewart. Adolescent sexual behavior in middle America revisited: 1970–1973. *Journal of Marriage and the Family* 36 (1974): 728–741.

Weideger, P. *Menstruation and Menopause.* New York: Knopf, 1976.

Glossary

Accommodation The process of equilibration through which one either modifies existing behaviors or adds new behaviors to one's repertoire of responding to the environment.

Achievement motivation (need to achieve—N Ach) According to motivation theorists, the need to obtain mastery and feelings of competence in solving problems and in interaction with others.

Adolescence Freud's fifth stage of development involving a resurgence of instinctual sexual drives, a desire to lessen parental attachments, and a variety of conflicts.

Afterbirth The final stage of the birth sequence during which the placenta, remaining amniotic sac, and what is left of the cord are expelled.

Aggression Behaviors normally associated with the feeling of anger.

Alienation A subjective feeling of lack of meaningful relationships with others.

Altruism Apparent unselfish behavior with no observable external reward.

Amniocentesis The procedure involving the removal of fluid surrounding a fetus in utero to study the fetal cells it contains.

Amniotic sac A fluid-filled cavity serving as a protective device for the embryo.

Anaclitic identification Identification occurring during infancy; used to explain attachment to the primary caretaker.

Anal stage The Freudian stage concerned with developing control of the child's environment, often through the bladder and bowels.

Anecdotal record Accounts of student behavior recorded by teachers on regular bases.

Anger The feeling of distress when a child is restrained.

Angry or hostile aggression A common form of aggressive behavior in which children will display hostility directly toward others, often in order to reinforce "tough" images of themselves.

Anomie A subjective feeling of separation of oneself from societal norms.

Anoxia A condition, sometimes occurring during the birth process, in which the full oxygen supply is not absorbed into the bloodstream; effects can vary from irritable behavior to death.

Assimilation The process of equilibration through which one responds to novel stimuli by using already existing modes of behavior.

Associative play A form of social play in which children imitate play behaviors of others.

Attachment The result of an infant's associating drive reduction with the primary caretaker, usually recognized as affectionate behavior.

Attention span The length of time an individual attends to any one given task.

Attitudes An individual's relatively permanent orientations toward factors in the environment; considered to be learned.

Autism A severe behavior disorder characterized by extreme withdrawal or unresponsiveness to others and often, in more serious cases, by self-destructive behaviors.

Autogenous Those behaviors, such as walking, that seem to appear without learning.

Autonomy vs. doubt A stage described by Erikson which, depending on the success of the individual's attempts to control the environment, can result in the person developing either positive or negative feelings about competence.

Babinski response A reflex found in neonates in which the toes fan up and outward when the sole of the foot is stroked.

Baby biography One form of recording observations of a child's development during the early years.

Behavior management A term used to describe procedures for altering behaviors based on the principles of operant conditioning.

Behavior-patterned abuse A variety of child abuse in which the parent cannot successfully cope with his or her own feelings of inadequacy and punishes the child for them.

Blastocele A cavity which forms in the zygote as it descends the fallopian tubes during the period of the ovum.

Blastocyst The term describing the zygote during the period of the ovum.

Borderline prematures Infants born from 37 to 38 weeks after conception; these infants are often susceptible to serious respiratory difficulties.

Caretaking The feeding, cleaning, caring for, and protecting of a child.

Case history A descriptive procedure used to study children which focuses on events in their past.

Causality The understanding that certain events have specific and necessary antecedents.

Cephalocaudal principle The fact that growth and development proceed from head to foot.

Child abuse The physical or psychological harm done to children by their caretakers through either direct administration of punishment or the withdrawal of satisfaction of basic needs.

Child-rearing practices The set of practices by which each culture and subculture raises its children.

Childhood schizophrenia A serious behavior disorder characterized by changing styles of behaviors, extremes of activity, and mood and verbal disturbances.

Chromosomes Rod-shaped bodies in cells containing the genes.

Chronic abuse The variety of child abuse occurring most frequently; chronic abuse reflects deep psychological problems of the parents.

Circular reaction Behaviors of young children progressing from simple repetition for repetition's sake through more complex problem-solving behaviors.

Classical conditioning Learning that occurs when a response associated with an unconditioned stimulus becomes associated with an initially neutral (conditioned) stimulus paired with the original stimulus.

Classically conditioned fear response The association of a fear response with a conditioned stimulus.

Classification The ability to group objects along one or more dimensions.

Cloning A genetic manipulation procedure through which cell nuclei are fertilized by other cell nuclei to produce an organism identical to that from which the original cell came.

Cognition The processes of thinking, understanding, and problem solving.

Cognitive strategies Internally organized skills governing a child's learning, remembering, and thinking.

Cognitive structure The term used by Piaget to describe the coherent organization of information to solve problems.

Cognitive (learning) styles Different approaches to organizing learning.

Compensatory role of peer contact Refers to children's reliance on age-mates to provide security, sources of attachment, and models for social behavior in the absence of adult caretakers.

Concept learning A form of learning that requires classification of stimuli according to shared attributes.

Concept of ability One's perceptions of one's academic and social skills.

Concrete operations A stage of thinking described by Piaget in which children still require the presence of concrete objects to solve problems.

Conditioning Learning that occurs through association between stimuli and responses, as in classical or operant conditioning.

Conditioned response In classical conditioning, a response elicited by a conditioned stimulus; in operant conditioning, a response reinforced by a particular stimulus that follows it.

Conditioned stimulus A previously neutral stimulus that, through pairing with an unconditioned stimulus, comes to elicit specific responses previously elicited only by the unconditioned stimulus.

Conscience or principle orientation Kohlberg's final stage of development of moral reasoning in which individuals develop personal senses of morality.

Conservation The Piagetian concept that, regardless of changes in shape or disbursement, the original amount of a substance remains constant.

Continuous schedule of reinforcement One in which a reinforcer is provided immediately after each desired response.

Control subject The subject in an experimental study who, while matched with the experimental subjects on relevant characteristics, is not subjected to the independent variable.

Conventional morality Piaget's second stage of the development of moral reasoning in which moral decisions are based on the attitudes of others toward the activity.

Conventional role conformity Kohlberg's stage of development of moral reasoning in which "right and wrong" are determined by conforming to authoritative sources.

Cooperative play The highest form of social play in which children rely on each other to successfully complete a period of play.

Co-twin procedure An experimental design in which one twin is subjected to the experimental conditions while the other twin acts as a control.

Creativity The ability to solve problems in new and innovative ways.

Crisis intervention The provision of assistance during crises which helps to resolve problems while reducing the immediate effects on the people involved.

Critical growth period The time during which specific tissues and organs display their more rapid growth in utero; during this period the body part in question is most susceptible to environmental influences.

Critical (sensive) periods Those times in an individual's development when the learning of certain behaviors occurs with relative ease.

Cross-sectional method A research procedure in which groups of individuals are avaluated of different ages and then compared.

DNA Deoxyribonucleic acid; a nitrogen-based compound that forms genes.

Day-care center A facility providing total child care during the day, normally for the children of working parents in our society.

Defense mechanisms Behaviors developed in order to decrease anxiety.

Defensive identification Identification processes through which individuals internalize the prohibitions of a model figure.

Deficit interpretation An approach to interpreting group differences which maintains that, for any combination of factors, one group is less able than another.

Delay of reinforcement The operant conditioning principle that states that the greater the delay of the reinforcer, the less its effect on the response.

Denial A defense mechanism characterized by refusal to acknowledge an anxiety-producing situation.

Dependent variable In experimental design, a change that takes place as a result of experimenter-controlled manipulation of the independent variable.

Descriptive child research Child research that occurs in natural settings; conditions are not manipulated by the researcher.

Development The process in which an individual changes from a simple to a complex, highly structured organism.

Developmental readiness   The readiness of an individual to perform satisfactorily certain behaviors, dependent on both growth and maturation.

Difference interpretation   An approach to interpretive group differences offered by environmentalists which maintains that certain differences are due primarily to variations in the kinds of learning individuals have been exposed to.

Direct primes   Suggested guidelines on proper behavior directed to a specific child.

Direct reinforcer   A procedure by which a teacher can directly provide reinforcement to a student for successful completion of a task.

Discipline   Strictly speaking, the class of behaviors whose purpose is to teach new behaviors or to teach control of one's actions.

Discrimination   In language development, the ability to apply linguistic rules to appropriate words.

Discrimination learning   Learning that requires the ability to perceive and act on differences between stimuli.

Disequilibrium   A state of cognitive unbalance that must be resolved for successful interaction in the environment.

Displacement   A defense mechanism characterized by hostility toward persons or objects weaker than the actual object of the aggression.

Dominant gene   A gene capable of determining the appearance of a certain trait in an individual, regardless of the contribution of the second gene.

Dramatic play   A form of play involving pretending to be various objects, both animate and inanimate.

Drive   An internal state, resulting from needs, which compels one into a state of activity.

Dyslexia   A common learning disability involving a variety of perceptual or organizational difficulties.

Early-intervention programs   Programs designed for preschool children which attempt systematically to help so-called disadvantaged children who have received little cognitive stimulation during infancy.

Ectoderm   The outer layer of embryonic cells; it gives rise to the skin, some mucous membranes, and the central nervous system.

Educable mentally retarded   The least severe level of mental retardation; the educable mentally retarded are capable of learning skills necessary to hold relatively simple jobs.

Egocentric speech   An early form of speech seemingly intended to serve one's own purposes rather than to communicate information to others.

Egocentric thinking   In Piagetian theory, thinking seemingly based on immediate perceptions and lack of ability to consider alternative points of view.

Ego differentiation   Erikson's term for the psychological separation of one's self from other people and objects in one's experiences.

Embryo   Term applied to the developing organism between the third and seventh week of prenatal development.

Embryonic area   The area between the amniotic sac and the yolk sac in which the embryo develops.

Embryonic period   The stage of prenatal development normally between the third and seventh week of pregnancy.

Emotional dependency   Feelings associated with those behaviors normally demonstrating strong attachment, such as separation anxiety, seeking approval, etc.

Enactive mode   Bruner's term for describing how young children habitually use one mode of responding to a variety of stimuli.

Endoderm   The innermost layer of the embryonic area which develops into lungs, bladder, alimentary mucosa, pancreas, and liver.

Environmentalists   Those psychologists who maintain that environmental differences are the main cause of variations of traits among groups of people as well as among individuals.

Equilibration   In Piagetian terms, a balanced set of ideas that can be organized in order to solve problems effectively, caused by the interplay of assimilation and accommodation.

Equilibrium   A state of cognitive balance resulting usually in the demonstration of social adjustment.

Eugenics   Term describing attempts to improve human genetics, both by selective mating and by reducing the probability of mating of individuals considered unfit.

Euphenics   The direct manipulation of genetic material by genetic surgery.

Excessively anxious children Children who exhibit behavior problems characterized by short attention spans, high levels of distractibility, hyperactivity, and disorientation.

Experimental researcher Researcher who manipulates aspects of the environment in order to measure resultant behaviors.

Experimental subject The subject in an experimental study who is presented with the independent variable in an experimental design.

Exploratory drive According to some motivation theorists, a need of living organisms to explore the environment.

Extinction The operant-conditioning procedure that causes termination of a learned response after reinforcers are no longer presented.

Extrinsic motivation Motivation inferred when behavior is directed toward goals external to the learning experience.

Family day-care home Usually state-licensed neighborhood homes in which children are cared for while their parents are working.

Fantasy play Play in which children's imaginations allow them to transcend the limits placed on them by reality.

Father-present delivery Delivery of a child with the father present.

Fear of competitiveness According to motivation theorists, an avoidance of competitive situations which results in a decrease in achievement motivation.

Fear of success According to motivation theorists, a desire *not* to succeed which results in decreased achievement motivation.

Fetal period The third phase of prenatal development lasting from approximatly the eighth week of pregnancy through birth.

Field dependence An approach to the perceptual organization of information in which it is hypothesized that individuals may be overwhelmed by the context within which a problem occurs; this often results in problem-solving difficulties.

Field independence An approach to the perceptual organization of information in which it is hypothe-

sized that individuals can isolate easily the important bits of information from the total context in order to solve a problem.

Finger and toe flexion The ability of the neonate to grasp objects pressed against the fingers or toes.

Fixation In Freudian terms, the arresting of the normal process of development due to unfulfilled basic needs.

Fixed schedule of reinforcement Schedule in which a reinforcer is provided only after a specified period of time has elapsed or number of responses has been emitted.

Fontanelles Six soft spots on the neonate's skull where the bones have not yet ossified or hardened.

Formal operations The Piagetian stage in which thinking can occur at an abstract level; the child no longer requires the presence of concrete objects for problem solving.

Friendship groups A small, fairly consistent group of individuals who regularly interact socially as a unit.

Gametes Sperm and egg cells.

Gametogenesis The process through which gametes are produced.

Gene The carrier of genetic information.

General factor theory of intelligence The theory that intelligence is a general, pervasive ability that facilitates a person's capability to do anything.

Generalization The process hypotheized by learning theorists through which stimuli or responses are associated with other similar stimuli or responses.

Generativity or self-absorption A stage described by Erikson, occurring during middle age, in which the individual is concerned about being productive or exhibits an excessive self-concern.

Genetic surgery The process of altering genes through repairing defective ones or replacing them with others.

Genital stage Freudian stage characterized by the desire to obtain pleasure through adult sexual gratification.

Genotype Characteristics or traits due to the individual's genetic makeup.

Growth Quantitative versus qualitative changes taking place in an organism.

Habituation The process, resulting from prolonged stimulus presentation, by which one ceases to attend to the stimulation.

Holophrastic speech An early form of speech in which single words are used to express complete thoughts.

Hyperactivity A condition characterized by erratic, restless behavior.

Iconic mode of responding Bruner's term for image-based representation built on partially-complete concepts.

Identical-twin study Investigations of sets of genetically identical twins, the purpose of which is to identify genetic or environmental influences on behaviors.

Identification A learning process through which children internalize both the behaviors and the standards of a model.

Identification with the aggressor Identification with model figures who possess power or authority.

Identity confusion Erikson's term for an unresolved identity crisis that results in adjustment problems, most common during the adolescent period.

Ideological experimentation Erikson's term for the preoccupation among adolescents with the meaning of socially accepted values, attitudes, etc.

Image-based thinking Piaget's term for the ability of individuals to represent to themselves both events that have occurred in the past and objects that are no longer in their view.

Imprinting A form of learning that occurs in a young animal and involves recognition of and attraction to its mother or adopted mother-figure.

Impulsivity A learning-style characteristic in which individuals respond quickly to a problem without first analyzing carefully its components.

Inclusion The ability to recognize "some" and "all" categories in a hierarchy—e.g., all birds are animals but only some animals are birds.

Independence The process of becoming less reliant on others for the satisfaction of one's needs.

Independent variable In experimental design, that which is manipulated in some manner by the experimenter.

Indirect primes Suggested guidelines for proper behavior that can include a shy individual while not singling him or her out for special attention.

Industry or inferiority A stage described by Erikson in which conflicts may arise between the individual's attempts to win recognition through production and any inadequacies in these attempts which may produce discouragement.

Infantile amaurotic family idiocy A specific hereditary defect of the nerve cells of the brain and spinal cord.

Initiative or guilt A stage described by Erikson in which conflicts may arise between the desire to exhibit newly discovered skills, such as motor control, and their consequences.

Inner speech Vygotsky's term for what he hypothesized to be nonverbal means used by children to control their own behaviors.

Instrumental aggression A common form of aggressive behavior in which individuals resort to antisocial behaviors in order to attain desired objects if less aggressive means are not successful.

Instrumental conditioning Synonym for classical conditioning.

Instrumental dependency Behaviors initiated in order to receive attention from others.

Integrity or despair A stage described by Erikson during which adults, if they have not yet developed a sense of order and meaning in their lives, feel a profound sense of despair over not having succeeded at this task.

Intelligence (IQ) test A measure of cognitive ability, normally composed of problem-solving tasks.

Interval schedule of reinforcement Schedule in which a reinforcer is provided only after the passage of specific time intervals.

Intervention programs Educational programs designed to alter the course of cognitive and language development of individuals who have, in the past, received inadequate cognitive stimulation.

Interview An observational tool consisting of orally administered questions that require oral responses.

Intimacy or isolation A stage of early adulthood described by Erikson during which individuals strive to establish emotional relationships; conflicts may arise if these relationships are not established, resulting in withdrawal and isolation.

Intrinsic motivation Motivation internally generated; the experience itself serves as the goal.

Intuitive stage Piaget's stage of thought involving image-based thinking and perceptual centration.

Karotyping A procedure for studying the number, form, and size of chromosomes in the fluid surrounding the fetus in utero.

Kernel (elementary) grammar Chomsky's term for the earliest, simplest linguistic rules.

Labor The process by which the baby is squeezed out of the uterus and through the vagina.

Latency stage Freud's stage during which people outside a child's immediate family become primary love objects.

Learning A change in behavior resulting from interaction with the environment.

Learning rate A measure of the speed with which learning of any given task takes place.

Learning styles Synonym for cognitive strategies.

Lebensborn Life source; a eugenics program developed by Nazi Germany to produce the "super race."

Levels of aspiration A individual's expectations for his or her own performance and predictions for success.

Linguistic utterances The earliest sounds made by infants in attempting to communicate with others.

Longitudinal study Study in which a group of individuals is evaluated periodically in regard to any specified characteristic over a period of time.

Love-oriented discipline Discipline using positive interpersonal behaviors, such as affection, as tools for teaching children.

Mainstreaming Placing special-needs children, when appropriate, in regular classrooms with regular teachers.

Maintenance system In cultural anthropology, the economic, social, and political structures that determine and perpetuate socialized behaviors in any society.

Marasmus A condition of some institutionalized infants that sometimes results from lack of adequate contact; consequences range from listlessness to death; also called "hospitalism."

Matching Piaget's term for the selection of stimulus input that directly corresponds to the child's cognitive structure.

Maternal attachment The psychologically close relationship between an infant and its primary caretaker, normally the mother.

Maturation Development that occurs regardless of environmental influences.

Meiosis All division that takes place during gametogenesis and in which reproductive cells are produced.

Mental combinations In Piagetian theory, the ability of a child to perceive relationships and solve problems without direct manipulation of materials in the environment.

Mesoderm The middle layer of cells within the embryonic area; cells of the mesoderm develop into blood, muscles, bones, and certain organs.

Midwife delivery Delivery assisted by a trained or experienced layperson.

Mitosis The process of cell division for all cells except the gametes.

Moderately premature infants Infants born thirty-one to thirty-six weeks after conception.

Mongolism A genetic abnormality resulting from the acquisition of forty-seven rather than the normal forty-six chromosomes per cell.

Montessori method An approach to education based on multisensory interactions with one's environment.

Morality The overt expression of social attitudes and values.

Moro (startle) reflex Rapid reaching upward and jerking of the arms; results from withdrawal of physical support from a neonate.

Mothering The earliest caretaking activities of an infant by the mother or mother-substitute.

Motivation Inferred internal processes, measured by goal-directed behavior.

Motivation theorist One who attempts to describe internal processes in order to explain behavior.

Motor skill An integrated series of movements for a specific purpose—e.g., playing a piano.

Movement theory Theory describing the specific movement behaviors through which a child must proceed in order to make a learned response.

Mutations A natural process involving the alteration of genetic makeup of the cells, sometimes resulting in defective genes.

Myelin The tissue forming sheaths around nerve fibers.

Need An internal condition of the individual, the reduction of which produces satisfactory adjustment to the environment.

Negative eugenics A process of genetic control involved the elimination of "undesirable" characteristics achieved through decreasing mating possibilities of those considered "unfit."

Negative reinforcer A stimulus that an organism ordinarily seeks to avoid or stop, resulting in the strengthening of escape or avoidance responses.

Neonate Term used to describe the infant during the first two weeks of life.

Obedience and punishment orientation Kohlberg's lowest stage of moral reasoning in which decisions are based on the axiom "what is approved is good; what is disapproved is bad."

Object-oriented discipline Discipline that uses objects as tools for teaching children.

Object permanence In Piagetian theory, the ability to recognize the fact that objects exist when not in one's visual field.

Olfactory sense Sense of smell.

Open-class words In early language development, words added to pivot words to form new sentences and to express new ideas.

Operant conditioning Learning in which a response is followed by a reinforcer that increases the probability that this same response will occur again under similar circumstances.

Operant response (conditioned response) In operant conditioning, the response that operates on the environment to produce a desired outcome.

Operational stage The Piagetian stage during which children are first successful at solving problems through direct manipulation of materials in their environment.

Oral stage Freud's first stage in which activities revolve around the mother, the nipple, and the thumb.

Overgeneralization In language development, the tendency of young children indiscriminately to apply linguistic rules inappropriately, resulting in common errors in speech.

Overt speech Vygotsky's term for verbalizations, ordinarily following what he called "inner speech."

Pain receptors Those sense organs that transmit sensations of pain to the central nervous system.

Parallel play A form of children's social play characterized by playing alongside others with no direct interaction.

Patterns of caretaking The culture-specific practices of infant care.

Patterns of infant competence The specific behaviors or characteristics of infants that are functionally related to the caretaking patterns of a culture.

Perception The process of interpreting stimuli sensed in the environment.

Period of the ovum The phase of prenatal development lasting until the second week after conception during which the zygote lives off its own yolk.

Permissive discipline A method of discipline in which a great amount of freedom is provided.

Phenotype The observable expression of the interaction between the genotype and the environment.

Pivot-class words In early language development, common words that form core parts of many linguistic utterances.

Placenta An area of the uterine wall through which food, oxygen, and waste pass between mother and fetus.

Polygenic traits Those characteristics determined by a number of genes in combination.

Positive eugenics The increase of "desirable" traits through selective breeding.

Positive reinforcer A stimulus following a response that results in an increase in the probability of that response occurring.

Power-assertive discipline Discipline involving the use of parental power and authority.

Preconceptual thought Piaget's early stage of thinking characterized by reliance on only partially complete concepts to solve problems.

Preconventional morality Piaget's first stage of moral development in which moral reasoning is based on the consequence of any given action, regardless of the intent behind the action.

Prehension The ability to grasp objects.

Premack principle A behavior-management procedure in which one uses a child's preferred activity as a reinforcer to strengthen the occurrence of a less-preferred activity.

Premature infant An infant born less than thirty-seven weeks after conception or weighing less than five and a half pounds.

Premoral Kohlberg's first level of moral reasoning, characterized by the conceptualization of "good" as that behavior which is rewarded and "bad" as that which is punished.

Prenatal research A method, usually descriptive, of gathering information about children through investigation of the child during the period prior to birth.

Preoperational thought According to Piaget, the thought processes of children aged approximately two to seven years, characterized by egocentrism and perceptual domination.

Prepared childbirth Childbirth involving special exercises and a minimal, or nonuse, of anesthetics.

Presocial egocentric stage According to Piaget, an early stage in the development of children's conception of rules; characterized by adherence to adult authority.

Primary circular reaction stage In Piagetian theory, an early circular reaction stage involving the repetition of simple behaviors; an early form of cognitive development in which children discover relationships between behaviors and consequences.

Primary needs Those internal conditions necessary for physical survival that can be met by reinforcers such as food, water, etc.

Primary reinforcer Stimuli necessary for physical survival, such as food or water.

Principled moral reasoning Piaget's third and final stage in the development of moral reasoning, characterized by logical consistency in moral judgments.

Profoundly mentally retarded The most extreme level of mental retardation; the profoundly retarded are helpless and require lifelong care.

Prohibition learning The learning of a society's "don'ts," often taught through identification.

Projection A defense mechanism characterized by attributing one's undesirable behavior to other people.

Proximo-distal The principle that development proceeds from the central nervous system to the body extremities.

Psychosocial Descriptive term for Erikson's developmental theory describing children's orientations to themselves and their social world.

Puberty The period of sexual maturity.

Questionnaire A research instrument through which an individual can either orally, or through writing, indicate responses to written questions.

Quickening The stage of gestation at which fetal movement is felt by the expectant mother.

Radiation Energy emitted from certain elements in the form of waves or particles.

Ratio schedule of reinforcement Reinforcement in which the reinforcer is provided only after a specified number of responses has been given.

Readiness The collection of growth and/or maturational competencies, as well as specific learned skills, that enable individuals to learn more efficiently.

Recessive genes Genes that must be paired during fertilization of the ovum with other, corresponding recessive genes if the individual is to exhibit any given trait determined by those genes.

Reciprocal interweaving The concept that stages of development are composed of repeated alterations of opposing or contradictory forces.

Reflectivity A learning-style characteristic in which individuals consider carefully all the components of a problem before posing a solution.

Reflexive smile The apparently spontaneous smiling of infants in response to being touched and to hearing a human voice.

Reflexive stage A substage of Piaget's sensori-motor period during which reflexive behaviors become more efficient.

Reinforcement In operant theory, any stimulus that increases the immediately preceding response.

Reinforcement schedule The procedures by which reinforcers are presented.

Repression A defense mechanism characterized by deliberately wiping from memory an anxiety-producing event; memory may be restored under certain conditions, such as hypnosis.

Respondent conditioning Synonymous with classical conditioning.

Responsive environment Moore's teaching procedure (e.g., Talking Typewriter) in which the source of motivation appears to be the children's knowledge that they are learning.

Restrictive-permissive discipline Pattern of discipline that alternates between domination and freedom.

Rh factor Genetically determined condition in which substances present in the red blood cells cause maternal and fetal blood to become incompatible.

Rh positive Description of individual having Rh factor in the red blood cells; the Rh positive fetus sends antigens into the mother's blood, resulting in a return of antibodies that can destroy the red blood blood cells in the fetal blood supply.

Role Socially prescribed pattern of behavior.

Role confusion The knowledge that a personally satisfying role is not available to an individual, coupled with that individual's desire not to accept anything less than satisfactory.

Role identity The process of understanding one's self, including strengths and limitations.

Role overload An individual's assuming of too many roles and resultant inability to perform them adequately.

Role-playing A form of play in which young children act out familiar adult roles.

Rooming-in The practice of keeping a newborn in the mother's hospital room.

Rooting response A typical behavior of neonates in which stimulation near the mouth results in movement toward the source of the stimulation.

Secondary circular reaction stage In Piagetian theory, a later circular reaction stage in which an infant's responses are made apparently in order to re-experience cause-effect relationships.

Secondary need Needs other than those necessary for physical survival which must be reduced for optimal development.

Secondary reinforcers Stimuli that are not necessary for reducing primary needs yet still influence behavior, such as social approval or money.

Self-accepted moral principles Kohlberg's third level of the development of moral responses in which moral judgment focuses on individual rights, eventually culminating in a personal notion of right and wrong.

Self-care skills Skills necessary for personal hygiene, grooming, and care, such as dressing, bathing, and feeding one's self.

Self-concept One's perception of one's individuality.

Self-esteem The value judgment given to one's self-concept.

Self-fulfilling prophecy The concept that individuals react to preconceptions of their abilities in such a way that those who are considered "bright" will show more progress than those considered "dull," regardless of actual abilities of the individual's involved.

Sensation Awareness of stimuli in the environment, made possible through the receptor organs.

Sensorimotor stage Piaget's first stage of development during which infants learn to respond to their environments through the senses and through mastery of motor development.

Sensory orientation A sensory mode most easily employed in learning; can be visual, auditory, kinesthetic, or some combination of all three.

Separation anxiety An infant's fear of separation from the mother or object of attachment.

Seriation The ability to sort objects in a series along one or more dimensions.

Severely mentally retarded Those mentally retarded individuals who, with intensive training, may be able to learn some self-care skills.

Sex-typing The individual's learning of socially acceptable behaviors for his or her sex.

Sex-role adoption Identification by children with either a male or female role.

Sex-role preference A child's conscious preference for toys, clothes, etc. deemed appropriate for males or females.

Shaping In operant conditioning, the step-by-step reinforcement of behavior with the end result of establishing a new behavior; also referred to as the method of successive approximations.

Short-stay delivery units Hospital facilities in which midwives deliver the baby; if there are no delivery complications, the mother's and infant's stay sometimes is less than twelve hours.

Sibling rivalry The child's competition with a new baby or other siblings for parental attention.

Sickle cell anemia A genetic disorder, primarily found among blacks, in which red blood cells are deformed.

Situational abuse Child abuse attributed to parental reaction to their own personal crisis situations.

Social play An advanced form of play involving more than one child in direct interaction.

Socialization The process of learning behaviors accepted and expected by one's society.

Socialized speech A form of speech designed to communicate information accurately to another person, often taking into account the listener's point of view.

Socioempathize The ability to recognize and respond to the attitudes of other members of a group.

Solitary play An early form of play characterized by interactions with inanimate objects, such as blocks or toys, rather than with other people.

Special education Separate educational programs designed to meet the needs of children with special needs.

Specificity In development, the principle that, as the individual becomes more complex, behaviors as well as physical development become more specific both in function and purpose.

Stage dependent An approach to the description of development that assumes development proceeds in specified stages that occur in a fixed, sequential order.

Stage of incipient cooperation Piaget's term for the stage in which children first desire to learn rules in order to win at a game.

Standardized population The sample of people whose scores on a standardized test determine the norms against which all people taking the test are compared.

Stranger anxiety An infant's fear of unfamiliar people.

Sublimation A defense mechanism characterized by substitution of acceptable behaviors for unacceptable ones.

Sudden death syndrome (crib death) A condition of uncertain origin that results in the sudden death of infants from three weeks to six months of age.

Suzuki method of teaching A method of teaching very young children to play the violin based on developing strong intrinsic motivation.

Swaddling The tight binding of infants' bodies with cloths to keep them motionless.

Symbolic play Piaget's term for imitative play in which an object "stands" in the child's mind for its real counterpart.

Symbolic representation Piaget's term for the preschooler's ability to use signs and symbols to represent objects in his or her experience.

Syntax Grammatical structure of language.

Tactile sense The sense of touch.

Tay-Sachs disease A genetically transmitted disease found among Ashkenazic Jews which causes rapid degeneration of the brain during the first six months of life.

Tertiary circular reaction stage In Piagetian theory, a final circular reaction stage in which the infant's repetitive responses are made in order to draw attention to themselves.

Trainable mentally retarded The level of mental retardation in which the individual can learn sufficient self-care skills to live successfully in the community rather than in an institution.

Trial and error stage An early Piagetian stage characterized by the development of object permanence.

Trophoblast The part of a blastocyst which gives rise to the amniotic sac and the yolk sac.

Trust The expression of confidence in the environment.

Trust or mistrust Erikson's first psychosocial stage, during which an infant either does or does not develop basic confidence in the environment; this stage influences later social and emotional relationships.

Umbilical cord The structure that carries food and waste products between mother and fetus.

Unconditioned response In classical conditioning, a response that occurs spontaneously upon presentation of a given stimulus.

Unconditioned stimulus In classical conditioning, a stimulus that, without benefit of learning, produces a given response.

Unsocialized and aggressive children Children characterized by hostile, disobedient, and destructive behavior.

Values Individuals' criteria for evaluating their environments; values remain relatively constant over time.

Variable schedule of reinforcement That in which the reinforcer is provided according to a schedule the subject cannot predict.

Vestibular sense Sense of movement and balance.

Vicarious pleasure The phenomenon by which individuals, through identifying with a model figure, receive pleasure from observing the model receive rewards.

Visual action A common characteristic of preschool thinking which involves the active use of manipulation in solving problems.

Volition According to Bruner, the voluntary control of the body in order to obtain a desired outcome.

Vospitanie Communist upbringing and morality; the long-term goal of Soviet education.

Yolk sac The structure that feeds the embryo until the umbilical cord is fully developed.

Zygote A fertilized egg cell.

Photo Credits

1, Marshall Henrichs; 3, Florence Sharp; 5, *Joseph Moore and His Family* by E. S. Field, courtesy of Museum of Fine Arts, Boston; 6, The Bettman Archive, Inc.; 9, Robin Gibson; 11, Photography by H. Armstrong Roberts; 12, Courtesy Rugh & Shettles, *From Conception to Birth: The Drama of Life's Beginnings,* Harper & Row, 1971; 19, Novosti Press Agency (APN); 22, H. F. Harlow, University of Wisconsin Primate Laboratory. Copyright © 1958 by the American Psychological Association. Used by permission; 37, Charles S. White, Jr.; 40, The Iconographic Collections, State Historical Society of Wisconsin; 43, Thomas D. McAvoy, *Life Magazine;* 44, Florence Sharp; 45, Florence Sharp; 48, Florence Sharp; 54, Stuart Johnson; 56, Lore Rubin; 57, Gesell Institute of Child Development; 63, Florence Sharp; 71, Talbot D. Lovering; 73, Rosemary Good; 75, Janice Gibson; 78, William B. Finch; 86, Florence Sharp; 88, Florence Sharp; 90, Florence Sharp; 91, William Hamilton; 93, Rosemary Good; 97, Charles S. White Jr.; 99, Lore Rubin; 105, Dr. Albrecht K. Kleinschmidt and Elsevier/North-Holland Biomedical Press; 111, Arthur M. Siegelman; 113, Marshall Henrich; 117, Historical Pictures Service, Inc., Chicago, Ill.; 127, Marshall Henrichs; 129, Florence Sharp; 130, Florence Sharp; 139, Florence Sharp; 153, Bruce Anderson; 156, Joan Stellwagen Henriksen, Cardinal Glennon Memorial Hospital for Children, St. Louis, Mo.; 159, Marshall Henrichs; 160, Marshall Henrichs; 163, Marshall Henrichs; 165, Marshall Henrichs; 167, Courtesy of New Yorker Films; 173; Florence Sharp; 177, Janice Gibson; 178, Jane Simkin; 181, Bruce Anderson; 182, Janice Gibson; 184, Lore Rubin; 190, Bruce Anderson; 191, Marie Demarais; 196, Bruce Anderson; 197 and 198, Copyright © 1969, William K. Frankenburg, M.D., and Josiah B. Dodds, Ph.D., University of Colorado Medical Center; 202, Jane Simkin; 211, Rick Smolan; 214, Lore Rubin; 217, Joan Stellwagen Henriksen, Cardinal Glennon Memorial Hospital for Children, St. Louis, Mo.; 221, Florence Sharp; 228, Novosti Press Agency (APN); 229, Janice Gibson; 232, Luiz Veiga; 232, Novosti Press Agency (APN); 235, Robin Gibson; 247 Florence Sharp; 249, Marie Demarais; 251, Robin Gibson; 258, Marshall Henrichs; 262, Janice Gibson; 264, Lore Rubin; 266, Susan Redlich; 269,

Rosemary Good; 273, Florence Sharp; 281, Susan Redlich; 283, Marshall
Henrichs; 288, Janice Gibson; 293, Helen Jeroslow; 294, Florence Sharp; 297,
Janice Gibson; 299, William Hamilton; 301 (right), William Hamilton; 301
(left), Rosemary Good; 303, Janice Gibson; 350, Janice Gibson; 313, Florence
Sharp; 315, Bruce Anderson; 320, Marshall Henrichs; 327, Janice Gibson; 330,
Robin Gibson; 332, Ambassador College Photo; 336, Lore Rubin; 337, from
Maria Montessori: Her Life and Work by Mortimer Standing; 340, Marshall
Henrichs; 349, Florence Sharp; 351, Marshall Henrichs; 359, Erika Stone,
Photo Researchers; 363, Anne K. Moon, Stock, Boston; 365, Rosemary Good;
366, Marshall Aronson; 374, Ellis Herwig, Stock, Boston; 375, Marshall
Henrichs; 385, Marshall Henrichs; 388, Marshall Henrichs; 392, Marshall
Henrichs; 393, Rosemary Good; 396, Helen Jeroslow; 402, Marshall Henrichs;
407, Florence Sharp; 414, Robin Gibson; 423, Luiz Veiga; 426, United Press,
International, Inc.; 431, Florence Sharp; 433, Marshall Henrichs; 437, Rick
Smolan; 438, Tim Carlson, Stock, Boston; 445, Robin Gibson; 446, Robin
Gibson; 461, Florence Sharp; 463, Cary Wolinsky, Stock, Boston; 465, Janice
Gibson; 472, Photo courtesy *Andover Townsman*; 475, Photo courtesy *Andover Townsman*; 481, Luiz Veiga; 483, Marshall Henrichs; 485, Photo courtesy
Andover Townsman; 487, Photo courtesy *Andover Townsman*.

Author Index

Berndt, E., 354, 380
Berndt, T., 354, 380
Bernstein, B., 254, 277, 316, 343
Best, D., 382
Bettelheim, B., 132, 475, 491
Bigelow, B., 362, 380
Biglass, E., 132
Biller, H., 255, 259, 277
Birch, H., 279
Birch, J., 449, 454
Birns, B., 226, 241
Blackham, G., 297, 309
Block, J., 477, 491
Bloom, L., 319, 343
Bodmer, W., 109, 132
Borow, H., 483, 491
Bowen, B., 419
Bower, G., 83, 102, 182
Bower, T., 207
Bowlby, J., 31, 45, 68, 195, 207, 216, 218, 240, 241
Bowes, W., 154, 160, 162, 170
Brackbill, Y., 76, 101, 192, 195, 207
Brackett, B., 167, 170
Bradbury, W., 431, 435, 454
Braine, M., 160, 170, 207
Brazelton, T., 162, 170, 241
Brenner, J., 490
Brent, S., 405, 419
Brewer, T., 150, 170
Bridges, K., 193, 194, 207
Brightman, A., 453
Brinkerhoff, M., 134
Broen, W., Jr. 479, 491
Bronfenbrenner, U., 31, 75, 101, 109, 132, 133, 210, 231, 240, 241, 242, 255, 256, 276, 277, 279, 283, 309, 310, 354, 370, 372, 379, 380, 382, 475, 486, 491
Bronson, G., 195, 207
Brook, J., 401, 419
Brothers, R., 428, 454
Brossard, M., 199, 207
Broughton, J., 207
Brown, E., 334, 345
Brown, R., 207, 323, 343
Bruner, J., 74, 101, 183, 207, 297, 310, 322, 324, 325, 330, 343, 344
Busk P., 374, 380
Bussey, K., 382
Bryan, J., 94, 103

Burchinal, L., 241
Butler, N., 151, 154, 170

Caldwell, B., 171, 201, 207, 213, 226, 241, 276, 306, 310
Callard, R., 200
Calverley, D., 419
Campbell, H., 171
Campbell R., 381
Cantoni, L., 278
Carey, S., 317
Carey, W., 214, 241
Carroll, J., 316, 343
Casler, L., 200, 207, 208, 223, 241
Caualli-Sforza, L., 109, 132
Cazden, C., 338, 342, 343
Charlesworth, R., 301, 310
Chavas, J., 419
Chen, H., 186, 205
Chess, S., 279
Child, I., 249, 280, 400, 416, 419
Chomsky, N., 322, 344
Chukovsky, K., 338, 344
Church, S., 42, 69, 123, 134, 187, 205
Churchill, J., 152, 171
Cicirelli, V., 332, 344
Claiborn, W., 416, 419
Clarey, S., 344
Clarfield, S., 455
Clark, A., 79, 101
Clark, D., 415, 419
Clark, K., 100, 101
Clark, R., 421
Clarke-Stewart, K., 214, 215, 219, 241
Clifton, R., 206, 207
Cody, J., 416, 421
Cohen, J., 241
Cohen, S., 272, 277
Cole, M., 330, 342, 344
Cole, S., 435, 454
Coleman, J., 373, 380, 476, 479, 490, 491
Coles, R., 31, 42, 68, 490
Collard, R., 208
Collins, J., 486, 491
Comer, J., 255, 277
Condry, J., 354, 380
Conger, J., 488, 491
Conger, L., 344
Cook, K., 257, 279

Hersher, L., 241
Herson, H., 456
Herzog, E., 357, 381
Hess, R., 254, 278, 329, 344, 419
Hetherington, E., 360, 381
Hewitt, L., 402, 420
Heyman, K., 486, 493
Hicks, D., 302, 311
Hilgard, E., 83, 102
Hilgard, J., 20, 32, 40, 41, 68
Hill, W., 102
Hiller, M., 118, 133
Hoedt, K., 450, 457
Hoffman, L., 242, 309
Hoffman, M., 278, 358, 381
Holley, W., 152, 171
Holmes, F., 267
Holmes, S., 272, 278
Holstein, C., 358, 381
Holz, W., 83, 102
Hony, A., 310
Horner, M., 402, 421
Horton, C., 31
Hosken, B., 302, 311
Howe, L., 132
Hsia, Y., 118, 124, 133
Hsu, F., 19, 32, 250
Huesmann, L., 380, 382, 492
Hulka, J., 151, 171
Hundley, V., 134
Hunt, J., 102, 109, 133, 243, 327, 344
Hunter, M., 95, 102
Hurlock, E., 39, 49, 55, 68, 301, 311
Hursh, D., 91, 102, 208
Huston, A., 257, 277

Ilg, F., 56, 67, 68
Ingle, D., 124, 132, 133
Inhelder, B., 53, 68, 318, 345, 390, 422
Iorio, J., 142, 171
Irwin, O., 186, 208
Isaacs, S., 291, 311
Itard, J., 67
Jackson, G., 373, 381
Jacobs, C., 371, 381
Jacobsen, L., 416, 422
Jaffe, B., 271, 278
Jalkanen, A., 481, 484, 492
Jankowski, J., 243
Jason, L., 443, 455

Jeffrey, W., 419
Jenkins, J., 344
Jensen, A., 107, 133
Jersild, A., 267
Johnson, N., 334, 344
Jones, G., 455
Jones, N., 455
Jones, R., 447, 455
Jose, J., 416, 421
Josselyn, I., 471, 492

Kagan, J., 91, 92, 99, 101, 102, 208, 209, 213, 219,
    240, 242, 251, 256, 268, 278, 302, 311, 395,
    400, 401, 421, 422, 470, 471, 472, 492
Kamii, R., 254, 278
Kandel, D., 487, 492
Kantner, J., 471, 492
Kanzer, P., 401, 422
Kaplan, B., 209
Kariagianis, L., 428, 448, 453, 454
Karnes, M., 333, 334, 344, 442, 445
Karson, E., 310
Kaufman, B., 453
Kaye, H., 192, 209
Keay, A., 142, 171
Kellaghan, J., 209
Kelly, J., 357, 381
Keniston, K., 53, 68, 354, 382, 476, 485, 492, 493
Kephart, W., 269, 278
Keppel, F., 202, 209
Kesson, W., 210
Key, M., 157, 171
Keyserling, M., 233, 242, 309
Kiely, F., 310, 382
Kipnis, D., 419
Kirchner, E., 382
Kirshner, K., 345
Kistiakouskaia, M., 200, 209
Klips, B., 345
Knepler, A., 487, 493
Koch, H., 263, 278
Kogan, K., 261, 279
Kohl, H., 88, 103
Kohlberg, L., 52, 61, 68, 69, 311, 469, 473, 493
Kohli, K., 124, 134
Koltsova, M., 192, 207
Korner, A., 180, 200, 209, 289, 311
Kornetsky, C., 155, 171
Kotelchuck, M., 278
Kron, R., 162, 171

Krug, D., 447, 455
Kubler-Ross, E., 51, 69
Kunz, P., 124, 125, 134
Kupers, C., 302, 309

LaGaipa, J., 362, 380
Lamb, M., 259, 278
Landis, J., 268, 278
Landreth, C., 183, 186, 193, 209, 220, 223, 242
Lane, P., 382
Langner, T., 442, 456
Lavatelli, C., 42, 69
LaVor, M., 425, 456
Lazarevic, J., 122, 134
Leader, F., 292, 311
Leboyer, F., 166, 171
Lefkowitz, M., 376, 380, 382, 492
Legg, C., 263, 278
Lehane, S., 206
Leizer, J., 367, 382
Lenneberg, E., 209, 323, 344
Leonard, M., 214, 242
Lesser, G., 487, 492
Lester, B., 202, 209
Levy, B., 370, 382
Levy, M., 486, 493
Levy, V., 92, 104
Lewin, H., 279, 289, 311
Lewin, R., 152, 171
Lewis, M., 158, 171
Lewis, O., 442, 456
Libby, R., 483, 493
Lichtblau, N., 151, 172
Liebert, R., 382
Liikanen, P., 376, 381
Lipscomb, W., 170
Lipsitt, L., 31, 176, 188, 192, 194, 209, 210, 317, 329
    345
Lipton, E., 176, 206, 209, 241
Little, A., 209
Little, E., 192
Locke, E., 94, 103
Loney, J., 455
Long, A., 439, 456
Lord, J., 79, 101
Lorenc, K., 43, 69, 217, 242
Loughman, R., 170
Low, S., 126, 134
Lowe, G., 464, 493
Lowell, E., 421

Luria, A., 322, 344
Lurie, O., 450, 456
Lyell, R., 487, 493
Lytton, H., 260, 278

Maccoby, E., 279, 290, 311, 359, 382, 401, 421
MacNamara, J., 209
Manes, A., 402, 421
Marcus, Jr., 230, 231, 242
Margolin, E., 259, 279
Markle, S., 96, 103
Markova, A., 390, 421
Marsella, A., 279
Marshall, E., 388, 421
Marshall, K., 443, 456
Martels, A., 171
Marx, J., 154, 171
Marx, M., 409, 421
Masland, R., 254, 279
Maslow, A., 87, 103, 408, 421
Matarazzo, R., 171
Maurer, A., 267, 279
May, M., 358, 381
McCall, R., 226, 242
McCandless, B., 302, 311, 493
McCarthy, E., 456
McCelland, D., 400, 401, 403, 421
McCormick, T., 119, 122, 134
McCullers, C., 361, 382
McFeatters, A., 374, 382
McGinity, D., 149, 172
McGrath, C., 130, 134
McGrath, N., 130, 134
McGraw, M., 44, 69
McKee, J., 292, 311
McKinney, J., 395, 421
McNeese, F., 444, 456
McPeake, J., 419
Mead, M., 4, 32, 129, 134, 227, 242, 486, 493
Meagher, D., 490
Mech, E., 271, 279
Meili, R., 31
Melnyck, K., 402, 421
Meredith, D., 255, 277
Merricks, D., 428, 448, 453, 455
Merrill, M., 8, 33, 94, 103, 411, 422
Messick, S., 394, 395, 421
Meyer, D., 102
Miller, N., 439, 454, 456
Miller, T., 356, 382

Miller, W., 209
Milton, G., 401, 421
Milunsky, A., 120, 122, 132, 134
Mitchell, J., 470, 493
Mogar, R., 170
Mohs, K., 279
Moltz, H., 43, 69
Mondale, W., 374, 382
Montessori, M., 75, 103, 336, 337, 388, 344, 421
Moore, M., 207
Moore, O., 88, 103
Moore, T., 343
Morgan, D., 142, 171
Morris, N., 150, 151, 172
Morrison, B., 103
Morton, M., 338
Moss, H., 421
Moulty, G., 399, 421
Mowrer, O., 103, 454
Murphy, D., 453
Murphy, L., 170, 172, 210, 213, 242, 243
Mussen, P., 31, 32, 39, 69, 309, 379

Najarian, P., 222, 241
Nash, J., 109, 134
Nations, J., 97, 103, 393, 421
Nelson, A., 434, 456
Nelson, K., 209
Neugarten, B., 442, 455
Nevis, S., 223, 241
Newberry, H., 12, 32
Nias, D., 366, 381
Nimnicht, G., 334, 345
Nortman, D., 151, 157, 172
Norwood, R., 457
Novak, D., 449, 456
Novy, M., 151, 171
Nugent, F., 450, 456
Nye, F., 242, 260, 277

O'Connor, M., 306, 311
Olson, M., 398, 422
Olver, R., 343
Osborn, J., 333 345
Osborne, E., 124, 134
Osser, H., 96, 102
Ounsted, M., 154, 172

Palermo, D., 344
Pallas, J., 210

Pannor, R., 279
Papousek, H., 193, 209
Parke, R., 360, 381
Parker, H., 365, 382
Passantino, R., 231, 242
Patterson, G., 85, 104, 276
Pavlov, I., 181, 182
Pearce, D., 311
Pearlin, L., 474, 493
Peck, E., 128, 134
Pederson, F., 243
Pedrini, B., 447, 456
Pedrini, D., 447, 456
Perry, D., 360, 382
Perry, L., 382
Peterson, F., 256, 279
Pettigrew, T., 468, 493
Phillips, D., 437, 456
Phillips, W., 92, 102
Piaget, J., 53, 60, 69, 172, 180, 189, 191, 210, 285,
    311, 318, 327, 345, 353, 363, 382, 390, 422
Pick, A., 96, 102
Piesach E., 419
Polkonis, P., 457
Pines, M., 335, 345
Pitman, J., 408, 422
Plummer, G., 155, 172
Plutarch, L., 134
Pohlman, E., 124, 128, 130, 134
Poulos, R., 382
Poussaint, A., 255, 277
Powledge, T., 123, 134
Premack, C., 84, 103
Pronko, N., 88, 103
Proscura, E., 345

Radin, L., 254, 278
Radpoff, L., 279
Rainwater, L., 129, 134
Ralston, N., 16, 32
Ramey, C., 201, 210
Rapoport, R., 127, 134
Rasmussen, B., 381
Rav, L., 243
Rawlings, E., 164, 172
Raynor, R., 76, 104, 210
Redl, F., 261, 279
Reed, V., 210
Reese, H., 31, 176, 188, 194, 210, 317, 329, 345
Reese, J., 455

Wallerstein, J., 357, 381
Wallers, J., 290, 311
Walters, R., 289, 309
Warburton, F., 408, 422
Waterhouse, I., 79, 101
Watson, J., 76, 104, 167, 172, 193, 210
Watson, S., 302, 311
Wattenberg, B., 135
Wechsler, D., 411, 422
Weideger, P., 494
Weisley, M., 382
Weissenburger, F., 455
Weithorn, C., 435, 457
Westlake, H., 64, 69
Whelan, M., 309
White, B., 215, 243
White, R., 398, 422
Whiteman, M., 419
Whiting, B., 280
Whiting, J., 249, 250, 253, 278, 400, 416, 419
Whitten, C., 210
Wickman, E., 370 382, 437, 457
Williams, J., 359, 382
Williams, T., 270, 280
Wills, J., 257, 280

Wiltz, N., 85, 104
Wishik, S., 151, 172
Woestehoff, E., 432, 457
Wohlwill, J., 53, 54, 67, 69
Wolff, P., 175, 176, 195, 210, 223, 243
Wolins, M., 210, 240, 242, 276, 279, 382
Woods, M., 356, 382
Wortis, H., 170
Wright, C., 310
Wright, H., 13, 33, 269, 280

Yaffee, S., 161, 171
Yarrow, L., 243
Yarrow, M., 351, 382, 493
Ysseldyke, J., 455
Yussen, S., 92, 104

Zehrbach, R., 455
Zelnick, M., 471, 492
Zentall, S., 435, 457
Zigler, E., 401, 422
Zimbardo, P., 436, 457
Zimmerman, R., 216, 242
Zook, E., 302, 310
Zwirner, W., 260, 278

Subject Index

Accommodation, 60, 189. *See also* Piaget's theory of cognitive development
Achievement motivation, 398, 471
Achievement motivation training, 403
Adolescence
  physical changes during, 463
  problem behavior during, 478–479
  psychological changes during, 464
  theories of, 485–486
Adoption, 271
Aggression
  development of (*see* Emotional responding)
  effects of socioeconomic differences on, 290
  overcoming, 307
  types of, 289–290
  unsocialized, 438
Alcohol, effects on prenatal development, 154
Altruism, development of. *See* Emotional responding
Amniocentesis, 119
Anaclitic identification, 218–219
Anal stage. *See* Psychoanalytic theory and stages of development
Anecdotal record. *See* Biographical research methods
Anger, development of. *See* Emotional responding
Anomie, 479
Anoxia, 158
Anthropological views of development, 249
Anxiety, excessive, 435
Arthur Point Scale, 411
Aspiration level, 399

Assimilation, 60, 189. *See also* Piaget's theory of cognitive development
Associative play, 301
Attachment, development of, 194–195, 216
Attitude learning. *See also* Learning
  in the school years, 351
  social, 353
Audition, of the neonate, 177
Autism, 441
Autogenous behavior, 41

Baby biography. *See* Biographical research methods
Bayley Scale, 197, 329
Behavior management, 83
Behaviorism
  behavior management, 83
  classical conditioning, 76
  conditioned response, 77
  conditioned stimulus, 77
  extinction, 81
  instrumental conditioning (*see* operant conditioning)
  operant conditioning, 78–79
  reinforcement, types of, 79, 82
  respondent conditioning (*see* classical conditioning)
  schedules of reinforcement, 81–82
  shaping, 82
  theories of, 76–84
  vicarious reinforcement, 98